Portable Property

Portable Property

VICTORIAN CULTURE

ON THE MOVE

John Plotz

PRINCETON UNIVERSITY PRESS

PRINCETON AND OXFORD

Published by Princeton University Press, 41 William Street,
Princeton, New Jersey 08540

In the United Kingdom: Princeton University Press, 6 Oxford Street,
Woodstock, Oxfordshire OX20 1TW

Library of Congress Cataloging-in-Publication Data

Plotz, John, 1967–
Portable property : Victorian culture on the move / John Plotz.
p.   cm.
Includes bibliographical references.
ISBN-13: 978-0-691-13516-8 (cloth : alk. paper)
1. English fiction—19th century—History and criticism. 2. Material culture in
literature. 3. Property in literature. 4. Personal belongings in literature.
5. Sentimentalism in literature. 6. National characteristics, British, in literature.
7. Expatriation in literature. 8. British—Foreign countries. I. Title.
PR878.M38P58   2008
823′.8093553—dc22   2007033548

British Library Cataloging-in-Publication Data is available

This book has been composed in Sabon

Printed on acid-free paper. ∞

press.princeton.edu

Printed in the United States of America

10   9   8   7   6   5   4   3   2   1

For Lisa

I crossed a moor, with a name of its own
   And a certain use in the world no doubt,
Yet a hand's-breadth of it shines alone
   'Mid the blank miles round about:

For there I picked up on the heather
   And there I put inside my breast
A moulted feather, an eagle-feather—
   Well, I forget the rest.

     —*Robert Browning, "Memorabilia"*

I always take 'em. They're curiosities. And they're
property. They may not be worth much, but after all,
they're property and they're portable. It don't signify
to you with your brilliant look-out, but as to myself,
my guiding-star always is, "Get hold of portable
property."

     —*Charles Dickens,* Great Expectations

Contents

List of Illustrations

Getting Hold of Portable Property

EMILY EDEN ONCE MADE the modest proposal that people would be much happier if they could forgo having children and instead give birth to "a set of Walter Scott's novels, or some fine china."[1] In India with her brother the governor general, the delivery of her beloved possessions seemed simpler still: "Sixty-five elephants and 150 camels will carry our little daily personal comforts, assisted by 400 coolies and bullock-carts innumerable."[2] Although Eden frequently voices the common English complaint that going to India meant being "dead and buried . . . in my hot grave,"[3] that grave would at least have been well stocked.

This book began as an attempt to understand Victorian writers who, like Eden, proclaim that their attachment to distant homes depends upon their portable property. Despite her gleeful enumeration of bullock-carts and elephants dedicated to her "personal comforts," Eden's Indian odysseys are not about accumulation for accumulation's sake. Instead, they mark her as an exemplary child of the Victorian era, when, as never before or since, trinkets and ornaments became the metonymic placeholders for geographically disaggregated social networks. All over "Greater Britain," Victorian lovers made elaborately braided hair-jewelry, parents decorated photographs of far-off children with hair-pieces woven from their actual hair, and letter-writers frequently enclosed palpable tokens attesting to an enduring attachment.[4]

In Eden's letters home, for instance, simple material wants—fans, a silver busk, flannel nightgowns—are specified and promptly forgotten. What recur are less easily assuaged demands: for example, "some English boxes, with new books and little English souvenirs from sister, nieces, etc."[5] A friend sends Eden a bracelet to be worn waking and sleeping, while another begs, "Send me a bit of your hair, my darling, and always bear me in your 'heart of hearts, as I do thee, Horatio.'"[6] Like the latest numbers of "Pickwick," these objects make a distant world just present enough to remind Eden how distant it truly is. My initial aim, therefore, was to explore why and how certain objects, artworks, and cultural practices came to serve as metonymic extensions of the home and family Victorians on the move had left behind.

How did Victorian England and its global extensions become a forcing bed from which portability emerged as a new way of imagining community, national identity, and even liberal selfhood on the move? I began by hypothesizing that infallible, unbreakable relics might operate as a moveable repository of both family feeling and of Englishness, a national identity understood metonymically as an extension of domestic ties. My quest for a complete catalogue of such properties, though, quickly encountered a problem: the age of triumphant (and triumphantly English) mementoes was simultaneously the apogee of English capitalism, with London doubling as the world's industrial engine and its central bank. Wallerstein and Arrighi describe the nineteenth-century dominance of an economic world-system based on the pure interconvertibility of commodities and capital, exactly contemporaneous with the world of well-beloved bibelots that fill Victorian novels.[7] This was not a case of simple succession, passionate fetishism followed by ruthless liquidity. It evidently was not the case that everything solid in one age (its curios and mementoes) melted into air in the next. Any conception of portability attuned to the concurrent dominance of what Hobsbawm succinctly labeled "Industry and Empire," had to account for valued pieces of portable property neither exempted from nor antecedent to capitalism's fluid markets.

Two ideas I had thought of as in conflict with one another—the allure of commerce and the allure of hoarded valuables-beyond-price—turned out to be deeply intertwined. It was precisely because the Victorian world came to seem increasingly flooded by fungibles and commodities that certain objects and cultural practices, not so much sacrosanct as especially supple, became repositories of mobile memory. Rather than the omnipresent fluidity that Marx's account of modernity predicts, the nineteenth century's turn toward fully globalized capitalism engenders in the cultural realm a heightened commitment to durable but moveable repositories of nonfiscal value. The key was to understand how certain moving objects turned into resonant pieces of portable property: what was the mechanism whereby certain objects (but not others: not Irish potatoes, not Indian cotton) came to be regarded as at once priceable and invaluable, fungible and nonfungible?[8]

The result of "capital's ability to generate wealth through circulation," Mary Poovey argues, was that Victorians began to "measure their worth not simply [by] the acres (or square feet) that surrounded them but by . . . a form of value that was always deferred."[9] This system might have kept money itself "imaginatively engaging,"[10] but it also generated a counterflow: Victorian writers began to speculate about, and conjure up, an alternative network through which protected objects and practices could move. Culturally resonant objects, if blessed with the right sort of domestic imprimatur, could be withdrawn from the ordinary rules of commodity circulation. Little wonder, then, that Victorian émigrés often carried with them a sprig of heather, or a copy of what became the ur-text of English "tales of locale," Gilbert White's 1789 *Natural History of Selborne*.[11] Although understood as partially withdrawn from the ordinary depredations of exchange, such objects gained their power only in motion. Back home on the heath, after all, nothing could be more common, more trivial, than a sprig of heather.

This doubleness means that culture-made-mobile was rarely so simple as it seemed. Victorian readers of Austen abroad knew they were doing more than merely recreating a domestic reading experience; precious relics overseas could connote family, England, and the prospect of ready cash all at once. In Charles Dickens's *Great Expectations*, when Wemmick tells Pip to "get hold of portable property!"[12] the heavy silver mourning rings he refers to may seem nothing more than cash-equivalents—like the sterling cutlery in *Our Mutual Friend*, which asks greedy visitors, "wouldn't you like to melt me down?"[13] But why does Wemmick carry them strewn about his person, and take care to remind Pip that each one tells a story?[14] Such portable reliquaries of departed clients are—like Wemmick's miniature castle, where he and his diminutive "Aged Parent" fire tiny cannons and run tiny fountains—a form of domestic retreat. But the rings go the castle one better, because they are virtually the only objects that can accompany Mr Wemmick, with his "post-office of a mouth," out into his grimly workaday world.[15] They let him recollect, at a touch, the perversely comforting narratives that somehow sustain him.

Like novels themselves, in fact, these rings are saleable objects also endowed (if regarded aright by a careful reader) with measurable narrative significance. That parallel—that even mourning rings might start to seem like novels under the proper cultural conditions—helped me to see that the novel lay at the crux point where dual conceptions of value collided in the Victorian era, and that the novel's aesthetic preeminence and cultural influence had everything to do with that centrality. Novels were precarious but crucial documents because they seemed to be in an impossible double bind, torn between being fungible objects—saleable commodities that made Trollope and W. H. Smith alike wealthy men—and the sublime effusions Carlyle called "vesture of a thought," with a value precisely dependent on exemption from commerce's usual laws. Getting hold of my subject properly, then, entailed understanding Victorian novels as a series of works *about* portable property that were also meditations on their own status *as* pieces of portable property. More than once I thought of titling this study "The Adventures of Portable Property, As Told By a Portable Property."

That this book exists at all is due entirely to the incredible generosity of an enormous network of friends and colleagues, who have given far more than I had any right to expect, and received far less than they deserve in return. Some offered suggestions at chance meetings; others participated in reading or writing groups that kept my hope alive at crucial moments; others were generous interlocutors or supportive colleagues and co-workers; others offered crucial practical and technical aid. Finally, my everlasting devotion goes to those friends whose friendship itself was a gift outright. The least I owe, and the most I can offer here, are my thanks to: Rachel Ablow, Liberty Aldrich, Sally Alexander, Amanda Anderson, Isobel Armstrong, Nancy Armstrong, Sam Baker, Tim Bewes, Mark Blackwell, Mark Blyth, Jonathan Bolton, George Boulukos, Wini Breines, Stuart Burrows, John Burt, Antoinette Burton, James Buzard, Mary Campbell, Deborah Cohen, Mary Jean Corbett, Danielle Coriale, David Cunningham, Lewis Dabney, Nick Dames, Theo Davis, Linda DeLibero, Andrea Dodge, Sharon Dolovich, Ian Duncan, Mary Esteve, Frances Ferguson, Elizabeth Ferry, Penny Fielding, Philip Fisher, Jen Fleissner, Billy Flesch, Nick Frankel, Catherine Gallagher, Eilenn Gillooly, Timo Gilmore, Robert Glick, Sarah Gracombe, Allen Grossman, Jonathan Grossman, Daniel Hack, Lisa Hamilton, Anna Henchman, Noah Heringman, Susie Herman, Neil Hertz, Susanna Hines, David Hollenberg, Lauren Holm, Jackie Horne, Jennifer Howard, Anne Humphreys, Shannon Hunt, Caren Irr, Dan Itzkovitz, Holly Jackson, Sarah and Roy Jacobs, Matthew Jordan, Phil Joseph, Amy King, Tom King, Peter Knight, Paul Kramer, Ivan Kreilkamp, John Kucich, Daniela Kukrechtová, David Kurnick, Sue Lanser, Yoon Sun Lee, Deidre Lynch, Ruth Mack, Peggy Mackenzie, Simon Manley, Sharon Marcus, Lucy and Alen Mattich, Sean McCann, Andrew Miller, Paul Morrison, Lisa Pannella, Rick Parmentier, Adela Pinch, Leah Price, Laura Quinney, Robert Reid-Pharr, Tom Reinert, Ben Reiss, Bruce Robbins, Alex Ross, Jennifer Ruth, Elaine Scarry, Linda Schlossberg, Cannon Schmitt, Hilary Schor, Bendta Schroeder, Eugene Sheppard, Gillian Silverman, Faith Smith, Alex Star, Jennifer Stern, Judith Stoddart, Ramie Targoff, Bianca Theisen (fondly remembered), Sasha Torres, Irene Tucker, Judith Walkowitz, Chris Waters, Joseph Wensink, Alex Woloch, Molly Wyman, Amit Yahav-Brown, and (last only alphabetically) Rachel Yassky.

Thanks are also due to Hanne Winarsky and her superb colleagues at Princeton University Press, to anonymous readers at *Victorian Studies*, *ELH*, and at Princeton, and to the following for financial support that made the project possible: The National Endowment for the Humanities, the National Humanities Center for a year-long residential fellowship in 2001–2, Howard Foundation, and the Norman fund at Brandeis for sabbatical support in 2005–6, and to all my colleagues and co-workers in the English departments at Johns Hopkins University and at Brandeis University. Permission to reprint illustrations from the Harry Elkins Widener Collection at Harvard Library, and from Anne S. K. Brown Military Collection, Brown University Library, is gratefully acknowledged. I also appreciate suggestions and criticism from audiences who endured early slivers of this project at the English departments of the following colleges and universities: The University of California, Berkeley; Brandeis University; Brown University; the University of Chicago; the University of Colorado, Boulder; Columbia University; Concordia University; The City University of New York; the University of Delaware; George Washington University; the University of California, Los Angeles; the University of North Carolina; and the Harvard Humanities center. Portions of chapter 1 previously appeared as "Discreet Jewels: Victorian Diamond Narratives and the Problem of Sentimental Value," in *The Secret Life of Things: Animals, Objects, And It-Narratives in Eighteenth-Century England*, edited by Mark Blackwell (Lewisburg, Maine: Bucknell University Press, 2007). Portions of chapter 2 previously appeared as "The First Strawberries in India: Cultural Portability in Victorian Greater Britain," *Victorian Studies* 49, no. 4 (2007). Portions of chapter 6 previously appeared as "Nowhere and Everywhere: The End of Portability in William Morris's Romances," *ELH* (Winter 2007).

Finally, my family ensured that this book turned from an idle daydream into the sort of portable property that can be picked up, put down, underscored, or overvalued. Intellectual inspiration from my mother, Judith, is imperfectly acknowledged in a few footnotes, but it will be obvious to anyone who knows her that her influence goes far deeper. What I owe my grandmothers, Helen Abrams and Helen Plotz, cannot ever be reckoned; the same goes for everything that ties me to my brother David and his family—Hanna, Noa, and Jacob. I am deeply touched by a decade of kindness from the Soltani and Farhadi families, especially from Mohsen and Shahnaz. It gives me incredible pleasure to report that the idea for this book began about a dozen years ago on a trip with my father, Paul, a doctor whose taste for long novels matches his passion for properly exhaustive case histories. Riding home from Vermont late at night, holding a flashlight awkwardly between my head and shoulder, I read him the opening paragraph of Joseph Conrad's *Victory*: "Both [coal and diamonds] represent wealth, but coal is a much less portable form of property. There is, from that point of view, a deplorable lack of concentration in coal. Now, if a coal-mine could be put into one's waistcoat pocket—but it can't!" In a lifetime of beyond-generous gifts from my parents, the moment was small but sufficient. Finally, I hope that my daughters Nelly and Daria will someday see there is more of them in this book than just their exercises in automatic typing. And I hope they will approve of a dedication that tries to say—without quite saying it out loud—everything to the one person everything depends on.

Portable Property

The Global, the Local, and the Portable

ONE UNIVERSALLY acknowledged truth about the Victorians is that they loved their things.[1] Deborah Cohen has recently argued that in nineteenth-century England moral uplift came for the first time to be associated with the accumulation and harmonious arrangement of possessions; home-decoration turned into a saintly affair.[2] The objects that pack Victorian parlors—aquaria, terraria, globes, books, and beetle collections among them—might seem to make bourgeois life into a collector's paradise, an alternative to ever quitting the home.[3] However, the titles of popular works such as Friedrich Ernst's *The Portable Gymnasium*, John Bartholomew's *Portable Atlas*, and Elizabeth Kent's *Flora Domestica, or The Portable Flower Garden* prompt us to tell the story slightly differently.[4] So, too, does a revealing fact: when possessions fill Victorian novels—so copiously that later readers describe themselves as swaddled by, drowning in, or suffocating under their weight—they generally serve not as static deadweights, but as moving messengers. Aquaria or collector's cabinets might be the Victorian repositories of choice, but the objects that fill them—bugs, mourning rings, or precious letters—acquire meaning primarily from their earlier peregrinations.

These are a few of their favorite things: Shakespeare's complete plays; an Indian pearl necklace sold to buy a copy of Samuel Johnson's *Works*; some unlabelled beetles bound for the British Museum; a monogrammed silver teapot; an Indian diamond with a "moony glow"; a Kashmiri shawl; a grandfather's chest of documents in various languages; a ruby ring, its provenance carved upon it in Farsi; an embroidered handkerchief in a silver box.[5] My argument is that Victorian novels made much of such objects, returned to them repeatedly, and interrogated their significance in a variety of puzzling ways, because of the novel's own status as an exemplary portable property. Themselves sentimentalized items, endowed with a fiscal and a transcendent value at once, English novels from the 1830s onwards took on the project of making sense of resonant but potentially marketable objects.[6]

They did so because so much of the novel's own cultural importance derived from its status as a text caught between fungibility and irreplaceability. In this introduction, I offer brief readings from novels by Eliot, Gaskell, and Oliphant, so as to explore three distinct ways that novels represent the curiously double nature of resonant pieces of portable property. The commonality I discern forms the basis for a claim that portability has significant features in common with, but is ultimately distinct from, both fungibility and from fetishism (that is, from an attachment to singular objects so profound, so willing to ascribe transcendent powers to a free-standing thing, that it resists conceiving of meaning as built up out of association and resonance). From those readings, I go on to ask why an England defined by both "Industry and Empire" was the logical breeding ground for a heightened attention to the problems of property's portability. My answer is that the problem of "staying English" within the wider realm that Dilke in 1868 called "Greater Britain" is addressed in novelistic representations of implicitly and explicitly *national* portable property. It is the existence of Greater Britain that requires not just a notion of portable cultural objects, but also of *asymmetry* in portability, so that the flow of culture-bearing objects from core to periphery is not counterbalanced or interrupted by a flow in the opposite direction. The capacity of an imperium to sustain that kind of asymmetry is a crucial component of its power.

It is vital to begin with a sense of the novelty of the developments that make Deborah Cohen call the Victorian English "the first people to be so closely identified with their belongings."[7] What Cohen calls "identification" arises, I am arguing, because certain belongings come to seem dually endowed: they are at once products of a cash market and, potentially, the rare fruits of a highly sentimentalized realm of value both domestic and spiritual, a realm defined by being anything but marketable. The best pieces of portable property can become, in effect, their own opposites. If the oddity of that development—the emergent rivalry between schemes of value being played out in single objects—is not immediately obvious, recall that in the eighteenth century, objects located front and center in novels belonged to a realm that might bear the name of sentiment or of exchange, but was in any case characterized by free, rapid, unproblematic circulation.[8]

The talking guinea at the center of Charles Johnston's 1765 *Chrysal*, for instance, is a hypostatization of the spirit of circulation itself. Chrysal accordingly calls forth formally congruent revelations about each character who holds him: each character's desire for the exchange value embodied within him is boundless, and effectively identical. Even the animated corkscrew in *The Adventure of a Corkscrew* boasts to readers neither of bottles opened nor bygone feasts, but its own price on the open market.[9] And objects endowed with putatively sentimental value may fare no better. As late as 1815, Jane Austen is caricaturing bathos, not sympathizing with pathos, when she has Harriet Smith lachrymosely catalogue her

"*Most precious treasures*:" a leadless pencil-end and a sticking-plaster she associates with the Reverend Elton.[10] When Harriet packages pencil and plaster in a cotton-lined "pretty little Tunbridge-ware box," itself wrapped in an "abundance of silver paper" and deposited in a larger parcel, she is as ridiculous as Elton himself, who is found cooing over "a precious deposit" Emma has given him.[11]

By 1830 (the chronology is explored in chapter 1, below), however, resonant objects began to appear in English novels in new ways. To understand why, it may help to notice that the word "portable" itself began to take on a new set of meanings and associations. Starting around 1830 both "portable" and "portability" begin to be used in increasingly abstract ways. Although there are at least two hundred book titles containing the word "portable" before 1833 (including a Psalter from 1600),[12] the first title to use the word metaphorically seems to be Joseph Gurney's 1833 *Hints on the Portable Evidence of Christianity*.

Gurney's preoccupation with portability's ambiguity sheds a great deal of light on the waxing importance of the concept to the intersection between economic and noneconomic valuation.[13] *Hints* begins:

> "Every man who reads the Bible with attention, and observes the value and excellence of the book—every man who compares what it says of mankind with his own experience, and marks the fitness of its mighty scheme of doctrine to his own spiritual need as a sinner in the sight of God—is furnished with practical proof of the divine origin of our religion. I love this evidence; I call it the PORTABLE evidence of Christianity." . . . The Bible is a portable book, and the Christian, whether at home or on a journey, ought always to keep it within his reach, and make use of it as his daily companion. Again—whatsoever be our place or circumstances, we all carry within us a knowledge of our own experience.[14]

But which sort of portability matters most: the physical portability (no quotation marks needed) of the Bible as a material book; or its metaphorical "portability," which depends on the applicability of its moral dicta in a potentially infinite variety of situations? Gurney refers to the Bible's physical advantages as a bearer of the good Word repeatedly throughout his tract, but those advantages are almost always linked immediately to a much less tangible sort of portability: the ease with which the Bible's lessons can be applied to the natural world, to moments of moral doubt, to cases of cognitive confusion, and so on.

Even at his most decisive, Gurney describes the Bible as simultaneously physical object and Word of God incarnate, permanently suspended between material and spiritual form: "Were that sacred volume more of a daily companion and intimate friend to us—did the words which it contains dwell in our hearts—did we 'bind' them 'for a sign' upon our hands, and as 'frontlets' between our eyes—our lingering doubts respecting Christianity and its doctrines, would soon fade away."[15] This may seem to be an injunction to physicalize one's relationship with the Bible, to make it ever more tangible in one's daily life. Yet the quotation marks around the various words that describe the Jewish ritual of wrapping tefillin underscore the distinction between making the Bible physically portable on one's person, and making it spiritually portable by taking it with one as a metaphysical passenger. The conventional distinction between the Old Testament "Word" and the New Testament "Spirit" is here reconfigured, via the quotation marks, as a distinction between merely carrying a book (Jewish literalism), and effectively internalizing the Bible's teachings (Christian spirituality).

If the best sort of metaphysical portaging of the Bible's ideas is to "bind" those ideas to readers, Gurney still imagines them as attached to that reader not as frontlets plain and simple, but as "frontlets," set off by quotation marks. Gurney's indecision is suggestive of the significant cultural transformation taking place around him: it is now the duality of any given piece of portable property that is the phenomenon that most bears remarking, and the parameters of that duality are what demand attention. And of all the places that such preoccupation comes to the fore, none is more striking than the lengthy and involved meditations on portability's dual aspect that come to define the Victorian novel.

LITERARY MATERIALS

The Victorian aesthetic practices that are shaped by the logic of portability are by no means limited to the novel, so a focus on how novels unpack these questions might initially appear arbitrary. The oft-noted Victorian predilection for quotation, for instance, derives partially from the sense that literary texts are designed to travel widely and hence ought to be useful in settings both congruous and incongruous.[16] Quotation, then, is one preeminent example of how literary texts can travel across historical, authorial, national and, not least, generic boundaries. Quotations might (or might not) come with generic markers attached to them but their diffusion hinges on their capacity to lodge in texts of any genre.[17]

Quotation, though, is far from the only way literary works are understood as attaining a kind of global mobility in the Victorian era; movement into other texts is not by itself success. Henry James, for instance, proposes that a successful novel has a curious untouchability derived not from its being quoted, but from its continuing ineradicable existence in readers' minds everywhere. Half-complaining, half-praising, James writes of Dinah Mulock Craik's 1856 *John Halifax, Gentleman,* that "we know of no scales that will hold [John Halifax], and of no unit of length with which to compare him. He is infinite; he outlasts time; he is enshrined in a million innocent breasts; and before his awful perfection and his eternal durability we respectfully lower our lance."[18] It is the content of other readers' heads, then, that makes a novel into a piece of properly portable property: its success depends on the knowledge that others will feel about the protagonist just as one does oneself.

Yet if such relentless generalizability—a Halifax in every head—was one side of the novel's nineteenth-century appeal, there was a converse, as well. How can such generality be reconciled with the realist novel's oft-applauded power to be local—locodescriptive, yes, but also particular, singular, individualized? Penny Fielding argues that Robert Burns's poetry is fractured by the implicit double burden of being at once extremely local and entirely detachable.[19] We might call this inherent paradox that of "absent presence." The more successful a text is at rendering a place palpable, the more it delocalizes the locale on which the representation is founded.

This particularity might seem irreconcilable with the attractive generality ascribed to literature. Portability, though, can solve the paradox—that literature is both locodescriptive and entirely separable from any given place—by providing a mechanism for inserting local mementoes into global circulation without detaching them from their original locale. Indeed, this sort of global mobility of local color might even be described as the forerunner of the fin-de-siècle international allure of American local color fiction that Brad Evans has recently described as "local chic."[20]

There is another crucial set of reasons why novels lie at the heart of Victorian reflections on portability. It was novel circulation that profited most from the triumphant explosion of book and periodical production and consumption that in so many ways shaped Victorian England. The novel profited especially from its association with new forms of rapid transit: some argue that the rise of railways, and concomitant emergence of W. H. Smith's stalls (Euston Station's was the first, in 1848), was the primary reason "sales of books and periodicals reached unprecedented levels in the 1850s."[21] The Smith stalls were prime distributors for Routledge's "Railway Library reprints," and also proved "instrumental . . . in devising the yellowback reprint of popular novels . . . forerunners of the twentieth-century paperback"; there were 35 Smith railway stalls by 1851, and 1,242 by 1902.[22] If the pious W.H. Smith II ("Old Morality") insisted on the installation of chained Bibles in every terminal, the commercial success of the Smith operation in truth depended on a profoundly mobile readership, for whom travel was an occasion for, rather than an impediment to, immersion in printed matter.[23]

What was true for the shortest of train trips was equally true for shipboard odysseys. Cargo allowances were miniscule for poor emigrants, and Bibles, prayer-books, and *Pilgrim's Progress* were likely the only books that poorer emigrants brought on Australia-bound ships. Still, Bill Bell notes that emigrant-oriented journals (*Chamber's Edinburgh Journal*, for instance) relentlessly praised books and periodicals not simply as "a continued flow of valuable and correct information" but also (as David McKenzie put it in 1851) as a means to "improve your heart and mind."[24] Bell argues that "the thousands of books, tracts, letters and newspapers that made their way to the colonies in the nineteenth century provided vital connections with familiar social values, serving for many to organize an otherwise unpredictable environment into recognizable patterns under strange skies."[25] Altick's and Bell's accounts are crucial in reminding us of how unashamedly attached Victorian readers could be to what Carlyle calls the "vesture" of the book—that is, its simply material shape.[26]

When Carlyle himself declared that "the thing we called 'bits of paper with traces of black ink' is the *purest* embodiment a Thought of man can have," he was finishing off a comparison between a book and a brick, a comparison that is quantitatively but not qualitatively to the book's advantage: both books and bricks are a mixture, in varying proportions, of the common stuff of earth and the ethereal stuff that flows through men's minds.[27] In fact, this focus on the material existence of a novel as book is one way of distinguishing debates about the portability of novels from Victorian debates on the status of other genres. Indeed, the rising tide of questions about what is "portaged" in a novel's portability is one of the indicators of the novel's centrality in Victorian debates on cultural mobility—a centrality that accords with what James Buzard has recently described as the novel's authority in demarcating national identity from the 1850s onward. Poetry, by contrast, seems at the time to have provoked fewer debates about the relationship between material embodiment and higher meaning, and hence to have been much less involved in the unfolding debates about literature's potential portability.[28]

Next to the arguments for focusing on novels as material objects, though, lies a complementary set of claims about the significance of Victorian novels as exemplary *texts*. The material realities of Victorian publishing and its enormous scale notwithstanding, hyperawareness of a printed page's material existence does not dominate the Victorian conceptions of reading, at least not in the ways that obsessions with the letter as material object might be said to shape the avant-garde works of the modernist era.[29] Novels were assemblages of signs, understood not as embodying a truth but telling a tale: the railway novel's lasting allure had (as Henry

James's remark about John Halifax suggests) more to do with the various other readers who might be imagined for it than with the object's own appeal. Moreover, the variety of forms in which a single novel might appear—serial, triple-decker, cheap reprint, and so forth—assured the impossibility of any single object being taken as metonymically representative of the sum of a text's potential.

A novel is no amulet, to be valued for some specific, nontransferable power that its actual physical possession confers. It is rather a curious combination of its material and its textual properties, readily assimilable neither to the world of commodities nor to the sublime realm of poetic experience. The necessity of occupying that contested middle ground is what both endangers and empowers novels in their effort to make sense of the ever-widening register of Victorian portable properties.

HOUSEHOLD GODS: THE MILL ON THE FLOSS

The English novel between 1830 and 1870 was defined by its obsession with objects represented as problematically endowed with sentimental and fiscal value simultaneously (as I argue in chapter 4, the triumphant acme of the "provincial novel" in England at this period is linked to this object-obsession, as well). The phenomenon is so widespread that it is worth beginning with an exclusionary example: what happens when George Eliot sets out a limit case, an object that fails to possess the kind of double portability that novels themselves do seem to possess? In *The Mill on The Floss* (1860) George Eliot's ruthless anatomy of Mrs Tulliver's attachment to irreplaceable familial artifacts perfectly exemplifies the work required to make a physically portable object seem culturally portable, as well.

After Mr Tulliver's bankruptcy and stroke, Maggie defends her father vehemently, and her brother Tom avows himself the inheritor of his father's beliefs, as well as his debts. Their mother, though, is discovered clinging, as a chapter title puts it, to "Mrs Tulliver's Teraphim, or Household Gods." Her husband's impending bankruptcy makes all her goods liable for auction, precipitating this impassioned monologue:

> "To think o' these cloths as I spun myself. . . . And the pattern as I chose myself—and bleached so beautiful, and I marked 'em so as nobody ever saw such marking—they must cut the cloth to get it out, for it's a particular stitch. And they're all to be sold—and go into strange people's houses, and perhaps be cut with the knives, and wore out before I'm dead. You'll never have one of 'em, my boy," she said, looking up at Tom with her eyes full of tears.[30]

Mrs Tulliver is haunted by her identifying "marking," doomed to be "cut" out of the cloth, or (telling repetition) "cut" by some stranger's knife in passing.

Maggie's memorable "Fetish" doll, which she passionately hammers at moments of rage, is a surprisingly flexible little object: it can represent any and all of Maggie's perceived tormentors. Rather than seeming a God incarnate, this fetish is a loyal accomplice to Maggie's remarkable emotional fluidity, capable of accompanying her, as a truly portable object should, through the outbursts that leave her "sobbing all the while with a passion that expelled every other form of consciousness—even the memory of the grievance that had caused it."[31] Mrs Tulliver, by contrast, has a resolutely unmetaphorical relationship to her things. Any object monogrammed with her initials or her family name seems an almost physically attached extension of herself. Her despair arises from realizing that she has had the bad fortune to find herself psychically enshrined in objects that can, as fiscal currents dictate, fly away.

Mrs Tulliver wants protection for her things and her name—she hopes to avoid seeing them enter into common circulation by selling them within the family. The irony is that her intense attachment is precisely what deters sympathy. Even her sisters feel disinclined to help her, since their own attachments lie elsewhere than those particular teapots:

> "Ah, dear, dear!" said aunt Pullet, shaking her head with deep sadness, "it's very bad—to think o' the family initials going about everywhere— it niver was so before: you're a very unlucky sister, Bessy. But what's the use o' buying the teapot, when there's the linen and spoons and everything to go, and some of 'em with your full name—and when it's got that straight spout, too."[32]

By Eliot's account, it is not Mrs Tulliver's teapots but her plight that might, properly handled, move both her relatives and her readers. Mrs Tulliver, though, cannot get her mind beyond the thing itself. Her primitive attachment to her property is so tenaciously complete there is no space for sympathy, either from her sisters or from the reader. In that sense, she is peculiarly ill-equipped, Eliot implies, to thrive in a world that requires at least formal protestations of affective commonality to act— the world, that is, of a Victorian novel.

This is unmistakably an exclusion marked by class status. Education's capacity to teach advancement-via-detachment threatens in time to teach Maggie (like Mary Garth or Dinah Morris) the flexibility that in the Victorian novel so often seems the necessary complement to capital's rhythm of accumulation and disbursement. Working-class primitive accumulation, though, is not the only class position spurned by portable property; the aristocracy, too, frequently seems hampered by a similarly primitive attachment to its outmoded, merely material possessions (in chapter 1, below, I examine how Trollope navigates between aristocratic and ascendant bourgeois passions for property). Lessons in having, letting go, and generating sympathy from others for one's act of renunciation are unmistakably part of the Victorian novel's intimate, if vexed, relationship to the process of bourgeois subjectivation.[33]

I am arguing that we ought to investigate ways in which cultural value is imagined circulating, in objects, practices, even in persons—even imagined as precisely inhering in that capacity to circulate, rather than in any detail of those two categories so beloved of economists, production and consumption. So why begin analysis here with a failure, a markedly subbourgeois version of primitive adhesion on Mrs Tulliver's part, leading to the dissolution of shared meaning in a welter of misunderstandings and commodification? Because by Eliot's account, Mrs Tulliver's downfall is her incapacity to see the doubleness of the portable property around her, the way that it can be simultaneously physical memento and metaphor for pathos. Recall that Gurney refuses to commit himself as to whether the "portable evidence" for Christianity consists of that palpable book called the Bible, or of the lessons that the book teaches. By contrast, Mrs Tulliver has plumped for the object, and nothing but the object, and accordingly found herself with nothing but her own objects to console her.

Eliot offers the hint of an alternative reading that would restore to Mrs Tulliver's possessions a kind of higher aesthetic resonance. That is, readers might be inclined to sense the poignancy of a female inscriber like Mrs Tulliver (or like the author herself) working so hard to leave such minimal traces on unrewarding material—the worked handkerchief, the engraved silver teapot.[34] Eliot is clear, though, that Mrs Tulliver does not participate in such imaginative extensions of the loss of her objects. Eliot's moral finding, then, is that a character (or a reader, or an author) who perceives only the physical mobility of a resonant object is missing the metaphorical possibilities inherent in its alienability, its sentimental transferability. Borrowing Gurney's language, we might say that because she is focused on the loss of her own personal set of well-beloved frontlets, Mrs. Tulliver cannot add the quotation marks: she does not see what it would take to make others think about their own "frontlets."

Eliot is not, however, proposing that property be detached from the body so as simply to be repudiated entirely. Mrs Tulliver's too-solid possessions do not constitute a plea for pure dematerialization. In *Daniel Deronda* (1876; I will analyze this work more closely in chapter 3, below), the shame associated with Gwendolen's sordid transaction with her emerald necklace is related to the problems that arise when personal possessions are treated neither as heirlooms nor as relics, but simply as alienable bits of potential cash. Gwendolen's pawning may not prostitute her outright, but is intimately tied to the very absence that the narrator is soon lamenting: that Gwendolen has no homestead from which to look up at the stars and imagine them as her own. Deprived of an imaginary grounding for her identity, Gwendolen begins her career potentially adrift in liquidity. Daniel's response to her action (tailing her, and returning the "redeemed" necklace) is, to Gwendolen, less a rescue than it is a rebuke for having misunderstood the delicate laws that mandate holding on to potentially disbursable valuables.[35] The balancing-act explored by Eliot leaves the best objects in a kind of Victorian analogy to Milton's Adam and Eve, "sufficient to have stood, though free to fall." Pawning, then, epitomizes the most grievous sort of fall out of portability that a semidetached possession can undergo.

INTERMITTENT PERSONALIZATION: CRANFORD

These Eliot examples pertain to objects that fail when they lapse into simple singleness, becoming a mere fetish (teapot) or mere fungible (necklace). A properly doubled object in a Victorian novel, though, looks quite different. In Elizabeth Gaskell's *Cranford* (1851–53), for example, we find a novel defined by a virtual armory of objects moving readily between and among rival schemes of value, objects whose status as both commodities and inalienable possessions marked them out not as spoiled hybrids, but as ideal sites of sentiment. Two questions shape *Cranford*: first, what sort of possessions are endowed with the most sentimental meaning? Second, what relationship do such objects have to the dangerous world of promiscuous circulation? Gaskell's quaint domestic appurtenances—the sucked oranges, the old lace eaten by a cat, the newspaper laid down to shield rugs from sunshine—have, as Andrew Miller warns, "often been misread as sentimental and nostalgic affection for the trivial details of the past."[36] In fact, the most telling bit of personal property in this highly domesticated novel is not domestic but international: the letter that the narrator writes to Miss Matty's brother Peter, in the hopes of fetching him home from India.

The crucial detail about this letter is that it is written to "the Aga Jenkyns" without certain knowledge that he actually is Mattie's brother Peter. Mary Smith, therefore, must carefully design "a letter which should affect him if he were Peter, and yet seem a mere statement of dry facts if he were a stranger."[37] The letter (like the novel itself) is capable of navigating Cranford's curious half-private, half-public world. Mary's letter simultaneously circulates as a piece of depersonalized freight in a worldwide postal system, and as a singular plea to the one who will feel the sentiment intended. It is as if the letter could be written in two entirely different alphabets, one saying "I am an impersonal plea from afar," and the other, "Your sister is in need of you."

The letter helps us discern the existence of a wide range of such doubly marked objects in *Cranford*: from the pearl necklace that the returning Peter liquefies into presents for Cranford ladies, to the nice, dry, grease-free tea that Miss Mattie deals in her double role as lady and merchant, to the worthless five-pound note that Miss Mattie redeems from a poor farmer (the note comes from "her" bank, so that she takes the failure personally). All these objects are capable of circulating as mere reified value, and yet simultaneously are endowed with a kind of sentimental energy that allows them to mean something particular, often even inarticulable, to individuals.

Cranford's treatment of Samuel Johnson illuminates the laudable duality attached to the best sorts of portable culture. Johnson's works represent, in *Cranford*, the boring bromides of an era before such properly enthralling novels as *Pickwick*. The ponderous apothegms of Johnson circulate in a boring because impersonal public sphere that is also associated with such mere fungibles as cash. Like cash and its (male) masters, Johnson fails to distinguish personalities in his "extensive view" of humanity, and supposes that individual variation can, or even ought to be, dispensed with.[38] Yet Mattie Jenkyns's gift of the collected works of Dr. Johnson to the narrator is the quintessence of poignancy, since it is done not out of any public motive, but to call to mind Mattie's deceased sister, who adored Johnson. As a gift, it has aura by association, and is more moving unopened than read.

The alignment offered between Peter's letter, the works of Johnson, and Gaskell's own novel does not mean that *Cranford* itself bids to become part of a universal realm of sentiment, through which the feelings of any afflicted reader for the sorrows of the Jenkyns family can flow. On the contrary, the claim to connection must be routed through at least a pretense to exclusivity, a space of domestic singularity whereby something that circulates with absolute abandon through a universal medium like the post is reimagined as circulating so that it reaches only its intended addressee: you, the singular reader. Think of Jane Eyre's passionate attachment to her singularized addressee—the "dear reader" is the only person as dear to her as Rochester.

Cranford, then, is a striking example of the Victorian novel's success in producing a public form of portable privacy. It postulates ties activated precisely because they are *my* ties of affection and no others. Many Victorian novels work to produce the feeling that the reader has a personal connection with characters that is denied to a hypothetical unsympathetic mass audience—to whom the novel would be, in *Cranford*'s terms, a "mere statement of dry facts."[39] And yet one is comforted in one's knowledge of shared sensation neither by the sense that the novel is merely singular nor simply that it is (as Benedict Anderson's notion of "parallel readerships" would have it) merely multiple, circulating through that big world of reified exchange in as many copies as the evening paper.[40] Rather, it is at once singular and multiple, private and public, sentimentally particularized and fungible. The sentimentalization of the works of Johnson, like the personalization of the five-pound note or the letter for Peter, provides a kind of security in sentimental objects, a way that beloved objects can partake in the best sort of circulation while remaining tied to the perceiving subject. Mrs Tulliver's teapots fail to evoke fellow feeling, in kin and readers alike, because this felt doubleness eludes her.

Conceptualizing the double life of property in this way helps to reveal what might be called the "intermittent personalization" of objects as a recurrent motif in Victorian novels. In *Great Expectations* (1861), this affects not just the mourning rings that Wemmick acquires as "portable property," but also the legacy paid out to Pip, cold cash warmed by his (mistaken, and yet foundational) belief that it is given him by Miss Havisham, and that it marks him out for Estella. And it transforms the chest of documents, "beautifully incised with Arabic lettering," that Daniel Deronda receives as a deferred gift from his grandfather. Deronda's notion of "separateness with communication" is perfectly figured in those documents, which allow him to be aligned with a great world borne in upon him by the documents, yet also encourage him to choose his learning because the documents seem to be family property.[41] In Victorian novels, almost all truly valuable objects come to be endowed with this double meaning, the appeal of which resides precisely in the disjunction that arises between the broadly shared, interchangeable, impersonal meaning and the poignantly personal aspect, which coexists with the former invisibly, or in ways accessible only to those who are already attuned to the sort of resonances that such personal associations produce.[42]

Haunted by Exchange: Kirsteen

> The gold thread that should run through all the years.
> —Oliphant, *Kirsteen*

The Victorian novel from Dickens to Conrad is permeated and defined by the sentiment that can be stored in redolent objects or practices moving through the ordinary coils of public (and often fiscal) circulation. By century's end, certain writers had begun to signal a mounting unease with the paradigmatic assumptions of portability. In chapter 3, below, for example, I argue that *Daniel Deronda* (1876) experiments with installing cultural knowledge deep within an individual's body, signaling that the provincial novel can no longer serve flawlessly as a vessel for the guiding assumptions of cultural portability. I also make the case in chapters 5 and 6, below, that an overtly antiportable logic pervades both the localism of Thomas Hardy's prose (and poetry) and the utopianism of William Morris's late novels.

Still, portable property's assumptions continue to structure a vast realm of mainstream fiction in the last third of the nineteenth century—for example, in Margaret Oliphant's (now nearly forgotten) *Kirsteen: The Story of a Scotch Family Seventy Years Ago* (1890).[43] *Kirsteen* is an evident response to the novels of Walter Scott: indeed, the title's echo of *Waverly, or, 'Tis Sixty Years Since* is confirmed by a staged reading of that novel midway through. Oliphant's preoccupation with the role played by information-laden trinkets certainly brings to mind Scott's battery of revelatory amulets, talismans, and broken necklaces. Yet there is a significant conceptual difference between the novelists. Scott's *aides-de-memoire* are portable properties in a very straightforward and decidedly unsentimental sense. Such amulets bear with them vital information rather than accumulating psychological weight: the heir to the estates in *Guy Mannering* (1815), for example, learns of his provenance by way of the locket worn around his neck.

Kirsteen, by contrast, springs to life with three linked items of portable property: a handkerchief monogrammed with Kirsteen's hair, a Bible with her initials written in it by her departed beloved, and a packet of money given her to make the trip to London. Each of these three items is initially endowed with value—use, ritual, and exchange value, respectively. It quickly becomes clear, however, that the initial valuation matters far less than the sentimental associations these properties gradually accrue. The gold hair/thread that Kirsteen uses to decorate a handkerchief with her lover's initials, for example, quickly becomes a transferable essence: her lover's parting words to her in turn become "the gold thread that should run through all the years."[44]

It is not surprising that such immediate metaphorization of the sentiment embodied in portable objects occurs with the signifying handkerchief. That a gift Bible should also be quickly sentimentalized—that is, valued for a lover's knot inscribed in it, but never opened otherwise—is mildly shocking, since the sacred value of the Testament is so quickly annihilated. The real marker of portable sentiment's importance to the novel, though, comes when cash gets reworked and metaphorized. The process is twofold: first, bank-notes are turned into "relic" objects like any other, so that their exchange value seems to be destroyed. Following that erasure, the cash is revivified by being made part of the new emotional economy that redefines it as a token of love. There is, for example, a loving bond between the loyal household retainer, Margaret, and her sister Jean, who had sent her cash so Margaret could travel from Scotland to London. Then Margaret gives that cash—and with it the force of the original sisterly love—to her beloved Kirsteen, who uses the money to serve its original purpose of financing a trip to London to see Jean.

> Marg'ret came back after a few minutes with a work-box in her hand. All kinds of things had come out of that box in the experience of the children at Drumcarro, things good and evil, little packets of powders for childish maladies, sweeties to be taken after the nauseous mouthful, needles and thimbles and scissors when these needful implements had all been lost, as happened periodically, even a ribbon or a pair of gloves in times of direst need. . . . [Margaret tells Kirsteen that her sister Jean] "sent me what would do for my chairges [to travel to London]. It was never touched by me. It took me a great deal of trouble to get Scotch notes for it, and here it is at the bottom of my box with many an auld relic on top of it." . . . She took from the bottom a little parcel in an old letter, folded closely and written closely to the very edge of the seal.[45]

Although all the signs point toward a sacrosanct relic—close-written words and a seal are mentioned—it is crucial that Margaret has already opened the letter, and changed the money that was enclosed into Scotch notes, after which she has reinserted those new notes into the letter.

This metamorphosis might simply read as a mere extension of the logic of finance, whereby cash that can buy one trip is used—as part of a fiscally minded gift exchange—to buy another instead (same ticket to London, different body traveling with it). That reading would link the novel to the interconvertibility of persons, types, and topoi that Deidre Lynch has shown to be central to the economy of character in the eighteenth-century novel. Every formal move described above, however, endows the logic of transference, metonymical association, and sentimental exchange with a kind of complicated, composite power that is deliberately opposed to the logic of fiscal exchange.

Kirsteen, forgotten though it may be, perfectly exemplifies the logic of Victorian portability (still going strong in 1890), because it showcases the ways in which the possibility of properly sentimental portability remains always haunted, like Margaret's work-box, by the specter of mere fungibility. At the bottom of the box, with "many an auld relic" on top of it, lie not the notes that Jean had sent Margaret but the Scotch notes that she had, with great trouble, exchanged for them. Objects that stage partial emergences from mere exchangeability, and incomplete translations into the realm of pure feeling, end up becoming become logical touchstones for novels (themselves instances of such divided value) seeking not a realm cut off from all fiscal logic, but a realm in which fiscal logic can be partially translated, imagined as contributor to a different sort of enduring value.[46] Such meditations are a powerful signal that even at century's end a logic that ties both national and sentimental identity to portable properties still thrives in mainstream Victorian fiction.

THEORIZING PORTABILITY

What each of these literary examples suggests is the inherent instability, in the Victorian age, of the opposition between fungible and relic object—an instability that is especially visible in novels, because of the precarious and yet prestigious middle ground they occupy. Understanding what it means for cultural properties to become portable may help generate a general account of which particular aspects of any given culture lend themselves to transmission, generalization, or replication in an age of worldwide mobility. That connection, which I explore in more detail in this book's conclusion, below, seems worth spelling out here, in order to clarify both the theoretical background of my study, and its potential implications for those studying similar problems in other disciplines.

One way to gain perspective on Victorian novels' representations of an in-between object comes from the vocabulary that anthropology has developed, after Mauss, for making sense of the relationship between gift and exchange.[47] Annette Weiner, for instance, moves away from Maussian insistence on networks of strict exchange reciprocity by positing a sort of property she intriguingly labels "inalienable possessions." Those possessions lie at the heart of the paradox of "keeping while giving"; namely, that "some things, like most commodities, are easy to give. But there are other possessions that are imbued with the intrinsic and ineffable identities of their owners which are not easy to give away. . . . The loss of such an inalienable possession diminishes the self and, by extension, the group to which the person belongs."[48] On the one hand, Weiner's model seems very helpful in understanding the centrality of the process of discrimination—distinguishing, say, fungible Irish potatoes from valuable English flowers—to Victorian novels. On the other, her insistence on the rigid distinction between ordinary trade goods and inalienable property works less well. Weiner even insists that "transfer" (within a family or other "group") is categorically distinct from exchange. In Victorian novels, though, objects like the Eustace Diamonds (see chapter 1, below) or precious English books Emily Eden reads in India (see chapter 2, below) or even a carefully preserved chest of Jewish documents in *Daniel Deronda* (see chapter 3, below) are valuable and narratable because they can seem ineffable and fungible simultaneously.

In a response to Weiner, Maurice Godelier emphasizes the fluidity of boundaries between various states of exchange, arguing that "alienable" or "inalienable" status attaches to particular objects only at certain times, and the particular relationship of any given object to exchange is potentially debatable. Godelier argues for

> the juxtaposition or even the addition of the alienable and the inalienable, for society is brought into existence and sustained by the union, by the interdependence of these two spheres, and by their differences, their relative autonomy. The formula for maintaining the social sphere is therefore not *keeping-while-giving* [Weiner's phrase], but *keeping-for-giving and giving-for keeping*.[49]

This formula sheds real light on a persistent Victorian novelistic suspension of valued objects between the twin imperatives of currency and inalterability: this has also been described as the ability of "inalienable commodities" to exist within "rival schemes of value."[50] The quintessential Victorian portable properties—novels, diamonds, family letters—are not, as Weiner's model demands, marked off as sacrosanct. Rather their difference is always tinted with potential sameness: were they not also potentially implicated in the ordinary flow of exchange, they never would have become portable repositories of meaning.[51]

Despite the subtlety of recent work such as Weiner's and Godelier's on the suggestively dual status of possessions, though, dominant social-scientific paradigms for treating worldwide circulation of culture and its objects often remain tied to a dualism that simplifies culture-bearing objects out of all recognition.[52] An unwieldy binary distinction between the local (or authentic) artifact, and the purely capitalized global commodity has, for example, profoundly shaped discussions focused on "things" or "objects" in the two decades following the provocative delineation of that field of study in Arjun Appadurai's edited collection, *The Social Life of Things*. Appadurai recently reaffirmed the basic binary that he sees differentiating global commodities and local authentic "things" (here, Indian):

> Things in India never lose some of the magic of their human makers, owners, or handlers. . . . [By contrast] the United States is the ultimate consumer, market, affluent, or image society . . . a peculiar veil of abstraction governs over the material life of societies like the United States. Abstraction in this context has several dimensions. The first is that no object or thing in this type of society is fully enjoyed for its sheer materiality. . . . No object is truly priceless, and indeed pricing the apparently priceless continues to be a deep American obsession.[53]

Even though Appadurai finds "India . . . a society whose material life is in the throes of deep change,"[54] he does not offer any way out of the binary he so violently denounces. Rather, he pins his hopes on the side of the binary that he has already classed as archaic. "In India, and in societies where the rule of the market is as yet incomplete, there is a certain chaotic materiality in the world of things that resists the global tendency to make all things instruments of representation, and thus of abstraction and commodification."[55] The continuing dependence on the simple distinction between a world of cultureless abstraction and an archaic material world leaves Appadurai here making the untenable claim that an unspecifiable resistance to abstraction and representation itself is the only way to fight an absorptive and evil market logic.

Adding "portable property" as a third term between "abstract commodity" and "autochthonous thing" may clarify the situation Appadurai is describing. Models of succession (relics succeeded by fungibles, or good Third-World materiality overwhelmed by evil First-World liquidity) necessarily understate the true complexity of simultaneous developments in the ways that objects are regarded. Despite Appadurai's argument (and Mauss's before him), the durability of sentiment, gift-giving, and memento culture in successful capitalist societies is *not* a residue of an archaic gift impulse lingering in a reified world. Rather, the account of portable properties I am proposing suggests ways in which the portaging of sentiment in beloved objects is a predictable, even a necessary, development in a world of increasingly successful commodity flow.[56] The more global such trade becomes, the faster the exchange of items between different regions becomes, the more need to develop auratic—or even somatic—forms of storing personal or familial memories.

PORTABLE HOMELANDS

> The Jews carried [the Bible] with them in exile like a portable fatherland.
>
> —Heinrich Heine, "Geständnisse"

Far from their retaining archaic objecthood in a deracinated world, the seemingly preextant "thingness" of the portable properties that Appadurai singles out for praise is as much a product of the modern world of global exchange as any software network or Coca-Cola franchise.[57] The really interesting questions about the legacy of European empires, then, have little to do with recovering authentic relationships with archaic things, and everything to do with making sense of the systems that for more than a century were able to represent English culture as a dominant form of *translatio imperii* that moved across the world in an unbroken wave, which suffered neither interruption nor undertow.

My argument about the centrality of portable properties to the logic of the novel, and the consequent centrality of the novel to the Victorian conception of what portable properties were, has up to this point centered mainly on the question of reconciling economic and sentimental value. But there are also some interesting implications for the cultural logic of Victorian empire-formation. Gauri Viswanathan has initiated a very productive line of inquiry by pinpointing "the irony that English literature appeared as a subject in the curriculum of the colonies long before [that is, in the 1820s] it was institutionalized in the home country." *Masks of Conquest* also "examine[d] the ways in which [the administrative and political imperatives of British rule] charged [literature] with a radically altered significance, enabling the humanistic ideals of enlightenment to coexist with and indeed even support education for social and political control."[58] While Viswanathan is interested in how literature was taught to Indians and other colonial subjects, I am concerned with contemporaneous English efforts to sequester the pleasures and powers of English literature and nationalize them, to make access to them as restricted as membership in Anglo-Indian clubs.

Such literary "clubability" was not always sustainable and its collapse (as Priya Joshi's work on the Indian circulation of English melodramas suggests) might result in a blurring of the lines between colonizer and colonized: such diffusion presents a powerful alternative to any model that posited a seamlessly successful portability of Englishness into an uncontaminated hinterland.[59] Regardless of its eventual success as a form of sequestration, however, recreating home had become a nearly sacred injunction for English émigrés by the middle of the nineteenth century. It was in the Victorian era that Jane Austen and William Shakespeare alike become reassuring embodiments of "dear old England" for nostalgic expatriates, and that afternoon tea on a foreign verandah came to stand in for England—although the tea might be Indian, and the cups Chinese willow-ware.[60] Victorian Greater Britons evidently valued objects (a trinket), locales (an "English" garden), and even practices (midday walks) that could in some way serve as a direct conduit back to a place nostalgically construed as an alma mater. A piano becomes the "shadow of a rock in a dusty land"; an Anglo-Indian girl picks the first fruits from "the first strawberry plant that ever grew in India" because they embody her distant homeland.[61]

Portability's efficacy as a mechanism of imperial expansion required the blessed dream of a distant redemptive locale. This accords well with Benedict Anderson's argument that successfully producing a sense of belonging at an empire's far-flung margin necessitated a retrospective reconstruction of national identity "back home."[62] It is also compatible with recent work arguing that (following Linda Colley's magisterial *Britons*) life overseas for Scottish and Irish subalterns was bolstered by looking backward to an hypostatized unity described both as "British" and as "English": it is significant, for instance, that within the first two paragraphs of Kipling's *Kim*, its protagonist is described as English, white, and Irish.[63]

What advantages does portable culture offer in protecting or producing a sense of group cohesion or individual identity on the move? The idea of portable property works as an alternative both to fluid cultural forms, which adapt themselves with chameleonic ease to every new setting, and to purely immobile bits of local life. Imagine, for instance, a late Victorian expatriate making a choice between three pastimes as repositories for national pride: football (that is, soccer), cricket, and Morris dancing.

To choose football means embracing the "global modernity" that Lafranchi and Taylor suggest is perfectly symbolized by that sport's rapid adaptation all over Europe and Latin America. Along with simplicity and the ready transferability of knowledge and personnel comes the capacity for regions or nations to develop their own "local styles"—but always within the confines of the same fundamentally simple sport.[64] Adopting football as a source of pride, though, is as risky as pinning your faith in a commodity like cotton: someone else might become a better manufacturer or player than you.[65] An innovator's own worst enemy can be success so complete that originator and imitator become indistinguishable.[66] In fact, once a practice has passed out of its originators' control, the temptation toward what might be called a "cultural sulk" arises; for instance, England's 1904 refusal to be a cofounder of the International Football Federation (FIFA), and its shunning participation in the World Cup until 1950.

Still, what if the only alternatives to having one's cultural markers voraciously globalized were to define one's identity by what is most inimitable, or simply unimitated?[67] Choose Morris dancing, for instance, and you align yourself with the quintessentially local, something as unlikely to be taken overseas as a ruin or a soil-specific crop. With only Morris dancing (or samphire eating, or pole climbing) to fall back on, it might prove hard to forsake football—or cotton, or Wedgwood china, or Fry's chocolate bars (invented 1847)—despite that ominous universalizability.

Enter cricket, a seeming compromise that is actually a third way. Cricket remains markedly English overseas: think of accessories like pads, whites, and the tea break; of argot like *wickets, googly, silly mid-on,* and *howzat.*[68] Yet cricket is also capable, like football but unlike Morris dancing, of a global journey as successful as that of Shakespeare, whom Carlyle describes as embodying England everywhere he goes.[69] It is reportable worldwide—there are two memorable Englishmen always desperate for radio or newspaper cricket scores in Alfred Hitchcock's *The Lady Van-*

ishes (1938)—yet always inescapably English. And even if England's dominance wanes, colonials ("Black Britons" or "Brown Sahibs") who adopt the game often understand themselves to be donning English garb and imbibing English mores.[70] It says a great deal about the patriotic force still ascribed to cricket as a metonymic piece of portable Englishness that the Bank of England in 1993 issued a ten-pound note inscribed with a picture of Charles Dickens gazing benignly down on "The Cricket Match Dingley Dell Against All Muggleton."

James Buzard's recent account of imperial autoethnography—that is, the scrupulous examination of one's own culture, performed by English writers at the height of British dominance—argues that dominant cultures are not just cataloguers of vanquished cultures, but also of their own ascendant national essence. His argument is that novelistic national introspection turns folkways into what might then be labeled "culture" (a process that, as his chosen example of *Bleak House* suggests, is rarely purely triumphalist).[71] This sort of homeland-based ethnographic introspection has historically struck scholars as incompatible with the Victorian notion of stage-by-stage cultural progress, which would seem to entail British dominance gradually exporting an admirable form of civilization that itself need not be interrogated as the mores of "lesser breeds" are. If imperialism succeeds by creating a reassuringly homogeneous space, an undemarcated realm where universalizing integration can follow a British model, then what reason would there be to examine English folkways?[72]

Brad Evans has recently charted early anthropological struggles to reconcile "particularist" and "diffusionist" accounts of cultural circulation. Even Boas, who is now remembered for advocating a homogeneous and stable "culture" as the basis for all evaluations of human society, early in his career advanced diffusionist hypotheses (derived from such Victorian scholars of tale-migration as Theodore Benfey) to explain how particular tropes, stories, and culture-bearing objects might move across seemingly impervious ethnic boundaries.[73] Such fin-de-siècle fluidity in theorizing the emerging concept of culture suggests that any monolithic notion of what makes a "people," a "tribe," or even a "culture" into a unit is perpetually "challenged by the circulation of the people and things they supposedly delimited across their conceptual borders."[74]

The flow of objects outward from England played a crucial role in exporting a restrictive, distinctive sort of Englishness through a world that stayed distinctively non-English.[75] The cultural value attached to markedly English portable property emphasizes the exceptional power (power potentially restricted only to English émigrés) that discrete objects can come to possess overseas. These pieces of property are meaningful not because they are capable of abetting the civilizing process, but precisely because they *do not civilize*; instead, they embody English culture, in its most particularist and nonteleological sense. Such objects can thus produce a sense of identity that travels without decaying, and also without spreading out, that is successfully exportable and yet potentially not diffusionist.[76]

My account of how particular objects come to be endowed with cultural value can, I hope, offer a valuable perspective on this object-by-object process. Because pieces of portable property can be examined separately for their capacity to move from space to space unchanged, my account can help to assess the significance of certain objects (novels central among them) in terms of those objects' ever-shifting relationship to the nature of cultural portability itself.

PORTABILITY IN EXCESS AND IN REVERSE

J. R. Seeley, in his 1883 *The Expansion of England*, complains that his contemporaries "do not perceive that . . . the history of England is not in England but in America and Asia."[77] It might seem hard to credit that at any point in the Victorian era the English could have seemed to have "conquered and peopled half the world in a fit of absence of mind."[78] The developing logic of portability in the Victorian cultural realm, though, suggests that so long as the aesthetic objects through which identity was constituted and solidified could both represent and engender a sense of seamless identity on the move, the "absence of mind" that allowed a culture to finesse or ignore its immersion into global circulation could continue.

Failure, in fact, is one of the most important available clues about portability. I earlier mentioned Irish potatoes as a kind of ne plus ultra of nonportability, the item that marks the limits of cultural portability by refusing to signify anything. Such noncompeting objects, though, are not the only counterpoint to successfully British portable property. More troubling to the economy of unidirectional cultural flow (typified by the enormous success that Wedgwood boasted with his blocky, distinctively English porcelain, sold to Anglo-Indians eager to set their tables with decidedly "domestic" plates)[79] is the possibility of counterflow: objects shipped from colonies to motherland with their colonial character still very much attached.

It is not hard to see why such objects are both problematic and likely. The very success of English-dominated global flow engenders a set of problems for the victors. How can distinctively English culture be passed along the waves of trade, if trade is constituted precisely by the interchangeability of items, their exchange value trumping all use?[80] Moreover, even granting its preservability in a marketplace of fungibles, how can "culture"—or national essence defined in any way other than racially—travel unchanged from the core to the periphery of the empire?

A notional portability that protects Englishness but forecloses on other national transmission mechanisms, then, is implicitly, and at times even explicitly, committed to pure asymmetry. If in the best of times portability is the mechanism ensuring that British culture survives unaltered overseas, at the worst of times the process can also go into reverse, sending from the edges of empire to its core artifacts still freighted with foreign meaning. Scholars have lately stressed the potent allure of such elements of foreignness incorporated into British culture.[81] There is some evidence as well, though, for contempt and for dread associated with the flow of objects from abroad to England (sometimes called "imperial panic"). Could such objects refuse to become commodities, and instead keep their "native" cultural essence about them?[82] In Wilkie Collins's *The Moonstone* (1868; discussed in chapter 1, below), that essence takes the form of three dedicated killer priests who will do anything necessary to repatriate the diamond in question.[83] And if the threat of reverse portability looms large, equally troubling is the specter of an English portability that works so well that it becomes simply diffusion (English culture as football, that is, rather than as cricket). Charles Dilke describes seeing, in Bombay, a play billed as "The Indian Romeo and Juliet." "The play had no Friar Lawrence, no apothecary, and no nurse; it was nothing but a simple Maratta love-tale, followed by some religious tableaux. In the first piece an Englishman was introduced, and represented as kicking every native that crossed his path with the exclamation of 'damned fool.' "[84] Dilke (about whom more will be said in chapter 2, below) is relieved that the Indian audience, having gotten England's notion of power so right (in the form of that native-kicker), at least manage to get its literary touchstone so wrong. Dilke is capable of waxing poetic for three paragraphs on the virtues of the English housefly and its capacity to beat New Zealand flies as thoroughly as English settlers have beaten the Maori.[85] Shakespeare, however, is global in a different way: he travels well *with* us, but let us not be too quick to wish him well among the natives.[86]

Philip Fisher has made the case that a desire like Dilke's—to keep the national culture national even as it becomes global—is more likely to be realized if that culture is stored in words than if it is embodied in artworks collectible and enjoyable without translation. By Fisher's account, literature's physical mobility does not allow it, like paintings, to move worldwide with cosmopolitan ease. Instead, like a ruin or an architectural tradition, literature assumes the ossifying role of embodying a national cultural heritage: if paintings are more like football, literature is more like cricket.[87] This helps explain the increasingly strident nationalism of the latter nineteenth century, and the emergence of a vehement and highly elaborated insistence upon racial difference among prominent English writers from the 1860s onwards,[88] correlated with the increasing focus upon a *written* aesthetic heritage as grounding English pride, and indeed English identity as a whole.[89]

Fisher's hypothesis may help explain the importance of portability not simply as a general description of transmissible culture in Victorian Greater Britain, but as a particularly vital structuring logic for literary texts.[90] It also bears stressing, though, that novels, no matter how nationalized, possessed another kind of doubleness that made them, as Benedict Anderson has recently argued, agents both of group formation and of disruptive anonymity, of a dissident solidarity tending to unsettle fixed divisions (in Anderson's terms, novels are sites of both "bound" and "unbound seriality"). If they were associated with their incarnation (in newspaper, journal, part, or volume) in ways that made them resonant, collectible, and endowable with personal or familial associations, their existence as texts is certified by their capacity to move across boundaries with a potentially unsecured, even unsecurable, diffusion.

Because novels were themselves defined by their uncertain status as portable properties, they became in the Victorian era a ground-zero for a wide-ranging exploration of what it meant for an object to travel simultaneously with ineradicably particular meanings, even national ones, attached, and simultaneously to stand for the potentially limitless fluidity of the marketplace. One implication was that novels could, as in the case of Jane Austen's works among the "Janeites," even travel with forms of meaning generated primarily in the process of circulation itself. It is such complicated results of simple initial impulses that I have tried to explore and explain in the chapters that follow.

CHAPTER ONE

Discreet Jewels: Victorian Diamond Narratives and the Problem of Sentimental Value

> Of all the precious articles that constitute the representative signs of wealth, jewels are those which contain the greatest amount within the smallest compass. Hence the ease with which they may be concealed from the most searching eyes, and conveyed mysteriously and easily from place to place.
> —A. de Barrera, *Gems and Jewels*, 1860

> The . . . peculiar, watery brightness of her eyes—in the corners of which it would always seem that a diamond of a tear was lurking.
> —Anthony Trollope, *The Eustace Diamonds*

THIS BOOK explores an era in which global capital flow simultaneously engendered new forms of fungibility and new sentimental attachments to objects that seemed capable of warding off that fungibility. Marx's commodities and Mrs Tulliver's linens grew up together, and the quest was on for ways to represent the far-flung movements of household treasures as antithetical to the simple exchange of commodities. The complicated relationship that grew up between trade-born fungibles and local repositories of identity sparked a search for ways to understand the movement of Victorian English goods and government overseas, to see that migration as something other than the pure dematerialization of objects into abstract value. Portability came to seem a way of loading cultural meaning into a potentially infinite range of objects. The best sort of culturally resonant properties—to revert to the sporting comparison I set up in the introduction—moved through the world more like cricket than like football.

Given how comprehensive a shift in thinking about portable property I am discussing, it may seem a waste of energy to examine in detail the ways that specific objects—teapots, letters, Bibles, or jewels—have been singled out as exemplary bearers of portable culture. The comparative dematerialization of the meaning of the word "portable" throughout the early nineteenth century (traced in the introduction) might also seem a reason to avoid an object-centered approach to understanding how Victorian notions of moveable value worked. With fewer "portable atlases" and more "portable evidences of Christianity," that is, what good are specific portable objects in beginning to investigate Victorian ideas about portability? Understanding how the Victorian age differed both from predecessors and successors, however, entails locating the spots in Victorian culture at which the interface between "culture" as a whole and its material substrates becomes most tangible: the places where totality meets particularity.

This chapter proposes, accordingly, that the preoccupation with portability in the mid-Victorian period is manifested in diamond tales as nowhere else. Those tales make a unique set of claims about the status of portable property in the Victorian era because of the diamond's status not as an object, but as a "thing."[1] My understanding is that in the emergent field of thing theory, objects or possessions turn into things only when they are located at troubling intersections between clear categories, thus defying ready classification. Harriet Beecher Stowe's original subtitle for *Uncle Tom's Cabin*, "the Man who was a Thing," is far more shocking than Uncle Tom's merely being called an "object," in part because "thing" is the term of choice for the extreme cases when nouns otherwise fail.[2]

"Things," then, are limit cases at which our ordinary categories for classifying signs and substances, meaning and materiality, appear to break down.[3] And diamonds, in the Victorian novel, are just such boundary-troublers. In their persistent refusal to turn either into pure liquidity or pure bearers of sentimental value, they can function as a byword both for the apotheosis of sublimely unique beauty (the "diamond of a tear" that authenticates the depth of an unassailably personal feeling) and for the supreme concretization of monetary value. In that doubleness lies their problematic status—and their enduring allure. Accordingly, some of the most interesting Victorian texts centrally concerned with value's portability are diamond stories: among them, Christina Rossetti's "Hero," Anthony Trollope's *The Eustace Diamonds*, and Wilkie Collins's *The Moonstone*.

MODERNIST "OBJECTIVATION"

The crucial role that diamonds are capable of playing in Victorian texts, where sentiment and cash value openly collide, stands in stark contrast to the role they play in texts from both earlier and later periods. One way to grasp Victorian distinctiveness in this regard is to consider the change in early twentieth-century thing-thinking perfectly exemplified by the development and success of the Rorschach blot. Rorschach's insight, in his 1921 advocacy and distribution of a set of "Rorschach cards," was that a "degree zero" of thingdom—in the form of blots painstakingly engineered to seem purely arbitrary—could elicit the true contents of test-taker's psyches.

> Not only did these cards talk; they did so in virtue of their form and color down to the smallest detail. If the blots suggested even a shard of human design, certain patients would seize on that fragment, losing their own ability to speak from within. For this reason, nothing was more important to Rorschach than creating and reproducing cards that would register as undesigned designs.[4]

In a recent article, Peter Galison locates the early twentieth-century problem of the "talking thing" not within the thing itself, but at the vexed boundary between self and world. Deciding what is "contained" in objects involves a series of prior, potentially ideological decisions about where you imagine human labor or human thought residing. The telling contrast with nineteenth-century conceptions of the thing lies in the modernist notion that the inner self is thoroughly and objectively mappable by its reaction to the external world. The Rorschach blot works only if the talkative object is so perfectly of the "objective" outer world that one can be sure that no other human agency was there before. Therefore, what one says about the objects marks one's encounter with the pure outsideness of the world: "The [Rorschach blot test] means that the functions of subjectivation (how subjects are formed) and objectivation (how objects are formed) enter at precisely the same moment. To describe the cards (on the outside) *is exactly* to say who you are (on the inside)."[5] The Rorschach blot belongs, in short, to a broader modernist conversation about the capacity of indisputably mute objects to "speak" the inner truth that they contain, a conversation that leaves little room for confusion about the moral or psychological state of the property owners who are construed by way of their belongings.

Consider George Simmel's famous 1908 text on "Adornment," which takes up the question of what jewelry, and diamonds in particular, have to say about their wearers.[6] Diamonds strike Simmel as the best example for talking about the way in which ornaments produce, both within the wearer and for observers, the sensation (or illusion) of "deep" or "genuine" character. For Simmel, jewelry is an exemplary instance of the way that the most personal of valuables is precisely the most impersonal, the most immersed in a shared knowable and priceable realm. On the one hand, through jewelry one establishes a sense of personal worth and identity. On the other hand, jewelry's

> very elegance lies in its impersonality. That this nature of stone and metal—solidly closed within itself, in no way alluding to any individuality; hard, unmodifiable—is yet forced to serve the person, this is its

subtlest fascination. What is really elegant avoids pointing to the specifically individual; it always lays a more general, stylized, almost abstract sphere around man—which, of course, prevents no finesse from
connecting the general with the personality.[7]

To Simmel, diamonds are the best of friends not despite their alienability,
but because of it. Simmel distrusts any account of "depth" that discerns
a personality distinct from the circulatory systems through which worldly
value is established.

The first historical distinction worth establishing in understanding Victorian portable properties, then, concerns the distance—or at least the
apparent distance—between a prototypically Victorian attachment to
portable objects and the modernist "objectivation" that is exemplified
both by Rorschach's blots and Simmel's diamonds. Dorothy Van Ghent
is not alone in arguing that Victorian objects—whether endowed with the
power of speech or not—seem both cozily personable and morally salutary. Pub chairs in Victorian novels invite readers to curl up in them, and
Christmas puddings address their consumers by reciting their ingredients
and their provenance; a sparkling grate and glowing fire seem to offer
intimate satisfaction only rarely produced by mere human companions.[8]

The Victorians "were the first people to be so closely identified with
their belongings," argues Deborah Cohen in a recent study that documents a distinctively Victorian linkage between moral improvement and
the possession of beautiful objects. Cohen's notion of "identification,"
though, is far from that implied by Simmel's diamonds, which possess
personality so that their owners need not. Rather, Cohen discerns a Victorian capacity to imagine one's personality as constituted out of a problematic back-and-forth between oneself and one's belongings. She discusses,
for example, Gladstone's profound anguish when selling a lifetime of collections ("the whole process has been a little death"), and a piece by art
critic Philip Gilbert Hamerton that ends with a clergyman proclaiming
approvingly that "we get so attached to some pieces of furniture that they
become to us as if endowed with a kind of affection themselves, and we
half believe not only that we love them, but that they love us."[9]

To analyze Victorian novels via any kind of thing theory, then, apparently requires focusing on the way that an object's singularity calls forth
unsuspected reservoirs of emotion. Such outbursts, clearly, are far removed from Simmel's argument that the love felt for one's jewelry is at
core nothing more than a reflection (objective, impersonal, predictable)
of that jewelry's market value. Simmel speaks of diamonds that do not so
much adorn their wearers as pick them out as "distinguished." Galison
speaks of the process of "subjectivation" occurring with Rorschach blots
as occurring only alongside the most extremely impersonal sort of "ob-

jectivation": seemingly intimate revelations about one's psyche, that is, are by the 1920s understood as produced only through one's alignment with the most palpable external forces. This is a long way from Gladstone's anguished "little death" at the loss of his bibelots.

The Victorian era might appear, therefore, precisely as far apart from its modernist successors as it is from its eighteenth-century forebears, those "object narratives" in which things speak on and on at great length so as to proclaim a fundamental identity between their consciousness and their exchange value. The very starkness of that apparent opposition, however, signals a certain deficiency in current accounts of Victorian convictions about sentimentalized objects. In Victorian sentimental-object narratives, we often find the passionate insistence that such objects contain hitherto undreamt of depths of personality. Alongside, though, runs an evident worry that just the opposite is the case—that such objects are no better than cold material, and that to waste human emotions on them is deluded, selfish, or sinful.

Geoffrey Batchen has shed some light on this problem recently with a series of acute readings of such Victorian oddities as photographic altarpieces to departed children, complete with actual hair from the child draped over the photograph as a kind of (grotesque) wig.[10] Batchen argues that photographs edged with the actual hair represented in the photos hint at an avowedly artificial conjunction of image and "reality." A Victorian advertising jingle perfectly elucidates the boundary status of these photographs: "secure the shadow ere the substance fade / let nature copy that which nature made."[11] Hair, like the photograph, is in some sense consubstantial with the person depicted—this "shadow" is made by nature, in direct contact with the now-absent person. The photograph, because it is the direct record of a bygone human life, thus becomes at once more than an object (because it contains parts of a human being) and yet also less than an object—because what is human in it is so intangible, so removed from the zone where interaction might take place.

Such photographs, like memorial rings, hair, jewelry, and a range of other Victorian "tokens," were commonplace ways to memorialize the absent or the dead. The knowing juxtaposition of copy and relic that these photographs employ does not square with the notion that the Victorians were simply more sentimental than the commonsense Smithians who preceded them and the cold, impersonal Modernists who followed them.[12] In fact, relics like a hairy photograph suggest the internal tensions already present within the Victorian notion of "sentimental objects." Thing theory's attention to the marginal object proves useful here: to Simmel, there was nothing marginal, nothing liminal, nothing troubling about the diamond that defined its bearer's character. His Victorian predecessors, though, saw an abiding tension between fiscal and sentimental value in diamonds. This becomes especially clear when we trace the nine-teenth-century fate of a popular eighteenth-century genre, the talking-object narrative.

TALKATIVE FOREBEARS

The seminal eighteenth-century talking-object narrative, Charles John-ston's *Chrysal, or the Adventures of a Guinea,* depends formally upon a chilly sort of "intuition" that allows Chrysal, a thoroughly peripatetic talking coin, to know the mind of every human being he encounters. There is an intriguing catch, though: Chrysal's (very Simmel-esque) act of mind-reading only works to the extent that those minds are obsessed with gold. Simply to be represented in the novel, then, already attests to a character's avarice. In fact, to have any sort of desire at all—aesthetic, romantic, or financial—is to be inserted into the libidinal economy over which Chrysal reigns.[13] *Chrysal*'s formal innovation (the intuiting coin who discerns what unites humanity) is strongly preserved in the object narratives that follow; in the eighteenth century, such narratives are gener-ally committed to erasing the distinction between the circulation of senti-ment—or desire, or any kind of amiable affection—and the circulation of cash.[14] This willingness to collapse barriers between cash and sentiment, to read avarice as an exemplary emotional state, accords well with eigh-teenth-century notions of both political and emotional economy.

Adam Smith's *Theory of the Moral Sentiments* (1759) describes sympa-thy between person and person as arising from the effacement of individ-ual particularity; in object tales as in other eighteenth-century novels, therefore, sentiment, like cash, comes across as pervasively liquid, produc-ing for sympathetic identification indistinct and generic, rather than sin-gular and memorably distinctive, characters.[15] If, as has recently been ar-gued, the "apparent visual scantiness" of eighteenth-century English novels (that is, the paucity of enumerated objects) can be traced to "an old, deep suspicion of description as something that got in the way of narrative," the objects that do appear are made *more,* not less, important by their "scantiness."[16] Objects can play the role of hero perfectly because their whole personality seems engrossed in their role as fungible pieces of the realm of exchange.[17]

In the early nineteenth century, however, the realms of sentiment and cash value start to become antithetical in new ways. A transitional object narrative, *Aureus: Or, the Life and Opinions of a Sovereign* (1824), re-vealingly begins with its protagonist, a particularly loquacious silver coin, drawing itself up into a flaming pillar and telling the narrator, "I am thy Sovereign."[18] The latent pun, however, hinges not on the authority that the king-coin has over the narrator, but on the fact that the coin is at once an exchangeable totem and a personable companion: the stress falls on *thy*, not on *Sovereign*. If Chrysal was a cold token of ultimately interchangeable desire, Aureus reveals himself as a sympathetic aid to two sisters trying to win the men of their dreams. Forsaking his fiscal duties as coin of the realm, and going out of his way to disparage the notions of cash exchange in general, Aureus steps in to set both sisters on the path to loving matrimony (by showing them they would be better off swapping fiancés). When Aureus goes to a watery doom in a shipwreck, the readers are encouraged to feel as much for his loss as they would for any vanished mariner.

By the time of *Aureus*'s publication, then, what had seemed two compatible discourses in eighteenth-century object narratives—cash and feeling—are beginning to look like antithetical versions of circulation (the saleable and the not-for-sale). It is not simply that one must trade love for money, as certainly happens in eighteenth-century narratives, but that the very move to treat things as exchangeable within a cash economy (rather than, as with the swapped fiancés, within a libidinal one) desecrates them. Love and money still circulate, but they must do so in incommensurable ways, and finding the circuits of love involves disavowing finance. Thus, successful movement in the circle of cash money proves an object's inability to be a bearer of sentiment—and vice versa.[19]

Adamant Objects

This tendency grows so pronounced in the Victorian age that the number of talking-object narratives proper falls off sharply: in thing theory's terms, we might hypothesize that the new doubleness of the realms of cash and sentiment made it harder for a talking object to be a narrator, since the peculiar status of that very narrator would have become a site of perpetual contestation and confusion. The proof of this change is to be found in those few object narratives that do emerge in the Victorian period: all represent their central objects as endowed with deeply sympathizable qualities, a turn toward object pathos that would have been unimaginable with Chrysal and his ilk. The Victorian era is not heavy on cash-conscious clocks or corkscrews, but it is masterful at churning out talkative objects that sweetly explain their own sentimental makeup.

This phenomenon unsurprisingly flourishes most in children's books. In Annie Carey's *Autobiographies of a Lump of Coal; A Grain of Salt; A Drop of Water; A Bit of Old Iron; A Piece of Flint* (1871), for instance, the reader is overwhelmed by a panoply of objects with distinct personalities, each as loveable as Chrysal is fungible. Even coal gets personalized:

"There are some members of our family of the name Lignite, who have preserved very distinct impressions of our former condition," a loquacious lump proclaims, thus encouraging his young readers to construct a genealogy not just for coal in general but for each lump in their own cellar.[20]

This pedagogical science book, though, with its chatty soap bubbles and orotund raindrops, is a far cry from, for instance, a typical Trollope novel, and the difference is a revealing one. Coal's Victorian status as a forgettable commodity makes it worlds apart from its carbon cousin, the diamond. The calm and witty banter of Carey's coal has little relationship to the high anxiety produced by the ultraportability of a Moonstone or a £10,000 necklace. The ways that this gap is explained are various, but each example makes the same fundamental point: this diamond, whether its value be defined by sentiment or cash, becomes a thing worth fighting over by virtue of its remarkable compression. De Barrera in 1860 calls the diamond "the greatest amount [of wealth] within the smallest compass"; Doyle in 1892 registers the same disparity between size and value when he has Sherlock Holmes call diamonds "the devil's pet baits."[21] The equivalence of years of harsh drudgery to a single, easily lost set of stones is the horrible point of Guy de Maupassant's "The Necklace" (1884), and a similar sort of calculation (stones traded for lives) gets played out in Victorian texts that range in mood from the gruesome to the coldbloodedly political to the fantastical.[22]

The distance between eighteenth-century object narratives and Victorian diamond tales is directly linked, then, to the changing relationship between cash and sentiment. Diamonds assume a significance that is at once determined by their exchange value and by a difficult-to-articulate rival—a sentimental value certified by the fond associations, the auratic or cultural resonances, that cluster round them. Diamonds, rather than being objects of pure sentiment or of pure cash, are at their most distinctive in Victorian novels when they are manifestly *riven*. Jane Panton's *Dear Life* (1886) makes this point by basing its plot upon two nearly identical rubies, which are distinguishable from one another only by a minute variation in the Persian inscription carved on them. That slightly vagrant line means the difference between rightful possession and felony, pursuit, and death.[23]

Consider, for example, a Victorian fairy tale in which, rather than a coin speaking and feeling as a person would, the opposite happens: a person becomes a coin-like object. The plot of Christina Rossetti's "Hero" (1870) turns on young Hero's being granted a wish by the Fairy Queen. Her wish "to become the supreme object of admiration" means that while her body is immobilized in Fairyland (also revealingly called Giftland) her spirit will in effect become a pure commodity, fungible enough to assume any shape so long as that object is the apple of some-one's eye.[24] The Queen "charm[s] her conscious spirit into a heavy blazing diamond—a glory by day, a lamp by night, and a world's wonder at all times."[25] Hero's spirit rushes off to be the hero of a story of dizzyingly swift transformations: her owner prefers his wife to her, so she turns into the wife; then he momentarily prefers an opera singer, so she becomes that singer and so on, down ignominiously to a valuable plant, and then a ruin. Hero's commodification then miraculously comes to an end, and her body (spirit presumably reattached) is returned to her father and her patient fiancé, Peter.

On the one hand, exchange value is figured here through the currency of "admiration"; on the other, sentimental value, unexchangeable but also irreplaceable, is embodied in the long-lasting "love" sanctified by Peter's worshipful possession of Hero's pure white body. The question the story asks is whether those two attributes can be radically dissevered from one another. Victorian diamond tales might seem to assert that the two are separate categories—and that the notion of portability represents a way to attribute to sentimental value some remarkable kind of staying power that is not besmirched by mere fiscality. Yet the true radical break between the two (pure domestic bliss versus pure fiscal rapacity) is impossible, or nearly so, for a Victorian text to imagine in practice.

The Victorian obsession with jewelry made out of a beloved's or a dearly departed's hair is a welcome reminder of what is at stake in diamond tales when sentimental and cash value come into direct comparison. For jewelry to be laden with affect is suitably Victorian; but it is equally true to the times for such jewelry to offer quick access to the world of fungibility, where esteem can be translated readily into property. A custom-made piece of jewelry in a Victorian novel is almost always de-fined simultaneously by its romantic significance and its cost.[26] On the one hand, such jewelry is meant to represent the potential transmissibility of affect. On the other, though, it has an ominously handy relationship to the coils of mere fiscal exchange: "the devil's pet bait's" are also (as Becky Sharp's machinations just before Waterloo remind the reader) the decamper's best friend. Thackeray is one Victorian writer who will have virtually no truck with the blurring of the line between sentimental and cash value: the decidedly unsentimental satire of Thackeray's *Vanity Fair* proposes to divide the world (with only the tiniest of exceptions)[27] be-tween Becky Sharp's cold-blooded cash calculations and the fetishistic adhesion to pure sentiment that Amelia represents. But in this as many other respects Thackeray stands apart from his peers. Perhaps the most representative Victorian view of diamonds as perpetual mediators be-tween cash and sentiment comes in a novel often read as Trollope's re-sponse to *Vanity Fair*, *The Eustace Diamonds*.[28]

More or Less than an Heirloom: *The Eustace Diamonds*

The Eustace Diamonds (1871) is best remembered as Trollope's Becky Sharp novel, in which Lizzie Eustace, queen of sharp dealing, vague deceit, and "perjury . . . committed in regard to one's own property," attempts to abscond with a £10,000 necklace stolen from her dead husband's estate.[29] The novel is equally concerned, though, with "the state of despondency into which [Lizzie] had fallen while the diamonds were in her own custody."[30] It is not just despondency, in fact, but diamond-induced irrationality that ends up being both "unnecessary" and "injurious" to her own cause and those around her—Lizzie is maddened by her diamonds.[31] When (in the midst of a complex plot that revolves around Lizzie's dastardly efforts to obtain legal title to a diamond necklace she has essentially stolen from her dying husband and is trying to keep away from her own infant son) she complains that the necklace "has been like the white elephant which the Eastern king gives to his subject when he means to ruin him," she tells an inadvertent truth about her (self-inflicted) plight.[32] At any time, Lizzie could relinquish her claim on the diamonds, knowing they would then descend to her son, and that she could enjoy uncontested possession of an estate that is worth more than the necklace. Instead, the diamonds she should either possess or relinquish possess her.

Lizzie's diamonds are potentially cash, but they turn out never to be fully detachable from various antefiscal systems. The diamonds are legally attached as "heirloom" (until the claim is dismissed), practically attached as vulnerable personal property (they shuffle in and out of a protective iron box), and sexually attached as the dower prize Lizzie uses to lure suitors.[33] Once Lizzie's relationship to the jewels becomes one of insistent avarice—once they stop being an ornament whose value can be shared or realized in Simmel's sense—they supply her neither the benefit of a proper name nor the flexibility of a common asset. In Rossetti's "Hero," objects speak to offer themselves for exchange with any other admirable object in the world: hold me or trade me, they say, behaving just as Marx prescribed. In *The Eustace Diamonds*, however, the necklace is rightly classed by the sage lawyer Dove under the heading of "property so fictitious as diamonds."[34] Dove means more by this than that diamonds are valued simply for being valuable. More unsettling still, their "fictitious" power lies in what they can make their possessors believe. The "risk of annihilation" Dove refers to is the vulnerability of jewels,[35] portable rather than landed property. New sorts of vulnerability, though, bring power. Lizzie is of interest because she attaches herself not to a lover (as Lucy Morris finally gives up her flexibility and attaches herself to Frank) but to the fictitious subject of the necklace.

D. A. Miller has pointed out that Trollope's novels generally depend upon a "merry war" that is depicted as merely a "belated copy . . . of a belligerent and heroic original," a "moderate schism" that allows plot to proceed by way of formal differences that cry out for a readily achievable resolution.[36] *The Eustace Diamonds*, though, presents the story of a woman who moves outside such narrow disputational bounds. To other characters in the novel, the crucial questions of intersubjective and economic behavior involve taking up, and letting go of, objects of transitory but engrossing interest. This is best demonstrated in the character of Lucy Morris, whose amiability is signaled by her remarkable capacity to attach herself serially to a variety of "causes" or "subjects." Lucy Morris is beloved for her ability to "take up your subject, whatever it was, and make it her own."[37] She knows better than anyone how to enter into and "be effective in the object then before her, be it what it might."[38]

Lucy offers a general ethical paradigm for how to navigate the shifting currents of an emotional economy, currents in which Lizzie founders. Lucy is "a treasure" because she enters into "objects" without personal interest. Other characters, less admirably, pursue their own interests (Lord Fawn, thinking of promotion) or their own passions (his sister Mrs Hittaway, who likes to boss her family about). Self-interested and benevolent characters alike, though, are united in their capacity to adhere to and detach from objects of interest: What will happen with the Sawab of Mygawb's pension? Does anyone truly favor Palliser's currency reform? What social scandal will occupy the Duke of Omnium's energy, so that he is not tempted to marry? This is the realm of Miller's "moderate schism" and it is filled with moderately egotistical or moderately selfless people, each happily flitting (or ponderously bumbling) from one "subject" to the next.

Moderate schism, though, is not the only terrain in this novel. By contrast, all Lizzie's attachments and detachments have a single center. A lawyer for the Eustace family declares that the necklace's capacity to lend itself to different meanings for different people is inherently problematic: "the very existence of such property so to be disposed of, or so not to be disposed of, is in itself an evil."[39] That assessment is true to the novel's logic: the fault is not Lizzie's but lies in her permanently uncertain relationship to the stones. She cannot help testing the limits of her power over them. Lizzie exceeds her life-tenure perquisites in other ways—for example, she lops down old trees on the Eustace family estate of Portray— but who could imagine a novel called "The Eustace Timber-Rights"? The necklace's iron box and patent key, the breathless trips up and down stairs it requires, and the almost sexual violations of her person it produces (in the way of searches, arrests, and robberies) all intimate that she is succumbing to the power of the necklace itself.

With such overattached objects—to return to the term I used in the introduction, above, to describe Mrs Tulliver's heirlooms—a character's self becomes so bound up in the object that it proves impossible to regain a salutary relationship to exchange.[40] In anatomizing the extremity to which such overattachment can proceed, Trollope is in some sense testing the fit between Victorian political economy and the tenets of Victorian (Millian) liberalism. After all, if an infinite variety of possible meanings—and accordingly, a practically infinite range of valuations—can be attached to any given object by various subjects, it might be hard to understand how objects can retain a transparently negotiable value.

Given what we know of the way commodities were appraised in the mid-Victorian era, why should it be a problem if different onlookers evaluate a given object differently? As Catherine Gallagher has recently argued, the (Ricardian) labor theory of value—predicated upon a pure and direct connection between the labor put into any commodity and its value—was under fire from several directions at midcentury. On the one hand, Ruskin argued against "abstract fungible values independent of their physiological utility" in favor of a valuation system that favored "biological regeneration. . . . Economic exchange [should] proceed from flesh back to flesh by the least circuitous route."[41] On the other hand, in 1871 W. S. Jevons published *The Theory of Political Economy*, "denying Ricardo's claim that labor is the source of value and making the counterargument that value arises instead from the interactions of consumers trying to maximize their satisfaction and producers trying to maximize their prices."[42]

There is no intrinsic reason, then, why individual diversity in valuation ought not arise, and indeed the exchange in commodities seems precisely designed to accommodate such diversity.[43] In *The Eustace Diamonds*, though, Trollope is pressing the question of disjunct valuation to such an extreme that he reveals a problem that is woven into the character of the commodity itself. By Trollope's account, once a commodity is endowed with a potential (but as yet unrealized) exchange value, the sentiment attached to it is necessarily shaped by its dual character as a tangible (lovable) object to its possessor, and as a fungible item in the flow of commerce. Accordingly, Lizzie's extreme, and extremely physicalized, attachment to the jewels, rather than simply marking one edge of the range of motivating "sensation" that Jevons and Richard Jennings had charted as the underpinning for the value of commodities,[44] demonstrates that any one relationship between an individual and a particular portable property can take on a new (and hence intrinsically narratable) life of its own.

Trollope had explored a similar problem in *He Knew He Was Right* (1869), in which a husband's suspicious misreading of his wife's behavior leads him to a clearly mistaken belief in her infidelity. In that case, Trollope ultimately resolves (or simply cuts) some of the knottiest complications by decreeing that his passionate belief in an unprovable adultery can only betoken madness. *The Eustace Diamonds*, too, has the option of representing Lizzie as pathological, like her other alter-ego, Lucinda,[45] whose disproportionate attachment to her devious aunt eventually drives her mad. Indeed, there does seem to be a lesson in Lucinda's deteriorated mental health: her incapacity to detach from her aunt is what drives her into madness on her wedding-day.[46] Trollope does not redescribe Lizzie's attachment as madness, though. Rather than being deranged, she has simply fallen under an object's thrall. Readers know that Lizzie's doppelganger, the ingénue Lucy, is good because her "diamond of a tear" springs into being out of sympathy for others' concerns.[47] By contrast, Lizzie's diamond is for her own eyes alone. Lizzie becomes increasingly devoted to the actual physical process of tending to the diamonds: "And she would keep the key of that iron box with the diamonds, and he should find what sort of a noise she would make, if he attempted to take it from her. She closed the morocco case, ascended with it to her bedroom, locked it up in the iron safe, deposited the little patent key in its usual place round her neck."[48] But this excessive incarnation of her possession is what dooms her. Even her own traveling companion begins to think, "Who would willingly live with a woman who always traveled about with a diamond necklace worth ten thousand pounds, locked up in an iron safe?"[49] Lizzie is not punished, as readers might initially assume, for being a bad girl. She is punished for being bad at being a bad girl.

Lizzie's trip to Scotland, her diamonds in tow, brings to the fore her incompetence in the most excruciating way possible. Carrying the diamonds with her in a heavy iron box, Lizzie feels her zone of vulnerability growing, so that the whole container, her entire carriage finally seems as vulnerable as the thing contained. Fending off the Eustaces' lawyer, Lizzie feels herself stripped almost naked in her effort to protect the jewels: "There was now a little crowd of a dozen persons on the pavement, and there was nothing to cover her diamonds but the skirt of her traveling-dress."[50] The diamonds' portability here is both sine qua non and curse:

> During the whole morning she had been wishing that she had never seen the diamonds; but now it was almost impossible that she should part with them. And yet they were like a load upon her chest, a load as heavy as though she were compelled to sit with the iron box on her lap day and night. In her sobbing she felt the thing under her feet, and knew that she could not get rid of it. She hated the box, and yet she must cling to it now. She was thoroughly ashamed of the box, and yet must seem to take pride in it. She was horribly afraid of the box, and yet she must keep it in her own very bedroom.[51]

In the chronic repetition of the word "box," the diamonds are transformed into an enormously enlarged zone of sexual vulnerability. By boxing the diamonds Lizzie has not managed to take them out of circulation, as deposit in a bank vault would imply. Instead, she has allied their movement with that of her own body, and made her own movement crushingly dependent upon the properties of her boxed jewels.

TROLLOPE'S BOX

Lizzie's relationship to her boxed diamonds suggests that her attempt to navigate the shoals of fiscal and personal value is not a dead end but a crux in Victorian notions about detachable personal property. This is not madness, but the everyday logic of portable objects taken to an extreme. The diamonds are designed to dangle between sentimental object and cash instrument, quintessential portable properties in their unsettling capacity to carry more than one sort of value at once. The oddly double nature attributed to those diamonds comes across all the more clearly when contrasted to Trollope's idea of the sort of property that moves to its allotted place in a fiscal system and gains value by staying put. Trollope's own voyages, as detailed in *An Autobiography*, were accompanied by a striking tranquility about his most valuable property, his writing. Trollope boasts of having gone off to Australia with a light heart—just after finishing *The Eustace Diamonds*—because

> I also left behind, in a strong box, the manuscript of *Phineas Redux*. . . .
> I also left behind me, in the same strong box, another novel, called *An
> Eye for an Eye*. . . . If therefore the *Great Britain* in which we sailed
> for Melbourne had gone to the bottom, I had so provided that there
> would be new novels ready to come out under my name for some years
> to come.[52]

A man who "never made any money selling anything except a manuscript" therefore shows himself adroit at the disposal of his one alienable property, so that his name can survive both the *Great Britain* and his body.[53]

There is, though, a crucial difference between Trollope and the lamentable Lizzie: he can detach himself from this object of interest, profit from it, and move on. Trollope's vault may not be inherently any safer than Lizzie's, but property stored within them is already half inserted into a system of alienable assets and affections. Like having a son halfway round the world, having novels available anywhere in the empire gives Trollope not a specially precarious identity, but—to judge from his serene confidence—a specially aggrandized one. Trollope is famously willing to put on display his own triumph in entering precious personal treasures into the marketplace—indeed, his autobiography became notorious for his blunt boasts about having turned genius into "product" and inspiration into income. Objects such as his manuscripts are unapologetically endowed with sentimental and cash value simultaneously, in a way that profits from the dual systems rather than, as with Lizzie's necklace, falling between them with a thud. By contrast with Lizzie's impersonal but uncashable diamond, Trollope's own mobile writings look like a laudable contribution to an economy that pays him in cash and reputation both.

Georg Simmel conceives of diamonds as (to borrow Galison's description of the Rorschach blot) sites where "subjectivation" lines up precisely with "objectivation"; diamonds make us feel "deep," that is, because we possess something that has deep value. In *The Eustace Diamonds*, the relationship between economic value and psychological depth is exactly the inverse: the problem with the necklace, by Trollope's account, is the way that it threatens to serve simultaneously as a marker of singular psychological depth and as a token of objective, impersonal value. This sort of unease about doubly valued objects recurs elsewhere in Trollope, as well. In *Can You Forgive Her?* (1864–65), when the cad George Vivasour flings a "love gift"—a ruby-and-diamond ring for his beloved Alice—onto the floor, one of the guard diamonds is dislodged.[54] George has just taken from Alice as a "heart" token a "little ivory-foot-rule" because, he proclaims vehemently, "nothing is too poor, if given in that way."[55] Given George's extravagantly displayed preference for sentimental over cash value, it might seem that Alice—who fears rather than loves George—will not be quick to recover the diamond, no matter how valuable.[56] After all, if true sentiment is what matters most, even such a pricey gem might well be insignificant. In fact, though "it was not that she had any desire for the jewel, or any curiosity even to see it,"[57] Alice spends a long time looking in the grate for the lost stone before carefully hiding the ring away.

Marx argues in *Capital* that anything kept purely for personal use, or even preserved solely within the familial economy, need have no relationship to exchange value at all.[58] Marx divides objects between those valued in the personal or familial realm and those that fatally bear the marketplace's brand on them; gain exchange value and you lose the possibility of parsing things according to one of the systems of archaic value. By Trollope's lights, though, George's violence in separating diamond from ring and his stupidity in thinking a thoroughly valueless folding ruler can be a suitable love token (for stupidity it clearly is) both stem from the same basic mistake. George has failed to grasp what the good Lucy Morris demonstrates with "a diamond of a tear . . . lurking" in her sympathetic and sympathizing eye. Diamonds are of value because they belong to a well-lubricated circulatory system in which emotions, like valuables, are poised to make the rounds. If the cash value of something as emotionally meaningful as a ring were to depart, so, too, would the sentimental value: even a cheap love token that Lucy gives to Frank is "purchased out of her own earnings."[59] Short of fantasized combustion, entombment, metamorphosis, or destruction, emotional and fiscal value cannot be dissevered from one another.

Lucinda may prefer a "gridiron" given with love to valuable silver, but in Trollope the separation of sentiment from value does not come so easily: by Trollope's lights, a gridiron would make a loving gift only if the giver were poor enough that the purchase were a real sacrifice.[60] Trollope possesses a Simmel-like conviction that the construction of a system of circulatable sentiment to run alongside the world of fiscal liquidity creates striking disjunctions that generally conceal the underlying homology between any object's cash value and its affective value. If those two values are not the same, they are still, in both Simmel's and Trollope's accounts, assembled out of the same logical elements and thus capable of standing in for, as well as contradicting, one another.

What for the modernist sociologist Simmel is an inevitable feature of the world's circulating systems, however, is for Trollope a site of a peculiar tension and unease, which must be made palpable before any resolution can be attempted. By focusing on the Eustace diamonds—which are never even described, let alone made aesthetically appealing to the reader in any way—Trollope sets out to provide a general account of something that can only ever happen to some particular individual about some particular object. Trollope, that is, wants to explore those moments where adhesion interrupts flow, where individual desires (for a diamond necklace, even) exist that the novel can point to but not hope to explain. If the novel's explanation for Lizzie's feelings about the diamonds were adequate, after all, the desire would no longer be just intimate personal property; it would be part of the circulating economy of the novel itself. Lucy's shifting interest in the Sawab, like Lizzie's various marital prospects, is a predictable articulation of a well-lubricated system. Lizzie's adhesion to her diamonds, though, is singular in a world of shifting occupations and possessions. She is locked down by the unexpected and almost unrepresentable vitality of the very portable property whose mobility ought to abet, but instead arrests, movement.

Such portable property in Trollope, then, precisely on account of its apparent banality, turns out to have a paradoxical capacity—not present in Simmel—to stand in for the very fact of particularity. Like persons, certain things come to be endowed with an abiding-because-indescribable strangeness within a world that threatens (as in Trollope's slightly later *The Way We Live Now* [1874–75]) to be full of nothing but fungible things and persons. The portability of the hypostatized object—whether it be a compelling necklace or an unpredictable fiancé—thus offers hope that both objects and persons retain a depth precisely defined by being beyond the representative reach of the novel itself.

PORTABILITY IN REVERSE: THE INDIAN RESIDUE OF *THE MOONSTONE*

In Rossetti's story, Hero is metamorphosed into commodity after commodity, producing a strong distinction between the desire for admiration—which creates commodified mutability—and for (effectively incestuous) love, which upholds perpetual sameness. *The Eustace Diamonds*, by contrast, treats its diamond necklace as an object that necessarily circulates uneasily between cash and sentimental value—an object that bears with it potentially all the memories of an heirloom and all the convenient amnesia of a letter of credit. This uneasy doubling turns out to describe a wider range of Victorian texts confronting the problem of portable valuables than does the sharp bifurcation of sentimental and fiscal value proposed in "Hero." One text that showcases the elaborate layering of emotive and mercantile considerations onto a valued object is Wilkie Collins's *The Moonstone* (1868), which Trollope clearly had in mind when he came to write *The Eustace Diamonds*.[61]

My argument has until now been confined to English examples, and domestic ones at that. Here, however, it makes sense to begin discussing how problems of Little England and Greater Britain intersect in the ways I sketched out in the introduction, above. It is true that a great many of the complications in *The Moonstone* arise simply from the tension between a diamond understood as a simple bearer of fiscal value and as the complicated intersection of various sentimental pressures. There remains, however, a crucial distinction to be made between Trollope's and Collins's object choice, a distinction in the *sort* of nonfiscal sentiment associated with the Moonstone. Collins makes sense of the range of anterior values associated with the central object in his novel by making the Moonstone into a portable metonym for India itself.

A decade after the Sepoy Uprising of 1857, with the English beginning to comprehend the true extent of "Greater Britain," it is hardly surprising that Collins could write a successful sensation novel by building his plot around an Indian object endowed with tremendous cultural significance (it had previously been pried from a holy statue, and three priests have lost caste so as to pursue it to England). The Indian origin of the jewel means that (all domestic intrigues and gambling debts aside) the terror associated with the mysterious followers of the jewel is redoubled by all the fiscal and military unease associated with imperial rule over India. But the way that Collins chooses to treat the moveability of Indian attachment to the Moonstone is one of the earliest suggestions that, starting in the 1860s, English and alien pieces of portable property alike will be deeply colored not just by overseas origins, but also by their potential extended life beyond native shores.

Recent critical attention to *The Moonstone* has often focused on the novel's relationship to the imperial environs (India) from which the diamond springs. Ian Duncan has described its "imperial panic," arguing that the novel documents a "demonic counter-imperialism" in the form of the incursion of the diamond and its defenders (the priests of the shrine it was stolen from) into England itself. When that incursion is repelled, Duncan argues, what is left is a "bright but fragile" restored "English domestic order," so that the "diminished solutions of domestic fiction" are counterpoised to a vast "world economy."[62] World-systems theory, too, allows one to understand the novel as representing the economic realities of Britain's worldwide "shadow empire," in which capital flowing through and out of London effectively sets the pattern for production and consumption worldwide. By the logic of a world-system centered in London, there is no particular reason for a diamond's alluring gleam to connote foreign danger, or for romantic fancies of young women or men to light on it with any deeper thought than concupiscence.

The Moonstone is structured around the sentimental attachments that Franklin Blake and Rachel Verinder form to a diamond lawfully attached to India. Rachel and Franklin's interest in the object—as family heirloom, as thing of beauty, as symbol of their love—is represented, intriguingly, as mild counterpart to, rather than an antithesis of, the mysterious forces that pull that diamond back to the East (forces represented both by the three priests who pursue it and the religious curse that hangs over it). Collins's readers would have been well attuned to such connections, and willing to suppose that English aesthetic appeal in England might be comparable to Indian religious yearnings. For all the objections to Collins's excessive "ingenuity" among English critics, not one of them echoes the charge made by the *Nation* when the novel was published in America: that the yellow diamond at the novel's center "might as well have been a black bean, or a horn button."[63] The diamond's specifically Indian history matters, and is treated with the kind of cautious respect—among English readers—that reveals the depth of consideration given to the question of what Indian portable property might look like.

Collins represents the diamond, then, as being a potent bearer of familial, romantic, and aesthetic power because (not despite) of its arrival from the Orient with a dangerous but enviably powerful set of Indian associations.[64] Rachel's passionate attachment to the diamond, like Franklin's somnambulant one, is a pale domestic imitation of that much stronger force from abroad—Duncan labels it "Asiatic romance." The crucial force of the aesthetic attraction in *The Moonstone*, then, resides in the affinity the stone creates between domestic and external desires. Both weak, domestic, aestheticized attraction to the gemstone and strong, long-distance, Hindu religious devotion to its divine power are placed on one side of the equation.

As I argued in the introduction, above, starting in the 1860s the capacity of Indian objects to possess or seem to possess this kind of powerful cultural residue might be called the threat of "reverse portability." But this kind of reverse is ominous enough that even in a sensation novel it does not go unchallenged. Against the idea of legible traveling Indianness setting up a living breathing presence in the heart of England—a portable empire—Collins sets the exemplars of total liquidity: European debt and European markets. Both Blake and Godfrey Abelwhite (thief and eventual victim of the Moonstone, respectively) are in debt—one accrued his debts on the Continent, the other looks to go there to clear them. Entangled in the global credit market, these two have one idea only: to get to Rotterdam (here understood as the diamond hub of the world-system) so as to liquidate valuables such as the diamond, or their own good name, or their family ties, and re-enter the free-moving stream of the marketplace. By the same token, the novel's opening threat, if Rachel refuses the poisoned gift from her uncle John Hearncastle, is that the stone will be cut up—its value will be increased when it is dismembered, because of a flaw at its heart—and sold to fund that ultimate form of pure fiscal mobility, "a professorship of experimental chemistry."[65]

The image of the flawed jewel only heightens an effect that Collins clearly strives for: the felt disjunction between diamond as money and diamond as site of sentiment. As long as the diamond remains uncut, the possibility of its double meaning is retained. The novel documents the period during which the stone, by being both potential cash and the instantiation of aesthetic value, also offers itself as a vulnerable marker of the fragility of both systems. Like the Eustace diamonds, the Moonstone is not only saleable but also damageable (burnable, cuttable, stealable) for as long as it stays intact. Translate it into some other form of value (let it cement a marriage, or fund a professorship) and it becomes merely a part of the smooth circulation of cash. So long as the Moonstone remains intact and in the house, though, on Rachel's neck or Abelwhite's person, it troubles the circulation of cash and sentiment both.

My claim is that the diamond's sort of durability makes *The Moonstone* a sterling example of a trend that troubles the logic of portability even at its acme in the mid-Victorian era. The logic of reverse portability is simple: if British expansion to India and elsewhere brings with it items like a "portable Bunyan," or the collected works of Shakespeare that, for Carlyle, make an empire, then what is to stop other objects making the journey in reverse?[66] *The Moonstone*'s very specific spin on "imperial panic" depends on the stone's being laden simultaneously with Abelwhite's cash covetousness, Rachel's aesthetic intoxication, and, below it all, a traveling Indian curse. What makes that threat so troubling is that its Indian executors (like the traveling caskets of earth envisioned in *Dracula* a generation later), rely on the very same neutral mechanisms of travel that Britons themselves rely on. The stone may arrive as pelf, but its guardians arrive like returning Anglo-Indians by Suez steamer.

This study as a whole, for reasons I outlined above in the latter half of the introduction, aims to move from considering how English economic thinking shaped notions of portable property into a reckoning of how imperial aspects of Greater British expansion changed the ground rules for evaluating the use and the durability of culturally resonant traveling objects. The imperial relationship between England and India, with its two-way traffic and one-way power dynamic, is a central reason why any account that sets out to tell the story of English sentimental objects also has to reckon with the ways that sentimentality about Englishness is always in large part a Greater British phenomenon. One way to see why this must be so is to consider what notion *The Moonstone* conveys about the viability of Indian culture making it to England unscathed.

Although there were a good many more Indian goods than Indian persons transported to England as early as 1868, still there was a small but significant Indian presence in England already by midcentury, coupled with a steady stream of Indian travelers.[67] Gandhi was one among many education-bound Indians when he arrived to study law in the 1888; on the political side, in 1892 Dadhabai Naoroji (1825–1917) was elected MP to represent not only Holborn but also, Antoinette Burton argues, implicitly the whole of India, as well.[68] What such traffic implies, and what *The Moonstone* goes out of its way to underline, is that English travel, with imperturbable assurance of adaptability anywhere, raised the alarming possibility that sauce for the conqueror likewise might be sauce for the conquered. If Indians could move to the West Indies as migrant labor (or into nabobs' townhouses as necessary chefs) their objects ought to be able to move through the British Empire with the same sort of cultural baggage attached to them as Dickens novels, altarpieces, or tea-services.[69] Salutary consequences for the imperial rulers might even follow: Western domesticity might (on the model of *Uncle Tom's Cabin*) be recapitulated everywhere by obedient subaltern races.

The Moonstone sees only murder at the end of that road. Collins's fantasy of a priest-haunted Indian jewel does *not*, however, prove there is an immense body of mid-Victorian "imperial-panic" texts; enthusiastic gushing over the wealth of Eastern goods at Liberty's (or, increasingly, at provincial marketplaces) far overshadows Collins's expertly packaged dose of sensation-mongering.[70] It is worth keeping *The Moonstone* in mind, though, because of the often surprising vehemence with which Anglo-Indian writers, from the 1820s onward,[71] deny that objects shipped from India to England can bear the essence of India with them. Instead, the Anglo-Indian texts analyzed in chapter 2, below, often strive to depict Indian-made objects as gaining real meaning only through their British associations. Even diamonds taken from the neck of a crown princess are treated, in Emily Eden's remarkable Indian travelogue, *Up the Country*, as two things only: cash for the Company, and a story to share with a sister. Anyone looking in homesick Anglo-Indian texts for redolent Indian objects like the Moonstone would be startled to discover the amount of space given over to describing what can be done with English objects sent to India; pages lavished on silver, whole entries given over to rhapsodies about the latest insipid (even willfully insipid) London dramas put on in memsahib circles. Equally surprising is the amount of ink spilled on one of the most modest portable properties I turn to next: English fruit transplanted to India.

CHAPTER TWO

The First Strawberries in India:
Cultural Portability Abroad

A CORDON OF INATTENTION

Strawberries first taught Harriet Tytler she was English. Born, bred, and married in India, the octogenarian Tytler in 1903 still described herself and her fellow Anglo-Indians as "exiles in a foreign land."[1] Her obdurate refusal of Indianness helps explain why one of her strongest memories is of being taken, at age eight, to see

> the first strawberry plants that ever grew in India. . . . Two of the plants had one ripe berry each. Of course everyone was delighted at the novel sight. No one touched them, but all expressed the desire to be Lord Auckland [and so] to have the pleasure of eating the first Indian strawberries. . . . No sooner had my father and his friends gone on, chatting away, than I thought I really must taste the strawberries. Accordingly, I picked and ate them both.[2]

Born in what she cannot conceive as her own land, raised to idolize an England known only through words, pictures, and stories, Tytler cannot resist the chance literally to ingest England.

That bit of strawberry theft exemplifies the cultural practices that allow self-styled exiles to think of England as a tangible alma mater, not a distant speck on the map. Such long-distance attachment allows Anglo-Indians to overlook their Indian surroundings, and helps explain cultural portability's importance in an imperial "contact zone."[3] Tytler's strawberries become sentimental objects in the service of a powerful national ideology not hindered but helped by the fact that the nation it serves is thousands of miles distant.

Margot Finn, E. M. Collingham, and others have recently drawn attention to the Anglo-Indian gift-exchange and alliance-formation with "indigenous Hindu and Muslim economic elites" in the eighteenth and early nineteenth centuries.[4] That affiliative fervor, however, disappears almost entirely in the Victorian era; from the 1830s onwards, the highly developed Anglo-Indian network of sentimental object-exchange—hair jewelry, association copies of Greek dictionaries, et cetera—almost exclusively connects blood-English circles of friends and relations.[5] Such long-distance national or familial connections could, as the strawberries suggest, thrive on modest as well as sumptuous substrates. Canadian-born Sara Jeanette Duncan's proudest claim, after two-plus decades in India, was that "there was no golden-rod in Simla till I went to America and got it. . . . And the warm scent of it, holding something so far beyond itself and India, something essential, [is] impregnated with the solace that one's youth and affections are not lost, but only on the other side of the world!"[6] For Duncan, these messengers of a life elsewhere function simultaneously as a breeze from the West, and a shield against the East.

The much-remarked capacity of Victorian writers to deploy ready-made Orientalist tropes to caricature and classify India, then, does not exhaust the resources of a colonizing nation in a contact zone. Gauri Viswanathan's injunction to "consider English culture first and foremost in its imperial aspect" requires making sense of the vast body of Anglo-Indian writing that, in preference to writing directly about India and Indians, goes out of its way to preserve the illusion that life in India is best understood as a (painful but necessary) continuation of Englishness abroad.[7] My argument is that the innovative Victorian conception of dematerialized portability (that is, the notion that abstract concepts like Englishness, race, or familial heritage can become metaphorically portable by being incarnated in crucial objects) allows physically portable objects to bear both national and familial heritage with them into Greater Britain.

Amartya Sen has proposed dividing European writing on and in India into three categories: "exoticist," "magisterial," and "curatorial."[8] A fourth category, though, "willfully inattentive," better describes some of the most memorable and widely circulated pieces of Anglo-Indian writing.[9] These India-made-easy texts prove useful in establishing a cordon of inattention, allowing English readers the option of imagining India principally via the sufferings of Anglo-Indians.[10] Three works published between 1843 and 1873 are illuminating examples: Julia Maitland's *Letters from Madras During the Years 1836–1839*; an anonymous memsahib memoir, *Overland, Inland, and Upland*; and Emily Eden's *Up the Country*. In each, the allure of portable Englishness is crucial in representing what English experience looks and feels like in the Raj; yet in each text, some attributes of that portability ultimately fracture and unsettle the national solidarity that portability putatively strengthens.

Why India?

A great deal of current work on the British Empire has—as Seeley does in *The Expansion of England* (1883)—stressed how vast and lucrative were the settler colonies where a "virgin-land" myth prevailed, and where, unlike India, virtually uncontested expansion of British culture into a razed hinterland was the order of the day. Such work emphasizes that

> in the United States, South Africa, Australia, and elsewhere, settlers sought to construct communities bounded by ties of ethnicity and faith in what they persistently defined as virgin or empty land. . . . They wished less to govern indigenous peoples or to enlist them in their economic ventures than to seize their land and push them beyond an ever-expanding frontier of settlement. . . . Such settler colonies . . . quickly became highly integrated into global markets, their prosperous immigrant populations supplying crucial metropolitan goods while enjoying considerable political autonomy.[11]

In colonies such as Australia and Canada, the lack of effort to understand extant native culture has been attributed to material causes (settlers' not needing to manage forced labor) and to cultural ones (the "desire for London" that meant any homegrown accomplishment, whether literary, sporting, or scientific, could only please Australians after it had been acclaimed back in the metropole).[12] A heightened sense of the importance of London mores sent abroad even inspires Janet Myers, in a recent study of Australian emigration and nation-formation to describe the establishment of bourgeois ideology in the Antipodes as "portable domesticity." Myers goes on to argue that such portability ironically becomes the basis for the invention of an Australian national identity that effectively borrows its structure from British domestic practice.[13] This idea—that national identity is achieved by slyly appropriating the imperial legacy and proclaiming it as the basis for a new autochthony—is akin to Benedict Anderson's argument that settlers in the Massachusetts Bay Colony first became Americans at the moment that they articulated a distinctive sense of their own Englishness.[14]

By such accounts, settler nationalism can look like the product of a series of transformations, performed in a cultural vacuum, that transform an original imperial English identity. It is crucial, however, to recall the indispensable role that Irish and convict populations played in producing Australian national identity—and, equally crucial to consider the significance, and the origins, of studious Australian obliviousness toward aboriginal culture.[15] Such deliberate oversights played a crucial role in the creation of new national identities on every imperial periphery. One reason that Anglo-Indian texts ended up circulating so widely in settler colonies and overseas holdings was that they explicitly addressed the problem of managing—and of ignoring—colonized populations. In every imperial contact zone, the English understood they were interacting with one or more vibrant subordinate cultures.[16] It was Anglo-Indians, however, who produced a series of influential texts about the obstacles to remaining

English abroad, texts that seem to have circulated as widely in other settler colonies as they did back in England, and that in time became tem-
plates for imagining a portable Greater British culture.[17]

It is Anglo-Indian writers who most fully describe English objects bearing salutary messages from afar, in large part because that portable meaning was the best line of defense against a dimly acknowledged nemesis:
autochthonous Indian culture—and behind that, more ominous still, the
specter of Indian portability in its own right.[18] India was, to Anglo-Indians
concerned both to administer and understand it, a periphery that threatened to define its own relationship to the metropole.[19] Tytler and her peers
adhere to an "English" identity that can only seem unproblematic and
entirely natural thanks to an immense effort on the part of thousands of
Britons in India to recall or invent distant metropolitan alternatives to
Indian realities. In Salman Rushdie's *Midnight's Children* (1981), Saleem
owns a toy globe stamped not with the phrase "made in England," but
"made as England."[20] It is a very Victorian formula. Anglo-Indianness,
which is not made in England but nonetheless has to function "as England," thrives on assertions of homesickness, nostalgia, or attachment
to absent England. Such claims, though, are always the product of liminal
interactions, most colonial precisely at the moment where they seem most
English.[21]

The need to disavow antagonism with nearby potential foes and to
redescribe one's actions as if they were oriented entirely toward keeping
faith with the distant metropole profoundly shapes, for example, the
Anglo-Indian gentleman's club. At first glance, such clubs may seem incar-
nations of the simplest sort of portability, an effort to replicate the life
their members had enjoyed in their Pall Mall or St. James clubs. A 1927
article about Indian clubs reported, for example, that "it is the practice
of European peoples to reproduce as far as possible in their settlements
and colonies in other continents the characteristic social features of their
natural lives."[22] As Mrinahlini Sinha puts it,

> "Clubland" as a whole served as a common ground where elite Europe-
> ans could meet. . . . These clubs represented an oasis of European
> culture in the colonies, functioning to reproduce the comfort and famil-
> iarity of "home" for Europeans living in an alien land. The cultural
> values that the club represented were understood as transplanted to the
> colonies.[23]

Clubland is far from simple, though. Sinha argues that such clubs are "a
privileged site for mediating the contradictory logic of Eurocentrism in
the creation of a distinctive colonial public sphere. . . . The clubland of
colonial India was thus not so much a 'hothouse' import from a sealed-
off national British culture as a response to the particular demands of its

colonial location."[24] For example, the fear that English women could not be trusted on their own "ensured that the European social clubs in India became immediately more vulnerable to the 'infiltration' of women than their counterparts in Britain."[25] Ironically, the only way to produce a space that can function "as England" is to people it with women, destroying the resemblance to London gentleman's clubs. There is also an analogous phenomenon that might be called "upclassing," by which middle-, or even lower-middle-, class Englishmen and women, condemned to comparative poverty and bungalow obscurity "back home," could enjoy a simulacrum of upper-class life in their Delhi or Calcutta clubs.[26]

The insistence on "remaining English" while abroad thus means inventing a camaraderie impossible back in London. This sort of exiles' solidarity helps shed light on recent work discussing Anglo-Indians as vectors "carrying India" with them back to England. Nupur Chaudhuri, for example, has argued that English "memsahibs" frequently turned into ardent proselytizers for Indian mores or menus when back home in England:

> Nineteenth-century memsahibs, to create a British lifestyle in the Indian subcontinent, seem to have collectively rejected Indian objects in their colonial homes and refused Indian dishes in their diets. [However,] the memsahib's negative attitude regarding the use of Indian goods and dishes was almost totally confined to the colonial environment.[27]

Returnees from India brought back with them elaborate recipes for Indian food, supplies of fresh curry powder, and Kashmiri shawls. In England, memsahibs could flaunt such extravagantly Indian imports as "the Late Baboo Sir Dwarkanath Tagore's Highly Esteemed Curry Powder."[28] In Anglo-Indian society, however, a premium was placed on the appearance of imperturbability in the face of rapid cultural changes—that is, on the capacity to remain aloof, superior, resolute. Charting the repudiation of India-glamorizing nabob culture that began in the 1820s (a chronology that tracks well with Finn's finding that "white mughal" practices of transcultural gift-exchange circles had declined markedly by the 1830s), Collingham describes the importance of markedly English dress among Anglo-Indians, and the surge in advertisements for canned and otherwise preserved food. Also part of the same story are the extravagant efforts among Anglo-Indians to avoid even those foreign goods that were treasured back in England. Josiah Wedgwood announced with amazement that his chinaware was valued more highly than genuine Chinese porcelain by Anglo-Indians; and in 1837, Frederik Shore reported that "some years ago, hardly anyone in Calcutta would place upon his dinner table any but the plainest white English crockery ware. Even English china was objected to for fear it might be mistaken for real China, and not perceived to be of English manufacture."[29] It was no longer enough for Anglo-Indians to do as they did in London; it began to seem necessary to do as they would have done in an England without imports.

Julia Maitland: So Curiously Different

In a Victorian Anglo-India characterized by such exaggerated efforts at establishing psychic distance from one's actual site of residence, it is perhaps no wonder that one of the best-known midcentury Anglo-Indian memoirs spends considerable effort describing her portable havens from foreign climes. In Julia Maitland's *Letters from Madras* (1843), only mobile Englishness seems capable of rescuing her from the dust, the heat, and the impositions of "native life." She describes the bliss of leaving, with her civil-servant husband, a Rajah's party:

> We stayed with him as long as we could endure the heat, din, and glare, and then went to our own rooms. There we found everything such a complete contrast to the native taste, that we could scarcely fancy ourselves only a hundred yards from all the Rajah's row. Our matee had lighted the candles, and placed our tea-things, books, and drawing materials on the table, all looking as quiet and comfortable as at home. I never saw anything so curiously different from the scene of the minute before: every feeling and idea was changed in an instant.[30]

Such moveable rooms are a saving grace for travelers abroad who reserve the right to define themselves by their extended community back home.

The Suez or Madeira mails, which supplied everything from portable beds and gymnasia to seeds and cheap India-paper editions of quintessentially English books (perhaps published, as Maitland's was, in the short-lived midcentury Murray's Home and Colonial Library or, after 1886, in the longer-lived Macmillan's Colonial Library), helped émigrés to establish their retreats.[31] When in 1846 John Kaye declared that "there is no country in which cheap and portable literature is more required" than India, it is possible that he had a native-Indian readership for English novels in mind (a readership that, as Priya Joshi has demonstrated, waxed through the nineteenth century and became crucial to the success or failure of various English publishing houses who aimed for dominance in overseas sales).[32] In calling for greater portability of reading matter, though, he certainly had in mind the reading requirements of those English subalterns driven to make hundred-mile journeys for the chance at a copy of *Waverley*.[33]

Able to sequestrate herself in a portable England every night, Maitland (a great-niece of Fanny Burney) presents herself as a traveling incarnation of everything European. In another Rajah's house, for instance, she becomes a Western art restorer:

> Penny-Whistle [the Rajah] was very fond of his pictures, and sent for some other great coloured prints of hares and foxes to show us. They had been given him by an Englishman long ago, and the colour was rubbed off in many places, so I offered to mend them for him, which greatly pleased him. While I was filling up the holes in his foxes' coats with a little Vandyke brown, he stood by crossing his hands and exclaiming, "Ah! all same as new! wonderful skill!"[34]

The "same as new" that Maitland can deliver speaks to the complicated doubleness of culturally portable objects. These prints, Maitland believes, are treasured for their very Englishness (even "Vandyke brown" is an English color here). Their repair therefore requires not artistic expertise—there must be far more skilled painters than Maitland in even a minor Rajah's court—but national authenticity.

This straightforward account of portable Englishness may seem entirely consistent with Maitland's own understanding of herself as detached from India and still connected to England. Yet even as Maitland reminds herself of England, she evinces considerable uncertainty about how detached she might or might not be from the English around her. She does not, like many of her peers, rail against the fatal climate and the untrustworthy servants. Rather, her habitual venom is directed against two foes: the Englishmen who arrive at her house unannounced to claim hospitality, and the Englishwomen who, having nothing better to do, exchange calling cards or meaningless chatter all day. "It is wonderful how little interested most of the English ladies seem by all the strange habits and ways of the natives; and it is not merely that they have grown used to it all, but that, by their own accounts, they never cared more about what goes on around them than they do now."[35] Here, the very durability that she seemed to treasure—her capacity to go out with her European paints, but return in the evenings to the quiet comfort of an English tent—is viewed from another angle. The capacity to go on being what one was back home—or rather, to expose oneself to nothing that might change that long-lost image of home—is not a blessing but a curse.

Nor is the Englishman's lot any better. Roles are distinct: women stay in the civil lines, while men extract a living from some form of grappling with "natives." Men, however, are as reluctant as women to be altered abroad. This manifests itself not in apathy and listlessness, but in a complementary sort of single-minded vocational avarice.

> As soon as three or four of them get together they speak about nothing but "employment" and "promotion." Whatever subject may be

started, they contrive to twist it, drag it, clip it, and pinch it, till they
bring it round to that; and if left to themselves, they sit and conjugate
the verb "to collect": "I am a collector—He was a collector—We shall
be collectors—You ought to be a collector—They might, could, should
or would have been collectors."[36]

Women insulate themselves, while men who do explore this brave new
world see nothing but the taxes they must collect. If the culturally redolent
objects that arrive from England are portable, what these men collect is
quintessentially fungible.

Maitland's contempt both for female withdrawal and for male incapacity to see anything other than cash makes her commitment to a portable
English identity an increasingly complicated one. In *A Passage to India*
(1924), E. M. Forster offers a stark binary between English conformists
(the subaltern Ronnie Heaslop) and rebels (the defiant teacher Fielding).
The meek and the mindless among the English sing the Anthem and attend
productions of banal London comedies, while Anglo-Indian rebels hold
themselves firmly aloof, seeking out Indian conversation and moonlit
mosques.

Maitland, though, refuses Anglo-Indian community without relinquishing Englishness. This double refusal highlights one of the most curious developments produced by notions of cultural portability in Greater
Britain: that, far from serving to underwrite a straightforward solidarity,
the allure of portability is often linked to its capacity to protect individual
writers *from* the very community that such portability is supposed to instantiate. Some of the most interesting texts produced in the Victorian Raj
reveal a remarkable interest in establishing almost as strong a detachment
from other Anglo-Indians as from "natives." That is, writers describe feeling divided from rather than united to the Anglo-Indian community—or
rather, united precisely in their disunity, so that these writers feel connected to fellow exiles precisely by their very sense of geographic and
social dislocation. Maitland manages to feel herself a rebel from Anglo-
Indian life without the danger of an active solidarity with "natives."

The result is that Maitland seems constantly on the lookout for activities that will distinguish her as much from her peers as from the vexing
natives. Naturalizing is one such outlet. If Anglo-Indian ladies take no
interest in the natural life around them, Maitland will retaliate by becoming a collector of a different sort, gathering beetles for the British Museum. That project establishes her detachment from lazy English ladies,
yet it avoids committing her to siding even with the Indians who play a
major role in her entomologizing:

> I have been trying to entomologize, as there are abundance [*sic*] of curi-
> ous insects. Mr Spence himself told me, before I left home, that the

insects of India were very little known; and that I could not fail to find many new specimens, especially among the smaller Coleoptera. It is impossible to go "*à la chasse*" oneself, so I employed the beggar-boys, who at first liked the amusement and brought me a great many, but they gradually grew tired of it, and are now too lazy to find me any more at all. . . . [They] will not give themselves the trouble even to put out their paws to take an insect if he crosses their path. They are indeed a lazy race.[37]

Maitland's collecting establishes her better-than-Anglo-Indian connection directly back to London, but also establishes her superiority to the natives whose "paws" render them only slightly more advanced than the beetles they fail to gather.[38]

Maitland is well aware, however, that her efforts at collecting are amateurish, and she is uneasy about the resemblance they might bear to the social time-wasting of her compatriots in India.[39] Maitland is at her most candid, it turns out, at moments when the very activities that she wants to think of as distinguishing her are revealed as very widely prevalent among Anglo-Indians. The central irony that shapes Maitland's time in India is that she sets out to detach herself from English men and women who themselves also want nothing more than to detach themselves from their Indian surroundings. Consider mail-call:

> For some days before the mail is expected all Madras is in a fever, speculating, calculating, hoping, almost praying, that it may arrive a few days, or even a few hours, before the usual time; and when it is known to be "in," the news travels like wildfire in all directions; peons are dispatched from every compound to wait at the post-office and bring the letters the instant they are given out, in order to gain an hour upon the general postmen; all other interests and occupations are forgotten; and many people will receive no visits, if there should chance to be any unfortunate beings so letterless as to be able to pay them.[40]

The pretense of important visits between families is dropped; in the rush to feel long-distance connections, it seems hollow to put energy into local ones. At this moment, Maitland's basis for distinction wanes: every Briton abroad turns out to share her aloof attitude toward exile community. Their removal from their homeland forms the basis for their solidarity. Ironically, though, that solidarity is best expressed in these moments of separation from one another.

Anglo-Indian cultural portability helps explain Maitland's simultaneous connection to and alienation from a cohesive national identity in exile. Drawn to the mails and to her attenuated ties back to England just like any other imperial civil-service wife, she nonetheless resists being

connected to those very people with whom she shares the stance of detachment. A parallel might be drawn between Anglo-Indian notions of portability and the kind of detachment that structures literary representations
of another sort of hermetic community: suburbia. Suburbia, too, is represented (in English texts dating as far back as Thomas De Quincey's "The
Household Wreck" [1838], but also in twentieth-century American writing) as a disavowed community. It is made up of those who arrive in the
suburb in order to escape the claims of community, only to find a community defined by each resident's insistence on his or her nonmembership.[41]
The parallel is underscored by the insistence with which Maitland (like
many of her peers) insists that she is not like other Anglo-Indians, since
her mental life derives from England itself, rather than from this simulacrum of England.

Maitland, though, is never as separate as she makes out, and there are
moments when a reader can glimpse her implicit attachment to the Anglo-
Indian community she seems overtly committed to scorning. In recording
her reaction to the death of the bishop of Madras, which occurs very
shortly after her own arrival in the city, she merges into the community
of Anglo-Indian mourners.

> *February 12th*—Everybody in Madras has been in real sorrow of late
> for the death of Bishop Corrie. They say he was the most useful person
> in all India, and the most beloved. He was thought to have more judg-
> ment, experience, and knowledge of the native character, than anyone
> else. Everybody of every class looked up to his wisdom and firmness:
> yet he was so gentle, benevolent, and courteous, that it was impossible
> to know him without becoming really attached to him. I used always
> to think I had never seen such a pattern of "the meekness of wisdom."[42]

Maitland's unacknowledged search for inclusion among Anglo-Indians
could not have found more nuanced expression in novelistic free indirect
discourse than it does here, in the slide from "[t]hey say he was" to "he
was thought" to "I used always to think"; third-person plural giving way
to passive impersonal and then to first-person singular. Maitland does not
merely align herself patriotically with that expatriate "we" who valued
the bishop. She goes beyond the loyally impersonal "it was thought" into
an assertion of her own as-if-personal connection to the bishop, and back-
dates her loyalty, so that her month in India becomes part of the timeless,
knowing residence of the "old-timer." The phrase "I used always to
think" is akin to Pip's observation that after his first visit to Miss Havisham's house he had daydreams of what "I used to do" as if he had
been going to the house all his life, not just once.[43]

Moreover, this passage reveals some of the difficulties involved in Maitland's claim that attachment to the homeland via portable property can

exempt one from the obligation to affirm a connection to one's immediate neighborhood. Maitland's implied incorporation into the "we" who mourn the death of the bishop of Madras suggests that it is difficult to avoid being conscripted into the social universe that portable culture conjures up. Maitland sets out to establish her own mail-routes, her own beetle brigade, buttressed by hostility toward Anglo-Indian hospitality and "collecting." She finds herself nonetheless drawn into the shared emotions of the community and into its apathy and listlessness, beginning to adapt the viewpoints and opinions of her nearest English neighbors.[44]

Maitland's unwillingness to knuckle under to her presumptive social role as hostess turns out to be representative of a certain logic actually inscribed in the paradigmatic portability that sustained Englishness, especially of the genteel memsahib variety, in India. That she feels impelled to incorporate herself into the shared mourning for the bishop does not, after all, mark a radical break from her claims not to be part of that community. It is a community founded in many ways on a refusal to be incorporated, built out of resistance to promiscuous mixing. Her inclusion in such a community partially depends on her book's pointedly proclaiming her distance from it.

Overland, Inland, and Upland

> What the eye does not see the heart does not grieve for.
> —A. U., *Overland, Inland, and Upland*, 1873

Such portability-abetted detachment is not only for those who loudly proclaim that they are not typical Anglo-Indians. It turns out to be a striking feature even of travel writings that go out of their way to proclaim their ordinariness, their conformity with the (English) custom of the country. *Overland, Inland, and Upland: A Lady's Notes of Personal Observation and Adventure* (1873), for example, epitomizes the prejudiced, partial, and studiously ignorant Indian travel books anatomized by Benita Parry,[45] in which everything Indian is ultimately found wanting in comparison to England. Indian flowers may be "superior" in color but they are inferior in scent, lacking what is "refreshing or wholesome"—except, that is, for "the homely fragrance of the old English marigold and southernwood, which do contrive to retain their character out there."[46]

Even *Overland, Inland, and Upland*, however, is haunted by the possibility that English culture may be too portable. Although A.U. is delighted by the possibility that marigolds carry their English odor unmolested (never mind that they are originally from Central America), she persistently worries that a yet more fundamental property will pass out of English control: Christianity. Catherine Hall's work on English evangelizing in Jamaica sheds considerable light on why it was in the British commercial and governmental interest to minimize, even to recoil from, Christian proselytizing in India.[47] A.U., however, is a fervent believer who claims to be delighted that India is slowly awakening to Jesus. Yet her every encounter with autonomous Indian Christianity is shaped by evident ambivalence.

This may be because it is only in discussing Christianity that A.U. must let drop her habitual cloak of indifference and ignorance about India. Describing a trip to Benares, she muses, "It was strange even then, and it seems stranger now that I am sitting quietly at home, to think of our position—English ladies, miles away from any other European, standing on a burning ghaut in that wild spot, speaking freely of the gospel to an educated Brahmin!"[48] And even more provocatively, in Calcutta:

> Once I had been watching a brilliant group of native princes, including more than one useful ally in the awful crisis of the Mutiny, who were eagerly discussing some topic of engrossing interest, when a native professor [that is, a Christian] who had joined in the argument, left the group and asked me to guess what they were talking of. . . . The doctrine of original sin![49]

Both passages are shot through not with delight, but a kind of shocked awe at Christianity's Indian incarnation.

Exactly how permeable has the barrier between Britons and Indians become? A.U. is hard pressed to square such moments of powerfully transmissible theology with the inherently malicious and deceitful nature of all Indians, and with her conviction that the English in India will always remain a race apart. If conversion has a capacity this potent, all barriers between the two nations appear breachable. A.U.'s solution relies on an extreme version of an assumption about cultural asymmetry that pervades Anglo-Indian writing: A.U. believes that the English are in India to bring civilization (or Christianity), but that the less they actually know of India while performing that mission, the better.

Too much knowledge is therefore repeatedly revealed to be a dangerous—or at least a nauseating—thing. A.U. reports on discoveries that English ladies made when venturing into their Indian kitchens: the pudding was boiled in a waistcloth, the sock was used as a strainer, butter was stuck on the cook's toe before being spread on bread, and so on. Instead of being an argument for greater surveillance, these are reasons for A.U.'s decision to close her own eyes:

> After facts like these, one can believe anything of a similar nature; but it is better for one's tranquility not to suffer the imagination to dwell on such topics in India. Dwellers in far-off lands must carry out the

adage, "what the eye does not see the heart does not grieve for," and judge what is placed before them on present merits rather than possible antecedents.[50]

A.U. is torn between two imperatives of survival in India: know what the servants are plotting (against you), but try not to dwell on what they are doing to (and for) you.

A.U.'s book, though, can only supply information, not ignorance. Still, if both information and ignorance are required in order to sustain a sense of one's own identity in India, perhaps it is possible to conceive of a form of knowledge that produces concomitant ignorance in its train. Emily Eden's *Up The Country* (1866), a redaction of her Indian letters and journals from a trip thirty years earlier, may have been the best-known book to ask what sort of portable property sufficed to keep one English in the Indian wilds. It is striking, then, that Eden's account of her Indian adventures is almost entirely about her efforts to keep herself connected to home, to family, and to English literature—and that those efforts sometimes entail an active effort to achieve ignorance about India and the Indians that surround her. Eden's writing suggests that the cordon of inattention can also turn into an active annihilator of what lies beyond the "civil lines."

"DEAR SHAKESPEARE": *UP THE COUNTRY*

Eden may be best remembered for the word she coined in the title of her 1859 novel, *The Semi-Detached House*.[51] *Up the Country*, though, describes a type of detachment seemingly far removed from such suburban concerns.[52] In India, Eden subsists on a steady diet of gossipy letters from home, mixed with an almost fanatical devotion to out-of-context quotation. Eden's work is at once exemplary and exceptional, pushing to an extreme the Victorian penchant for quotation (discussed in the introduction) as a way to instantiate portable Englishness. A recent critic has described her as strengthening her nostalgic patriotism overseas by immersing herself in the works of Jane Austen, who becomes "a stabilizing touchstone of pure English character and language, a centring, norming instrument."[53] Eden not only plays on Austen's prose to describe the weather ("cool, but not too cool"), she also bases character sketches on *The Pickwick Papers*, and turns back to Shakespeare to describe a Cawnpore famine.

Scholars have speculated on how Eden's six years in India shape *The Semi-Detached House* and *Up the Country*.[54] The changes in Eden's thinking that occurred in the three decades between visit and publication, though, can also be seen developing in her 1844 book of captioned

sketches, *Portraits of the Princes and Peoples of India.* Something between a rich woman's folly and a commercial venture (Dunbar says that
"all their friends begged for copies . . . and the edition was soon sold,"
but there seem to be fewer than thirty extant copies), these pictures are a
revealing record of Eden before she turned from a run-of-the-mill depicter
of the mysterious East into a brilliant (and enormously popular) anato-
mizer of Englishness in India.[55]

Like those memsahibs who returned bearing shawls, curry, and recipes,
Eden leads off *Portraits* with some gloriously outré Oriental sketches of
bearded fakirs and shy youths. Even in 1844, however, traces of the future
Eden surface. Her captions are filled with the sort of insider information
that the sister of the governor general might be expected to possess.[56]
A picture representing Indian animals and their trainers, for example, is
supplemented with an arcane note detailing the regal provenance of these
particular hawks and hounds.[57] Even a delicate sketch of a "Young Hill
Rana . . . a good looking, pleasing boy" is accompanied by a diplomatic
gloss: "These Hill chiefs are feeble in character, and divided in interests
and possessions; and they and their people fell easy prey to the Nepalese
. . . till they were relieved . . . by the conquest of the Hills by the British
government."[58]

The final picture of the collection, however, is a subtler account of the
English status within, and yet apart from, India. "Lord Auckland receiving the Raja of Nahum in Durbar" (fig. 2.1) has a caption taller than the
plate itself (42 lines, or about 400 words) that goes into numbing diplomatic detail on the order of reception, including the "trays of presents
brought by the Native Chiefs for the Governor General" that are "lifted
up during the interview, and replaced by others, containing return presents from the Governor General to the Chief."[59] It omits to mention,
though, the detail that secures both the imperial and the domestic character of Eden's brother, the governor general: his lambent dog. The various
attendant Indian lords, occupying the blurred fringes of the vividly colored picture, serve as an exotic, chivalric, yet reassuringly subordinate
Indian aristocracy. The governor and his lapdog, though, are rendered in
fine detail at center stage. Eden is evidently already beginning to discover
that the pleasures and challenges of establishing enduring Englishness
overseas are the most interesting thing she knows about India.

Twenty years later, when Eden took up the task of collating, redacting,
editing, and rewriting her "journal letters" from her long-ago Indian so-
journ, Anglo-Indian deprivation had become her central theme. The most
poignant and vivid moments in *Up the Country* have nothing to do with
Indian glamour. Eden strives instead to evoke what English objects meant

Figure 2.1 Emily Eden, "Lord Auckland receiving the Raja of Nahum in Durbar"; *Portraits of the Princes and Peoples of India* (1844)

to a homesick traveler. Lost mail, miraculously salvaged journals, and redemptive glimpses of artworks that evoke the distant world of London are her only comforts. Thus a shipwreck glimpsed from afar is notable not for its human cost, but principally because "I expect my box of clothes, which was to come this month, was in her."[60] As it turns out, though, something has been saved:

Wednesday Feb. 19.

A jewel of a man in a small boat came floating up with a yellow dâk packet in his hand, which he put on board—two letters from G. and W.O.[61]

It is moments like these that Eden remembers and chooses to report. Not because of anything Indian in them, but because the man—made a jewel by his mission—delivers letters from her absent brother.

In a letter from Simla, Eden makes explicit her attachment even to her own letters:

I sent off another lump of Journal last Saturday, but somehow I feel none of those last letters are sure of reaching you. They will be drowned going overland, after the contrarious way of the world. We might have had your April packet by this time, but the Bombay dâk has not been heard of at all for five days, and it is supposed the rivers have overflowed and that all your dear little letters are swimming for their lives.[62]

In situations such as this one, Eden seems to value letters or paintings more highly than the lives of those nearby.[63] A flood, for example, matters for the irreplaceable (painted) faces it might have washed away, not for the lives lost downstream: "Giles rushed in at the head of a valiant band of khallases (Indian housemaids of the male gender), and carried off my books and pictures, and nothing was hurt, only you know your face might have been entirely washed out, which, as there is not another like it within 15,000 miles, would have been an irreparable calamity."[64] Eden's homesickness, poignant as it is, also reveals her commitment to remain, like Maitland or A.U., detached from India, lest its culture come to life as powerfully as English objects do.

Although Eden never explicitly taps into the "imperial panic" evident in the Indian plot of Wilkie Collins's *The Moonstone*, she is clearly worried by a possible counterflow of resonant Indian objects into England. In an empire committed to free traffic between England and India, and especially committed to the extraction of Indian wealth whenever possible, Indian objects inevitably threatened to carry the same sorts of meaning with them back to the metropole that English objects carried to the imperial periphery. Such dangerous reciprocity is especially at issue in Eden's case. As the senior sister of the governor general, she embodied the power of England and the East India Company in one crucial way: she became her brother's designated receiver of gift jewelry from subjugated Indian rulers. Since gifts given to her are really intended for the East India Company's coffers, she finds herself becoming a convenient peg on which tribute can be hung. In a sense, she is the *ur*-collector, with an imperial duty to understand Indian treasures not as cultural property but as pelf.[65]

In describing her accumulated loot, Eden contrasts the ingenuousness among her givers—grateful Indians moved to express their emotions through jewels—to cool calculation on the English side. On a visit to one Rajah whose wife is only eight years old, for example, the initial awkwardness of the human encounter is quickly covered over by a catalogue of jewels, which is then followed by a fiscal reckoning:

She [the child Ranee] was so shy, she would hardly let us see her face, but the old woman talked for her, and the presents filled up the time, for the rajah had ordered that she should put all the jewellery on us with her own little hands. I had a diamond necklace and a collar, some native pearl earrings that hung nearly down to the waist, and a beautiful pair of diamond bracelets, and the great article of all was an immense diamond tiara. . . . They were valued altogether at 2,400 £., the mere stones. F.'s were of different shapes, some very pretty, but not so costly, but altogether it was an immense prize for the Company.[66]

There are three distinct phases in the transfer, and each works to strip the jewels of any Indian aura they might initially be imagined to possess. First, the dimly articulated emotions of the native gift-giver; which then give way to the mechanical problem of Emily herself as laden with jewelry ("I had a diamond necklace," not "she put a necklace on me"). Then comes a final (cash) calculation before the stones are sold at Delhi. Here, then, is another conjugation of the trope of "collection": Eden's stones end up seeming more like bank notes than like the beetles that Maitland gathered for the British Museum.

A less valuable sort of Indian gift, however, presents a trickier problem. Since Kashmiri shawls seem more personal than the jewels actually intended not for her but for the Company, Eden does sometimes contemplate keeping such shawls for herself or her relatives.

> The July overland came in yesterday and I have got your nice *fat* letter from Newsalls, and the Journal of your last month in London. . . . The third year I shall be at home, to hear all about it, which will be amazingly good fun; and in the meantime you cannot imagine the treasures these Journals are. Only think how pleasant! An old Colonel Skinner, a native as black as this ink, whose life you can see in Miss Roberts's book, writes to W. that "if the Miss Edens do not wish to mortify an old soldier, and bring down his grey hairs with sorrow to the grave, they will accept a pair of shawls he has ordered for them in Cashmere, and which have just arrived. If they return them, he shall imagine they look upon him as a native, and not as an old British soldier." Nothing evidently could be more palpably indelicate than to refuse them. I am the last woman in the world to hurt anybody's feelings by returning any shawl, to say nothing of a white one, made on purpose in Cashmere; and if he had thrown in a scarf, I should have thought his appearance and complexion only too fair for a British soldier.[67]

The racial comedy here hinges, overtly, on the possibility that Eden's judgment on color can be bought by white shawls. The better the shawls, she jokes, the whiter Colonel Skinner will seem.[68]

The proximity of this anecdote to her sister's dangling London diaries is the real key, however. This is a moment where Eden feels her detachment slipping. The chance to accept a real present, not to be sold in Delhi for the coffers of "The Company," allows her to imagine what it would mean to relinquish feeling attached to a London that is at least two years in her future. The satisfactions of the shawl—not as a glamorous Indian transplant, but worn right here and now, in India—might actually have the effect of making Skinner appear not "black as ink" but instead white as the shawls he brings. The diaries and their promise of future relief deflect that threat, but they do so imperfectly.

"Mental Friction"

Eden had an acute sense of the psychic price she paid for her refusal to accommodate herself either to "native" India or to Anglo-Indian life. Skinner's shawls notwithstanding, Eden is increasingly bored by Indian jewels, less and less connected to an émigré community whose dull theatricals and uninspired lovemaking cannot replace London. At low points, her letters and journals pinpoint the yawning dissatisfaction that reliance on redolent objects from abroad can bring.[69] In the doldrums out along the Ganges, she finds herself rereading, for the third time, a beloved memoir brought out from England. In a moment of eerie doubling, she notices that the author, too, says that his Indian time was largely spent with old books.

> I declare I never hear in society anything that can be called a *thing*—not even an Indian thing—and I see in Sir James Mackintosh's *Life*, which I am just finishing for the third time, that, in his Indian journal, there is nothing but longings after home, and the workings of his own brain, and remarks on books; whereas, in his English and Paris journals, there are anecdotes and witticisms of other people, and a little mental friction was going on.[70]

Paintings, letters, and journals are of such great importance precisely because "mental friction"—talking with others who will see and describe things differently—is impossible in India, where "natives" are outlandish, and fellow English are, as Maitland also had noted, trapped in the same listless, newsless state as Eden herself.

Eden thus finds herself in the odd position of deploring her dependence on books, and yet glorying in the relief from her surroundings they can provide. If her central concern in *Up the Country* is anatomizing the ways in which she feels her nostalgic attachment to her English friends and family, it is striking how often that (intimate and personal) nostalgia is expressed intertextually. If she is not complaining of the short supply of letters from home she is imagining how the latest Dickens work is going down in London. Moments in which she thinks of a dear friend at home are often less poignant than moments in which she can make her Indian experiences cohere with what she reads about in Dickens. For example, in expressing her delight with *The Pickwick Papers*, she rebukes a correspondent for not telling her more about it sooner. "It is odd how long you were writing about *Pickwick*, and yet I felt all the time, though we are no judges of fun in this place, that it must be everywhere the cleverest thing that has appeared in our time."[71] Two things stand out here. First, the apology for being in India, where "fun" like Dickens can not be judged. Second, the insistence—even before reading it—that *Pickwick* will know no boundaries.

Hence the oddity of the phrase, "it must be everywhere the cleverest thing." What does it mean for something to be clever "everywhere"? Nothing, unless one is worried that jokes might founder in the arid air abroad. Having praised *Pickwick*, Eden is virtually required to prove its everywhereness by doing what she repeatedly does in *Up the Country*: making quotation into a kind of guide to the country around her.

> I had laughed twenty times at that book. Then there is always a quotation to be had from *Pickwick* for everything that occurs anywhere.
>
> That Mr Q., of ——, who has been living with us for a month, and who admires Chance [Eden's horse], as a clever demon, but is afraid of him . . . [is, for example] so like Pickwick, and his "good old horse."[72]

Quotation, then, is the lifeblood of *Up the Country*. Eden, though, remains uncomfortable with that fact. On the one hand, it allows her while abroad to wrap herself in the mantle of those distant English writers whose words of wisdom can be stretched to cover even Indian disasters. Witnessing an Indian famine, she muses, "as usual, dear Shakespeare knew all about it. He must have been at Cawnpore at the time of a famine." In proof of that deliberately incongruous claim she quotes *Romeo and Juliet*, "Famine is in thy cheeks."[73] On the other hand, she remains deeply ambivalent about the kind of "mental friction" that can be generated by a life grown dependent on the printed page alone. Similar ambivalence, interestingly, is associated with the quotation-mad Jewish character at the center of Eden's most celebrated work, *The Semi-Detached House*.

THE SEMI-DETACHED HOUSE

Unease about loss of mental friction, I am arguing, is crucial to making sense of how literary quotations are used as immunization against India in *Up the Country*. *The Semi-Detached House*, though, tells the story of prophylactic quotation in a slightly different way. Initially, incessant quotation in the novel has one clear purpose: to single out impostors. The tendency toward out-of-context quotation is often a racial marker: the Jewish Baroness Sampson, for example, is censoriously described as "doing [that is, playing] Cleopatra, minus the Nile."[74]

Misquotation's value as shibboleth, however, is undercut by the presence of another Jewish paragon of quotation and misquotation: English-born Rachel Montenero. At first, Rachel's alien religion appears inherently offensive, and her artificial efforts to dress up life with quotation egregious. It soon becomes clear, though, that Rachel's quotations are meant to be taken both literally and literarily. When she moans out poetry, she really is expressing some kind of heartfelt anguish, aesthetically mediated though it might be. Surrounded by mendacious and hardhearted relatives, but herself passionate and child-loving, her only outlet for real feelings lies in the words of Byron or Shelley. Eden the novelist and Rachel Montenero the performer, then, are alike in understanding that the habit of quotation can be something like assuming a role that others have laid out for one to play.

Rachel's Shakespearean quotations ultimately turn out to have the power of being eerily, aptly descriptive of the circumstances around her. One small triumph comes when she describes an upcoming party to Mrs Hopkinson (a down-to-earth, lovable English character) as "a tedious brief scene, and very tragical mirth, and hot ice and wondrous strange snow."[75] Mrs Hopkinson immediately glosses Rachel's remark sympathetically: "But Rose says she was only quoting Shakespeare, and of course what Shakespeare says must be right, and, besides, I should like to taste hot ice."[76] Ironic Rachel teaches even the ingenuous Hopkinsons to respect the solace that she finds in Shakespeare.

Shakespeare is a mantle Rachel wears against this gray, threatening England—much as Eden wrapped him round her against the aridity of India. She even finds herself deeply attached to a young boy (the son of her suitor, Mr Willis) in large part because he enjoys babbling and garbling lines from Shakespeare back at her: "Nebber shake your golly locks," he tells her (that is, "never shake thy gory locks at me!").[77] Rachel sternly reminds herself, "It would not do to marry poor Mr Willis on the strength of that one quotation."[78] She soon does just that, however, converting her taste for (mis)quotation into the middle-class respectability she covets.

The salient irony is that Rachel is not abroad: she is in England quoting English writers for comfort. That disjunction clearly causes Eden pause. In India, "quotation" might justify anything, but picking a mate by way of Shakespeare seems less comprehensible in an England that ought to be generally filled with "mental friction." Perhaps Eden sees Rachel as mired in a permanent India, surrounded by unsavory relatives from whom quotation is her only solace. Yet in the heart of the country is this half-foreigner, using English verse to hold England at bay.

Perhaps Eden is implicitly playing out a comparison between the anomie of semi-detachment in English India, and the deracination of London's "bran' new" suburbs, where either a Jewess and a cultured returnee from India might find herself adrift in a sea of identical bungalows.[79] That interpretation would line up not only with my analogy between Maitland's Anglo-Indian society and suburbia, but also with a recent argument that Eden "perfectly captures the character of a suburb . . . and successfully implies that a patently artificial place is best regarded with a breeziness indicating that it has no depths to plumb."[80] Detachment comes in many forms, and it might be as necessary to wrap oneself in quotation as protection against Dulham as against Delhi.

PORTABILITY GONE POLITICAL: DILKE AND ACTON

> Our citizenship of the great Anglo-Saxendom . . . [preserved England from] the curse of small island countries which would otherwise make us Guernsey a little magnified.
> —Charles Wentworth Dilke, *Greater Britain: A Record of Travel in English-Speaking Countries during 1866 and 1867*

> A man . . . lives not only in the spot which he personally occupies, but in every spot to which he may extend his action, or to which he may conceive it possible that his action should be extended. And so, wherever over the world British influence penetrates, or can conceive itself penetrating, there, and not in the mere islands where we have our footing, Great Britain lives.
> —David Masson, "Politics of the Present, Foreign and Domestic," 1859

Meditations about cultural portability at work in Greater Britain were not confined to India, but India was evidently their forcing bed. In the decades that followed Eden's and Maitland's fledgling efforts to describe the essence of out-of-England Englishness, the notion of traveling Englishness had entered the journalistic and political mainstream with a vengeance: seeing it at work requires looking no further than the illustrious Whig Charles Dilke, and the redoubtable Tory Lord Acton. In its translation to the realm of political action, the notion predictably gained some features (an obsession with the futurity of Englishness abroad is one) and lost a few others. Most notably, the pragmatically political writers who played out visions of expatriate English community were much less attuned than Maitland, A.U., and Eden to the inevitable tensions that arose between individual and community when nationality was defined by distance. These later writers, that is, omitted an exploration of the ways that self-conscious exile and the capacity to differentiate oneself from one's surroundings (that is, even from "English" society: differentiation even from fellow émigrés) could become central to a Greater British identity.

Charles Dilke's 1868 *Greater Britain*—profoundly influential on "imperial" writing of the latter Victorian period, especially on Seeley's *The Expansion of England*—is probably the clearest example of the immense confusion that spawned repeated mid-Victorian meditations on the powers and pitfalls of English portable culture abroad.[81] The enormously popular first book of a young Whig aristocrat (who might have become prime minister if divorce had not derailed his career in the 1880s), *Greater Britain* explores the worldwide export of English blood, customs, and portable high culture.[82] Dilke finds that British germlines run strong in Canada and Australia, that British customs are still prevalent in politically independent America, and that British rule of law is still guiding the "cheaper races" all over South and Southeast Asia. He also sees the triumph of English portability at every level, down to the microscopic.

The book's most memorable chapter, "The Two Flies," turns on the omnipresent superiority of British mores, manners, objects, persons, and even animals, to softer, smaller, weaker colonized subjects.

> The English fly has had to contend not only against other English flies, but against every fly of temperate climates: we having traded with every land, and brought the flies of every clime to England. The English fly is the best possible fly of the whole world, and will naturally beat down and exterminate, or else starve out, the merely provincial Maori fly. If a great singer—to find whom for the London stage the world has been ransacked—should be led by the foible of the moment to sing for gain in an unknown village where, on the same night, a rustic tenor was attempting to sing his best, the London tenor would send the provincial supperless to his bed. So it is with the English and Maori fly. . . .
>
> Even the Pakeha flea has come over in the ships, and wonderfully has he thriven.[83]

English portable power controls the gamut from opera to fly, from economic system down to single laborer. Such triumph is simple for Dilke to describe in the White Commonwealth: Australia, New Zealand, and Canada are, by his account, unproblematically peopled with white Britons. Portability's success, though, becomes a potential problem as soon as Dilke leaves the portion of the globe that is both under British political control and populated by blood English.

In India, Dilke begins to worry that cultural portability might work so well that nothing, not even racial divides, can check English culture's expansion. Recall the passage analyzed in the introduction, above:

I had not been two days in Bombay when a placard caught my eye, announcing a performance at the theatre of "Romeo and Juliet, in the Maratta tongue;" but the play had no Friar Lawrence, no apothecary and no nurse; it was nothing but a simple Maratta love-tale, followed by some religious tableaux. In the first piece an Englishman was introduced, and represented as kicking every native that crossed his path with the exclamation of "Damned fool:" at each repetition of which the whole house laughed. It is to be feared that this portion of the play was "founded upon fact."[84]

Dilke's gloss on the play is revealingly odd. Does the absence of Friar Lawrence and the Nurse really disqualify this from being Shakespearean? What relationship does that kicking bully have to Shakespeare—for Dilke or for the Indian audience? Dilke's willingness to leave such questions dangling seems cognate with his willingness to suspend judgment on the larger question that lies beneath: is he celebrating the globalization of English people, English culture, or the English state?

Dilke finds in America, too, "a protean middle term, neither distinct from nor quite the same as Britain."[85] It is no longer ruled directly by the Crown, and it is peopled with the various European immigrant communities, who prove only partially amenable to British cultural and political imprinting. Yet *Greater Britain*'s most controversial claim is that the United States is the last, best hope of England's great expansion. The argument—unheard of in the 1860s, increasingly accepted by the end of the century—is built on the shifting sands between cultural and racial accounts of "Englishness." The shiftiness of Dilke's racial-cultural notions begins early: the second sentence of the book's preface reads, "If I remarked that climate, soil, manners of life, that mixture with other peoples had modified the blood, I saw, too, that in essentials the race was always one."[86] After proposing that blood can be modified, though, he corrects course, asserting that some quality of sameness ("the race was always one") allows one to recognize English blood kin abroad.

That apparent resolution, however, soon falls away:

The idea which in all the length of my travels has been at once my fellow and my guide—a key wherewith to unlock the hidden things of strange new lands—is a conception, however imperfect, of the grandeur of our race, already girdling the earth, which it is destined, perhaps, eventually to overspread.

In America, the peoples of the world are being fused together, but they are run into an English mould: Alfred's law and Chaucer's tongue are theirs whether they would or no. There are men who say that Britain in her age will claim the glory of having planted greater Englands across the seas. They fail to perceive that she has done more than found plantations of her own—that she has imposed her institutions upon the offshoots of Germany, of Ireland, of Scandinavia, and of Spain. Through America England is speaking to the world.[87]

This model of the "race," which Mill singled out for particular criticism in correspondence with Dilke, is conceptually confused.[88] Is it the blood of England that is spreading abroad, or its culture, or its institutions?[89] Dilke's confusion bespeaks an age where the possibility of a globalized culture presented almost infinite opportunities for English commerce, English religious fervor, and English political ambitions. Yet was it truly Englishness that was spreading abroad? Might the "nation" not be altered out of all recognition, its bloodlines or its culture polluted?

Such forays into portable Englishness, moreover, were not restricted to the Whig side of the aisle. A durably influential 1862 article by Lord Acton, "Nationality" (from it comes Acton's best remembered pronouncement: "exile is the nursery of nationality"), helped guide English conservatives bent on reconciling a powerful worldwide British state with an innately inalterable English national identity.[90] "Nationality" begins by criticizing an unlikely trinity—Napoleon, Metternich, and John Stuart Mill—for treating nationalism ("more absurd and more criminal than the theory of socialism") as an admissible basis for state-formation.[91] It goes on, though, to mount a passionate defense of a British Empire that should neither permit national autonomy nor suppress subordinate nations' sense of identity. Rather, Acton believes that England will flourish abroad if it overcomes the

> French [notion of] nationality . . . founded on the perpetual supremacy of the collective will [and implements instead the English system, which] tends to diversity and not to uniformity. . . . Private rights . . . are preserved by the union of nations. . . . The presence of different nations under the same sovereignty is similar in its effect to the independence of the Church in the State. . . . It promotes independence by forming definite groups of public opinion, and by affording a great source and centre of political sentiments, and of notions of duty not derived from the sovereign will. . . . That intolerance of social freedom which is natural to absolutism is sure to find a corrective in the national diversities, which no other force could so efficiently provide.[92]

National identity works best when the state itself contains multitudes of nations—and "the nationality formed by the State, then, is the only one to which we owe political duties, and it is, therefore, the only one which has political rights."[93] The English state can establish itself everywhere as the avatar of modernity. Meanwhile, English people themselves circulate widely through that transoceanic state, educated by cultural diversity but not themselves altered—much as A.U. imagined Christianity triumphing without her having to think about or talk with its Indian acolytes.

The result of such contact, Acton argues, can be a worldwide British domain that will profit subordinated nations as well—if they can relinquish their desire for a state to correspond to their nationhood.

> It is in the cauldron of the State that the fusion takes place by which the vigour, the knowledge, and the capacity of one portion of mankind may be communicated to another. Where political and national boundaries coincide, society ceases to advance, and nations relapse into a condition corresponding to that of men who renounce intercourse with their fellow-men. . . .
>
> Those states are substantially the most perfect which, like the British and Austrian Empires, include various distinct nationalities without oppressing them.[94]

English rule makes the ruled aware of their own national status—they are manifestly different from their rulers, and should be happy to be so. It does so, however, without making them want to cast off those rulers, since it is to their advantage to be leavened by contact with a manifestly greater nation, even if it means being ruled by the English state. Acton, then, actively depends upon the portability of Englishness. On the one hand, citizens of the expansive British state can be relied upon to continue being a part of their natal nation ("the nation derives its rights and its power from the memory of a former independence").[95] On the other, contact with their mobile English rulers is guaranteed to change them for the better.

Dilke's Whig brief for the portability of English culture within a Greater Britain revealingly converges with Acton's case for the conservative virtues of an omnipresent British state benignly guarding various inferior national identities. Dominion overseas is ensured if the English can learn to move abroad, among strangers, changing minds and mores as they go, without themselves being changed. Like the Pakeha flea, they can simultaneously embody their empire and spread the news of its arrival. The ability to detach oneself from one's surroundings, then, also endows the English with a newfound capacity to move without seeming to move— perhaps even without realizing that they have moved.

Anglo-Indian writers, though, had already told this story. That curious capacity to move without relinquishing Englishness is already at work in the writings of such Anglo-Indians as Julia Maitland and Emily Eden, for whom detachment from their Indian surroundings is a matter of course. Maitland and Eden, though, register an unsettling development that Dilke and Acton have no space for in their political précis of the emigrant condition. Both Eden and Maitland notice, even revel in, their detachment from the very traveling community that supposedly underwrites their being abroad. Theirs is a curious balancing act, whereby one invents a cultural aura of "Englishness" to justify abroad things or practices (a piano, a garden) that at home do not speak of Englishness in any way.

Emily Eden's notion of portable, quotable Englishness becomes most interesting, and most difficult to parse, when it addresses the question of whether culturally resonant objects might go on resonating even within Britain, when seemingly more powerful forms of communal association ought to be able to overcome them. Eden does have a peculiarly Anglo-Indian preoccupation with the extent that literature—turned into memorized quotations—could substitute for the "mental friction" of home. Yet Eden's work also underscores a general mid-Victorian disposition to shape questions about the durability of cultural property sent into danger zones not in Simla, but in the barren wastes of semi-detached houses around London. The uniformity in English culture that proved so useful for Anglo-Indian imaginings of the distant homeland thus seems to have an important domestic effect, as well. Eden's sense of the threatening deracination of the suburbs might well be a valuable first clue to approaching the problem of imperial portability come home to roost. Eden's alter-ego, the Shakespeare-quoting Jewess trapped not in India but in barren Dulham, suggests that familiar problems of Greater British portability can occur even within England.

Eden's tentative link between Indian and English experiences of cultural detachment, however, raises many more questions than it answers. Are there ways to ensure that the English abroad enjoy all of the virtues and suffer none of the pitfalls of such detachment? Appadurai has described the establishment of émigré lives in strange places as the "production of locality"; what would such locality-production entail for Britons overseas? One possibility, explored in a remarkably wide range of mid-Victorian texts, was that novels might become meaningful sites of cultural authority by producing a common *provincial* England, an England made up of a repeating patchwork of Austen country towns.[96] The mid-Victorian upsurge of confidence in the provincial novel, I argue in the following two chapters (briefly in chapter 3, and at length in chapter 4) depends in vital ways on the notion of a seamlessly portable Englishness that can circulate both within England and beyond to a notionally expansive Greater Britain (which Dilke describes as including not only settler colonies, such as New Zealand, and imperial holdings, such as India, but also the United States).[97] Between the 1850s and 1870s, the metonymic claims of provincial writing reach their apex—a county, or a town, or even a few genteel "country" families—can seem to stand in for England as a whole. The remarkable powers of adaptability that the notion of Greater Britain displayed are surprisingly bound up with the new importance that comes to be attached to the idea of a reassuringly homogeneous (and hence exportable) provincial England.

Two very important alternatives to the provincial novel arise in the late 1860s, however. First, there occurs a brief revival of widespread interest in the notion of an England defined by singular, distinct, internally differentiated *regions*, each generative of a culture that requires as much work to make it to London unscathed as English culture does to reach India. Blackmore's 1868 *Lorna Doone* is the proof-text for both the possibility of such a regional revival (which would have been akin to the full-blown triumph of "local color" writing in America during the last third of the century) and for its ultimate demise, which sheds a great deal of light on the competing claims of coherent national identity and regional autonomy—and on the relationship that regionalism and provincialism have to the underlying logic of cultural portability.

The second new avenue through which cultural transmission seems to occur in the late 1860s is of a quite different order: race. Dilke's confusion about whether Englishness is an acquired set of customs or a bloodline is symptomatic of a general confusion in the late 1860s. Eden's fiction is premonitory: Rachel's curious relationship to English culture hints at the enormous changes that a newly empowered racial thinking was to wreak on notions of cultural portability in the decades to come. But Eden's conception of Rachel's Jewishness is different from what is to follow: had the novel been written a decade later, perhaps her ardent passion for Shakespeare as protection against decultured Dulham would have turned into a penchant for quoting Maimonides instead. The early 1870s produced a novel best understood as a distinctively unsettled set of experiments, exploring ways that even culture invisible to outsiders might be carried by individual members of a nation or a race: George Eliot's *Daniel Deronda*.

CHAPTER THREE

Someone Else's Knowledge: Race and Portable Culture in *Daniel Deronda*

> [Mordecai] would begin to repeat a Hebrew poem of his own, into which years before he had poured his first youthful ardours for that conception of a blended past and future which was the mistress of his soul, telling Jacob to say the words after him.
> "The boy will get them engraved within him," thought Mordecai; "it is a way of printing. . . . My words may rule him someday. Their meaning may flash out on him. It is so with a nation—after many days."
> —George Eliot, *Daniel Deronda*

> As to the Jewish element in *Deronda*, I expected from first to last in writing it, that it would create much stronger resistance and even repulsion than it has actually met with. But precisely because I felt that the usual attitude of Christians towards Jews is—I hardly know whether to say more impious or more stupid when viewed in the light of their professed principles—I therefore felt urged to treat Jews with such sympathy and understanding as my nature and knowledge could attain to.
> —George Eliot to Harriet Beecher Stowe, October 29, 1867

THE ECONOMIC AND SENTIMENTAL VALUE attached to objects in motion produced an avalanche of Victorian texts exploring new notions of cultural portability. Diamond stories opened ways for novelists to reflect upon the logic of social exchanges that at once interfere with and help to constitute putatively sheltered domestic tranquility. And a range of Anglo-Indian travel writings—whether focused on palpably portable properties like strawberries or on the literary quotations that could craft a sense of continuous selfhood in England as also in India—explored both institutional and idiosyncratic alternatives to the ominous fungibility of market transactions. The novel, I have been arguing, is the logical breeding ground for reflections on cultural portability in large part because its own form—the self-sufficient but mimetic narrative, bound in covers but free to roam—makes it an ideal inhabitant of this world of portable cultural property. Novels are not fixed to a certain place, like monuments, sacred battlegrounds, or fabled national landmarks. The material mobility of literary texts and the mental transport they license allow their readers to conceive of the transactions connected to an era of "flexible accumulation" by combining immersion in the everyday with sanctioned retreat.[1]

In the 1870s, that flexibility is tested by the gradual development of quasi-racial accounts of identity formation. Whether influenced by Darwinian thinking, the Governor Eyre controversy, or Great Britain's newly articulated status as imperial nation, novelists began to approach the question of racial identity and its relationship to national culture in new ways.[2] Such changes in English society at large sometimes resulted in novelists bucking the limitations imposed by the provincial novel. In other cases, the impetus to alter the novel's form and its reach evidently stemmed from a reinvigorated wish to locate what is distinctive about individuals or about cultures, to disentangle the threads that constitute a community and see how fundamental is the role played by such pieces of culture-constituting property as novels themselves.[3]

George Eliot, in the early 1870s, starts experimenting with a quasi-racial conception of portable culture, initiating an important shift in European conceptions of narrative's relationship to national and racial identity—a shift that culminates in the deterministic narratives of fin-de-siècle Naturalism. Eliot is especially noteworthy among such writers, however, because *Daniel Deronda* (1876) is utterly original in asking what happens when culture is internalized so successfully that it enters into the body of the consciously nationalized subject. In brief, Eliot proposes that acquiring (or coming into) a national culture can transform a character so completely that he will not only become opaque to other characters, but actually disappear from the narrator's own line of sight. In other words, the acquisition of a fully racial identity may entail that a character's personality, individuality, and all his accoutrements and peculiarities vanish from the reader's sight. It is the possibility of such complete internalization that underlies Mordecai's conviction that his Hebrew poems can lie dormant within Jacob (who is both Anglophone and boyishly oblivious) until "[t]heir meaning may flash out on him." Acquired culture has not quite become racialized, but it has been redefined as an inescapable inheritance with this curious feature: that culture has an entirely different meaning for those within the charmed circle than it does for those without. *Daniel Deronda* accordingly certifies its status as a realistic novel not by heightening its attention, but by *withdrawing* its gaze from Daniel's interior, once his Jewishness is revealed.

Daniel Deronda suggests, in other words, that any given nation's portable culture will be visible only to those already within the charmed circle that such a national culture generates. Those on the outside might accordingly fail to recognize even the bare fact that what is being transmitted is a form of culture. Outsiders might, indeed, even understand the process of transmission as a kind of racial inheritance. Those on the inside of the national culture, however, possessing both the "nature" and the "knowledge" for limitless access, will find that their feelings and their intellectual comprehension are sharpened by their newfound "partiality." Objects, texts, and practices formerly inaccessible will suddenly become part of the lore of the tribe, available to sense and sensibility alike in a new way. The existence of tension between insider knowledge and outsider bafflement itself is not new: George Borrow's 1851 *Lavengro*, for example, is a quasi-ethnographic account of English gypsies very concerned with marking the limits of what an English fellow traveler can hope to discover about even the friendliest of gypsies. *Daniel Deronda*'s striking innovation, however, is to situate the narration, the reader, even the novelist herself, as both insider and outsider, by way of a formal withholding, an exclusion of the narrative itself from knowledge, in such a way that the reader can witness Daniel experiencing things for which the novel itself, by definition, can have no words. Some of the novel's most revealing moments, accordingly, are those moments in which everything of importance in a scene is hidden, not just from the Christian outsider, but from Eliot and her readers as well. This is a novel that can produce not just knowledge, but also the experience of palpable ignorance, an ignorance shared between novelist and reader. It is a novel in which portable properties can become so portable because they are located entirely within characters, visible only to those who already belong within the privileged circle of national belonging.

Struggling to make sense of a nationality that has begun to take on certain aspects of a racial identity—the words "nation," "people," and "race" begin to seem almost interchangeable in the novel—Eliot imagines a durable and transferable culture that is a body of portable properties legible to the cognoscenti and the born insiders; those not in the know will see a mere blank wall concealing what can come to look like an immutable, or even genetically transmissible, heritage. The letter from *Cranford* I discussed in the introduction, above, was written so that if the addressee truly were a long-lost brother, that letter would read as a passionate plea, but would seem "a mere statement of dry facts if he were a stranger."[4] Eliot's account of Jewish culture can be seen as an extended and explicitly nationalized version of just such bifurcation between sentimentally attuned insider and merely objective outsider. The result is that not only the novel's reader but also Eliot and her narrator become outsiders to some of the novel's most intimate and crucial scenes, frequently to disturbing effect.

In "The Modern Hep! Hep! Hep!" (the final essay in *Impressions of Theophrastus Such*, her final book), Eliot proposes a close analogy be-

tween Jews and the English in their new global peregrinations.[5] That analogy's efficacy lies largely in the conceptual asymmetry Eliot proposes between those who can make sense of a culture from inside it (those to
whom its essential aspects have been made portable) and those who can
only gaze at its exterior lineaments with puzzlement. By Eliot's account,
Jewish culture, made not so much cosmopolitan as internationally durable, offers to insiders an illuminating web of connections, along with a
ready map for discerning connections with other insiders.[6] Insider knowledge provides a way for Jacob to recognize rote memorization as ancient
wisdom, for Mirah to recognize nonsense syllables her mother taught her
as Hebrew, and for Daniel to recognize Mirah as his destined bride via
purely somatic associations. This is the significance of Mordecai's pouring
Hebrew poetry into Jacob's ears while he sits—his characteristic pose in
the novel—"reaching out and surveying the contents of his pockets," as
if everything of value he accumulates (a knife, a poem) could be tucked
away in some hidden pouch either upon or within his body.[7] In this novel,
Eliot experiments with the idea that successfully portabilized national culture can be pocketed, as it were, going so far inward as to be either invisible or illegible to those on the outside.

ON BEYOND PROVINCIALISM

I want to consider *Daniel Deronda* not only in relation to the Greater
British problems I laid out in the previous chapter, but also in relation to
the most straightforward way for novels to carry Englishness into that
Greater British terrain: namely, to generate a readily generalizable provincial English setting, a Carlingford, Barchester, or Middlemarch. The particularity of setting (this country house and no other, this particular set of
named sisters) insisted upon in the Victorian provincial novel never presented an impediment to the act of metonymy whereby it stood in for
English country living as a whole. The rest of the English countryside may
be geographically discrete from "our village" (the felicitous title to the
sketches Mary Russell Mitford began publishing in 1824), and yet remain
that village's topological and social doppelganger. *Adam Bede* (1859) and
Middlemarch (1871–72) are by this metric as provincial as Oliphant's
"Chronicles of Carlingford" (1861–76): the provincial novel's affirmation
of a national identity underwritten by particular and yet generalizable rural
landscapes predominates in each. Appreciation of *Middlemarch*'s landscapes is not restricted (as in *Lorna Doone*, about which I shall have more
to say in chapter 4, below) to those who know the particular trees that
grow there, or where to catch its most delicious fish. Rather, Eliot hyposta-

tizes a generic Midlands reader who, by a metonymic sleight of hand, becomes any reader capable of appreciating a beautiful countryside:

> Little details gave each field a particular physiognomy, dear to the eyes that have looked on them from childhood: the pool in the corner where the grasses were dank and trees leaned whisperingly; the great oak shadowing a bare place in mid-pasture . . . mossy hills and valleys with wondrous modulations of light and shadow such as we travel far to see in later life, and see larger, but not more beautiful. These are the things that make the gamut of joy in landscape to midland-bred souls—the things they toddled among, or perhaps learned by heart standing between their father's knees while he drove leisurely.[8]

Like Austen's "Midland Counties of England," *Middlemarch*'s landscapes are defined not by a qualitative difference from the rest of provincial England, but by the mere fact of physical disaggregation (same fields, different places).[9] Provincial England is the space that keeps its character by being spread out, and thus exists in a state of perpetual disconnection from itself.

Daniel Deronda, however, as Ian Duncan has argued, rejects such provincial logic:

> Eliot brings the provincial novel to its fullest development and beyond, to its mid-1870s point of dissolution. . . . [*Daniel Deronda*] narrates the failure of the genre associated with provincial and country-house settings, the female bildungsroman. The novel engineers a catastrophic split between its domestic plot of courtship and provincial life, and its world-historical plot directed to an alien nation, Israel.[10]

Eliot offers a wide variety of textual signals that the sureties of provincial logic will no longer hold (which perhaps helps explain why the novel "did not become popular in Britain," at least in comparison with Eliot's other novels).[11] For example, the well-known passage bemoaning Gwendolen's deracination—sometimes taken to signify Eliot's continued commitment to rootedness—also signals that the novel will not remain beholden to its provincial setting.

> Pity that Offendene was not the home of Miss Harleth's childhood, or endeared to her by family memories! A human life, I think, should be well rooted in some spot of native land, where it may get the love of tender kinship for the face of the earth, for the labours men go forth to, for the sounds and accents that haunt it, for whatever will give that early home a familiar unmistakable difference amidst the future widening of knowledge: a spot where the definiteness of early memories may be inwrought with affection, and kindly acquaintance with all neighbours,

even to the dogs and donkeys, may spread not by sentimental effort and reflection, but as a sweet habit of the blood. . . . The best introduction to astronomy is to think of the nightly heavens as a little lot of stars belonging to one's own homestead.

But this blessed persistence in which affection can take root had been wanting in Gwendolen's life.[12]

On one level this is a genuinely ardent provincialism, proclaiming that a fabricated "natural home" is better than none at all. If belief that the stars in the night sky belong to "one's own homestead" is evidently false, such a belief in the primacy of one's local impressions can still serve the developing mind as an aid to wider comprehension.

Yet this passage from the third chapter stands in a somewhat uneasy relationship with the first chapter's opening: Gwendolen gambling among rootless cosmopolites in a German casino.[13] Not only does the novel—as Conrad's or Ford Madox Ford's so often do—unfold in a restless, transitional hotel setting, Eliot even opens with an epigraph insisting all beginnings (in science, in life, and certainly in fiction) are equally fictive.

Men can do nothing without the make-believe of a beginning. Even Science, the strict measurer, is obliged to start out with a make-believe unit, and must fix on a point in the stars' unceasing journey when his sidereal clock shall pretend that time is at Nought. . . . No retrospect will take us to the true beginning; and whether our prologue be in heaven or on earth, it is but a fraction of that all-presupposing fact with which our story sets out.[14]

Following two chapters after a beginning that disavows all beginnings, the narrator's pronouncement, "Pity that Offendene was not the home . . ." is just as wry as another instance of seeming narratorial regret about Offendene's deficiencies, coming a few sentences later: "One would have liked the house to have been lifted on a knoll."[15] There is real nostalgia for the lost possibilities of an Austen novel here; but with that nostalgia comes a sense of stakes deeper than Gwendolen's matrimonial accommodation—stakes that ensure the novel will not long remain confined to midland scenery and marriageable cousin plots.

NATIONAL "PARTIALITY"

> For he might have been a Roosian,
> A French, or Turk, or Proosian,
> Or perhaps Itali-an!
> But in spite of all temptations

> To belong to other nations,
> He remains an Englishman!
> —William Gilbert and Arthur Sullivan, "For He Is
> an Englishman," *H.M.S. Pinafore*, 1878

If the novel's range and scope is no longer determined by the geographical confines of its provincial setting, its parameters must be set in some other way. From early on in *Daniel Deronda*, pure universal benevolence is ruled out as an adequate substitute for that impossible dream of an always-present Offendene. It is true that the ideal reader must begin a novel by universally sympathizing. That does not mean, though, that Daniel's desire to be purely receptive, open to any and all sensations, is admirable. Sir Hugo warns him early on, "It will not do to give yourself to be melted down for the benefit of the tallow-trade."[16]

Daniel is no sooner ensconced in the neutral receptivity Hugo censures, in fact, than the novel starts urging him into some kind of embodiedness. Out rowing on the Thames, he may be open to the universe. After rescuing Mirah, though, he grows accustomed to the idea that some kind of allegiance is what will enable him to make sense of the world. "The scent of violets" comes to exemplify experiences foreclosed to the pedants who only accumulate a "dead anatomy of culture," but are a welcome second nature to the person who has avowed, or discovered, an inward partiality.

> He was ceasing to care for knowledge—he had no ambition for practice—unless they could both be gathered up into one current with his emotions; and he dreaded, as if it were a dwelling-place of lost souls, that dead anatomy of culture which turns the universe into a mere ceaseless answer to queries, and knows, not everything, but everything else about everything—as if one should be ignorant of nothing concerning the scent of violets except the scent itself for which one had no nostril. But how and whence was the needed event to come?—the influence that would justify partiality, and make him what he longed to be yet was unable to make himself—an organic part of social life, instead of roaming in it like a yearning disembodied spirit, stirred with a vague social passion, but without fixed local habitation to render fellowship real?[17]

Without partiality, beautiful aromas evanesce. A completely impartial understanding of the violet fatally misses its aroma—that is, it fails to be an aesthetic understanding.

If Eliot goes out of her way to disavow an older kind of rootedness, then, it is not because she advocates deserting all sorts of localization. She seems rather to have in mind a new sort of "fixed local habitation" to survive such disruptions. James Buzard has recently argued that *Daniel*

Deronda "anticipates the dynamics of nativism and modernism" in later American realist and Naturalist texts.[18] The comparison to the determinism (sometimes economic, sometimes racial) and typological rigidity of a Zola or a Norris novel is an intriguing one. *Daniel Deronda* does, after all, appear during the upheaval in racial thinking in the early 1870s.[19] Early elements of such a shift may have begun a quarter-century earlier,[20] but it was not until the mid-1870s that there arose a welter of explicitly racialized works premonitory of the run-of-the-mill racial thinking of the fin-de-siècle. There is no denying the emphasis Eliot places on a mysteriously inward component of portable culture: if Jewishness requires documents, it also requires a "sweet habit of the blood" to interpret them. It does seem worth stressing that Eliot's notion of a fully internalized Jewish identity remains distinct from the fully racialized account of heritable (and unavoidable) identity evident in many novels of the early twentieth century. Still, the portability of a national culture in the 1870s looks much more dependent on inner predispositions than it previously had. Eden needed to read *Pickwick* before she knew it would appeal "everywhere"; Daniel's inward convictions about his national heritage ultimately require no such verification.

In *Daniel Deronda*, such explicitly racial thinking is readily recognizable in what Eliot herself labels the "Jewish element."[21] From early in the novel, Jewish identity explains both the affiliation and detachment of characters. Even when they themselves do not know it, it is racial connection that brings characters together. Demonstrating her vocal abilities to Daniel, Mirah initially sings innocuous German and Italian songs. She then launches into a new kind of sacred text: "the Hebrew hymn she remembers her mother singing over her when she lay in her cot." Daniel responds to the song's potential sacredness with apt reverence: he would like to hear it only if "you think I am worthy to hear what is so sacred."[22]

> "I will sing it if you like," said Mirah, "but I don't sing real words—only here and there a syllable like hers—the rest is lisping. Do you know Hebrew? Because if you do, my singing will seem childish nonsense."
> Deronda shook his head. "It will be quite good Hebrew to me."[23]

The terms of Daniel's acceptance signposts the games that the novel plays with Jewish lore and learning. The words, nonsense or sense, are simply "good Hebrew" as far as the polite outsider can hope to tell. "Mirah crossed her little feet and hands in her easiest attitude, and then lifted up her head at an angle which seemed to be directed to some invisible face bent over her, while she sang a little hymn of quaint melancholy intervals, with syllables that really seemed childish lisping to her audience."[24] Though it is the absent mother who bends invisibly over Mirah, labeling this song a hymn suggests the overlooming face might be God's, as well.

It is almost as if Judaism's matrilineal descent makes the mother not only the arbiter of identity but the divine presence itself.[25] Both Mirah and Daniel emphasize that the meaning of the words is not at the core of their experience of the song. Mirah remarks that "if I were ever to know the real words, I should still go on in my old way with them."[26] Mrs Meyrick's response to Mirah's song—"A mother hears something like a lisp in her children's talk to the very last"—registers the way that any performance calls forth aspects of the listener's, as well as the singer's, inner nature (that is, she credits Mirah with simulating, in the song, the way that a mother would have heard her child's lisping voice).[27] Daniel's response— "The lisped syllables are very full of meaning"—inverts that logic: he knows that the song has meaning although (or precisely because) that meaning is foreclosed to him. Mirah's song has (to modify a remark of Kafka's) an infinite amount of meaning—but not for us.

Seeing Daniel moved, Mirah speaks of a deep-flowing river, glimpsed only by other Jews: "'Oh, was it great to you? Did it go to your heart?' said Mirah, eagerly. 'I thought none but our people would feel that. I thought it was all shut away like a river in a deep valley, where only heaven saw—I mean—'she hesitated, feeling that she could not disentangle her thought from its imagery."[28] Daniel assures her that he, too, can see it. There is, though, a twist to Daniel's assurance. At this point in the novel, both he and the reader believe that his capacity to sympathize with Mirah's national feeling is part of his overly promiscuous, downright readerly nature. Both he and the reader turn out to be wrong; it is Daniel's own Jewishness that gave him access to the river. The character who started the novel seemingly consumed by excessively fungible emotions turns out to exemplify the advent of a newly potent portability: a cultural identity so deep that it, like Mordecai's poem in Jacob's memory, can sink below the surface and become a permanent treasure.

This sort of submersible national culture is occasionally on display in the novel in its positive form, as when Mirah's lisped syllables strike a chord in Daniel. Equally important, however, are the cultural items visible only by way of their absence, or their indescribability. Eliot is committed to narrating the register of objects that cannot properly be appreciated by the outsider, and which are best approached with that decorous incomprehension put into play when Daniel calls Mirah's nonsense syllables "quite good Hebrew to me." Thus when Daniel and Mirah are married, a daughter of the pawn-broking Cohen family attends in what is described, for the benefit of Christians making sense of a veiled Judaism, as a "new Sabbath frock"—although the wedding takes place on a Sunday. The Cohen baby can be described as "teething intelligently at home" only because it is an accepted feature of the Cohens that their children behave with intelligence, whether the activity permits intelligence be applied to it or not: from an outsider's perspective, teething is as liable to look intelligent as reciting Hebrew.[29] Of the wedding itself, readers learn that "naturally, they were married according to the Jewish rite."[30] Just as naturally, however, nothing of that rite is described.[31]

It is as if the novel disaggregates everything marked as "Jewish" into two categories: done exactly like a Christian, and hence not in need of description; or, so unlike Christian practice as to be indescribable. Alongside the indescribability of difference, then, is a different sort of indescribability: details about events, emotions, thoughts, or even words meaningful only to Jews are tellingly omitted. Hebrew disappears from the novel: not printed, not transliterated, and rarely even translated, it is instead paraphrased or glossed over altogether (unlike various untranslated snippets of German, Italian, and French). This is most striking in the novel's final paragraphs, which describe Mordecai's death by withholding one quotation—Mordecai's recital of the Shema—and providing another in its place.

> "Where thou goest, Daniel, I shall go. Is it not begun? Have I not breathed my soul into you? We shall live together."
>
> He paused, and Deronda waited, thinking that there might be another word for him. But slowly and with an effort Ezra, pressing on their hands, raised himself and uttered in Hebrew the confession of the divine Unity, which for long generations has been on the lips of the dying Israelite.
>
> He sank back gently into his chair, and did not speak again. But it was some hours before he had ceased to breathe, with Mirah's and Deronda's arms around him.

> Nothing is here for tears, nothing to wail
> Or knock the breast; no weakness, no contempt,
> Dispraise, or blame; nothing but well and fair,
> And what may quiet us in a death so noble.[32]

Milton's "Samson Agonistes" might seem to operate here as a suggestive analogy to the feelings the represented Jews are having in their own particular way, out of direct observation. Yet it seems a very peculiar way to arrive at that analogy. While Milton's subject matter (the death of a powerful Jew) does resonate with the scene, the poem has no directly discernible relationship to Mordecai's own prayer. In place of some kind of correspondence to Mordecai's own words, it supplies another account of what the reader is seeing and feeling.[33] If this is meant to establish an analogy, then, it is one pointedly constituted out of disjunction between two powerful cultural systems, each of which has texts that will resonate at moments of high feeling.

This passage marks the culmination of an intriguing pattern. Eliot establishes an unscrutinizable national interiority by elaborately staging a withdrawal of the novel's gaze from scenes that might shed light on the interiority of a character who is experiencing a moment of national consciousness. Eliot stages this withdrawal repeatedly: a vivid prelude to a scene is followed by a somewhat removed account of its crisis, followed by complete narratorial withdrawal from the moment of utmost revelation. So a scene of interior debate rendered in free indirect discourse is followed by a scene simply rendered on the level of social interaction, which in turn is followed by the disappearance from observation and representation that occurs when a truly national sentiment is attained. For example, just after the meticulously detailed story of Lapidoth's theft of Daniel's ring (vividly rendered in free indirect discourse from Lapidoth's perspective) comes a brief social scene, narrated from far above, that leads Daniel to propose marriage. This is followed by Mirah and Daniel finally coming together in a space outside the complications of language, "meeting so fully in their new consciousness that all signs would have seemed to throw them further apart."[34]

As the novel proceeds, it is not just Mirah and Daniel's ecstasies that are foreclosed, but the inner workings of Daniel's mind altogether. The realist novel characteristically defers certain forms of representation as a way of heightening verisimilitude, just as (by Michael Fried's account) the "absorbed" figure in realist paintings experiences something precisely denied to the viewer herself.[35] Here, though, Eliot introduces an apologetic evacuation of authorial knowledge from a central locus within the novel—the protagonist's own consciousness. The only contemporaneous novel that experiments with such a radical withdrawal from its putative central consciousness is *Madame Bovary*.[36] The portable essence that defines Daniel's identity is not cognate with the kind of information that might be encoded in a novel, or a chest of documents. The feelings generated within the nationally inaccessible characters are not—as in the case of the text that proceeds by way of carefully prefigured gaps in representation—an "open secret" to the reader.[37] Their distance from both Christian readers and the Christian novelist is exactly the point: nothing can be further from the (presumptively Christian) reader's mind than a sense of what is in Deronda's own at such moments.[38]

CRITICAL DISTANCE

The distance between the reader's position and Deronda's sparks considerable ire among Eliot's contemporary readers. By disappearing into a national plot, Daniel attains a cultural portability that looks truly racial—

since no outsider to his "people" can hope to penetrate, meaning that no reader of the novel is expected to make any more sense of his inner state than Eliot herself does. Bemused or irate, critics ask if there is any content to Daniel's beliefs: what sort of actions ought to follow from them? What did Mordecai mean to tell him? Such questions predominate from the early notices through Leavis's famous broadside: "As for the bad [that is, Jewish] part of *Daniel Deronda*, there *is* nothing to do but cut it away."[39]

Critical frustration with Daniel as he is depicted late in the novel stems from his having entered into a destiny that must remain a mystery to his readers.[40] Not because they are Christian: certainly, English readers could recall entering into Jewish or Muslim characters' minds (in Scott's novels if nowhere else). Rather, the walls are drawn up against Deronda because Eliot suggests he is right to conceive of his partiality as definitive, right to think that his attachment to a single race is what makes him uniquely able to gather knowledge about it. With its master tongue represented as a mess of syllables to lisp or to recite without comprehension, Judaism has become the lingua franca that Daniel can hear—but one the reader, the rest of the characters, and even Eliot herself cannot speak. This is not the end of the line for the notion of cultural portability I have been tracing from the 1830s: it is simply where such portability slips below the visible surface of the text, and becomes hypothetical, visible to readers only through approximations—or through cover-texts such as "Samson Agonistes." Or perhaps it is where the notion of a portable national culture (Maimonides for Jews, Milton for the English) becomes a kind of ghost trace, felt only as a disturbance on the surface of the text, a something that stands between the reader and full, complete "sympathy" with characters whose lineaments are gradually growing dim.

Contemporary critics feel that implied exclusion keenly. Even the largely positive account by R. H. Hutton specifies that:

> The *ideas* and creed of the man, on which, in a case like this, so very much turns, are too indefinitely and vaguely sketched to support the character. Before such a being as Mordecai could seriously have proposed to restore nationality to the Jews, in order that they might resume their proper mission of mediating, as religious teachers at least, between East and West, he must have had a much more defined belief than any which the author chose to communicate to us.[41]

Hutton, then, doubts even the existence of the "mission" that putatively terminates *Daniel Deronda*. That doubt suggests that critics feared Eliot, in withholding knowledge, had also foreclosed on the novel's accepted capacity to present individual consciousness fully. If in *Middlemarch* she had been guilty of making the community's life and its ideas too painfully present within the text, she is here guilty of having gestured to ideas that not only are not represented, but cannot even be conceived at the level of the text.

Critics are quick to pick up on implications for how empathy would be permitted or baffled within a novel "nationalized" in this new way. Henry James's famous attack on *Daniel Deronda* notes the irony in Gwendolen yearning after the very thing Daniel attains:

> The very chance to embrace what the author is so fond of calling a "larger life" seems refused to [Gwendolen]. . . . Her finding Deronda pre-engaged to go to the East and stir up the race-feeling of the Jews strikes me as a wonderfully happy invention. The irony of the situation, for poor Gwendolen, is almost grotesque, and it makes one wonder whether the whole heavy structure of the Jewish question in the story was not built up by the author for the express purpose of giving its proper force to this particular stroke.[42]

That is, Gwendolen is thwarted by the very same fact—Daniel's Jewishness—that brings an end to Daniel's early receptiveness. Given the sort of ultrareceptivity toward Mordecai Daniel manifests, Gwendolen's being "forsaken" may seem a kind of split within the idea of sympathy itself. Mordecai's seeking spirit finds response in Daniel, once his heritage is known; but Gwendolen's spirit is repulsed for the very same reason. What looked like the carrying capacity of sympathy—that it enabled one to enter into the nature of another, and work selflessly for that other's benefit—turns out only to be exercisable when ethnic lines abet the connection.[43]

Such a reading would certainly help to explain why, after *Daniel Deronda*'s late turn to what has been called "national epic,"[44] it so pointedly refuses older forms of cultural portability. Sentimental fetishes are scattered as freely around the early pages of the novel as they are in earlier novels such as *Middlemarch*: there is little to separate Henrietta Noble's attachment to Will Ladislaw's "tortoise-shell lozenge-box" from Mab Meyrick's mock resolve to "carry [Daniel's] signature in a little black-silk bag round my neck to keep off the Cramp."[45] But such fetishes disappear from the latter half of *Daniel Deronda*; indeed, they more than disappear—objects that might serve as relics are pointedly introduced so as to be excluded. Daniel embodies the people whose wanderings make them a paradigm for England's own newly expansive wanderings over the globe. Rather than requiring a renewed commitment to "most precious treasures"—documents, amulets, or fetishes—Eliot turns the hoary resurrected-documents plot on its head.[46] Daniel's ascent into a timeless national identity requires the mediation of no documents: at least, no documents that will make any sense to the reader.

Victorian readers contemplating the triple resonance of Daniel's documents—as a familial legacy, as palpable treasure-trove, and as a set of stories not unlike the story they themselves are reading—would likely have felt a revelation at hand. When Daniel actually takes delivery of his grandfather's papers, though, Eliot marks the moment as at once vital and nugatory. The chain he discovers is "electric," suggesting a meaningful connection reestablished—and yet that electricity is entirely Daniel's own.

> The moment wrought strongly on Deronda's imaginative susceptibility: in the presence of one linked still in zealous friendship with the [long-dead] grandfather whose hope had yearned towards him when he was unborn, and who though dead was yet to speak with him in those written memorials which, says Milton, "contain a potency of life in them to be as active as that soul whose progeny they are," he seemed to himself to be touching the electric chain of his own ancestry: and he bore the scrutinizing look of Kalonymos with a delighted awe, something like what one feels in the solemn commemoration of acts done long ago but still telling markedly on the life of to-day. Impossible for men of duller fibre—men whose affection is not ready to diffuse itself through the wide travel of imagination, to comprehend, perhaps even to credit this sensibility of Deronda's; but it subsisted, like their own dullness, notwithstanding their lack of belief in it—and it gave his face an expression which seemed very satisfactory to the observer.[47]

The electric connection Daniel feels depends both on his superior "fibre" and on his Jewish blood. It does not, however, depend in any meaningful way on what the chest contains. The papers themselves, treasured as association copies but persistently reluctant to yield up any sort of quotable, or even paraphrasable, meaning, end up operating as a kind of novelistic foil. They are brought in to advertise their superfluity.

"I shall live": Surmounting and Succumbing to Time

Documents or no, Daniel is by novel's end so well insulated, so far removed, that it is almost impossible for the reader to comprehend him, let alone feel sympathy for him. Yet this disappearance from the reader's eye is accompanied by no moral opprobrium, no lapse, no overt cognitive transformation. Rather, Eliot disengages Daniel from readerly sympathy principally by charting his discovery of a way to opt out from the unfolding present in which the novel's action takes place. The Jewish Daniel falls out of synch with the slow but incessant forward march of time that the novel itself, and its readers, cannot do without. The "make-believe of a beginning" might be dispensable for systems of knowledge (like astronomy) that can look at sidereal and terrestrial evolution sub specie aeternitatis. Sequence within a novel, though, is inescapable. That readers suspend the temporality of their own lives to assume that of the novel might complicate their experience of its sequentiality, but certainly does not negate it. Readers' ardent attachment to Gwendolen, and the distance they feel from Daniel, stems in part from the way that Eliot moves to represent escape from temporality in the character of Daniel—and the impossibility that Gwendolen, even for a second, can make a similar escape.

Daniel's Jewishness makes an epistemological difference—readers, like Eliot herself, might know something about Judaism, but never the crucial things that Daniel knows and means to act upon. His Jewishness also makes an ethical difference—because he is Jewish, he ought to love Mirah, but ought not stay close to Gwendolen. Both these developments are mapped by way of Daniel's ascent into a new relationship to time. The language of immortality and eternal recurrence surrounds Daniel. Mordecai passes away, yet he is with Daniel. Daniel's alliance with Mirah quasi-incestuously cements what he and his ancestors already were with what he and his descendants certainly will be. Even his answer to Gwendolen's question about his return to England—"If I live . . . *some time*"—suggests his indifference to the location and duration of his future work in the world.[48]

Eliot's template for the kind of enlightened timelessness that Daniel attains can be found as far back as her first contribution to *The Westminster Review*, which praises the ideal scholar as possessing "a wonderful intuition of the mental conditions of past ages with an ardent participation in the most advanced ideas and most hopeful efforts of the present."[49] Anchored in the present, this is a mind that ranges freely over past occurrences and deploys them to imagine how present ideas might advance into a hope-filled future. In *Middlemarch*, Eliot offers a horrifying account of what it might mean to get scholarship wrong—but it is not a description of a dry, withered scholar trapped in the past. Rather, it is Casaubon's curse—due largely to his ignorance of contemporary German scholarship—to be trapped not in the actual past, but in his own chimerical sense of what that past was.

By contrast, Daniel's immersion in what he eventually discovers to be his true past (a grandfather, a scholarly heritage, and so forth) is an indispensable part of his progression into the future of those he calls "my hereditary people." When he tells his mother, for example, that "the Christian sympathies in which my mind was reared can never die out of me," he immediately adds: "But I consider it my duty—it is the impulse of my feeling—to identify myself, as far as possible, with my hereditary people, and if I can see any work to be done for them that I can give my soul and hand to, I shall choose to do it."[50] The reference to his "Christian sympathies" might seem to bespeak a partial distance from his Jewish identity here. Those "sympathies," too, however, are marshaled precisely to indicate how fully he will devote his present to discovering the people who now define his past and bettering their future. This adherence in his future to the dictates of a past allegiance does not strike Daniel—as it strikes his mother—as a loss of freedom, acquiescence to the dead hand.

The success of Dorothea Brooke at the conclusion of *Middlemarch* depends on her learning how to put to use her "far-reaching sensibilities" within the narrow boundaries of her own parish. Daniel's success at novel's end almost seems the opposite. His nationality has taught him not to have "far-reaching" but rather narrowly focused sensibilities, attuned to the needs of "my hereditary people" alone. Rather than applying those sensibilities within a well-delineated province, he is liable to turn up anywhere in a world that is as open to wandering Jews as to the conquering English—those being the two nations licensed to roam the globe at large.

If Daniel's final location is thus deliberately undefined as to space and time, he refuses to see it that way. By his account, his discovery of his heritage has cleared him to go anywhere and to feel equally present in memories of a Jewish past and daydreams of a Jewish homeland yet to be. When his mother reveals the (to her mind dreadful) fact of his Jewish birth, she places his genesis in a quirky past participle: "I relieved you from the bondage of having been born a Jew."[51] Gwendolen's response to the same revelation is also in a convoluted past tense: "What difference need that have made?"[52] But Daniel's response to the Alcharisi places the news within a permanent present, understood as both biology and destiny: "'Then I *am* a Jew?' Deronda burst out with a deep-voiced energy."[53]

It might seem logical for Eliot to juxtapose Daniel's collapse of past and future against the temporal dilations involved in Grandcourt's ennui, a version of eighteenth-century aristocratic nonchalance run amuck. Yet the operative distinction that the novel repeatedly raises is between Daniel's ambitions toward pure diachrony and Gwendolen's entrapment in an enduring and unendurable present. The reader is repeatedly reminded how incapable Gwendolen is of managing time and its effect upon her. Gwendolen is adrift not in the past but in the dreadful present progressive, in which history is available to her only as whatever memory happens to loom up: "Things repeat themselves in me so. They come back—they will all come back."[54] The gothic implications of such haunting would be clear, even without the painted panel at Offendene to drive the point home.

While Daniel has all of time at his disposal, Gwendolen is all too acutely aware of the moment-by-moment nature of the present. There is immense agony implied by the word "quite" in a sentence like, "[W]hen [Daniel] was quite gone, her mother came in and found her sitting motionless."[55] It is this imprisonment that gives rise to the temporal confusion in Gwendolen's most memorable expressions of her grieving hope: "I said . . . I said . . . it should be better . . . better with me . . . for having known you."[56] The sentence moves, ellipsis by ellipsis, from a past where she "said," to what might be a hypothetical or a potential future ("should be better") glimpsed from that past, a past to which "having known you" returns.

Gwendolen accordingly appears to represent an Englishness not yet quite ready to take on the sort of atemporal dislocation that allows Jewishness to weather all the perils of global dislocation, whether as a diasporic or a "colonizing" people. It seems apt, therefore, that Eliot's final word on the Jewish/English national question, five years later, bemoaned the perils of remaining isolated within the tortured temporal present, and advocated that Jews and English alike discover a way to carry their culture with them anywhere.

Liberty and Nation: Eliot's Last Words to Mill

> Every Jew should be conscious that he is one of a multitude possessing common objects of piety in the immortal achievements and immortal sorrows of ancestors who have transmitted to them a physical and mental type strong enough, eminent enough in faculties, pregnant enough with peculiar promise, to constitute a new beneficent individuality among the nations, and, by confuting the traditions of scorn, nobly avenge the wrongs done to their Fathers.
> —George Eliot, "The Modern Hep! Hep! Hep!"
> *Impressions of Theophrastus Such*, 1879

Once race and culture come to seem so potentially intertwinable, the portability of national culture can take on a wide range of new forms. Viewed through this new lens, problems of psychological introspection can be reshaped into problems of national mobility. Rather than grappling with the formal demands of provinciality that dominate the early pages of *Daniel Deronda*, Eliot's last book, *Impressions of Theophrastus Such* (1879) begins by meditating on subjectivity's pitfalls. "Looking Inward" explores the overly sympathetic subject's incapacity to establish an abiding selfhood based either upon permanent introspection (how can you trust your own gaze?) or on reference to the outside world (how can you trust your sense of others if you cannot even be sure about your own interior?). It is these pieces a contemporary review called "careful but unsympathetic analyses of certain phases of human character: admirable dissections, no doubt, but life has fled under the scalpel."[57] The book's final essay, though, "The Modern Hep! Hep! Hep!," suggests that immersion in a national identity can resolve such worries. National solidarity, figured as Jewish, is the mediating mechanism that can assure that individual introspection actually resonates with a past, present, and future community. From a different starting point, *Such* arrives at a terminus it shares comfortably with *Daniel Deronda*.[58]

Many early reviews contained a version of *Fraser's* complaint that "the vague personality through which George Eliot has thought fit to speak is little better than a masquerade costume . . . a nobody."[59] Critics, though, were not entirely deaf to Eliot's notion that shared national culture might serve as a way of alleviating some of the worries created both by provincialism and by excessive introspection.[60] Eliot's commitment to sustaining that simultaneous attention to affinities and contrasts, in fact, is what persuades her to conclude "The Modern Hep! Hep! Hep!" by picking a quarrel with John Stuart Mill's *On Liberty* (1859). Eliot is convinced that any cohesive culture will contain within it shared cultural properties that might make no sense to an outsider, but all the sense in the world to someone within its confines. The cultural insider can thus find a comforting connection where an outsider hears only hollow words, or sees only meaningless gestures. It is thus not individual but *national* difference that should be universally protected.

> Pagans in successive ages said, "These people are unlike us, and refuse to be made like us: let us punish them." The Jews were steadfast in their separateness, and through that separateness Christianity was born. A modern book on Liberty [that is, Mill's *On Liberty*] has maintained that from the freedom of individual men to persist in idiosyncrasies the world may be enriched. Why should we not apply this argument to the idiosyncrasy of a nation, and pause in our haste to hoot it down? There is still a great function for the steadfastness of the Jew: not that he should shut out the utmost illumination which knowledge can throw on his national history, but that he should cherish the store of inheritance which that history has left him.[61]

Eliot is not merely suggesting that national idiosyncrasies ought to be respected as much as individual ones. To Eliot, Mill's defense of mere individualism actually looks actively misguided when compared with the virtues an autonomous nation possesses.[62]

Eliot explores what it might mean to respect Jews not as individuals but as a distinct culture apart. This kind of respect, though, rooted as it is in a corporate definition of a united nation, cannot readily be compared to the sort of respect that *On Liberty* argues is merited for anyone holding distinct views—simply because they are his or her own. At the end of both *Daniel Deronda* and *Theophrastus Such*, stances taken by individuals acting as members of groups become a kind of loyal adherence; but readers are pointedly excluded even from the grounds for agreeing or disagreeing with their choices.[63] Such choices might be motivated by reasoned choices, but they are arrived at by pathways sometimes obscure even to the most studious outsider. Eliot in the mid-1870s is a paramount practitioner of an art that binds people together on the basis of potentially limitless sympathy, an art seemingly designed to uncover the obscurities of others' motivations. Both *Daniel Deronda* and *Theophrastus Such*, however, conclude by proposing that it is the "idiosyncrasy of a nation" that must be protected.[64]

This might well be the best explanation we will find for Eliot's curious withdrawal in the face of Jewishness, manifested not only in the depiction of Daniel, but also in Eliot's notable eagerness for Jewish approval of the novel. Despite Eliot's extensive research for the novel, and her evident erudition in Judaic matters,[65] a letter to David Kaufmann responding to his "George Eliot und das Judenthum" suggests the sort of sanction she craves:

> Certainly, if I had been asked to choose *what* should be written about my book and *who* should write it, I should have sketched—well, not anything so good as what you have written, but an article which must be written by a Jew who showed not merely sympathy with the best aspirations of his race, but a remarkable insight into the nature of art and the processes of the artistic mind. . . . I confess that I had an unsatisfied hunger for certain signs of sympathetic discernment, which you only have given.[66]

Sympathy here is what can be extended between people over the content of beliefs that they need not—even cannot—discuss.

In a sense, the disappearing Daniel turns into a "Saint Somebody" after all, by becoming the face Eliot puts on a Jewish learning that is at once hers and not hers. Paradoxically, Daniel's ascent into nationality offers the novelist herself a chance to perform the exceptional experiment of disqualifying herself from describing, representing, or even understanding one of her own creations. Viewed in this light, Eliot's letter to Kaufmann is a poignant reminder of how thoroughly she intends the novel to establish the existence of a kind of portable identity that is representable, within the novel, only by the sort of lacuna with which the novel concludes: the excision of the Shema, and the substitution of "Samson Agonistes." The "sublime selflessness" Gallagher describes as the apotheosis of Eliot's art is thus figured at the novel's end by the substitution of someone else's poetry for Eliot's own prose.[67]

Cultural portability as it had been shaped in the novels of Trollope, Collins, or Emily Eden is profoundly altered by the end of *Daniel Deronda*. Daniel's new persona has all the virtues of fixity and reliable transtemporality that the national epic can offer. That portable identity, however, has the concomitant disadvantage of denying the novel reader any insight—by analogy or homology—into Daniel's character. The reader who might have imagined that the novel could render a mental state like Gwendolen's real in the words of the novel itself would never make that mistake about the rendering of Daniel's national state.

By the end of *Daniel Deronda*, cultural portability seems at once apotheosized—because racial heritage makes it a given that culture, too, is transmissible—and potentially annihilated. That is, the laudable transmission established by novel's end requires that no mechanism of transmission will be visible to the outsider. Does this mean that the knowledge seemingly conveyed in Mirah's lisping song, Jacob's rote memorization, or in Daniel's inaccessible books is simply null, a cipher for the participant in the culture as much as it is for the excluded and bemused reader? If so, culture has more or less been replaced by race. Yet it is hard to square that reading with the status of Eliot's own text. After all, if there is nothing to represent, and potentially nothing to represent it with, it is not clear what representational work the novel itself has just done. It is difficult to accept that, like the cover verse from Milton, the entire novel is intended to project a sort of shadow Jewishness on a screen where Christians can view it—while underneath, in some unrelated way that is fueled only by nature and not by knowledge, authentic Jewishness proceeds.

Daniel Deronda stands at a crucial volta in the English novel's relationship to cultural portability. After Eliot, there are certainly still novels whose basic lineaments are entirely defined by the assumptions of cultural portability spelled out previously in the introduction—Oliphant's *Kirsteen*, for example, dates from 1890. A variety of factors, though—including the explicit imperialism of "Greater Britain," the hardening racial categories of the last quarter of the century, and an evolving sense of the limitations inherent in various forms of cultural transmission from core to periphery—combine to generate within post-1876 English fiction a variety of strong challenges to the logic of portability. The final three chapters of this book accordingly focus on writers who made their dissatisfaction with some of the guiding tenets of cultural portability overt, albeit in profoundly different ways.

Chapter 4 considers R. D. Blackmore, who attempts in *Lorna Doone* and its unsuccessful successors to infuse a regionally specific sort of local color writing into his novels—but without entirely forgoing the sort of effortless portability (largely manifested in readily universalizable characters and predictably recapitulated romance plots) that had been the hallmark of the mid-Victorian provincial novel. Blackmore exemplifies what might be called unsuccessful early adaptation, a search for new forms of cultural portability that he thought Greater Britain might demand. Perhaps responding, by the end of his career, to the enormous success of American local color writing in the last third of the century, Blackmore was a novelist struggling to modify the fictional formulae he had inherited.

The final two chapters, though, analyze two writers whose fiction is deeply shaped by a determined effort not to adapt and thrive, but to break violently from the long-held verities of cultural portability. In chapter 5, I argue that Thomas Hardy, from his first novels of the early 1870s, discovered a new sort of locodescriptive writing that fused deep readings of landscape with meticulous descriptions of the radically diverse observers who register those landscapes. Hardy was committed to writing novels "of environment and character" that were neither regionalist nor provincial—and might be called "localist" by virtue of their obsession with the importance of registering how differently various individuals make sense of the world. Hardy came to believe central to the logic of the novel ought to be the question of attention: who notices what, when, and why? His conclusions about how such attention was initially formed, then shaped and modified by the environment, led him to an account of how individuals were suspended within their cultural settings that could not have been further apart from the portability that shaped the mid-Victorian novelistic mainstream.

In chapter 6, I make a contrasting case: that William Morris, whose mantra of socialist solidarity was the notion that an injury to one was an injury to all, came to believe that portability foundered on its claim that *any* meaningful difference between persons existed or ought to exist. Morris was looking, in both *News from Nowhere* (1889) and the strange utopian romances of the 1890s, for an aesthetics that could represent sameness between people, and hence the absurdity of attempting to create cultural artifacts that would circulate only among a privileged few. Morris's rejection of portability's logic was complete, and the vitriol directed against the oppressive, elitist "local color" logic of the novelists who preceded him unmistakable. If George Eliot pushes cultural portability to its logical limits in an attempt to square it with the newly emergent logic of deep national/racial identity, and Blackmore strives to create an English regionalism that is as portability-centered as the provincial novel, Morris and Hardy are the first Victorian writers to refuse, point-blank, portability's master logic.

CHAPTER FOUR

Locating *Lorna Doone*:
R. D. Blackmore, F. H. Burnett, and
the Limits of English Regionalism

ABSOLUTE LIVING

Eliot's memorabilia, Gaskell's letters, Trollope's necklace, Eden's quotations: are these anything more than Victorian oddities, bits of portable property afloat by chance in the era's most capacious genre? Grant that portability proves a powerful paradigm for novelists such as Trollope, preoccupied with the ways that sentimental value can adhere to objects seemingly defined by their fiscal nature only; grant that Emily Eden would be preoccupied with deciding how literary quotations could constitute an Englishness on the move; even grant that in setting out to represent the unrepresentability of Jewish culture, Eliot is exploring how deeply portable culture can be embedded within a racialized body. Taken separately, these instances hardly prove a widespread novelistic obsession with portability. Why would the same logic apply to novels in which locale is everything, novels defined more by their setting than by incident or characters? What need would such novels have for the play of portability?

I argue in this chapter, however, that the logic of portability is unmistakably at play within locodescriptive fiction of the sort that seemingly disavows mobility altogether. An inherently antiportable form of locodescriptive fiction could well have flourished in England in the last third of the nineteenth century—as regionalist, or "local color," writing flourished in America—but such a form did *not* emerge. English regionalism is the dog that did not bark. Its silence has a great deal to say about the surprisingly pervasive and durable hold that the notion of portable national culture had upon the thinking, and the novel writing, of the day. This was, in fact, a hold so durable that iconoclastic later writers like Thomas Hardy and William Morris still thought it worth their while to thunder against portability's guiding assumptions.

It is not that examples of nascent English regionalism are entirely absent. In Richard Doddridge Blackmore's *Lorna Doone* (1869), every tree that narrator John Ridd sees, every sheep he owns, and every wrestling throw he makes are recruited as arguments for Exmoor's inimitable nature, and for John as the personification of Exmoor. This representation of a thoroughly and persistently local mindset could easily be mistaken for the exact antithesis to portability's fluid gyrations. The timing looks right. Eliot and Blackmore, after all, both recognized at roughly the same time that the English provincial novel was nearing a crisis point, and both recognized a readership (and thus a market) for innovative accounts of the relationship between a readily moveable national culture and counter-vailing forces of locality and particularity. Eliot's final experiments, I have argued—*Daniel Deronda* and the peripatetic essays of *Theophrastus Such*—explore whether portable culture might be carried far enough inside an individual that it became a kind of bodily, as well as spiritual, heritage. In an age when antiquarianism, often of a highly regionalist bent, flourished, nothing could seem more logical than Blackmore's forsaking all motion and locating authentic experience in the singular realm of inimitable Exmoor.[1]

It was portability, though, not locality, that made *Lorna Doone* immortal. The ecstatic reviews; the popular success that by 1871 had erased memories of poor initial sales (in 1897, for example, there was a print-run of 100,000, "all of which were sold within one week"); the spike in popularity of the name Lorna between 1870 and 1920; the spate of early films: all of these result not from Exmoor's charms, but from the "undying" romance between stolid, common, burly John Ridd and delicate Lorna Doone, a love story that makes "one forget it is not of one's own age."[2] Blackmore's ambition, consistent with the cultural authority that adhered strongly to the provincial novel (but not at all to regional-minded antiquarian writing), is to juxtapose the demands of locale and of character, resulting in a striking interplay between the Exmoor landscape and the essential ethereality of a single character (Lorna) capable of flowing over such a landscape unchecked. Perfect geographic determinism meets perfect fluidity, and neither blinks.

Blackmore's success with *Lorna Doone* tells half the story of what happens to the sort of locodescriptive fiction that might seem set to undermine portability altogether. The other half is told by the critical and popular failures that followed, as Blackmore labored, Pevsner-like, to write the novels of English regional identity he thought must be the logical successors to *Lorna Doone*.[3] Blackmore's failure to follow *Lorna Doone* with other bestsellers reveals the near-impossibility of regional fiction flourishing in England in the same way that it did in late nineteenth-century America. Blackmore could not, as his later writing poignantly demonstrates, understand why England was not ready for what America was experiencing: a tremendous upsurge in regional writing. His failures as much as his success, then, can clarify the crucial role portability (and especially the potency of imperial portability) played in determining how novels were read, and what sorts of novels achieved cultural preeminence in the last third of the nineteenth century. Blackmore ignored the most obvious sign that his success had little to do with local color: in contemporary English reviews, his zeal and care in rendering the landscape and folkways of Somerset and Devon forms an acknowledged but rarely valued complement to what reviewers truly want from Blackmore: the free-floating passion and timeless beauty of evanescent and aristocratic Lorna.[4] True, one early reviewer praised landscapes that "have been photographed, as it were, upon the retina of a plastic imagination."[5] And another found in "the local aspects of Somerset and Devonshire . . . [s]uch a wealth of plenty and comfort and warmth that the reader is made to feel as if he had been carried far away from London, and was breathing in the pure air of Exmoor, and luxuriating in the good country fare so well and vividly described."[6] Contemporary English reception in the main, however, tended to praise Blackmore's success in differentiating sharply between the smooth beauties of his heroine and the comparative roughness of the landscape below.

Margaret Oliphant's influential review set the tone. In it, she chides Blackmore for an excessive attention to the regional peculiarities of seventeenth-century Devon, complaining that there are too many "details simply as details [in the novel's] narrative of every walk taken, and every change of season." *Lorna Doone*'s success, she opines, is that Blackmore brings eternal moral and psychological lessons home to the reader: "[I]t is a real life that is set before us—not certain tricks of manner which pass away, but an absolute living. . . . A book full of the truest nature and beautiful thoughts."[7] By Oliphant's account, then, the logic of cultural portability persisted more or less unmodified even in a novel that deviated from the successful formulae of the provincial novel and struck out into the uncharted fields of regional peculiarity.[8] Oliphant reads *Lorna Doone* as committed, like her own novels, to a version of cultural portability that emphasizes how readily feelings and thoughts can travel from place to place, borne by the right sorts of sentimental subjects.[9]

Oliphant certainly underestimates how hard Blackmore labors to establish his tale's place, time, and folkways: Lorna's universality depends upon the novel's efforts to produce a sense of inimitable locality, an effort that no review of the book has ever ignored entirely. Still, Oliphant's influence is striking. After her review, *Lorna Doone* is generally praised among English Victorian readers and critics for its universal romantic appeal; in 1906, when Yale undergraduates voted it their favorite novel, it was surely John's romance with Lorna they had in mind, not Exmoor's sheep.[10]

The previous three chapters in this study—examining how the logic of cultural portability shapes diamond narratives, Anglo-Indian travel writing, and novels of national consciousness—have largely focused on the mobility of items of value, both within a domestic English economy and in Greater Britain beyond. My claim is that *Lorna Doone* experiments with a half-renunciation of that logic, but does not go far enough to make the novel an exercise in antiportability. *Lorna Doone* suggests that even the sort of stability and immobility associated with locodescription and the chronicling of folkways—when accompanied by the sort of "absolute living" that Oliphant values in the depiction of Lorna—abets rather than undermines portability's logic.

On the one hand, the logic of cultural portability I have described in the preceding chapters accords well with Oliphant's praise of Lorna's "absolute living": anything true of her, that is, would be true anywhere and at any time. Yet, on the other hand, like the locodescriptive poetry of Robert Burns discussed in the introduction, a novel's portability is dependent upon some hypostatized *fons et origo*, different in kind from all the places to which the novel circulates—in this case, Exmoor. A novel— whether understood as a material object or as an assemblage of signs (that is, a text)—might seem a poor choice to reconcile the uniformity of a print-mediated public sphere and the uniqueness of a single, memorable place. *Lorna Doone*'s subtle exploration of the relationship between detachment (ethereal Lorna) and location (Exmoor), however, proves remarkably capable of preserving both circulation *and* singularity.

Provincial versus Regional

Lorna Doone's innovations are best understood by comparing it to the provincial novels it bid to supplant.[11] In the novels of Trollope and Eliot (pre-*Deronda*), a Barchester or a Middlemarch becomes readily metonymic of an England of which readers mainly know that it is neither modern nor London. As Ian Duncan puts it:

> Regional fiction specifies its setting by invoking a combination of geographical, natural-historical, antiquarian, ethnographic, and/or sociological features *that differentiate it from any other region.* A provincial setting is defined more simply by its *difference from the metropolis.* . . . Thus, while "regional" implies a neutral or even positive set of multiple local differences, "provincial" connotes a negative difference, based on a binary opposition, expressed as a generic or typical identity, within which any particular provincial setting may take the place of any other.[12]

At the beginning of the nineteenth century, some writers who might be called regional novelists (for example, John Galt and Elizabeth Hamilton) appear on the Celtic fringe, working through the paradox Franco Moretti has described at work in the historical novel: "to represent internal un-evenness, and then to abolish it."[13] Duncan, however, argues that provincialism held sway in England until around 1870:

> In the great novels of Gaskell, Trollope, and Eliot the provincial county town or parish becomes the generic and typical setting of a traditional England, responsive to the pressures of modernity (politics, debt, fashion, crime) that have overwhelmed metropolitan life, but resisting or absorbing them—if only ambiguously, if only for a time.[14]

Provincial novels figure a given locale—a parish, town, county, or even country—as England writ small.[15]

Consider, for example, how neatly Gaskell's *Wives and Daughters* (1864–66) handles the problem of arbitrary placement in its opening two sentences:

> To begin with the old rigmarole of childhood. In a country there was a shire, and in that shire there was a town, and in that town there was a house, and in that house there was a room, and in that room there was a bed, and in that bed there lay a little girl: wide awake and longing to get up, but not daring to do so for fear of the unseen power in the next room; a certain Betty, whose slumbers must not be disturbed until six o'clock struck, when she wakened of herself "as sure as clockwork," and left the household very little peace afterwards.[16]

Down to the servant "Betty," whose remark about "clockwork" and name are unmarked by dialect or ethnicity, this passage suggests that all general claims derive directly from the nature of one's immediate, but ultimately generic, surroundings. Small wonder that in Gaskell's novels trips overseas are dealt with off-stage, their presence marked, at best, by unspecified bits of botanical or taxonomic observation alluded to in a love-interest's letters home.

In the best-known Victorian attack on provincialism, "The Literary Influence of Academies," Matthew Arnold critiques the dazed complacency of the English province-dweller, caught in his own small world at a great remove from the vibrant life of the metropolis, and hence incapable of sharing in the universal realm of thought.[17] Arnold is contemptuous principally of the provincial's various deficiencies: "the note of provinciality as caused by remoteness from a centre of correct information" irks Arnold, as does "the note of provinciality from the want of a centre of correct taste."[18] But Arnold's indictment of provincial failure to cohere has a problem. Any truly successful provincial novel—*Middlemarch*, for example—is predicated upon the iterability of provincial experience, and on the national coherence of various provinces, divided by geography but united by a shared sensibility.[19]

Arnold claimed to fear the provinces because they led to isolation and disjunction; he seems to be underestimating, though, the implicit and even explicit generalizability of provincial novels, which gloried in the ultimately sychronizable nature of experiences unfolding all over England in, say, identical cathedral towns. If novels offered, in place of the "ideas of . . . the first order," a sentimental experience of a "more common" order, then the "violent" and "hard-hitting" nature of the provincial writing Arnold excoriated might stem from its conviction of a new kind of common sense—in place of the common understanding that Arnold valued.[20] Rather than the sanction of an academy, the devotee of the provincial novel seeks another sort of agreement in judgment: even in one's archaic backwater, one can be true to the spirit of the nation in ways that erudite metropolitans cannot match.

My argument in preceding chapters has been that the logic of portability is indispensable to the provincial novel as practiced in mid-Victorian England. Making use of *auratic commodities* (as the readings of significant objects in Gaskell, Eliot, Oliphant, Trollope, Collins and Eden suggest), but also of *detachable locales* (singular and yet ultimately interchangeable), these novels take advantage of a public sphere that market forces and middle-class ideology have made ideal for the widespread circulation of novels as vehicles both of entertainment and of moral instruction. Provincial novels perfectly exemplify the logic of portability because they neither seize on that openness to represent or instantiate a "public sphere" characterized by pure transparency nor do they offer a kind of antithetical, cloistered, and cloistering privacy, a vision of domestic bliss that entirely excludes the dangerous ebb and flow of a promiscuous public sphere. Rather, their characteristic generation of spaces that are well demarcated, yet imaginatively attached to the reader's own life, allows novels to have the best of public circulation and bounded privacy alike. Proof of the consistent appeal and centrality of provincialism in the mid-Victorian era can be found, for instance, in the comparatively dim reception afforded to Emily Brontë's *Wuthering Heights*, highly esteemed for its regionalist features by later generations.[21]

The complications arising around 1870, when many critics have argued that the provincial novel dies off, do not, it seems to me, finish off either the provincial novel or cultural portability in England. The effect that regionalism had in America at just the same time certainly demonstrates how very likely it was that just such a reversal might have occurred in England as well. But it did not. The fact worth explaining, then, is that the English provincial novel's commitment to the double logic of portability—to representing, that is, singular locales that could readily be not merely analogized but actually homologized to the nation itself—found support in unexpected quarters, even among the quasi-regional novels that seemed certain to bury provincialism in England, and to lead to an American-style regionalism.

AMERICAN REGIONALISM

The honored verities of the provincial novel, critics agree, come under ferocious assault from about 1870 onward. With Gaskell dead, and Trollope's jeremiads focused on the sins of London, provincialism is often described as giving way to a renewed regionalism. I propose instead that the waning provincial novel gave way to an array of other formal and conceptual experiments, but that those experiments (such vocal opponents as Hardy and Morris notwithstanding) remain committed, at least through the turn of the century, to some variation of the logic of cultural portability I traced in earlier chapters. In fact, *Lorna Doone* is a crucial test for the regional novel's revivability (as also for the provincial novel's mortality), because there are so few other English novels from this period that could be described as regionalist even at a stretch. Although Richard Jefferies's tightly focused works, for example, seem regionalist at first glance, his interest in local color details pertains almost exclusively to the natural, and not the social, world.

The comparison to contemporary American novels that tread the same terrain can, it turns out, shed a great deal of light on English provincialism's refusal to go quietly. Given the evident overlap between the British and American literary marketplaces at this juncture (an overlap so thorough some have even proposed Anglo-American literary production and consumption is really a single field of study), the difference between the durable and vigorous success of "local color" writing in America and the fate that *Lorna Doone*–like books met in England is quite striking.[22] It is telling, in other words, that national differences would manifest themselves so strikingly around the question of regionalism's comparative importance—even while other features of the era's literary production suggest that such national differences matter comparatively little.[23]

Max Keith Sutton speculates that "Blackmore may have influenced the romantic regional fiction of the United States, where his story of outlaws was immensely popular."[24] If *Lorna Doone* did have an impact, though, it was because the seed fell on fertile American ground (while in England it fell on stones). On the western side of the Atlantic, the disintegration of provincial unity—Cooper's prairies and Irving's bucolia—into regional heterogeneity proceeded rapidly in the last three decades of the century. Starting in the decade following the Civil War, "local color" comes into its own in the 1880s and 1890s; its luminaries include Sarah Orne Jewett, Mary Wilkins Freeman, Hamlin Garland, and Charles Chesnutt, as well as such later avatars as Owen Wister, John Fox, Willa Cather, and even William Faulkner. The American novel's turn from provincialism to regionalism had, as recent critics such as Richard Brodhead and Amy Kaplan have argued, the surprising result of reinforcing national cohesion rather than disaggregating it.[25] Not confined to the aesthetic domain, the upsurge in local color bespeaks a major shift in how the relationship between locality and nation was understood in the culture as a whole.

In 1908, Josiah Royce looked back over four decades of American writing and summarized its case for what in England is called "regionalism," but Royce labels "provincialism."

> By the term "provincialism" I shall mean, first, the tendency of such a province to possess its own customs and ideals; secondly, the totality of these customs and ideals themselves; and thirdly, the love and pride which leads the inhabitants of a province to cherish as their own these traditions, beliefs and aspirations.[26]

To Royce, the capacity to create such a provincial attachment is the basis of the colonizing process that made Britain, and is poised to make America, a world power:

> It is the especial art of the colonizing peoples, such as we are, and such as the English are, to be able by devices of this sort rapidly to build up in their own minds a provincial loyalty in a new environment. The French, who are not a colonizing people, seem to possess much less of this tendency. The Chinese seem to lack it almost altogether.[27]

With an argument virtually unimaginable in an English context, Royce goes on to specify how provincialism within America can form the basis of a powerful national feeling—but only to the extent that the validity of provincial attachment is preserved *apart* from, rather than being sublimated into, a merely general national sentiment:

> If in our own country . . . there are some of us who, like myself, have changed our provinces during our adult years, and who have so been unable to become and to remain in the sense of European countries provincial; and if, moreover, the life of our American provinces everywhere has still too brief a tradition,—all that is our misfortune, and not our advantage. . . . The tendency toward national unity and that toward local independence of spirit, must henceforth grow together. They cannot prosper apart. . . . Provincialism, like monogamy, is an essential basis of true civilization.[28]

Scholars have stressed the role of local color in a nation that was both expanding exponentially westward and looking anxiously back eastward to justify such expansion.[29] Local color writers wanted to supplement—or even replace—a formal or procedural liberalism with a "deep" notion of culture, one drawing from profound wells of archaic custom, wells to be found in exemplary backwaters: Down-East Maine, or the Appalachian recesses where Elizabethan English lingers.[30] Thus Owen Wister's *The Virginian* (1902) features a match between a Virginia-born cowboy and a Vermont schoolteacher—but it is set in Montana, on the frontier where America's distinct cultures (Southern chivalry, Northern erudition) can be at once merged and preserved.[31] John Fox's *The Trail of the Lonesome Pine* (1908) leads coal and steel barons to the rustic glens, where an angel-faced beauty still sings operatically in Shakespearean English in much the same way that the "old natives" (that is, the first European settlers of America) did. Such American works delineate a capacious overall national framework that sanctifies rather than dismantles local cultural peculiarities, making the region not into an antithesis to the nation but its forerunner and mainstay—precisely by virtue of the difference between regional and national identity.

Brad Evans has argued recently that "local chic" can be pushed further, so that

> regionalism . . . had less to do with a sense of place than a dynamic of circulation. . . . [For example, William Dean] Howells positioned the local as a highly aestheticized global commodity, one that was flung into a kind of transnational aesthetic where it traded on the visual and visceral pleasures attendant to a dislocation of the self.[32]

Evans stresses the "transnational" dimension of such "chic" because he is interested in tracing the ways in which local color can become a metonym for folkways as a whole, understood to be dislocatable and transportable in more-than-national ways. The dispute between Evans and such interlocutors as Kaplan (for whom regionalism's local details eventually underwrite a consolidated national culture, not a diffuse international one) is fascinating. But the key question for our purposes is why there exists no legible tradition of English local color writing that could be subjected to the same analysis and debate, no body of regionalist writing that might be taken to stand in, metonymically, for the national essence, no particularist narratives of quirky local color that could attain the kind of circulating "transnational local chic" Evans describes.[33]

The absence of such a tradition in England tells us a great deal about how profoundly portability—especially its imperial implications—shapes the logic of Victorian novels. In America, local chic was vital to constructing an account of a nation that had deep cultural wells that nonetheless flowed together to form one great, common pool. James Buzard's compelling argument that a wide range of English novelists engaged in an "autoethnographic" mode of self-examination and nation writing might seem to make a vigorous English regionalism along American lines look indispensable.[34] Yet the era in which local color fiction should logically have arrived—with *Lorna Doone* as its *fons et origo*—instead saw a confusion surrounding provincial verities, but no new locodescriptive genre emerging as an alternative. After *Lorna Doone*, no deluge, barely even a trickle.

Ultimately, my argument is that England's anomalous position within a Greater Britain that began at the Welsh and Scottish borders precludes the kind of particularizing anatomies that became the lifeblood of American fiction in the last third of the nineteenth century. Seeing why this is so, however, requires a closer look at the persistent difference between American regionalism and its English not-quite-regional counterparts. Michael Elliot has recently made the case that one of American regionalism's proof-texts should be *Louisiana*. This 1880 novel about backwoods North Carolina was one of the first successes of the Manchester-born (but Tennessee-dwelling) Frances Hodgson Burnett, who is now best known for *The Little Princess* (1905) and *The Secret Garden* (1911).

Elliot argues that the novel perfectly embodies regionalist fiction's perennial preoccupation with deciding between "culture as cultivation and culture as local identity."[35] Narrated by two New Yorkers interested in the "novel" challenge of "stud[ying] the North Carolinian mountaineer 'type' with the enthusiasm of an amateur," *Louisiana* is about the difficulties involved in preserving local identity once civilization arrives to supersede it.[36] When the novel's eponymous heroine marries one of the New Yorkers, she insists on retaining as precious relics, in a locked back room, her father's parlor furnishings, "strange ugly furniture . . . and bright-colored lithographs."[37]

Burnett's brand of American regionalism relies, in other words, on a museum of residual "cultures," in which cultural difference can be retained, and yet at the same time archived—such cultural relics are neither to be compared to nor integrated into that other, higher culture (that is, civilization), but instead held apart for remembrance's sake.[38] Louisiana's commitment to secretly curating her familial heritage (vulgar as her mementoes would appear to outsiders) is perfectly continuous with Royce's notion of the perfect harmony, in a triumphant America, between "national unity" (marrying into high culture) and "local independence of spirit" (the residual backroom museum).

There is, though, an interesting twist to the story. The agreement between the views of Royce and Burnett's *Louisiana* only highlights the divergence between Burnett's American regionalist novel of 1880 and the two English provincial novels that she had published in the previous three years. Drawing heavily on memories of Burnett's English childhood, *That Lass O' Lowrie's* (1877) and *Haworth's* (1879) fared far better in England than in America, and were hailed by English reviewers as remarkable documents of Northern life, earning Burnett not only inevitable comparisons to Gaskell (presumably increased by her *Cranford* imitation, *A Fair Barbarian* [1881]) but also to Disraeli and Dickens.[39] Most striking in retrospect, though, is the sharp contrast between Burnett's commitment to a doubled notion of culture (as local identity, on the one hand, and civilization, on the other) in such American novels as *Louisiana* and the decidedly "*un*local color" notion of culture in her earlier Lancashire novels.

In neither *That Lass O' Lowrie's* nor *Haworth's* is the notion of an independent English working-class or regional culture broached, even though both meticulously detail working-class lives, speech, and cultural conditions. Instead, working-class life in these novels is persistently defined by *lack*: of food, books, and comfort, but also of "softness," kindness, and religion.

> They had lived among the coal-pits, and had worked early and late at the "mouth," ever since they had been old enough to take part in heavy labour. It was not to be wondered at that they had lost all bloom of womanly and gentleness. . . . There was no element of softness to rule or even influence them in their half savage existence.[40]

That Lass o' Lowrie's superficially resembles *Louisiana*, in that both novels elevate a poor lower-class girl to a marriage with a rich man from a softer part of the country.[41] Yet when Joan Lowrie comes to marry the engineer Derrick, she takes with her to the gentle South neither a working-class culture nor a museum of resonant properties. When she finally flees the hard life of the pits and factories, the note she bears to a genteel savior down South reads, "Give her the help she needs most. She has had a hard life, and wants to forget it."[42] In the book's final line, Joan even goes that sentiment one further, refusing to marry Derrick until she has acquired culture—defined as the gentle, softening education only middle-class residents of southern England can provide: " 'Give me th' time to make myself worthy—give me th' time to work an' strive; be patient with me until th' day comes when I can come to yo' an' know I need not shame yo'. They say I am na slow at learnin'—wait and see how I can work for th' mon— for th' mon I love.' "[43] Joan possesses nothing either to offer to the larger culture or to hoard for herself.

In *That Lass O' Lowrie's*, a kindly treated working-class woman will marry a middle-class man and learn to be genteel; in *Louisiana*, by contrast, a kindly treated backwoods American girl will marry a middle-class man, but construct a museum. The differences between these two novels, separated by only three years, are worth dwelling on in some detail because they align so perfectly with the differences between English notions of cultural portability, as incarnate in the provincial novel, and the American counterpart embodied in local color writing. In *That Lass o' Lowrie's*, culture is understood as a distinctly middle-class possession, handed down only to the most compliant members of the working class—and foundering on the barren ground of Joan's sullen, unresponsive peers, who gradually disappear from the novel. In *Louisiana*, though, the notion of what makes culture portable has undergone a distinctively American evolution toward the "local chic" Evans describes. In *Louisiana*, material culture matters as much as it does precisely because there is a poor, primitive, and residual local culture that needs to be preserved; therefore, it can linger on only in the barest sort of abject artifacts.

That Lass o' Lowrie's is the sort of provincial novel that need not rely excessively upon the sorts of auratic objects I have focused on in previous chapters (by contrast, the hoarded lithographs that conclude *Louisiana* are an instance of the kind of overly adhesive objects that Eliot goes out of her way to excoriate in the passage from *The Mill on the Floss* I analyzed in the introduction). In *That Lass O' Lowrie's*, it is quite striking how little specific material objects matter in the overall flow of culture from South to North. The letter that Joan brings with her to her southern savior merely has to mention her name for her genteel interlocutor to know (by prior arrangement) what is to be done with her; possession is less than one-tenth of that object's significance. Louisiana's commitment to her museum of "culture" indicates an awareness that, without these particular, ferociously guarded objects there might be no way to guarantee cultural continuity. At the end of *That Lass O' Lowrie's*, however, a monolithic and genteel national culture can be invisible precisely because it is not vanishing but thriving. Southern English culture requires no material props to travel the length of the country.

The comparison between *That Lass O' Lowrie's* and *Louisiana* highlights the memorable divergence between American and English provincial/regional fiction in the last decades of the nineteenth century. In America, it became commonplace for regionalist novels to imagine that remnants of archaic (Anglo-)American culture might be preserved in remote backwaters, and then brought out to underwrite future accomplishments. However, in England (the Celtic fringe is a different story)[44] the provincial novel's success still depended on locales that straightforwardly stand in as metonyms for an ideal national gestalt. Because the provinces stood for an inexhaustible treasury of old, even archaic, national virtue, provincialism was not weakened but strengthened by the community's resistance to signs of (putatively homogenizing) modernization: to railroads in *Middlemarch*, to the male world of Drumble banks and bank fraud in Gaskell's *Cranford*, to the nosiness of newspapers in Trollope's *The Warden*. English provincialism succeeded as an ideal not by marking out regions as particular, but by creating a uniform space onto which various "two nations"–style binaries could be layered: two classes, two political parties, even the two zones of North and South, with their ever-shifting boundary.[45] Burnett's novel exemplifies the failure of regionalist logic to find a foothold in England.

LORNA DOONE AND REGIONALISM

Given such a national predisposition against regional fiction on the American model, Oliphant's description of *Lorna Doone* as a slightly torqued version of the provincial novel is readily understandable. She believed that Blackmore (like Burnett, or like Oliphant herself) was ultimately committed to replicability and detachability, and to that dream of pure convertibility—into a common culture of English gentility—that shapes the end of *That Lass O' Lowrie's*. *Lorna Doone* relies on the distinctive features of Devon, true. Oliphant, though, reads it as an all-inclusive English story about the inevitable triumph of shared bourgeois values, simply making use of a backdrop that readily lends itself to generalization or abstraction. Given its resemblance to provincialism on such key questions as its universal love plot, its dependence on stock romance characters, and its interest in incongruously Victorian plot devices (for example, an industrial-scale gold mine opened in the very heart of Exmoor), how antiprovincial can *Lorna Doone* really be?

The story is not quite so simple, however. The very features that make reviewers like Oliphant praise Blackmore's sense for "absolute living"— Lorna's perfections or the Victorian entrepreneurism that drives John Ridd—are memorable precisely because in this novel they are laid, incongruously, across the top of a highly particularized rural economy with little place for delicate ladies or capitalist ventures. The gold mine goes bankrupt, John's plans for undercutting a neighboring egg-farm come to nothing, and Lorna remains perpetually out of place, best able to help in the Ridds' busy kitchen simply by lending her spirit and her cheer to its hustle and bustle.[46]

Lorna Doone plays out provincial novel tropes to perfection, in short— but it goes on to insert a distinctive regional setting just below that provincialism. For such incongruity to register, moreover, *Lorna Doone* requires what few Victorian novelists strive for: accuracy to local detail that will ring true enough to ignorant outsiders that they will feel at once included and excluded in the implicit readership. This commitment to local verisimilitude first makes itself felt in speech patterns and the rendering of the natural world. John Ridd's own speech, for example, requires a kind of prickly policing at all times. When Lorna gently imitates John Ridd's speech, he bristles and exaggerates its distinctiveness:

> I did not altogether like the way in which she said it, with a sort of a dialect, as if my speech could be laughed at.
> "Here be some," I answered, speaking as if in spite of her.[47]

Such acts of defiant local identity are buttressed at every turn by the sort of natural details that Oliphant thought purely superfluous, but that are actually central to the novel's aims. An 1875 letter from Thomas Hardy, whose writerly domain was a scant fifty miles from Blackmore's Exmoor, writes to applaud Blackmore not for his platonically unreal Lorna, but for his trees. More than a hint of professional jealousy is evident when he writes, "Little phases of nature which I thought nobody had noticed but myself were continually turning up in your book—for instance, the marking of a heap of sand into little pits by the droppings from trees was a fact I should unhesitatingly have declared was unknown to any other novelist till now."[48] Hardy's letter is useful in attuning the reader to what rarely survives into abridgements or film adaptations: vivid descriptions of natural phenomena. An Exmoor stream is

> napped with moss all around the sides and hung with corded grasses. Along and down the tiny banks, and nodding into one another, even across main channel, hung the brown arcade of ferns; some with gold tongues languishing; some with countless ear-drops jerking; some with great quilled ribs uprising and long saws aflapping; others cupped, and fanning over with the grace of yielding, even as a hollow fountain spread by winds that have lost their way.[49]

The death of John's father is announced when an old retainer makes "a noise in his throat, like a snail crawling on a window-pane," and trees on the verge of bloom are "frayed and flaked with light, casting off the husk of brown in three-cornered patches."[50] Such details are the building blocks for a kind of regional particularity that provokes in the reader admiration and frustration in equal measure. Admiration for the vivid rendering of physical presence, frustration because of the credo—often explicit—that one has to have been born in the region to appreciate its beauties properly. Blackmore really does intend Exmoor as a site apart. The novel accordingly thrives on moments at which an instance of thoroughly local culture is simultaneously offered for readerly pleasure and barred from enjoyment in any other way. John meditates repeatedly on his favorite dish, pickled loaches, for instance, but he carefully makes the point that its pleasures are not for just any reader-come-lately: "There are many people, even now, who have not come to the right knowledge what a loach is, and where he lives, and how to catch and pickle him. And I will not tell them all about it, because if I did, very likely there would be no loaches left, ten or twenty years after the appearance of this book."[51] The reader may read about but never taste Exmoor's red deer; may speculate on loach, but never know where to catch or how to cook them.

There is a curiously double effect to this sort of arm's-length nostalgia, whereby poignant childhood pleasures are detailed but then labeled as available only to residents within the novel, rather than readers of it. On the one hand, this sort of specificity tends toward the supernumerary realism, the proliferation of details relevant by their very irrelevance, that Barthes locates at the heart of the novel's effort at indexicality. On the other hand, however, Blackmore already reveals here what will eventually turn into a full-blown case of nostalgia so passionate that it might even (as with his 1884 tirade against socialism, *The Remarkable History of Sir Thomas Upmore*) turn into a xenophobic rant. Blackmore's aim—to welcome the reader in only far enough to demonstrate that no reader can understand this the way that the author does—is made explicit, for example, in the first pages of a slightly later Blackmore novel, *Alice Lorraine: A Tale of the South Downs* (1875).[52] The opening lines welcome any reader attuned to natural beauty:

> Westward of that old town Steyning, and near Washington and Wiston, the lover of an English landscape may find much to dwell upon. . . .
> Any man here, however sore he may be from the road of life, after sitting awhile and gazing, finds the good will of his younger days revive with a wider capacity.[53]

As a novelist increasingly eager to draw (decreasingly eager) readers, Blackmore astutely begins by addressing a potentially universal audience. Yet within a few sentences, Blackmore restricts enjoyment of the landscape to the (male) patriotic English viewer: "Into his mind, and heart, and soul, without any painful knowledge, or the noisy trouble of thinking, pure content with his native land and its claim on his love are entering."[54] After a few more exclusionary criteria, Blackmore eventually arrives at a far narrower account of who will appreciate the land he is sketching. The ideal reader is redefined as a man setting out to discover his own childhood, a land he knows so well that words are more or less superfluous to the experience:

But to those who there were born (and never thought about it), in the days of age or ailment, or of better fortune even in a brighter climate, how at the sound of an ancient name, or glimpse of faint resemblance, or even on some turn of thought untraced and unaccountable—again the hills and valleys spread, to aged vision truer than they were to youthful eyesight; again the trees are rustling in the wind as they used to rustle; again the sheep climb up the brown turf in their snowy zigzag. A thousand winks of childhood widen into one clear dream of age.[55]

That childhood "winks" become "one clear dream of age" conveys perfectly the text's dilemma. On the one hand, Blackmore is invested in a dreamlike singularity, the irreproducible distinctness of experience for the one old man who, coming home, feels and knows this place all the better because he never thought about it on first experiencing it. On the other hand, the "one clear dream of age" almost seems to be consistent with the earlier passages that promise a path for any reader—any man, Englishman or local yokel—to apprehend this landscape by following the text's instructions. It is in just such oscillations that Blackmore's fiction is habitually suspended.

Blackmore is aided in navigating this gulf between authentic place and ersatz global medium, though, by an essential novelistic irony: with the notable exception of Lorna, Blackmore's characters travel well in readers' memories precisely because they travel so poorly within the story itself. Take the moment at which John Ridd seems poised to escape his lumpen agricultural existence: his trip to London. John notably fails to profit from commercial opportunities laid open by the trip, fails to learn London argot, and even comes to regard himself as contaminated by the experience of migration. His only response to his neighbors' desire for an experience of London by proxy is contempt: he hates having become a traveling curio touched by the capital's majesty. "If I coughed, or moved my book, or bowed, or even said 'Amen,' glances were exchanged which meant—'That he hath learned in London town, and most likely from His Majesty.'"[56] Such glances fall away when John's acquaintances gather that they will learn nothing of London from him. His imperviousness is not only his charm—it is his *métier*, and the novel's. Only by asserting repeatedly that taking the lad out of Devon does not take Devon out of the lad can Blackmore convey his sense of the ultimate impermeability of regions to one another. John may seem chastened when he discovers that his fame (as wrestling champion of Devon) does not extend as far as East Somerset: "[I]t vexed me a little that my great fame had not reached so far as Bridgwater, when I thought that it went to Bristowe."[57] His chastisement, though, lies at the root of his pride, as well. Such narrow demarcation ensures John respect within his knowable community.

It is inevitable, then, that along with Blackmore's West Country brags—the unsurpassed flavor of red deer meat, the exploits of Tom Faggus the legendary highwayman, and so on—the novel features a well-marked and well-advertised zone of withholding. Without secrets, there is no sense of a region: unless there are locked doors, there is no way to know that local knowledge has any kind of substantial peculiarity about it. At a crucial moment in his death struggle with Carver Doone, John reports that "I grasped his arm, and tore the muscle out of it (as the string comes out of an orange)." Before the reader has recovered from that grisly image Blackmore takes the time to insert a footnote, reporting "a far more terrible clutch than this is handed down, to weaker ages, of the great John Ridd."[58] The pattern: a vivid description, followed by the claim that a yet more lurid fact has been withheld—is a common one. When John says that a penciled letter from Lorna will lie in his coffin with him, for instance, he also refers to something else so precious that he will not even name it.[59] (He thus also raises the further possibility that beyond the mentioned-as-unmentioned object there might be a purely unmentionable object, and so forth ad infinitum). And yet—by the logic of the paradox that does so much work in American regionalism and so little in England—that impermeability precisely becomes the salient way that the novel succeeds in conveying the essence of Devon to outsiders: its resistance to transport defines its portability.

LORNA ABOVE ALL

It might now sound as if *Lorna Doone* shifts all the way from provincialism to regionalism, discarding metonymic generality in favor of memorable peculiarity. Portability and the provincial novel, that is, might look supplanted by regional fiction, as seems to have occurred in America from the 1870s onwards. Reading *Lorna Doone* in that way, though, would risk omitting its heroine, which no abridgment or adaptation has ever dared. Lorna, as Oliphant admiringly noted, positively floats over Exmoor. Still, it is worth noting that the incongruity of such clinging-vine femininity in a rough rural setting did startle and displease some contemporary reviewers:

> Charming as she is, if we were inclined to take grave exception to anything in the book, it would be to this very character of Lorna; not because it is not beautiful, but because it is not natural. . . . [She is] one

of those self-perfecting, self-sufficing women who grow up pure, re-
fined, and accomplished in the midst of vice, vulgarity, and neglect.[60]

By that reading, Lorna belongs not in a "real" Devon, but in the land of
"fancy." And in certain ways, Blackmore himself seems to agree. Lorna
almost always appears set against a backdrop that emphasizes the perfect
purity (and portability) of her beauty: "Lorna, in her perfect beauty, stood
before the crimson folds, and her dress was all pure white, and her cheeks
were rosy pink, and her lips were scarlet."[61] There is a curious charac-
terlessness about Lorna. While they do sometimes reveal her lovely form,
for example, her dresses invariably reveal far less about her interior life
than they do about the nature of those around her. One white dress of
Lorna's, for example is successively admired (by John's good sister Anne),
scorned (by the brainy, impish sister Lizzie), and envied (by Lorna's rival
for John's love, Ruth). Readers learn a great deal about all three from
their reactions to Lorna, but they learn nothing about Lorna herself.[62]

In short, Blackmore's commitment—within what may seem a regional
novel on the American model—to the portability of Lorna herself, that
gliding fairy, produces a striking set of operative disjunctions. These disjunctions cause some reviewers to delight in Lorna's eternal womanliness,
and others to recoil from her incongruous, transparent overgenerality.
Both Lorna's body and her mind are required by Blackmore's logic to be
always on view—as the acme of John's fantasy about ideal womanhood—
and yet in such a way that no particular details emerge. The result is that
Lorna hovers over the landscape, providing a kind of gorgeous feminine
counterpoint to its earthy reality, and in turn deriving from that backdrop
an additional piquant charm—that of remaining herself always, no matter
how out of place.[63]

The illustrations to an American edition of the novel (published the
year of Blackmore's death) strikingly exemplify the strategy of superimposition or juxtaposition that the novel depends upon. The edition contains
many straight photographs of the physical beauties of Exmoor and its
peasants (generally photographed from the back). It also contains, in
strong contrast, a few simple engravings of climactic moments. A curious
pattern emerges, however—those schematic engravings almost always
follow a realistic photograph depicting the same locale: for example, the
photograph of "The Wizard's Slough" (fig. 4.1) is followed four pages
later by the sketch of "Then the little boy ran to me, clasped my leg, and
looked up at me" (fig. 4.2).[64]

Moreover, figures are painted on top of several of the photographs,
with no effort to hide the insertion. The effect is to heighten the feeling
of superimposition of "fancy" on top of "fact."[65] Thus "At the head of
the Waterslide" (fig. 4.3) is a blurry image of the hidden back entrance to

THE WIZARD'S SLOUGH

Figure 4.1 "Wizard's Slough"; *Lorna Doone* (New York: Harper's, 1900)

"Glen Doone," overlaid with the image of an indeterminately rural girl.[66] Factual landscape merges with fiction here, a juxtaposition made all the more striking by the fact that this composite photograph, too, has its straight complement: two pages earlier is another waterslide photograph, this one sharply focused but unpeopled (fig. 4.4).

Small wonder that even those who praised Blackmore for his "fancy" often singled out for special notice passages that were in fact sober descriptions of unmistakable Devon landscapes.[67] Like the illustrators of the Harper's edition, readers frequently sensed that Lorna's beauty was an outgrowth of the backdrop against which she sat—since Lorna herself was such a void. Yet in responding to such beauty-via-juxtaposition, readers found themselves thrown back on the resources that the provincial novel had provided: to assert that beauty came from "fancy" insofar as it escaped the knotty idiosyncrasies of local fact.

Lorna's name itself even becomes a site of dispute between regional and provincial approaches to the story. The persistent tension in the novel between Lorna's ethereality and John's (or Exmoor's) stolid solidity is also figured in her manifest indifference to her four names—Lorna Doone, Lorna Dugal, Lady Lorna, and finally Lorna Ridd. This debate might seem settled in favor of regionalism and its particularities when the novel

"THEN THE LITTLE BOY RAN TO ME, CLASPED MY LEG, AND LOOKED UP AT ME."

Figure 4.2 " 'Then the little boy ran to me, clasped my leg, and looked up at me' ";
Lorna Doone (New York: Harper's, 1900)

ends with John proudly announcing that he always knows how to tease
Lorna back into a sense of her dependence upon him: "And if I wish to
pay her out for something very dreadful—as may happen once or twice,
when we become too gladsome—I bring her to forgotten sadness, and to
me for cure of it, by the two words, 'Lorna Doone.' "[68] Naming Lorna's
captors, John thrusts her back into her unwelcome past as a prisoner of
the Doones, when she had a body linked to privation, corporeality, and
a disreputable local past. John feels triumph because he has returned her
to a time when she depended on him: before she had gained whiteness,
gained the name Lady and renounced it, and gained disembodying mater-
nity by becoming the domestic center of his ample bourgeois farm—a
farm that significantly contains territory formerly part of her gothic
prison, Glen Doone.

The neatness of that solution—in which a middle-class male interlocutor gains the power to name his enchanting faery—is bogus, however.
Lorna Doone may seem retrospectively bodied by her captivity, but when
she was a child, she had (as those Harper's illustrators astutely discerned)
already floated ethereally above the landscape. In fact, by recuperating
Lorna's status as "Lorna Doone," John is naming the novel as much as

AT THE HEAD OF THE WATER-SLIDE

Figure 4.3 "At the Head of the Waterslide"; *Lorna Doone* (New York: Harper's, 1900)

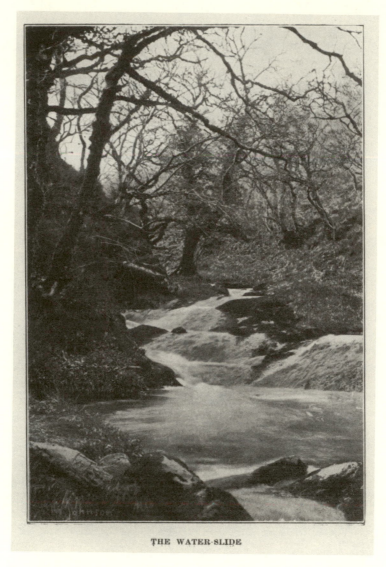

THE WATER-SLIDE

Figure 4.4 "The Waterslide"; *Lorna Doone* (New York: Harper's, 1900)

he is naming her past. The effect of that doubling is to remind readers that they share with John a pure pleasure in her title: she is the Lorna who belongs with the Doones, and the cure for sadness lies both in knowing the glen she sprang from, and in recognizing the portability that can lift her free of it by novel's end.

In short, my claim is that the new sort of locodescriptive romance that Blackmore developed in *Lorna Doone* never foreclosed on Victorian notions of cultural portability in the way that American local color writing did. The logic of cultural portability changed greatly in late-nineteenth-century America, as regionalist fictions opened up a new way to think about mobile mementoes like the "bright-colored lithographs" that Burnett's Louisiana preserves as aides-de-memoire.[69] By allowing the salvageable remnants of regional folkways to be folded into a national "culture" precisely by way of their distinction from mainstream national values and mores, local color writing offered an exceptionally flexible mechanism for incorporating cultural diversity into a national public realm. On the other side of the Atlantic, however, the popularity of *Lorna Doone* (which depended, I am arguing, on the interplay between geographical locality and Lorna's detachability) suggests that such local color flexibility, just such integration of deviant regions into a national mainstream, proved profoundly *un*welcome in the English context. Blackmore's inability to replicate *Lorna Doone*'s success, moreover, is a valuable clue to the important ongoing distinction between two nations whose literary products in many other ways increasingly converged during this period.

BLACKMORE AFTER LORNA DOONE

After the breakout success of *Lorna Doone*, Blackmore never produced anything that even approached its popularity or critical acclaim. *Lorna Doone: A Tale of Exmoor* was gamely followed (one dismal review surpassing another) by *The Maid of Sker* (1872); *Cripps the Carrier: A Woodland Tale* (1876); *Mary Anerley: A Yorkshire Tale* (1880); *Christowell: A Dartmoor Tale* (1881); *Kit and Kelly: A Story of Middlesex* (1890); *Perlycross: A Tale of the Western Hills* (1894); and finally, three years before his death, *Dariel: A Romance of Surrey* (1897). Blackmore's addiction to a model of regional romance tells us something about the effects that a peculiar combination of cultural forces can have on the trajectory of a writer unfortunate enough to match readerly requirements early in his career, and never again succeed in doing so. His decline, though, has a great deal more to tell us about why the exact mixture of local color and romance plots that flourished in America so relentlessly failed in England—though for a brief moment around 1870 it had looked fated to triumph.

With *Lorna Doone*, Blackmore believed that he had established his expertise at the sort of inversion effect that made American regionalism a successful variation on the logic of portability. In American local color writing, the region's inaccessibility to those from outside its folkways is precisely what makes it such an important building block of national unity; in fact, such idiosyncrasy becomes a new basis for cultural portability. It is thanks to local color writing that Royce could observe in 1908 that "the tendency toward national unity and that toward local independence of spirit, must henceforth grow together."[70] Blackmore seems to have believed that he had arrived at a version of American local color that might pan out in England.

Yet he was doomed. His failure may have stemmed in part from his own growing uncertainty about the roots of *Lorna Doone*'s appeal. In a late poem, for example, Blackmore describes trying to sell *Lorna Doone* to a "Gentleman from the West" in three ways: a rural eclogue (too much like America, the Gentleman grumbles); a religiously uplifting sublime (too dull, the Gentleman scoffs); and finally as a flaming sensation novel:

> "Who hath with ease is difficult to please;
>   Yet I can show thee wilder sights than these
>   The flash of falchions in the moonlit glen,
>   The caves of murder and the outlaw's den."

To which the "Gentleman" eagerly responds:

> "Bravo! That looks more like a proper fit!
>   I love to see a fight of real grit."[71]

Blackmore's conviction that regionalism can be saved by an infusion of sensational adventure systematically undermines his quasi-sequels to *Lorna Doone*.

Blackmore, however, was doomed by more than a poor grasp of his audience's tastes. Given the absence of purely regional novels following him, Blackmore was right to worry and to waver: he must have hoped for more and better sequelae than John Meade Falkner's *Moonfleet* (1898).[72] *Lorna Doone* is not an instance of American regionalism set adrift in England, or, for that matter, an early instance of either a coming or a resurgent English regionalism (here I part company with Duncan and the current scholarly wisdom about the fate of the provincial novel circa 1870).[73] Instead, it is a novel that—by dint of a powerful new sort of incongruity effect—combines the durable portability of provincial-novel characters with the memorable distinctiveness of regional-novel settings. That is, *Lorna Doone* seems to offer a way for regionalism to take hold in England; but in fact, its success depended much more on those provincial features that I have described as clustering around the figure of Lorna herself. By this reading, the incongruous placement of Lorna on top of a regional-novel plot allows Blackmore not simply to double his audience (detail-lovers over here, fancy-worshippers over there) but to redouble it:

the incongruity involved in Lorna's ethereal attachment to Exmoor is the real basis of the novel's immense appeal.

Blackmore putatively renounces the logic of the provincial novel by employing the inverted logic of American local color, whereby regional peculiarity leads to, rather than competing with, national cohesion: distance, oddness, and incommensurability hence become key parts of national amalgamation, rather than threats to it. Such regionalism, though, is counterbalanced at every key step by Lorna's own role in the novel. The result is that Blackmore altered, but ultimately preserved and strengthened, the logic of cultural portability that at bottom defines the provincial novel. Far from tolling the death-knell of the provincial novel or of portability's empire, then, Blackmore laid out a way for regionalism's most powerful features to be imported into a later form of the provincial novel.

The puzzle that confronts latter-day scholars, therefore, is not why provincialism came to an end in England with *Lorna Doone*, but rather why it did not. Why, that is, did cultural portability's unmistakable commitment to the grounding homogeneity of English culture have to be preserved between 1870 and 1900, despite a host of good domestic reasons to think that such moveable homogeneity no longer adequately described Englishness? Blackmore's novel and its reception, taken together with the dismal reception of his later novels, suggest how very dependent the late-Victorian realm of letters was upon the notional unity of England and English culture.

There is moreover, a telling irony behind this notional totality of Englishness, an irony we should be prepared for by the evidence presented in chapter 2, above, for Anglo-Indian dependence on the exportability of pure Englishness. The irony is that the need for a totalizable, unfragmentable Englishness is far stronger overseas, in Greater Britain, than it is within England itself. I am arguing, in other words, that Blackmore's uneasy combination of locodescription and ethereal idealism was possible around 1870 because the omnipresent awareness of a Greater British hinterland had made it impossible for local color (along American lines) to flourish in domestic novels. In an age just learning to call itself "imperial," that is, a provincialism that totalized England would always trump the sort of regionalism that threatened to fragment it.

James Buzard has made the case that "culture" (in that noncivilizational, folkways-oriented sense that Elliot identifies in *Louisiana's* museum of paternal flotsam) came to seem, in the mid-Victorian era, just as much an English attribute as one belonging to distant colonized peoples. Buzard argues convincingly that one corollary of the importance of English "culture" is that the "autoethnography" performed in works by Brontë or by Eliot (hence, potentially in any novel) is what gives the novel its vastly augmented authority in the midcentury. It is worth noting, though, that the "protoethnographic principle of structure" that operates in novels such as *Bleak House* works, on Buzard's account, by way of its potential totality; the whole of England must be somehow included in the account for any of its authority claims to resonate and to carry.

Such totality would have been deflected, even interrupted, by the sort of regional-writing tradition that flourished in America.[74] The reasons for regionalism's failure have everything to do with the way that England, autoethnographed or not, comes to stand in a unique geographical and conceptual relationship to the Greater Britain that it both centers and defines. While its metropolis might be the center of acute investigation of the *Bleak House* variety, any attempt to disaggregate its provinces further would result in the potential erosion of the most salient, most valuable piece of portable property of all: England itself, understood as the possession that is metonymically carried or sent abroad attached to every item that is "made as England." The danger of English regionalism is that local color writing on the American model might look like a way to fragment an England that can only do its conceptual work within Greater Britain by continuing to exist as an isomorphic totality. This kind of fragmentation would not have been a problem in America, because regional peculiarity becomes a common currency through which Americans can come to define themselves. But such diversity within England itself seems to have been too threatening to thrive.

On beyond Provincialism: Burnett and Others

The remaining two chapters of this book tell the story of two writers who, between 1870 and 1900, find separate avenues of disengagement from a narrow logic of provincialist portability: Thomas Hardy, by discovering a way to fragment the totality of England into a potentially infinite series of locales; and William Morris, by finding a way to repudiate the notion of geographic specification altogether. It is worth pointing out, however, that the impasse I have been describing, which stalled regional fiction in England for more than a generation, was only decisively broken in mainstream and popular fiction after 1900. It is equally notable that the popular-fiction breakthrough was accomplished by a pair of foreign-trained "English" novelists: Rudyard Kipling and Frances Hodgson Burnett.[75] Even then, though, the sort of regionalism that arose remained profoundly colored by the assumptions of cultural portability that I have been arguing deter Blackmore from attempting a purely local color form of regionalism. In Kipling's *Puck of Pook's Hill* (1906), for example, nothing other than the local folkways of Southeast England (incarnated in the genius loci, Puck) can safeguard a shared English patrimony. The workings of the plot to bring about the indispensability of the local to the national are quite ingenious: at a crucial moment, Pook's Hill turns out to be right next to Runnymede, home of the Magna Carta. Puck thus becomes a crucial figure in the creation of English national pride because of the role he plays in the Magna Carta's signing—yet without ever relinquishing his role as the platonic local informant.

Kipling's ingenuity in creating what might be called "provincial particularity" is followed in its turn by the immense success of Frances Hodgson Burnett's *The Secret Garden* (1911).[76] Burnett as English regionalist might seem an unlikely development. After all, with both the English provincialism of *That Lass O' Lowrie's* and the American regionalism of *Louisiana* behind her, Burnett, in her 1893 autobiography, *One I Knew Best of All*, laid out an ambitious new writerly agenda, one that seemingly disavowed locale altogether. As the autobiography told it, "Story" was to be Burnett's pole-star, and the explicitly Wordsworthian capacity to reconstruct, in perfect detail, her own childhood memories was to teach her how every child thought: the "one I knew best of all" referred to in the title turns out to be her own child-self, universally generalizable into childhood's true psyche.[77]

Even in *One I Knew Best of All*, though, geographic and class constraints quickly emerge: "Story" turns out to be the peculiar property of those who read their parents' books growing up. Moreover, its true possession is restricted to those children who learn by contact with social inferiors—but there is no suggestion that such transfers might be two-way. Burnett, for example, prides herself on having acquired Manchester street slang, but native speakers of such argots (along with those dull middle-class children who fail to read adventure books) are explicitly excluded from resemblance to the "one I knew," and thus from access to the Platonic essence of childhood.

"Story" as Burnett defines it captures the instrumental uses of a properly controlled regionalism perfectly, because any given (middle- or upper-class) child's access to "Story" depends upon learning to make use of some sort of regional knowledge as the first step on a path toward cosmopolitan knowledge—a path open only to privileged visitors, never for their native informants. Burnett's commitment both to a generalizable "Story" and to the allure of geographic specificity eventually leads her to Emily Brontë's *Wuthering Heights*, which becomes the departure-point for *The Secret Garden*, a novel about two upper-class children in need of nature and moral nurture that Yorkshire alone can provide.[78] Building on an enduring English legacy of national cultural portability (profoundly divergent, I am claiming, from an American novelistic mainstream transformed by four decades of local color writing) Burnett successfully reframed *Lorna Doone*'s simultaneous commitment to local singularity and detached universality. Like Royce, Burnett avowed that the great colonizing nation begins with intact provinces. Burnett, however, devised a new means by which to preserve both regionalism's foibles and provincialism's generalities: by finding a way to produce two floating upper-class characters who can learn what they need of local ways, and then continue their passage outward into Greater Britain.

The Secret Garden, though, is written not under Gladstone, but on the eve of World War I, when the relationship of "Little England" to its peripheries was imagined in entirely new ways. Unlike Blackmore, Burnett did not suppose that having a peculiar attachment to one special locale disabled the industrious acolyte from learning its ways and putting them to use elsewhere. Instead, Yorkshire argot becomes the medium through which Burnett imagines Mary and Colin (especially Colin, as a male suited for professional advancement) preparing themselves to find their vocations in the vast imperial hinterland, from which Mary came and to which Colin is headed. To speak "quite broad Yorkshire" becomes Mary and Colin's highest aspiration, because it seems the only way they can learn about the landscape they are in. When Mary says of a summer afternoon, "I'll warrant it's th' graideliest [that is, finest] one as ever was in this world," she demonstrates the sort of grammatical competence that wins the approval of her native informant: "Dickon grinned, because when the little wench tried to twist her tongue into speaking Yorkshire it amused him very much."[79]

Much as Lorna's immortality depends on her dislocation from Exmoor, *The Secret Garden*'s canonization as adolescent bildungsroman seems predicated on mastering Yorkshire and Yorkshireness—but only from the perspective of the sort of outsider who can come in, learn the flora and the lingo, and apply those lessons across the world. Burnett's Colin, cured of his invalidism by Yorkshire, is only too eager to follow Mary's lead in assimilating, and hence improving upon, the native's speech, be that speech Yorkshire, Indian, or African (just as Burnett describes herself as a child "mastering" Manchester urban argot so that she could speak it as a foreign tongue, while street urchins who taught her remained disappointingly monoglot). Even the supplanting of the autochthonous Emily Brontë by the cheerfully deracinated Burnett can be seen as another instance of the same movement: the newcomer flatters sincerely by imitating, but the imitation has (in Burnett's eyes, at least) vast advantages over the land-bound original. In a sense, Burnett saw herself as having produced a properly portable version of *Wuthering Heights*.

Perhaps *Lorna Doone* survived, then, because it was the English instantiation of an American predilection for rendering a place with such loving detail that its far-distant re-creation came to seem not only possible but necessary. It was in Boston in 1912, after all, that the heroine turned into a cookie, and in New Haven that she was voted immortal. *Lorna Doone* looks, retrospectively, like a logical moment for a British tradition of local color to assume much the same importance that it was to assume in America over the next three decades. That this experiment succeeded so wildly in Blackmore's first novel, though, and then suffered such crippling oblivion offers a rare opportunity to parse the negative spaces of literary history.

Blackmore's own poignant opening to *Alice Lorraine*—in which he imagines that landscapes come into their meaning precisely at the moment that one returns, knowingly, to what one had imbued involuntarily and deeply as a child—marks exactly the road that the English novel did not travel. The allure of portability is predicated on making culture accessible for consumption, not only for the person lucky enough to have been there at both its inception and its unrolling, but also for those whose formal membership in the group (Englishmen, presumptively) entitles them to "recover" the culture in all its particularity, as if it had been theirs to begin with.

I began this chapter by arguing that Victorian notions of portability mandate against the emergence of any form of English local color writing, and ended by saying that it took Kipling and Burnett to demonstrate what American-style regionalism could do within England proper. That does not mean, however, that no late-century alternatives to the provincial novel and to cultural portability existed. Long before century's end, Thomas Hardy takes up Blackmore's notion of a heterogeneous England, divided rather than united by its folkways and geography. Hardy's radically localized conception of novelistic characters and actions could, it transpired, be successfully realized only if he found a way to dismantle systematically the entire architecture of Victorian portability. That act of disassembly lies behind much of what is distinctive about Thomas Hardy's fiction and poetry alike. His antipathy to the notion of portability explains some of the opprobrium he faced in his day—and his staying power since.

CHAPTER FIVE

Going Local: Characters and Environments in Thomas Hardy's Wessex

THOMAS HARDY'S CHARACTERS have rarely been called "portable"; they have, though, often been dubbed puppets. Whether ruled by the whim of "the President of the Immortals" or by the ironclad "fact of individual unfreedom," Hardy's characters can appear so determined by overarching forces that they finally become indistinguishable from their surroundings.[1] His finely developed eye for the agricultural seasons and climatic exigencies of Wessex has long struck readers as proof of his indifference to the nuances of individuated human experience. Henry James, for one, detects little in Hardy beyond "a certain aroma of the meadows and lanes—a natural relish for harvestings and sheep-washings."[2]

From the first appearance of *Desperate Remedies* in 1871 down to the present day, in fact, few readers have expressed any interest in whether Hardy follows the provincial novel's lead on the question of cultural portability. To most of his readers, Hardy has appeared either so enmeshed in the determinism that Darwin's theory made possible or so besotted with the facticity of the natural world that his characters become little more than cogs in the vast Wessex machine. Such readers might, for instance, point to the somber, geographical, and impersonal sentence that begins *The Return of the Native* (1878)—"A Saturday afternoon in November was approaching the time of twilight, and the vast tract of unenclosed wild known as Egdon Heath embrowned itself moment by moment"—and go on to point out that the novel's first chapter ends, 1,500 words later, without a single human being appearing.[3]

It is little wonder this account of environment trumping character appealed to critics who deplored Hardy's philosophical materialism, or accused him of seeing no meaningful distinction between human existence and the rest of the universe: "Humanity, as envisaged by Mr Hardy, is largely compounded of hoggishness and hysteria."[4] This reading also proved congenial, though, to those early critics who praised Hardy's knowledge of Wessex's "nature and man" for the accuracy of its renditions of a bygone community's mores. In the condescending plaudits of such critics, Hardy's Wessex yokels are of interest simply as one aspect of the region's natural bounty—perhaps resembling similarly picturesque natives of far-flung colonial holdings in the Andamans or the Canadian West.[5]

One problem with this interpretation of Hardy, though, is that in the Wessex edition of 1912 Hardy labeled his principal works "Novels of Character *and* Environment." The balance implied in that phrase is crucial. Environment is complementary to (rather than determinative of) character in Hardy, a fact that underlies Hardy's abiding interest in how differently individuals make sense of the world they share. Only in uncovering the significance of Hardy's experiments in the heterogeneity of individual acts of attention can scholars make sense of his deep-seated antipathy to the legacy of cultural portability inherited from the Victorian novel, as well as make sense of the ways he found to replace that portability with a novelistic economy based as much upon diversity in various characters' forms of attention as upon the brute environmental facts.

This chapter makes the case that a feature of Hardy's poetry long noted by critics—his interest in the particularity of what any individual notices about the world—is vital in understanding his prose.[6] Hardy notices noticing, in all its diverse forms. I am claiming—against those who foreground Hardy's obsession with environment—that his obsession with how different individuals orient themselves in the world is crucial. Hardy's anatomy of noticing explains why character and environment are mutually exclusive and equally indispensable features of his novels. It also helps explain why his novels make mockery of the art of cultural portability that works so successfully in Victorian provincial novels—and in the various other sorts of realist novel that I have described in earlier chapters. Because Hardy conceives of perception as an entirely particularized capacity, and because he believes that the knack of noticing things in a certain way is the only meaningful cargo individuals can carry with them anywhere (so that they literally carry their locales with them, wherever they go), he is the first widely read and respected Victorian novelist to dismantle the flexible assumptions that undergird the novelistic investment in cultural portability.

The passionate attention to noticing that I am describing is present, in poetry and prose alike, throughout Hardy's long career. In his *Life* (published only posthumously), for example, Hardy describes meeting the aged Mrs Procter, who strikes him as a contemporary only when she is recalling her past: "Into her eyes and face would come continually an expression from a time fifty or sixty years before. . . . You would talk to her . . . and believe you were talking to a person of the same date as yourself, with recent emotions and impulses." When she rejoins the present, though, she suddenly seems eons away: "You would see her sideways when crossing the room to show you something, and realize her, with sudden sadness, to be a withered woman whose interests and emotions must be nearly extinct."[7] It is the act of attention Hardy attends to here, not the object attended to (which is after all invisible to everyone but the recollector). In fact, it is only when Mrs Procter is dwelling in the past that Hardy feels that he shares a present with her: bring her forward to a shared space-time, and she feels unutterably distant.

Ultimately, Hardy's interest in individuals' diverse ways of attending to the world seems to leave him deeply skeptical about the sorts of cultural portability that his novelistic predecessors had embraced in one form or another. Hardy characters *do* travel heavily laden, but it is not detachable culture—songs, letters, mementoes, or ethnic markers—that weighs them down (in the way that portable properties weigh heavily in the work of Trollope, Collins, Eden, Eliot, and Blackmore analyzed in previous chapters). Rather, characters' inescapable, untransferrable, and unavoidably diverse ways of perceiving the world travel with them. A nosey parson can correlate revealing physiognomy and dusty genealogies anywhere he goes ("'throw up your chin a moment, so that I may catch the profile of your face better. . . . That's the D'Urberville nose and chin—a little debased'").[8] When he passes along his findings, however, he does not also pass along the capacity to replicate, or even to grasp, them in the same way he does. The best model in Hardy for the futility of supposing that one's own way of seeing the world is transferrable might be the religious sign-painter in *Tess of the D'Urbervilles* (1891), whose rock-painted slogans ("THY, DAMNATION, SLUMBERETH, NOT. . . . THOU, SHALT, NOT, COMMIT—") are justified by his pious remark that he leaves the "application" to his readers.[9] The mixture of indifference and (in Tess's case) guilty turmoil that he leaves behind him is not caused by his readers having understood the "application" of his signs, but by their having noticed and "applied" it in ways undreamt of by the painter.

Hardy's refusal to portray religious instruction as traveling any better than the stones it is painted on marks his repudiation of the foundational metonymies that undergird the logic of cultural portability instantiated in the Victorian provincial novel, and the realist novel more generally, before him. In its place, Hardy has little to offer for moral comfort beyond Clym Yeobright's blindly microscopic preaching. He does, though, have in mind a way of understanding perceptual heterogeneity that has some decided advantages over the provincial novel when it comes to representing a world defined by the perennial localization of all individual sensations.

NEITHER PROVINCIAL NOR REGIONAL

From *Desperate Remedies* (1871) to *Jude the Obscure* (1895), and from *Wessex Poems and Other Verses* (1898) to *Winter Words* (1928), Hardy fought a pitched battle against the Victorian provincialism outlined in the last chapter, against imagining that all of rural England could be met-onymically instantiated in place-specific writing.[10] Yet Hardy's rejection of the provincial novel's assumptions about cultural portability does not make him, any more than R. D. Blackmore, into an American-style "local color" writer. Hardy, that is, does not understand his novels as sites where national unity arises (ironically) from regional heterogeneity.

There is, moreover, a crucial difference between Hardy's novels and those of Blackmore. Blackmore rejects "local color" because he remains attached to purely idealized characters (exemplified by Lorna Doone) whose gliding detachment from rocky local landscapes is what keeps Blackmore's novels attached to the guiding logic of cultural portability. Loveable as Tess, pathetic as Jude, or moving as Michael Henchard might be, Hardy's conception of character militated against any ready identifi-cation of his protagonists or their fates with general humanity. Hardy's novels in fact depend upon the impossibility of any truly admirable char-acter's being available as a piece of readily portable culture, a site of in-stant sympathy for distant readers. The very difficulty of sympathy with a character like Henchard is exactly Hardy's aim, and that difficulty is one of the clues that makes clear Hardy's stubborn refusal of the various sanctioned shortcuts in novel-composition that the guiding logic of cul-tural portability had made possible.

In its place, Hardy proposes a difficult epistemology (and ethics) built out of the perception of unbridgeable gaps in perception. Hardy fre-quently goes out of his way, in fact, to air his distrust of any traveling or diasporic community that relies on portable properties of any sort to sanction its self-conception. In place of the traveling cultural communities that George Eliot's late work cautiously proposed as a model for diasporic Englishness, Hardy offers sly satires on the notion that any sort of geo-graphical affiliation could be preserved on the move. Asked to address some encouragement to the Society of Dorset Men in London, for in-stance, Hardy tells them there is only one certifiable resident of Dorset to be found in London: "St. Paul's is built of Portland stone [and] is almost as much Dorset as [a Dorset man]. . . . [I]t stood, or rather lay, in Dorset probably two hundred thousand years before it got here."[11] The identity claims of blocks of Portland stone make more sense to Hardy than do the claims of those who think that a regional identity is something to keep proudly alive in the promiscuous metropolis.[12]

Hardy's searing description of Donald Farfrae's predilection for singing about Scotland makes evident how little he trusts a conception of "travel-ing culture" that would find in patriotic music the basis for a durably mobile nationality. Just arrived in Casterbridge, Farfrae brings both self and audience near tears with:

It's hame, and it's hame, hame fain would I be,
Oh hame, hame, hame to my ain countree![13]

Farfrae performs as if he had a portable Scotland in his breast: one home-body responds, "If I loved my country half as well as the young feller do, I'd live by claning my neighbour's pigsties afore I'd go away!"[14] But that response presumes a nonexistent relationship between Farfrae's performance and his feelings. Farfrae has no intention of returning "hame," and to take actual descriptions of the Scotland he left behind would be as foolish as supposing that Dorset men kept their original natures in transit in the same blockish way Portland stone does.

Both contemporaries and later critics have stressed that Hardy is committed to representing a Wessex complete with its own distinctive dialects, customs, and populace.[15] Hardy collaborated with the Dorset photographer Hermann Lea to produce *A Handbook to the Wessex Country of Thomas Hardy's Novels and Poems* (1905) and *Thomas Hardy's Wessex* (1912); Hardy reportedly even looked into getting the word "Wessex" copyrighted.[16] Reviewers of his day accordingly pegged him (all Hardy's disclaimers notwithstanding) as a rural writer pure and simple, whose vocation is to draw "a series of rural pictures full of life and genuine colouring," to depict an "immobile rural existence," and to "describe[] the burning rick-yard, or the approaching thunderstorm, or give[] us the wonderful comicalities of the supper at the malthouse."[17] The result of that attention to natural and folkloric details, though, was to leave the misleading impression that Hardy, despite his explicit and repeated repudiations of the idea, envisioned Wessex as a charming countryside packed with predictably feckless "Hodges."[18] If Blackmore failed to delineate a distinctively English way of demarcating regions for special attention, Hardy can be said to fail in the opposite quest: to make his readers understand that his attachment to a given region is purely heuristic, intended to simplify the limits of the perceptual universe that he describes.[19] The irony, then, is that Blackmore was a failed regionalist delineating a regionalism that never came into being, while Hardy, in disavowing a merely regional basis for his fiction, is rewarded with a laureateship of British regionalism as unwarranted as it is unwanted.

If Hardy is no regionalist, what does he propose as a replacement for provincialism? Partially because of the rush toward regionalism in anatomizing Hardy, and partially because of later critical interest in Hardy's relationship to Darwinism, social determinism, and Naturalism,[20] not enough attention has been paid to his interest in foregrounding the limits of perception, and to the ways in which such limits sharply undermine any purely regionalist element to his writing. As Hardy put it in 1902: "Unadjusted impressions have their value, and the road to a true philosophy of life seems to lie in humbly recording diverse readings of its phenomena as they are forced on us by chance and change."[21] From the beginning of his career Hardy's writing explores the perceptual and cognitive dissonance that shifting perspectives generate. My claim is that understanding Hardy's commitment to the radical divergence of individual perceptions clarifies his hostility toward locodescriptive regionalism. At the same time, it explains his unrelenting assault on the notions of cultural portability (and concomitant assumptions about sentimental value) that had sustained the English novel for more than a half-century.

In what follows, I argue that three features of Hardy's writing make his perspectivalism (and antipathy toward cultural portability) especially clear. First and most broadly, his recurrent interest in anatomizing the same scene viewed from multiple perspectives, which is linked to his interest in what it means for characters, as well as for readers, to notice others noticing things that they themselves had already failed to notice. Second, I argue that Hardy's noteworthy syntactic awkwardness often stems from his efforts to register the discrepancy between what it means for something to occur and what it means for some character to register its occurrence. Rather than stylistic flaws, that is, some of his typical inversions and passive constructions result from his efforts to micromanage the reader's understanding of the relationship between an occurrence and how that occurrence will strike a given observer. Third, I am interested in his poetry's commitment—underscored as well by his own illustrations for that poetry—to the idea of a landscape that is memorialized, but memorialized only for one observer. These three innovative features of Hardy's writing evidence his willingness—which went well beyond Blackmore's half-eschewal—to jettison the notions of cultural portability that undergird the provincial novel's version of national community.

A bit of intellectual history proves useful in framing an approach to the three distinctive aspects of Hardy's writings I want to emphasize. All three innovations in his writing are clearly linked to late nineteenth-century changes in notions of perception's relationship to the material world. That different people cannot fail to notice different things in the same situation is a venerable dictum: in the thirteenth century Rumi is already referring to the story of the five blind men and the elephant (each grabs a different body part, and comes to a different conclusion about an elephant's nature) as "ancient Hindu wisdom." Jonathan Crary argues, however, that only beginning in the late nineteenth century do "individuals define and shape themselves in terms of a capacity for 'paying attention,' that is, a disengagement from a broader field of attraction, whether visual or auditory, for the sake of isolating or focusing on a reduced number of stimuli."[22] Perception is understood as a both physically and psychologically fraught process, characterized by inevitable lacunae, absences and oversights that complement the sustained attention that permits one to notice anything at all.

> Normative explanations of attentiveness arose directly out of the understanding that a full grasp of self-identical reality was not possible and that human perception, conditioned by physical and psychological temporalities and processes, provided at most a provisional, shifting approximation of its objects. . .
>
> An immense social remaking of the observer in the nineteenth century proceeds on the general assumption that perception cannot be thought of in terms of immediacy, presence, punctuality.[23]

By the turn of the century, psychology and related sciences were dominated by the problem of the relationship between individual acts of perception and the nature of the world outside.[24] No wonder Gertrude Stein groused, "They used to universalise consciousness now universalise attention."[25]

Such ruminations might have been codified in Berlin or Cambridge laboratories, but their origins lie elsewhere.[26] While "Hardy's engagement with . . . monism, dualism, positivism, materialism and idealism is less than systematic,"[27] he is nonetheless one of the first British writers to explore this "problem of attention" systematically, and his conclusions underlie his understanding of fiction's capacity to represent both the world and other minds.

First Feature: Diversity in Perception

Hardy's Wessex is populated by various characters—cobblers, doctors, farmers, nobility, weak-sighted jewelers, and astronomers—each of whom notices different things about the world that surrounds all of them alike. Just as every writer "is what is called unequal; he has a specialty . . . [on which] he fixes his regard more particularly,"[28] so, too, does every Hardy character specialize, in ways that will always remain mysterious to others on some level. Taken to an extreme, Hardy's account of how we move singly through a shared world can even look like radically monadic skepticism. By the 1910s, Hardy seems to have arrived at the gloomy conjecture that individuated perception rules out any shared conception of the phenomenal world: the mere fact of noticing that someone else has noticed something is as close as we come to solidarity. In "Afterwards" for example, Hardy raises the possibility that certain kinds of perception may actually die when their possessor does:

If, when hearing that I have been stilled at last, they stand at the door,
   Watching the full-starred heavens that winter sees,
Will this thought rise on those who will meet my face no more,
   "He was one who had an eye for such mysteries?"

And will any say when my bell of quittance is heard in the gloom,
   And a crossing breeze cuts a pause in its outrollings,
Till they rise again, as they were a new bell's boom,
   "He hears it not now, but used to notice such things?"[29]

The speaker hears the bell's outrollings and their cessation when the wind shifts—others might not. If they do notice that acoustic intermittence, they will associate it with the speaker—after all, when he was alive, his interlocutors would have noticed his noticing such interruptions. With him gone, however, there seems no guarantee that the interrupted bell will even register. The problem of noticing the world and the problem of noticing others noticing the world are intimately linked, but they are not identical.[30] At the core of Hardy's novels lies his conviction that observing others experiencing a certain sensation is not the same as experiencing it oneself.

The effect of that differential observation, I am arguing, is that Hardy's Wessex looks less like a pre-extant region than it does a space within which various diverse forms of noticing can go on. One important result of that conception of Wessex is that the sort of portability that undergirded both Trollope's Eustace diamonds (which travel through England sustained by passion and cash value alike) and that valuable letter in *Cranford* (which could go anywhere in the world, guarded by the fraternal love that would sanctify it when it was read) no longer apply in Hardy's universe. In this cosmos, only people carry interpretive mechanisms with them, and any given piece of property can mean only what the observer who chances upon it wants it to mean.

Hardy's reputation as the spokesman of a real geographic entity called Wessex, though, seems to persist in obscuring his general skepticism about how divergent forms of individual perception can be integrated within a single work.[31] The result is that pieces by John Barrell and Raymond Williams that arguably remain the most influential accounts of Hardy's fiction misdescribe his work in crucial ways, and thus end up underestimating the significance of Hardy's attack upon Victorian ideas of cultural portability. Barrell's "Geographies of Hardy's Wessex" notes gaps between different sorts of perception exercised by different persons, but explains those gaps by describing a single gap, that between outsider/readerly knowledge and native experience. He argues that characters who are embedded within the world of Wessex cannot possibly grasp what's known by outsiders, but they can experience that world as no outsider could:

> The reader can certainly grasp from Tess that there is . . . local knowledge, in Hardy's Wessex if not in nineteenth-century Dorset; but he can grasp only the notion of its existence, not the knowledge itself. . . . The striking incongruity between Tess's view of the Vale of Blackmoor and the traveller's . . . emphasise[s] the impossibility of the traveller's crossing the space that separates him from Tess, and preserve[s], on either side of that space, the twin myths of an original, unified sense of space, and of an alienated geography.[32]

Readers are blessed with potentially universal forms of knowledge, "alienated geography." They are, however, excluded from the local apprehension of the landscape, which can only indirectly be described in the novel itself because it belongs to a milieu they no longer occupy.

Barrell's account presumes that Hardy is pointing out a gulf between readerly comprehension and the mythic knowledge of the heath-dwellers: that familiar binary between authentic but inarticulate natives and fluent but superficial travelers. The problem with Barrell's account, however, is that once you start spotting gulfs between different sorts of perceivers in Hardy, you cannot stop.[33] Barbers misunderstand apple-growers, preachers go astray thinking they understand farmers, a speculator in "small profits frequently repeated" cannot hope to have mutually comprehensible conversations with a man who once sold his wife.[34] The reason one of these gaps (between alienated travelers and unified rural denizens) strikes Barrell as qualitatively distinct from the others is only that Barrell is strongly committed to discovering a dichotomy between native and outsider, a dichotomy that Hardy himself is very far from intending.

Raymond Williams, by contrast, is no fan of such bifurcating chasms. In his influential account of Hardy in *The Country and the City*, Williams instead emphasizes Hardy's dislike of the mythology of a seamlessly archaic Wessex, and pointedly denies that a historical or perceptual chasm yawns between Tess's primitive Wessex and the London connoisseur. Williams reads Hardy as fascinated by his ambiguous relations with the Dorset he had largely but not entirely left behind. Openly linking his own intellectual trajectory to Hardy's, Williams characterizes Hardy's oeuvre as defined by his "attempt to describe and value a way of life with which he was closely yet uncertainly connected."[35] William's insight about Hardy's omnipresent uncertainty (that is, Hardy wonders whether the writer is part of the land he describes or detached from it, and applies, by extension, the same question to reader) helps explain the delicate oscillation, continually enacted in Hardy's prose as much as in his plotting, between such apparent binaries as learned and common or urban and rural.

There is a problem, however. Williams's investment in linking Hardy's struggle to the fate of common working people of rural England leads him to argue that "shared work, in the 'run of years' " is central to Hardy.[36] His account of Hardy's attachment to "the continuity not only of a country but of a history and a people" usefully undoes the false binary between the autochthonous and the educated that Barrell established, and restores the importance of the middle orders and in-between sorts whose stories Hardy laboriously chronicled.[37] Williams's stress on continuity, though, can discourage the critic from looking at the discontinuities and evident perceptual gaps that do yawn between Hardy's characters. The despair in "Afterwards," which is already present in Hardy's fiction, albeit in somewhat different form, stems from Hardy's conviction that even minimal reassurance—others will remember how you used to perceive the world—is lacking. Absent the sort of solidarity that stems from the conviction others united to you by labor will perceive the world just as you do, it is not so clear what kind of commonality is on hand to constitute a community.

Ultimately, neither Barrell nor Williams has a satisfactory explanation for Hardy's commitment to diversity in point of view. Hardy was committed to such multiperspectivalism by his notion that individual human perception could no longer "be thought of in terms of immediacy, presence, punctuality" (to borrow Crary's description of the late-century interest in anatomizing attention).[38] There is a sunny side to this kind of argument for the impossibility of believing in any single perspective on the world. Hardy avows, for example, in a rare moment of optimism, that recognizing the ongoing diversity of experience might serve any individual as a hedge against prejudice and dogmatism. In an 1883 article, Hardy conjectures that a "visitor . . . obliged to go home with" a typical farm laborer of Dorset would find that "variety had taken the place of monotony" and "that Hodge, the dull unvarying, joyless one, has ceased to exist for him. He has become disintegrated into a number of dissimilar fellow-creatures, men of many minds, infinite in difference. . . . They cannot be rolled together again into such a Hodge as he dreamt of, by any possible enchantment."[39] Those who have been exposed to distant climes, then, if they recognize the lesson being presented to them, will henceforth learn to see that part of the world as manifold, not uniform.

What makes for an upbeat lesson about rural diversity, however, can also present fertile ground for unavoidable misconceptions and mutual misunderstanding. From his earliest writing, Hardy strives to elucidate how perspectival difference radically transforms any given view, with the result that misunderstanding can spring up absolutely anywhere. For instance, a minor military parade in *The Trumpet-Major* (1880) is watched by the ingénue Anne Garland and Mr Loveday the miller; the paraders include Anne's two suitors, one of whom is the miller's son John. Also present are blasé Budmouth spectators and, arriving late, John's sailor brother Bob:

In those military manoeuvres the miller followed the fortunes of one man; Anne Garland of two. The spectators who, unlike our party, had no personal interest in the soldiery, saw only troops and battalions in the concrete, straight lines of red, straight lines of blue, white lines formed of innumerable knee-breeches, black lines formed of many gaiters, coming and going in kaleidoscopic change. Who thought of every point in the line as an isolated man, each dwelling all to himself in the hermitage of his own mind? One person did, a young man far removed from the barrow where the Garlands and Miller Loveday stood.[40]

Each of these perspectives is shaped not just by geography but also by social place—age, vocation, attachments, gender, and so on. For instance, the last thing that any local would see in the soldiers is mental hermitages. Still, Bob's perception of "every point in the line as an isolated man" is not wrong: a loner himself, used to the easy come-and-go of a sailor's life (like the peripatetic Newson in *The Mayor of Casterbridge*), Bob is uniquely suited to perceive psychic isolation beneath the visible unity of the parade. Meanwhile, the Budmouth crowd, good on spectacle and weak on long-term psychological commitment to their neighbors, are well poised to see the kaleidoscopic change—red, blue, white, and black—that characterizes their usual relationship with the soldiers who rotate in and out of Budmouth for duty.

Readers notice what the three observers notice, but something more as well—the reader's observation is not just of the crowds, but also of the observers themselves. The novel is always a step ahead of any individual character's acts of observation because the narrator is always a redacting force. Even when only one viewpoint is presented, the novelist behind knows that other observations are possible. Yet it might also be said that the novel is a step behind, as well, anchored as it is to acts of perception known to be partial and circumscribed. Attending to the novel in order to see the world is a bit like looking at a football crowd as the ball moves toward the net; you know if the ball goes in, but what you experience is not exactly the goal itself.

It is not that Hardy's novels deny perception can be transmissible at all. They are shot through with memorable passages in which a character's description of a noticed detail is so vivid that the reader seems to overshoot the mind and enter the instant itself—as when Retty Priddle sees Izz Huett "put her mouth against the wall and kiss[] the shade of [Angel's] mouth" on the wall behind the whey-tub.[41] Characters can also serve as one another's signposts, passing perception between them in an almost (though never perfectly) flawless way—in *Desperate Remedies*, for instance, Cytherea's fainting alerts other churchgoers that her father has just fallen past the open window.[42]

Even in such moments, Hardy perennially doubts and undercuts the way that the "application" of any observation can pass from one person to another. This is most obvious with outlanders: melancholy, silent Hussars; French exiles; and rusticated London ladies, each possessing an impossible-to-assimilate way of looking at the world. The exemplary transplant might be the polar birds who appear to Tess in Flintcomb-Ash:

> Gaunt spectral creatures with tragical eyes—eyes which had witnessed scenes of cataclysmal horror in inaccessible polar regions of a magnitude such as no human being had ever conceived, in curdling temperatures that no man could endure. . . . Of all they had seen which humanity would never see, they brought no account. The traveller's ambition to tell was not theirs.[43]

Or the engineer in *Tess of the D'Urbervilles*, following his machine around the country, obedient only to his machine's needs, and blind to the world beyond the moving strap that connects his "portable repository of force" to the local threshers: "He was in the agricultural world, but not of it. . . . He spoke in a strange northern accent; his thoughts being turned inwards upon himself, his eye on his iron charge, hardly perceiving the scenes around him, and caring for them not at all."[44] This engineer is an extreme example of Crary's "concentrated attentiveness," seeing only as far as the limit of his own trade.

There is a germane comparison here to the novelistic tradition Hardy had inherited: the role played by such incomprehensible foreigners in Hardy's novels is quite distinct from the role generally assigned to the "stranger" in the Victorian provincial novel. In such novels the stranger is a figure whose very alienness serves as reassuring proof of how well familiar domestic rules apply (for example, the eventually assimilated Herr Klesmer in *Daniel Deronda*). Whether cast out (like Emilius the cozening Jew in *The Eustace Diamonds*) or folded back into domestic circles (like Signor Brunoni in *Cranford*, who is revealed to be good old Mr Brown, after all), the legible alterity (as Simmel described it so acutely a generation later)[45] of the "stranger" provides a ready way to locate his/her significance. In Hardy, by contrast, an engineer's or a circumpolar bird's alienness remains so complete that the very fact of coexistence in the same physical world can look like an essentially nugatory accident.

If this kind of disconnection were simply a foreigner's deformation in Hardy, little might follow from it, beyond a sense that Hardy exemplified some sort of regionalist xenophobia. Nothing could be further from the case, however. The miscomprehension figured in that detached engineer is potentially universal. There is communal solidarity in Hardy, built up in slow degrees by shared custom or by endless reiterative talk. But such solidarity always has to reckon with disjunctions in perception between even the closest of friends. Hardy depicts a world fragmented not simply between earthy laborers and distant observers of "landscape" (Barrell's account) but between all the various viewers capable of noticing different things. A cobbler knows an old customer's daughter by the inherited look of her foot, a barber recognizes at once an affinity between an aristocratic and common head of hair, an astronomer sees a "meridional line" appear on his wife's cheek when she's injured. By the same token, people who travel over wide distances reveal the fundamental uniformity of their perceptions: wherever they go, their journeys are in some sense local, since they bring their rules for perceiving with them.[46]

In *Two on a Tower*, such adhesive locality is represented at its most dilated and its most contracted. The entire night sky of the Northern Hemisphere defines the true locale of the astronomer Swithin St. Cleeve, while a few small fields form the whole world of his antithesis, the barley-encrusted Amos. Yet there is no qualitative difference between their respective relationships to their locales, since each is acutely attuned to what happens within his demarcated domain—and indifferent or oblivious (like the threshing engineer and his "portable repository") to what lies beyond. Amos (the variant he generally goes by, "Haymoss," nicely underscores how well and truly defined by his fields Hardy means Amos to be) invariably sticks to his own locale. And yet so, too, in a sense does Swithin, whose efforts to remain well and truly immersed in sidereal evolutions might bring him, in any order "to the observatory of Cambridge, United States . . . [or] the observatory of Chicago; . . . the observatory at Marseilles . . . Vienna—and Poulkowa, too."[47]

To Swithin's forsaken lover, such wanderings seem an abysmal exile. Swithin himself, however, barely notices he has moved at all: such rotation in the same hemisphere, along more or less the same line of latitude, strikes him, if at all, as mere minor tinkering with his apparatus. The difference between his arriving at a European or an American observatory means as little as the difference between employing one lens and another. What to other characters look like almost unimaginably vast wanderings to Swithin matter as little as the stopovers in Wessex do to polar birds, or the chaos beyond the dynamic strap does to the concentrated thresher.

Could we call this kind of internalized set of perceptual rules a form of cultural portability, analogous to the traveling Jewishness that Eliot seems to show entering into a character's body and becoming part of his mobile identity? This would entail arguing that astronomy itself is the portable body of knowledge that travels along with the itinerant astronomer, which might seem a plausible enough extension of the kind of traveling Englishness that I argued Eden, Maitland, and their peers struggled to cloak themselves in. By my account, though, Swithin's total astronomical obsession is not cultural portability at all. Instead it signals Hardy's interest in the sort of radically incoherent modes of noticing the world that accompany the fin-de-siècle revolution in perception Crary describes. What Swithin bears in his trained eyes is a way of seeing the world, but not one that lends itself to any kind of metonymical associations with the place he has left, or any cultural affiliations with those he has deserted. Sidereal knowledge, exactly like the agricultural specialization of the sort that binds Amos to his fields, becomes the symbol of how profoundly individual acts of attention differ in a world that is as effectively fragmented as it is fundamentally unitary.

SECOND FEATURE: THE SYNTAX OF NOTICING

The world in Hardy is manifestly there to be noticed, but that alone cannot ensure that people with radically divergent ways of noticing will arrive at a shared sense of that common world. What, then, does serve to unify divergent perceptions, so that a common world emerges? Cultural portability had one set of answers, which depended on the pre-extant sharing of a set of learned assumptions about England in general: readers know what Barchester looks like because it already, and only, exists in a shared (national) imagination.

Hardy, though, required a different set of tropes to account for his various distinct characters agreeing upon a shared world. One solution might be a kind of authorial solipsism: he asserts at one juncture, for example, that "characters, however they may differ, express mainly the author, his largeness of heart or otherwise, his culture, his insight, and very little of any other living person."[48] That credo, however, does not seem to prevent Hardy's characteristic kaleidoscope of divergent forms of observation in rapid succession. Within a single page, Hardy will first describe what something looks like viewed from below, then how it appears to a jealous lover, or by a man losing his eyesight. At the very end of *The Mayor of Casterbridge* (1886), for instance, Hardy takes the time scrupulously to detail the appearance of the merest sliver of wedding dancers and musicians visible to Henchard through a door.[49]

Gillian Beer has made the case that "Happiness and hap form the two poles of [Hardy's] work."[50] Yet the abyss between the facticity of the material world and the isolated nature of any one character's perceptions of that world is equally important. There is an unavoidable disjunction between Hardy's impetus to capture the world as it is, and his instinct to notate when, where, and by what observer such capturing takes place. So it is not surprising that some of Hardy's most glaring syntactical peculiarities derive from just this tension. In the opening chapter of *The Woodlanders* (1887), Hardy channels all observation about Marty Southy's village through the dim perceptions of Mr Percomb the barber, who is on the lookout only for hair. Elaborate periphrastic language works to remind readers that Percomb is the one doing the noticing, but also to tip them off that much remains to be seen that Percomb himself fails to see properly: "Only the smaller dwellings interested him; one or two houses, whose size, antiquity, and rambling appurtenances signified that notwithstanding their remoteness they must formerly have been, if they were not still, inhabited by people of a certain social standing, being neglected by him entirely."[51] The syntax allows Hardy to describe the places fully before explaining that they were "neglected by him," persuading readers to treat key sensory details as clues—before they discover those details are not clues for Percomb.

The same applies to the "smells of pomace" that follow:

> Smells of pomace, and the hiss of fermenting cider, which reached him from the back quarters of other tenements, revealed the recent occupation of some of the inhabitants, and joined with the scent of decay from the perishing leaves under foot.
>
> Half a dozen dwellings were passed without result. The next, which stood opposite a tall tree, was in an exceptional state of radiance, the flickering brightness from the inside shining up the chimney and making a luminous mist of the emerging smoke. The interior, as seen through the window, caused him to draw up with a terminative air and watch. The house was rather large for a cottage, and the door, which opened immediately into the living-room, stood ajar, so that a ribbon of light fell through the opening into the dark atmosphere without. Every now and then a moth, decrepit from the late season, would flit for a moment across the out-coming rays and disappear again into the night.[52]

Hardy is often criticized for passive formulae like "were passed without result," but the purpose of this passive phrase and the attendant inversion is evident. They are meant to defer attention from the observing subject of the passage for as long as possible, and then restore him abruptly to the reader's attention.

By halfway into this second paragraph, the syntax has righted itself, but the basic problem remains—Percomb ignores what matters most to the reader. One of those magisterially impersonal sentences about the landscape that opened *The Return of the Native* would not do here, however. As so often in the novels, Hardy requires an observer for the place to exist. Everything important here is made significant by being seen: even the appearance of the moth as it flits across the "out-coming" light requires an audience. That this interpellated observer will not have appreciated that flight as the narrator hopes the reader will is embarrassing (hence the twisted syntax) but is not an insoluble problem. There are only differentially perceptive embodied subjects in this universe, no Smithian common man, and no *sensus communis*. Yet that is no reason for Hardy to give up on depicting the world as it unfolds itself to barbers and Londoners alike. Committed as he is to registering both the nature of the common matrix that holds his characters and the diverse ways in which those characters come to perceive that matrix, his prose reflects his ongoing engagement with the doubled nature of the world that fiction lays before its readers.

In Hardy's poetry, however, a sustained attention to the same problems sets him looking more deeply inward. His poems sometimes come across, then, as dim signals transmitted imperfectly from a speaker unsure if what he or she feels can ever be understood, let alone shared. Nonetheless, the interaction between some of Hardy's *Wessex Poems* and their accompanying illustrations shows that Hardy remains deeply fascinated by the problem of how parallax views, distinct apprehensions of the same universe, can be reconciled with one another—or, if not reconciled, then strikingly juxtaposed.[53]

Third Feature: Depicting Attention in Verse and Drawings

Hardy's experiments with diversified perception and fragmented forms of noticing may be visible throughout his work, but in his poetry those experiments place far more emphasis on how profoundly isolated any person's observations will be from any other's. Vernon Watkins has described Hardy's poetry as "dominated by time" (as opposed, that is, to the eternity of religious poetry).[54] The contingency that defines Hardy's poetry, however, is not simply historical; in his poetry, experiences are often so completely lodged within their subjects that the reader's challenge is not to recapture the experience, but simply to make sense of what the speaker must be experiencing.[55]

> But our eye-records, like in hue and line,
> Had superimposed on them, that very day,
> Gravings on your side deep, but slight on mine![56]

It is hard to conceive of sharing tastes, moral judgments, and affection when the same "hue and line" will result in different observers being imprinted with different "[g]ravings." That Hardy wrote this particular lyric after an outing with his wife—the second subtitle of the poem in manuscript, "She speaks," establishes that it is *her* impressions, not his, that are "slight"—underscores the omnipresent possibility of painful incomprehension that his poetry repeatedly aims to establish.[57]

Again and again, Hardy reflects on the inherent lack of correspondence between one person's associations with a given place or object, and the nature of that place as it will appear to an outsider—an outsider who is thereby invited to witness, but not exactly to share, the speaker's sensations. In "Green Slates" (1925), for example, the speaker maps an inescapable association in his own mind:

> Green slates—seen high on roofs, or lower
> In waggon, truck, or lorry—
> Cry out: "Our home was where you saw her
> Standing in the quarry!"[58]

This is one of many poems that stress the limitations of such associations—readers might be able to share a poetic experience, but they certainly cannot do so in front of the relevant green slates.[59]

Many of Hardy's poems, then, are committed to a profoundly individuating account of perception, so that the difficulties in any person's comprehending another's situation are what come across most clearly. But the thirty pen-and-ink illustrations that accompany Hardy's first book of verse, *Wessex Poems and Other Verses* (1898), reveal Hardy's fascination with the demands that divergent perspectives make on any individual trying to put together a picture of the world. These drawings have attracted little notice: "primitive in execution, and frequently inspired by a somewhat mortuary imagination" is a typical contemporary assessment, while Millgate says they vary between "hauntingly effective" and "relatively crude."[60] Nonetheless, they reveal deep and sustained attention to the relationship between the narrating observer, the thing observed, and the reader or viewer positioned so as to observe that observer's act of observation.

The drawing that accompanies "She," for instance, shows a dark form shadowed against a church wall, obviously looking in (fig. 5.1). Yet the poem describes not that observer, but the funeral going on before her eyes.

> They bear him to his resting-place—
> In slow procession sweeping by;
> I follow at a stranger's space;
> His kindred they, his sweetheart I.
> Unchanged my gown of garish dye,
> Though sable-sad is their attire;
> But they stand round with griefless eye,
> Whilst my regret consumes like fire![61]

The family looks at him and mourns; she looks at them and judges their mourning insincere. The onlookers to the drawing, meanwhile, stand back at a yet further remove, so that they can only grasp the funeral the

Figure 5.1 Thomas Hardy, "She"; *Wessex Poems and Other Verses* (1898)

poem describes by way of the grieving back. "She" feels welcomed to grieve by the family's absence of mourning, while the onlooker is conversely shut out by her intensity of feeling. Onlookers can know the anguish associated with some other person's "personal and local" (Hardy's phrase) grief. Yet in the drawing the speaker's head fills the only gap by which anyone placed behind her could hope to gaze at the procession she describes, so that the reader-viewer's knowledge of her mourning is precisely what prevents him or her from sharing in it. Any viewer can appreciate the church beyond, thanks to Hardy's best architectural draftsmanship. But the subject of the poem itself is hidden—behind the subject of the poem.

The illustration to "Her Initials" also plays a game of concealment, seemingly offering up what the poem withholds, but only at the price of withholding what it seemingly offers up (fig. 5.2). Here is the poem in its entirety:

> Upon a poet's page I wrote
> Of old two letters of her name;
> Part seemed she of the effulgent thought
> Whence that high singer's rapture came.
> —When now I turn the leaf the same
> Immortal light illumes the lay,
> But from the letters of her name
> The radiance has died away![62]

Hardy's characteristic TH is on the right hand page, while on the left are a legible but smaller pair of initials: Y-Z, markers of a past association now ended as absolutely as the alphabet. Between them lies the "immortal" poem, which is the only visible piece of writing that does not continue to carry meaning with it, because it is thoroughly illegible. What the speaker experiences is embodied in a pair of initials now lost to view;

Figure 5.2 Thomas Hardy, "Her Initials"; *Wessex Poems and Other Verses* (1898)

what the reader experiences is a poem that will not die; what the viewer of the illustration perceives is two sets of extant initials. Marjorie Levinson has recently described Hardy's poetry as "a body of work that appears not to solicit or even to acknowledge reading . . . withdraw[ing] from reading without a hint of condescension, self-absorption, or even self-awareness. One might say that it has Hardy's name all over it yet lacks the intentionality we associate with signature."[63] But reading seems both acknowledged and solicited here; "Her Initials" invites readers to look and to read at the same time, to take up the printed page as an object for perception.

Levinson is perhaps responding mainly to Hardy's notion that readers must make sense of the poem in a way understood to be categorically different from how the speaker or author experiences it. That sense of categorical difference is foregrounded, in a deliberately puzzling way, in Hardy's illustration to "In a Eweleaze near Weatherbury," a poem about a place that still keeps its shining perfection in the speaker's memory, though the person who triggered that sentiment has long since vanished (fig. 5.3). The poem begins:

> The years have gathered grayly
> Since I danced upon this leaze
> With one who kindled gaily
> Love's fitful ecstasies![64]

The illustration of the site of these vanished happenings is unremarkable—except for the pair of glasses sketched on top. They do not distort the image at all, nor is the poem confined to depicting what is behind them. The glasses seem to say, "Simply remember that someone drew this,

Figure 5.3 Thomas Hardy, "In a Eweleaze near Weatherbury"; *Wessex Poems and Other Verses* (1898)

and was tired, and took off his glasses and rubbed his eyes and went back to work."

Still, having the glasses *not* distort the landscape underneath is another form of trompe l'oeil. Hardy is asking viewers to recall the observer, but simultaneously to look at the observable scene.[65] Like the dark back in "She," the glasses instruct readers to observe scene and observer simultaneously, but with a sense of the discrepancy between the two chores. This is "Character *and* Environment" with a vengeance, and it brings to mind Mr Percomb, who, through Hardy's twisted syntax, became the unwitting bearer of all sorts of information about decrepit moths and ancient buildings, even though those very moths and buildings were "neglected by him." That is, like Percomb's observations, this drawing actually maps broad vistas, and also goes out of its way to show an undistorted snippet of that vista glimpsed through an observer's glasses. While the glasses span only a small portion of the drawing, everything depicted in that drawing (and in the poem beside it) will enter the reader's consciousness.

Hardy's drawings thus allow viewers to glimpse in his poems the same multiperspectival world his novels had constructed. By juxtaposing these apparently hermetic lyrics with illustrations that are complementary in unsettling ways, Hardy is not undermining subjective testimony, or trying to turn the monadic chamber of the speaker's mind into an inescapable catacomb, as happens in Gerard Manley Hopkins's late "terrible sonnets." Rather, he is approaching from a different direction the question of diverse ways of noticing that had shaped his prose for so long. That he remained committed to highlighting the disjunction between observer and world observed as he moved into the purely poetic phase of his career is a valuable clue to how seriously Hardy continues to take the fragmentation of perspectives. It is also a reminder that Hardy has little faith in the convey-ability of information that was taken for granted by writers of novels of cultural portability. Hardy has, that is, none of the security that allows Blackmore to sketch the transparent lineaments of Lorna and be certain that his readers will not just believe in her, but love her passionately. In its place, he offers a series of experiments in the limits of perception, and the hope that beyond those limits, some sort of objectivity might prevail.

CONCLUSION: GONE LOCAL

In Hardy's cosmos, attention can only ever be local, but that locale is potentially infinitely expandable. Hardy once wryly proposed, "One might argue that by surveying Europe from a celestial point of vision— as in the *Dynasts*—that continent becomes virtually a province—a Wessex, an Attica, even a mere garden."[66] Beneath the joke lies Hardy's conviction that any locale has its own scalar properties, and its own rules for perception. Hardy says that Hodge will disappear when the involuntary guest stays in Dorsetshire, but he also notes that upon that guest's return to London, some kind of "typical" agricultural figure will be conjured up all over again, once the vivid variegation of real Dorset life has receded into the indistinct distance.

Hardy's recurrent problems with converging or clashing viewpoints, tangled syntax, and layering of divergent sensoria signal his uneasy awareness of the abiding challenge involved in amalgamating (without quite reconciling) individuals' emplacement in their perceivable locales. Even his novels are, like the empirical world, potentially subject to this diverse attention. Readers' vividly realized perceptions might all derive from black marks on white pages, and yet consist, mentally, of kaleidoscopic bands on solders' legs, or old Roman roads, or apple trees glimpsed from above, or even of the earth-bound segment of a meridional line that when projected upwards also bisects the transiting Venus. Diverse as this attention is, however, Hardy is definite that it should not be mistaken for noticing the same phenomena in the world proper. Noticing a bell's "outrollings" when Hardy describes them in "Afterwards" cannot easily be equated with noticing the same intermittent sound on a Sunday morning when the wind is shifting.

The result of that difference (between sensations conjured by a printed page and the same sensations conjured up by the world beyond) is that Hardy does credit his readers noticing *something* in his words, but does not believe that such noticing means that his novels have become a truly portable Dorset (or Wessex). Hardy makes that clear in an 1895 preface to *Far from the Madding Crowd*, in which he reflects on the fact that his success in popularizing the word "Wessex" has replaced his own "partly real, partly dream-country" with a "a modern Wessex of railways, the penny post, mowing and reaping machines, union workhouses, lucifer matches." Yet Hardy asks "all good and idealistic readers to forget this, and to refuse steadfastly to believe that there are any inhabitants of a Victorian Wessex outside these volumes in which their lives and conversations are detailed."[67]

Hardy's refusal to entertain the notion that culture can be imagined as embodied in culturally valuable portable property—even in one of his own novels—is intimately linked to his conviction that there is only one thing that can travel successfully with a character, and that that one thing remains untransferrable: a way of noticing the world. Hardy's insistence on the ultimate individuation of attention amounts to something quite different from the passionate resistance to over-individuation in William Morris's late romances. Morris's works, I argue in the next chapter, aim to prove the moral idiocy of believing in the portability of any sort of culture, because any such claim inevitably depends on invidious distinctions between rich and poor, and the creation of differences that disrupt the just and true solidarity of human existence. Morris's refusal is thus at once fundamental and tactical, a political nullification of fictive conventions that he sees as abetting and continuing a bourgeois reign over England. His alternative is to invest his artworks with a socialist conception both of personhood and of aesthetic representation.

Hardy's refusal of the durable mobility of a Deronda or the ethereally ideal quality of a Lorna has none of the political vehemence evident in Morris's romances. In place of cultural portability, though, Hardy's novels offer a universe knowable only in the most circumscribed and deceptive ways, because each perceiving mind inhabits a body shaped by the sheerest contingencies of social and physical circumstance. Like the thought that Nietzsche says "comes when it wills, not when I will it," noticing is something that happens to characters in Hardy, not something those characters intend. It is one of "life's little ironies" that Hardy's characters continue to be held responsible for what they notice or fail to, even though they lack any meaningful capacity to control what they do or do not notice. Although nothing is more mobile and more durable than any given character's capacity to notice the same sorts of things wherever one goes, that consistency across space and time offers none of the reassurance that, for earlier writers, had been housed in shrines as frail as an English strawberry in India, the ethereal Lorna's ideal beauty, or the portable Judaism that sustained Daniel Deronda.

CHAPTER SIX

Nowhere and Everywhere: The End of Portability in William Morris's Romances

> Nothing, like something, happens anywhere.
> —Philip Larkin, "I Remember, I Remember," 1954

THROUGHOUT THE NINETEENTH CENTURY, local truths seemed the novel's distinctive contribution to the Smithian project of producing effective sympathy. A letter tucked inside a set of stays, the unmistakable set of a heroine's mouth, a whispered cockney version of the Lord's Prayer—each generates generality from extreme particularity:[1] no type without the individual, no general rule without the proper noun, the named character who strikingly exemplifies it.[2] Tolstoy's claims that each unhappy family is unhappy in its own peculiar way, for example, requires him to produce a new and unfamiliar piece of domestic unhappiness that can be recognized, precisely on account of its novelty, as another avenue back toward a shared human condition. Romantic desire is so central to the Victorian novel's modus operandi because there is no emotion more defined by the concurrent *locality* of its application (I love this person alone), and *universality*—for each character and each reader, some distinct love-object, desired in an all-too-common way.

William Morris, though, recoils against the notion that an investment in poignant particulars is the best avenue toward the universal.[3] He sees the penchant for arriving at general rules via personal sorrows not as the novel's acme but its Achilles' heel. Morris's indictment of the genre, indeed, is strongly reminiscent of Hannah Arendt's argument a half-century later: novels promulgate a corrosive kind of public discussion of the private problems of the body and its emotional apparatus. By her account, novels displace politics from its proper place by moving properly local griefs into a shared social realm.[4] They plug in compassion where solidarity is required, and replace judgment with soul-shivering empathy.[5] Exemplarity there must be, but it is judgment, understood as the capacity to apply the correct general rule to individual instances, that allows us to move outward from the exemplar to the type.

Morris and Arendt share a distrust for aesthetic works that claim to put local circumstances into global circulation. In Morris's 1891 *News from Nowhere*, an unlikable character gets the Dickensian nickname of

Boffin the Golden Dustman because he has a penchant for digging around in the ugly dust of the past: "[H]e will spend his time in writing reactionary novels, and is very proud of getting the local colour right, as he calls it."[6] Another reactionary old man embraces the "fun" of Thackeray's *Vanity Fair*, while his more enlightened interlocutor explains disapprovingly that novels belong to a time when "intelligent people had but little else in which they could take pleasure, and when they needs must supplement the sordid miseries of their own lives with imaginations of the lives of other people."[7] These characters are mocked because they, like the realist novels Morris spurned, imagine that poignant individual details can be conduits to universal knowledge.

In the previous chapter, I argued that Thomas Hardy discovered one effective way to refuse the pervasive logic of portable properties: reject the possibility that an agreed-upon and readily accessible realm of culture existed, through which particular resonant objects (art objects prominent among them) could serve to transmit meaning from place to place for the right set of co-cultured people. This chapter explores an antithetical refusal of portability: Morris's denial that novels—or, indeed, any art objects—can convey poignant, peculiar details about any individual's feelings. Instead, he makes the case that to think of novels as containing real human beings, with real sufferings, is radically to misunderstand what any artwork can possibly contain.

As might be expected from a founder of the Arts and Crafts movement (and arguably the first industrial designer), Morris's formal experiments—both in *News from Nowhere* and the subsequent prose romances—are not arguments against art per se. His attachment to "that great body of art, by means of which men have at all times more or less striven to beautify the familiar matters of everyday life" does,[8] however, explain why Morris was unprepared to rank fiction as an exemplary art form.[9] The imperative to "beautify" the familiar springs from Morris's conviction that the work of art forms a material *part* of human lives, rather than simply representing those lives. Morris, in his novels as much as in his fabrics, is not committed primarily to mimesis but to beauty: "Everything made by man's hands has a form, which must be either beautiful or ugly; beautiful if it is in accord with Nature and helps her; ugly if it is discordant with nature and thwarts her."[10] The best art cultivates an "intense and overweening love of the very skin and surface of the earth."[11]

Morris sees himself, in fact, as refuting one of the Victorian novel's core assumptions: that personal identity and cultural privilege are portable properties, and that characters' capacity to retain a durable sense of self even when amongst strangers is what engenders readerly empathy. Imagination properly exercised does not, by Morris's account, allow things or persons to become (the phrase is George Lamming's) "natives of our person."[12] Morris believed that the novel's paradigm of sanctioned identification with certain people was problematic because it underwrote *dis*-identification elsewhere. And he made his case against dominant Victorian conceptions of the novel's form and purpose in large part by producing (not just writing, that is, but also himself illustrating, typesetting, and publishing) his late romances, which aimed to move readers toward a kind of universal identification with beauty distributed consistently over a beautiful world.[13]

Alex Woloch has recently argued that nineteenth-century realist novels are centrally defined by a tension between their readers' "ability to imagine a character as though he were a real person, who exists outside of the parameters of the novel, and [readerly] awareness of . . . highly artificial and formal aspects of the narrative structure."[14] Literary analysis of the realist novel, then, ought to proceed by "establishing a relationship between the referential elaboration of a character, as implied individual, and the emplacement of a character within a coordinated narrative structure."[15] Woloch proposes to do so by analyzing

> The *character-space* (that particular and charged encounter between an individual human personality and a determined space and position within the narrative as a whole) and the *character-system* (the arrangement of multiple and differentiated character-spaces—differentiated configurations and manipulations of the human figure—into a unified narrative structure).[16]

When applied to Morris's romances, that approach fails. Morris rejects the logic of "character-space," rejects even the idea of minorness, rejects the implicit pathos caused, in the realist novel, by the "squeezing" of "an actual human being placed within an imagined world."[17] By removing from the late romances the poignant peculiarities of psychology that make readers feel a character's restriction by his or her world, Morris refuses the tension Woloch sees as definitive of the realist novel.

Instead, Morris proposes that characters be thought of as systematically flat, placed within the novel to fulfill the demands of its plot rather than to represent the excessive human individuality or alterity that makes for poignancy in the realist novel. Because Morris's romances are conceived as a radical break from the realist tradition, though, this disjunction between Morris's writing and the exigencies of character-space confirms, rather than undermines, Woloch's account. The silence and indifference that have greeted the romances—barring a brief revival spurred by fantasy novelists in the 1970s—speak as well to Morris's abiding strangeness, his uneasy relationship to an English prose fiction tradition heavily indebted to the logic of portable properties he sets out to undo.[18]

In Hardy, I argued, portability's logic fails because rather than making shared sense of a common world, finding the highest meaning in some culturally resonant set of transmissible objects, each character makes sense of the ambient world as his or her distinct sort of perception permits. In Morris's late romances, by contrast, characters carry nothing meaningful with them, because the grounding for all meaning is to be found within the world itself. There is nowhere to run, because everywhere a character goes, the same fundamental conditions apply. In a world fully defined by what Woloch calls "character-system," Morris believes the anguish associated with felt restriction of "character-space" need never arise.

The quasi-poignant end of *News from Nowhere*, where Guest sees and feels his chances for Ellen vanishing before his eyes, never recurs in the romances, because love triumphs and tribulations are fully folded within the overarching constraints of the tale (its overarching system, you might say). As a result, good and bad outcomes alike are understood primarily for their role in forging the human solidarity that arises from shared appreciation of the beauty incarnate in the tale itself—or in the actual printed book that is the tale's material avatar. In Morris's fiction, where interior depth of character never arises, the resonance of portable properties vanishes. Rather than functioning as auratic bearers of a never-fully-shareable meaning, portable properties become another set of beautiful surfaces, memorable only for their place in the interplay of forms through which the text's aesthetic value is constituted.

EVER SINCE CHARTISM

Morris's late romances are not a *de novo* response to Victorian mainstream fiction. Rather, they are a response to, and continuation of, a tradition of Chartist novels and short stories now largely forgotten, but cherished by Morris and his socialist circle.[19] That fiction (which flourished in the 1840s and 1850s) is marked, like Morris's late romances, by diverse and unsettling experiments with the delineation of individual character. Chartist fiction often features initially sympathetic characters whose idiosyncrasies are gradually erased as they come to stand in for the larger body of struggling English workers. These characters' initial individuality, that is, gets progressively subordinated to their typicality of the greater body ("the people") they represent.[20]

This progression is evident, for instance, in the ending of what has been called "the first working-class novel," Thomas Martin Wheeler's *Sunshine and Shadow*.[21] Wheeler spent thirty-six of the novel's thirty-seven weekly "communions"—it was published in 1849–50 in the Chartist newspaper the *Northern Star*—delineating his protagonist, North. But he concludes by dropping the pretense that North is an actual person (indeed, the similarity between the names "North" and *Northern Star* already points to the hero's Everyman status).[22] Instead, he deposits the responsibility for living as a post-1848 worker firmly back in readers' laps. Denying that the story of any individual working man—including the novel's hero—would possess any interest apart from its representation of the shared Chartist struggle, Wheeler urges a consciousness of shared bodily suffering, and a solidarity that springs from commonality above all.

> The spirit of despotism is still in the ascendant, and we still bow beneath its influence; but all hope is not lost, the earth still labours in the pangs of travail, and will ere long give birth to a new and better era; the spirit of freedom is again taking wing. Men walk wistfully abroad, and hold their breath in the deep ponderings of suspense. These are not the hours to waste in idle dalliance; we must be up and doing, or when the time comes, we shall again be found unprepared.[23]

By this account, North recedes, becoming only a minor member of a whole class whose composite story must be told. The effect is antifictive: to disavow the protagonist's importance makes good Chartist doctrine, but problematic storytelling. Wheeler admits this, yet he gamely plunges on, trying to make Chartist doctrine palatable.

> In quitting our simple tale, we seem like parting with friends, and with these reflections delay the minute of final separation. We have endeavoured to prove that Chartism is not allied with base and vicious feelings, but that it is the offspring of high and generous inspirations. . . . We might have made our tale more interesting to many, by drawing more largely from the regions of romance, but our object was to combine a History of Chartism, with the details of our story.[24]

That disclaimer effectively evacuates Woloch's "character-space" altogether, leaving in its place "inspirations" that can only be systematic and aggregative, rather than particular and poignant.

My hypothesis is that the high road that runs from Chartist writing to Morris, which has been vividly traced through Morris's poetry by Anne Janowitz,[25] also connects Wheeler's antiparticularizing fiction to such obscure Morris romances as *The Story of the Glittering Plain* (1891); *The Wood Beyond the World* (1894); *The Well at the World's End* (1896); *The Water of the Wondrous Isles* (1897; posthumous); and *The Sundering Flood* (1897; posthumous).[26] These books offer a dream of mutuality linked to the same critique of private property and of "local" differentiation between persons that structures *News from Nowhere*. In their renunciation of even as minimal a novelistic protagonist as "Guest," however, the romances take a further step away from both the conventions and the political underpinnings of Victorian realism.

Object Lessons

John Stuart Mill's liberalism, Jürgen Habermas has argued, arises from a crucial mid-Victorian change in notions of political representability: Mill envisions a deliberative democracy predicated on *necessary*, rather than merely contingent, exclusions of certain social classes from both deliberation and suffrage.[27] That notion of necessary exclusion helps explain Hannah Arendt's hostility toward the role that novels play in constituting, and justifying, the "social" realm.[28] Novels allow readers to establish a basis for sympathy with other insiders—precisely by using the potent tool of sympathy to represent the downtrodden, excluded, and wounded, whose fate could be publicly mourned even while their voices remained barred from the polity. This kind of ready sympathy promotes a sense of fictive inclusion, often within national boundaries—as if the novelistic representation of, say, the beaten wife of a drunken brickmaker could serve as a substitute for working-class parliamentary representation.

This sort of substitutive representation depended, moreover, upon a set of necessary and yet generally unspoken exclusions even from aesthetic representability itself: such exclusions are justified and understood by way of the logic of portable properties earlier chapters have traced through writers such as Collins, Trollope, and Eden. Such novels emphasize the virtues of a portable cultural heritage, I am arguing, so as to justify their characters' indifference to the lives and activities not bundled into the right sort of portable vehicle. The novel, with its moveable feast of "local color," is thus (from Arendt's perspective at least) an essential part of reaffirming, or even engendering, the temporary barriers that forestall solidarity in real life.

My claim is that by rejecting the realist novel's logic of distinctive personality and its attendant exclusions, Morris offers a new model for the sympathy that artworks can engender, one founded on the refusal to admit abiding disjunctions between persons. One way to understand the Victorian novel is as the genre that fuses particularity and generality by positing hidden personal motivations and then (whether by first-person narration or free indirect discourse) revealing those motivations to the reader, while hiding them from other characters. Morris, though, refuses to admit the very existence of the epistemological deficit upon which such revelations are predicated.

There is no hidden knowledge to be uncovered in Morris's late romances. Ralph, for example, the hero of *The Well at the World's End*, can safely assume that all his companions will know that in a given forest-glade he lost his beloved; it is as if the glade itself revealed that truth. The space between objects and persons, or places and persons, turns out to be the same for everyone: there is no sentimental road to deeper sorts of associations between one person and a place or object. The result is that particular sentimental associations, with auratic commodities and persons alike, are systematically refused. Time and again in the late romances, an object that seems at first glance to be sentimentally endowed is shown *not* to be what the Victorian novel would demand it be: a deeply meaningful piece of private property, redolent with one person's associations. For example, a pair of shoes is presented as a love-offering in *The Water of the Wondrous Isles*. "Any man," though, can appreciate the beauty of the shoes—and of the beautiful maiden whose feet they contain—in exactly the same way their recipient does: "They [the shoes] were daintily dight with window-work and broidery of gold and green stones, and blue. And forsooth it was little likely that any man should stand before her a minute ere his eyes would seek to her feet and ankles, so clean and kindly as they were fashioned."[29] Aesthetic impulses must always precede moral or sentimental reactions, and a sense for beauty always supersedes purely personal responses to a given object.[30]

Morris is so insistent on this convertibility because he wants to show that the central mistake of his own age is to prize objects as if one's ownership of them made them something special. Indeed, it is not just a mistake to prize objects because one owns them; it is a mistake to develop personal associations with one's possessions, rather than appreciating all the world's objects in equal measure. In *The Well at the World's End*, Ralph occasionally finds a sign that he is on the trail of his beloved, as, for example, a "fine green cloth embroidered with flowers" that she used to wear. When he finds it, though, he spends as much time admiring the fine workmanship and great beauty of this cloth as he does reflecting on her probable proximity.

This approach to possessions begins to appear in *News from Nowhere*, which in this respect, as in many others, serves as a sort of laboratory for Morris to develop a hybrid version of an idea that will emerge in the romances as a full-fledged antinovelism. Early in *News from Nowhere*, for instance, Guest goes in search of a pipe. He is offered the most beautiful pipe in a store. What if I should lose it, he asks the little girl behind the counter, who replies, "What will it matter if you do? Somebody is sure to find it, and he will use it, and you can get another."[31] The most noteworthy distinction made between persons up to this point in the novel, apart from that between men and women, is between smokers and nonsmokers. Now, however, readers are asked to suppose that this pipe can be anyone's pipe, valued exactly the same by nonsmoker B (who will perhaps "use" it only by gazing at it admiringly) and smoker A.

News from Nowhere makes the case, moreover, that if other people are suffering in ways that we ourselves have not—if the world, that is, has set up insuperable barriers between one somatic experience and another—

then no amount of aesthetic work will cross that bridge, and it would be gross indecency to try.[32] Morris's memorable description of the poet as an "idle singer of an empty day" relates to the poetic responsibility to produce an object equally delightful to all viewers anywhere.[33] "Story" and "story-telling," by contrast, are two of the most excoriated words in *News from Nowhere*.[34] It was only in the unhealthy nineteenth century, the wisdom character Hammond explains in *News from Nowhere*, that "there was a theory that art and imaginative literature ought to deal with contemporary life." Fortunately, Hammond continues, "they never did so"—because there is no real possibility of indexical reference between artwork and the world, imagined as a series of dismal encounters with objective referents.[35] All those artworks that imagine such a connection give up on their real role, which is (like a Morris and Co. textile) to "sharpen our dull senses" by a beauty that derives from an "accord with nature."[36]

By Morris's account, the best sort of art in a happy society will absolutely fail to convey any aspect of another's suffering. He is rejecting, then, or beginning to reject, the novelistic assumption that there is any mode of representation capable of making a suffering character's feelings present to the reader.[37] The best musical performance one can imagine, Hammond explains to Guest, is a woman singing about deprivation and misery without arousing any answering empathic pang in her audience:

> "To hear the terrible words of threatening and lamentation coming from her sweet and beautiful lips, and she unconscious of their real meaning: to hear her, for instance, singing Hood's 'Song of the Shirt,' and to think that all the time she does not understand what it is all about—a tragedy grown inconceivable to her and her listeners. Think of that, if you can, and of how glorious life is grown!"[38]

This is a striking choice of example, one that Morris's contemporary audience (the novel was first serialized, after all, in a socialist magazine) would have been hard-pressed to read without a wince of recognition. Hood's 1843 crowd-rousing lament on dehumanizing female labor is famously filled with bloody imagery and sustained rhetorical melodrama:

> It is not linen you're wearing out,
>   But human creatures' lives!
>   Stitch—stitch—stitch,
>   In poverty, hunger, and dirt,
> Sewing at once, with a double thread,
>   A Shroud as well as a shirt.[39]

Morris makes an example out of a song almost impossible to imagine stripped of semantic content, because that is the most radical way of advancing his claim that art should properly aspire to a non-narrative function. In a world where suffering has passed away, the song can cease to mean anything, except to a determined memorialist, and can simply, delightfully be.

The brief against pity is deliberate even in *News from Nowhere*, and becomes, I am arguing, pervasive in the romances that follow. Morris, like Arendt, indicts empathy because it operates as a replacement for other, more political, sorts of engagement. Pity might motivate individuals singly, but when it becomes the basis for political action—Arendt's example is the Rousseauistic fervor of the French Revolution, where collective will was mistakenly held as a replacement for an intersubjectively constituted solidarity—it gets in the way of a more fundamental basis for human connections. Pity forestalls, that is, recognition of the human uniformity that is precisely attested to by surface differences, by the infinite individual variations that make "plurality" the basis for cohesion.[40]

EQUALITY OF CONDITION

> A reform in art which is founded in individualism must
> perish with the individuals who have set it going.
> —William Morris to Andreas Scheu, September 5, 1883

According to *News from Nowhere*, the arts of the nineteenth century are crippled by their felt obligation to depict present suffering. The "record of the so-called arts of the time before Equality of Life" is so sordid because such arts are the product of the rich feeding ghoulishly off the poor's "pinched and sordid lives."[41] When a character is reproached with failing to enjoy himself in the "easy-hard work" of haymaking, he is told that he must be "wanting to nurse a sham sorrow, like the ridiculous characters in some of those queer old novels."[42] The sorrows of a novel are by definition sham, because they consist of morbid inward self-examination, when the real problems of life exist outside, in the structures of inequality. Recognizing the "true equality of condition" is what will make us treat one another like what we truly are—incorporate extensions of one another's being.[43]

Morris's commitment to "equality of condition" produces in his romances an egalitarianism so pure that the differences between persons seem to disappear. Strikingly, this depersonalization proceeds not by the elimination of romantic desire and sensual beauty from the texts, but rather from a new way of generalizing such desire. Particular bodies do not disappear from the romances; if anything, the attention to carnal detail grows, so that the notably decorous insinuations of Victorian romance plots are replaced by an aesthetic at once undecorous and *un*insinuating. Bodily beauty is frankly described and treasured, and yet from it follows none of the romantic intrigues that it would provide in a Victorian novel.

The late prose romances, though, have been punished for their pointed rebuke to individual sensibility—by contemporary critics and readers, by latter-day scholars, even by Morris's own family. The late romances' pre-occupations with the beauties of landscapes and of the human form are frequently seen as excursions into indulgent fantasy that leave Morris's socialist praxis behind.[44] Phillippa Bennett, by contrast, has described the appreciation of beauty in Morris's romances as a form of "wonder."[45] We might also describe Morris's attunement to beauty (and his willed blindness to suffering) as a sort of aesthetic promiscuity.

In the late prose romances, Morris is not so much eradicating the idea of a central romantic love as he is exploring ways in which it can be generalized. Not one but a hundred men can kiss the Beloved in *Child Christopher and Goldilind the Fair*; in *The Well at the World's End*, a whole nation finds its desire realized in the just reign of a beautiful but self-effacing ruler.[46] The omnipresence of lavish kisses is a way for strangers to express their admiration for a beautiful man or woman: phrases like "since he had kissed her so sweet and friendly, like a brother" recur in each of the romances.[47] Morris is committed not to obliterating but to universalizing the bonds of romantic love. He wants all persons to feel the same sort of deep emotional bond to one another that lovers now mistakenly believe separates them from the rest of the world. What Morris describes as "[s]ocialism seen through the eyes of an artist" is not an indifferent aesthetic hedonism, but a deliberate program for obliterating the social differences that make real life, the life lived outside of tales, into such a present agony.

In the late romances, accordingly, those who turn sexual desire into grounds for jealousy are profoundly misguided. Many of the most passionate and far-gone lovers are figures of fun. The amorous monk in *The Well at the World's End* loves his "Lady" so devoutly that he is convinced, falsely and against all evidence, that "she weareth a hair" (that is, a hair-shirt) beneath her gown, and is as devout a Christian as he.[48] In his mad love, he has replaced the object of his devotion with himself (he is the only hair-shirt wearer in the book) and so what purports to be flattery of his lady is really only a form of self-indulgence.

Nineteenth-century socialism is generally understood as deeply indebted to Marx's critique of capitalism's classed structure, which relegates the working class to the role of mere bodies.[49] By Marx's account, this relegation ensures the rupture of sensibility between people placed in different relationships to power (in Lukács, this is transmuted into the notion of the labor-produced class consciousness of the proletariat).[50] Socialism differs from liberalism, then, in its insistence that the bodily component of a worker's experience is a true component of the lived social world, rather than simply an impediment to participation in a realm of unfettered public discourse. Marx's notional attachment to a sphere of sanctioned privacy—as in his notion of a future marriage freed of economic shackles—might even implicitly rely on the suffering of working bodies as proof that capitalism's "objectivity" is the force destroying a zone of subjective intimacy.

Morris approaches the problem of shared or unshared bodily experiences differently. In *News from Nowhere* incipiently, and overtly in the later romances, the recognition of a virtually indistinguishable common humanity becomes an avatar of eventual shared corporeality. Like the Naturalists, Morris foreswears characters possessed of psychological depth, through whom readers might attempt to experience narrated events as if they themselves had been present. Unlike the Naturalists, however, Morris is not committed to a form of impersonal description that results from "the domination of capitalist prose over the inner poetry of human experience, the continuous dehumanization of social life, the general debasement of humanity."[51] Naturalism—generally accounted the fin-de-siècle's most socialist literary form—insists that if the sufferings of the "common people" continue long enough, those people are successfully made into nothing more than cogs in a machinery designed to grind them small for others' benefit.[52]

Morris takes hold of the other side of the word "people" and postulates, contra Naturalism, that distinct social roles are as illusory as any other bit of cruel "local color" that the masters of the nineteenth century have superadded to essential human resemblance. In Hardy, I argued, portable properties become irrelevant because the location of perception within persons is so complete that no shared world of auratic commodities could satisfactorily make what individuals experienced cohere. In Morris, by contrast, there is no radical distinction between persons. In fact, there is a radical *absence* of distinction, the implication of which is, again, that portable properties have no role left to play—because there has ceased to be any geographical or psychological gap for the objects to cross.

Morris's turn toward this form of impersonality—it might even be better labeled superpersonality—is consistent with his "artist's socialism": "Art cannot have a real life and growth under the present system of commercialism and profit-mongering. I have tried to develop this view, which is in fact socialism seen through the eyes of an artist."[53] Morris's socialism drove him to decide that he ought to *exclude* the corporeal suffering of the working classes from his art; he aims not to feel others' suffering, but instead to envision their shared future happiness. This sentiment, most famously expressed in the 1894 essay "How I Became a Socialist," commits him to attacking the idea that people should have different minds, different bodies, differently constructed feelings, different desires, and even different thoughts from one another, which in the better world of the future will no longer be the case.[54]

> Well, what I mean by Socialism is a condition of society in which there should be neither rich nor poor, neither master nor master's man, neither idle nor over-worked, neither brain-sick brain workers, nor heart-sick hand workers, in a word, in which all men would be living in equality of condition, and would manage their affairs unwastefully, and with the full consciousness that harm to one would mean harm to all—the realization at last of the meaning of the word COMMONWEALTH.[55]

"Equality of condition" might seem to mean the sharing of actual bodily anguish. Suffering, though, is infrequent in the romances, since Morris imagines artworks are designed not to inflict pain, but to produce pleasure (as his effort to imagine a pain-free future for "Song of the Shirt" suggests). So, for instance, a lovesick knight follows Birdalone through the forest in *The Water of the Wondrous Isles*: "He strove to be somewhat merry of mood, and to eat as one at a feast; but while his heart failed him, and he set his teeth and tore at the grass, and his face was fierce and terrible to look on; but Birdalone made as if she heeded it not, and was blithe and debonair with him."[56] Although "she looked on him pitifully,"[57] the important action is her refusal to share his love-mad mood, lest she encourage him to go further. Others' sufferings, then, are overlooked so that all characters can return to a shared emotional plane.

Morris's attachment to "equality of condition" is best expressed, from *News from Nowhere* onward, in his studied refusal to grant psychological depth; in Woloch's terms, Morris refuses the notion of "character-space" and embraces the cohesion promised by "character-system." Norman Kelvin even argues it is not so much the persons as the house in *News from Nowhere* that underwrites Guest's "intimate aesthetic experience" of the future. By Kelvin's reading, visiting future frees us from complicated human dynamics, and facilitates instead sensuous relationships with beautiful surfaces.[58] There is, by the same token, a telling moment in *News from Nowhere* when Guest finds himself falling in love with Ellen, the most arresting in a succession of unearthly beautiful women he encounters. "[Ellen] was not only beautiful with a beauty quite different from that of 'a young lady,' but was in all ways so strangely interesting; so that I kept wondering what she would say or do next to surprise and please me."[59]

So far, the incident reads as a novelistic description of the depth of feeling in one person called out by another's perennial mystery—my beloved has features invisible to ordinary perception. Morris now returns to that account and revises it strikingly: "Not, indeed, that there was anything startling in what she actually said or did; but it was all done in a new way, and always with that indefinable interest and pleasure in life, which I had noticed more or less in everybody, but which in her was more marked and more charming than in anyone else that I had seen."[60] What seemed startling in her, then, was only a "charming" version of the novelty of this whole world, and she is principally his point of entry to an entire world filled with an "interest and pleasure in life" that she exemplifies rather than possessing uniquely.[61] All the deeper feeling is an outgrowth of Guest's initial attraction to world rather than personage. If you wish to know why someone else appeals to you, look to the surface attributes of their speech and behavior, rather than mistakenly parsing those surfaces as concealing some deeper meaning.

It is worth noting here that Ellen's faux-depth distinguishes Morris's approach sharply not only from the Victorian psychological realist novelists whom he follows but also from the Victorian romance and fantasy tradition to which the romances may seem to belong. Even profoundly odd novels in that tradition—for example, George McDonald's *Phantastes* (1858)—do not envision, as Morris does, mutual incorporation erasing all differences between persons. In a fantasy novel Carole Silver has shown was one of Morris's inspirations, W. H. Hudson's *The Crystal Age* (1887),[62] the exceptional/typical object of desire is constructed along familiar Victorian lines. Like Guest, the narrator, Smith, has just arrived in the future from nineteenth-century England:

> After a first hasty survey of the group in general, I had eyes for only one person in it—a fine graceful girl about fourteen years old, and the youngest by far of the party. A description of this girl will give some idea, albeit a very poor one, of the faces and general appearance of this curious people I had so strangely stumbled on. . . . Her eyes . . . proved to be green,—a wonderfully pure tender sea-green; and the others, I found, had eyes of the same hue. . . .
>
> The exquisite form and face of this young girl, from the first moment of seeing her, produced a very deep impression.[63]

Here, the "poor idea" that the picture of the girl gives of the group at large is derived from the slippage between her exceptional beauty and the more ordinary (though still great) beauty of those around her. Hudson cannot decide if he is writing about the world or the girl—she typifies her people's green eyes, yet she also stands apart. Rather than her serving as a passage toward an understanding of the world as a whole, then, she is a unique and exclusive love-object for Smith. Indeed, his ultimate failure to fit into the utopian community turns on the incapacity of future humans to understand the redemptive intensity of the exclusive romantic love he feels for this girl. In Hudson's novel, as in the "machine-life" of Edward Bellamy's *Looking Backward* (1889),[64] the discovery of an exceptional beloved individual has the effect of obscuring, not illuminating, the world she inhabits.

In Morris's romances, by contrast—because they extend the logic of Guest's love for Ellen-as-world or world-as-Ellen—every man and every woman who is not deluded and wrongly possessed by monomania worships great beauties in identical ways. The pleasure involved in gazing at such beauties need not derive from a corresponding sense of disgust in looking at something else: the world might, like a perfect wallpaper design, simply be so satisfying to see in all its aspects that a non-exclusive beauty prevails. "Oh! but thou art beautiful, O earth, thou art beautiful," cries another beautiful Morris heroine at one point.[65] Such beauty needs no divisions. Art at its best is part of the process whereby we come to understand, and thus arrive at the true equality built into, the world itself.

Such universal fellowship also translates, in the curious logic of the romances, into a kind of Newtonian law of equivalence of affect—and effect. Just as persons resemble one another, so, too, do their actions resemble one another's, and it is a mistake to divide any one person's actions sharply from any other's. In *A Well at the World's End*, for example, an old lady points to the place where a thief had previously been sitting: " 'He sat just where sitteth now yon yellow-headed swain.'. . . Then she was silent, but the young man at whom she had pointed flushed red and stared at her wide-eyed, but said no word."[66] The young man apparently flushes from the excitement of sitting in the same place the villain had been. Later, however, his flushing is explained: he, too, had tried to steal the same necklace the thief had gone after, but at a later date. In the logic of the tale, his villainy and his having sat in the villain's chair are parts of one and the same disorder. Even evil here is made into another form of mutuality, an alliance that overleaps separate bodies and questions of ordinary social connection between persons.

The relationship between world and individual is the same, albeit with a different valence, when it comes to kissing: the personal turns global. People are constantly being embraced (willingly, reluctantly, or while sleeping) with kisses. Such kissing, or embracing, is freely practiced between heroes and their applauding throngs, even between young women and their various (unloved) admirers, so indiscriminately that the line between hero and throng or lover and beloved blurs. Morris means this "queer old" form of republicanism to be understood as a political affirmation that differences fall away at contact, rather than as carnality run amok.

One way to grasp what Morris gained as a writer when he was able to separate himself from Victorian novelistic conventions is to consider his earliest efforts at fiction, which are fundamentally swamped by the challenge of depicting both the beauty of the world as a whole and the abiding alterity of other minds housed in other bodies. Morris's early fiction is in essence a series of troubled (and troubling) meditations on how a beautiful body is linked to the "soul" that might or might not dwell within it. Descriptions of Clara, the heroine of his unfinished 1871 *Novel on Blue Paper*, for example, stress the beautiful nature of "those eyes, that body"—but then hasten to add that those eyes and that body are beautiful because "her soul has made" them so.[67] Still, after dwelling with such lavish detail on the adorable visibility of Clara's body itself (both heroes gawk unashamedly at her barely clothed form), Morris cannot supply an interior to match—or rather, an interior with all the passionate but modest depth a Victorian novel requires. The novel seems to falter precisely because Morris is astonished, possibly even slightly ashamed, to discover that he has nothing but cliché to describe Clara's personality, while making every effort to render her bodily beauty in loving detail.

The lesson Morris learnt from that juvenile failure seems to have been that an artwork's greatness resides not in the inaccessible inner recesses of heroines' souls, but on the surface, the depthless surface, of the page. The last line of *News from Nowhere* makes this insight explicit: "If others can see it as I have seen it, then it may be called a vision rather than a dream."[68] Just as a selfish individual desire is nothing—it might lead one to hallucinate that one's beloved is wearing a hair-shirt—so, too, do merely individual dreams evaporate, while visions verified by others' similar experiences endure.

I'll Teach You Differences

Morris is offering a socialist critique of the novel's dependence upon difference—linguistic, ideological, class, racial, or even psychological. By his account, the durable value of portable properties is doubly doomed. First, because artworks themselves have a value that depends upon their existence as beautiful (and potentially interchangeable) parts of the "skin and surface of the earth"; second, because the appeal of resonant portable properties (a beloved pipe, a valuable edition of Shakespeare) depends upon thoroughgoing distinctions between persons that Morris dislikes and denies.[69]

Morris's antipathy to the differences that divide humanity would be vitiated, however, were he simply to ignore or evade the mundane fact of human distinction, and the gaps such distinctions bring. If suffering in a factory bends backs and sours temperaments, it might seem myopic or cruel to dwell on human commonality at the expense of what disaggregates humanity. Social roles—defined by gradients of power and strata of class privilege—deeply define not just an individual's personality, but even the ways in which he or she perceives the shared world. Even if Morris wants to argue that such classifications stem from fatal political mistakes in the modern world, and that they form a vivid scar tissue on top of a common humanity, such classifications must still be mapped, even in order to discern the true, shared human life beneath.

Morris's account of why Hood's "Song of the Shirt" will eventually seem beautiful, however, clarifies his insistence on commonality at the expense of difference. There will come a day, Morris believes, when even that poem's aesthetic attributes will emerge unscathed by the incidental horrors of social inequity it documents. In that day, its appeal will derive from something entirely intrinsic to the artwork itself—but only if "threatening and lamentation" are pushed down, if historical conscious-ness and objective referent are traded in for an entirely different way of acknowledging the song. This kind of acknowledgment must stem from a consciously achieved obliviousness to the suffering with which the poem was once associated.

This notion owes a debt to, yet is ultimately distinct from, the role envisioned for the artwork in Chartist fiction. Chartist novels, from their beginnings in Alexander Somerville's *Dissuasive Warnings to the People on Street Warfare* (1839) to Ernest Jones's *De Brassier* (1851–52) were caught up in the minutiae of a daily struggle. Or, even worse, they were beleaguered, like Ernest Jones's late novels, by the ill-fitting garb of con-ventional melodrama, with its dependence on suffering bodies tied to lovelorn souls.[70] By contrast, Morris refuses both the immediacy of con-temporary political struggles and the confines of "timeless" love or "un-forgettable" passions, turning instead to an unexpected solution: forget-ting.[71] "My vision . . . is of a day when . . . the words 'poor' and 'rich,' though they will still be found in our dictionaries, will have lost their old meaning; which will have to be explained by great men of the analytical kind."[72] Were we to remember we would be forced to internalize others' sadness. So it is better, in the face of a world of inequities, for art to help us forget. By itself that claim for forgetting—worker's woes, suffering past, even the bodily inscribed differences that make some of us workers and others lords—seems to do little. Here the teaching and unteaching of differences in Morris becomes crucial.

Only what is first understood can be forgotten. So Morris's vocabulary lessons go out of their way to describe words whose formerly highly dif-ferentiated meaning has been or will be lost. For example, Morris relies heavily on the words "carle" and "quean" to describe men and women.[73] An angry common man proclaims at one point in a late romance that "churl" (a variant on Morris's favorite synonym for "peasant," "carle") is just another way to say "earl," and vice versa.[74] Those who note such class differences (those who care if a man is "churl" or "earl") will always be locked in linguistic disputes about how priority is to be established.

Once the human race in general has been trained to forget the alternative readings, however, as it forgot the suffering described in "Song of the Shirt," then "carle" will emerge as a catch-all. As the final lines of "The Folk-Mote by the River" put it, the erasure of the terms comes only with the oblivion after revolution:

> And yet in the Land by the River-side
> Doth never a thrall or an earl's man bide
>
> . . . .
>
> And we live on in the land we love,
> And grudge no hallow Heaven above.[75]

"Thrall" and "earl's man" disappear simultaneously, and in their place appear "manfolk" lost in the battle that actually turned them from thrall or earl into simply dead men. Thus the lowliest serf and the highest lord occupy the same category, under different headings—because the words are racinated together, the true correspondence between them shines through the temporary disjunction.

C. S. Lewis praises the "doctrine of generality" under which Morris's descriptions avoid specifics and ascend immediately to Platonic forms.[76] Lewis seems not to notice, though, that generality is constantly arrived at via particularity. "Carle" and "quean," in their capaciousness, are anything but "general" words. "Carle" means both a peasant and a man, and it can imply both surly and slovenly (like a peasant) and tough, vigorous, and reliable (again like a peasant, or perhaps simply like a man); while "earl" lingers by the transom, suggestively. The analogy holds for "quean," which gives the word "queen" (for effeminate men), and even "queening," as well as meaning "sluttish." Yet the word's first meaning is "woman" and "womanly." In choosing a word that has connotations running from negative to merely descriptive to highly positive, Morris is not sticking to some transparent earlier language. Instead, he is pointedly invoking contrast so as to overcome it.

This might be the primary reason that there are no Babels of tongues in Morris's romances. Characters almost always speak one another's "latin." Given the generally medieval matrix of the romances, calling its common language "latin" seems a way simultaneously to preserve specificity and generality—Latin is a specific tongue, but also a medieval passe-partout. There are no foreign languages in this world, because only within a matrix of a common human speech can difference itself be registered. Only if "carle," "earl," and "churl" mean similar but distinct things within a single semantic code can the revelation of their uniformity strike readers.

Morris delights in creating different categories only in order to shut down the differences between them. One of the Nowhereians offers this version of converging differences: "[L]et us take one of our units of management, a commune, or a ward, or a parish (for we have all three names, indicating little real distinction between them now, though time was there was a good deal)."[77] The differences of the past have to be forgotten, and the very process of forgetting them is what produces a new and better world. That finality, however, is reached by promulgating, and then incorporating, the old divisions—just as the historical "change" that brings Nowhere into being comes via a class struggle, between the "people" who rule and the "people" who serve them. Churls and earls share their humanity only when history has been learned, then left behind. For Morris, etymology is part of the trick played on the suffering common folk by history: the endless discovery and promotion of difference is part of a conspiracy to blind readers to sameness beneath.

In his antietymologies, Morris might implicitly be picking a quarrel with the prevalent Victorian taste for jingoistic etymology, promulgated in such widely circulated works as Richard Trench's 1851 *The Study of Words*. For Trench, the durability of words bespeaks an intimate, or even an organic link between their form and their meaning. The perdurability of language's greatness helps in reckoning up a goodly Burkean heritage:

> Language is the amber in which a thousand precious and subtle thoughts have been safely embedded and preserved. It has arrested ten thousand lightning flashes of genius, which, unless thus fixed and arrested, might have been as bright, but would have also been as quickly passing and as perishing, as the lightning.[78]

Coupled with this account of how individual greatness lingers in language is an account of how a culture organically builds on its strengths:

> Far more and mightier in every way is a language than any one of the works which may have been composed in it. For that work, great as it may be, is but the embodying of the mind of a single man, this of a nation. The *Iliad* is great, yet not so great in strength or power or beauty as the Greek language. *Paradise Lost* is a noble possession for a people to have inherited, but the English tongue is a nobler heritage yet.[79]

This echoes Carlyle's *On Heroes, Hero Worship and the Heroic in History* by taking a single phenomenon (here, the English language) as the proof of a *national* solidarity that cannot be otherwise established.[80] Noble heritages can be a reliable way to register, or to engender, differences between nations.

Morris, by contrast, repeatedly makes note of the differences within a set of signifiers, simply so as to assert that underneath that difference sameness runs. These experiments with collapsing apparent difference also dominate the various games and experiments in Morris's typography. Consider the opening and closing pages of *The Story of the Glittering Plain*, which was published first in a widely circulated magazine edition in 1890, but for its Kelmscott edition received a new title: "The Story of the Glittering Plain which has been also called the Land of the Living Men or the Acre of the Undying. Written by William Morris." Notice the curious interchangeability in Morris between related words: "land" and "acre" are distinct, yet in this case they will be the same; ditto with "living" and "undying." The final words appended to the end of the novel convey the same lesson:

> Here ends the Tale of the Glittering Plain, written by William Morris, & ornamented with 23 pictures by Walter Crane. Printed at the Kelmscott Press, Upper Mall, Hammersmith, in the Country of Middlesex, & finished on the 13th day of January, 1894.
>
> KELMSCOTT
> Sold by William Morris, at the Kelmscott Press.

This interchangeability does not quite extend to the distinction between "written," "ornamented," and "sold." It might as well, however, since all three are descriptive of operations performed on an essentially continuous artwork by a vertically integrated production studio.

The physical layout of the Kelmscott books themselves also makes the claim for the establishment of distinguishable differences, intended to be at once noticed and overcome.[81] It is not simply the way that, as on the title page of *The Glittering Plain*, the "I" and "t" that form the text's first word ("It has been told . . .") are located, respectively, within the surrounding ornament, and inside an autonomous illuminated chamber (fig. 6.1). Nor is it merely the way in which the illustrations may be coterminous with their bordering, or even the way that later in the same volume, instead of periods Morris sometimes inserts a leaf, prickly or smooth, as a paragraph division. Nor is it wholly the way that some paragraphs not coincident with chapter or section breaks are nonetheless marked with illuminated capitals, woven as well as pierced by tendrils in much the same way that the tendrils of the illumination itself weave round and occasionally pierce the text (fig. 6.2).

All such visual vividness, such erection and overcoming of differences (between border and text, between letter and leaf), helps the reader conceive of a future in which an illuminated manuscript or a Kelmscott book will bring the same pleasure Nowhereians get from hearing "Song of the Shirt" or gazing at a beautiful pipe.[82] Morris is ambitious to produce an aesthetic and hence a political totality, even at the cost of distinctions

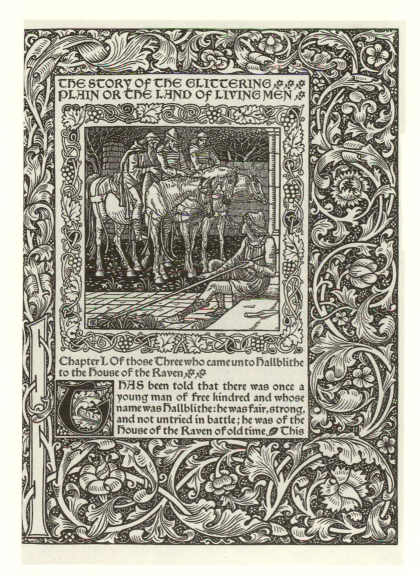

Figure 6.1 William Morris, from *The Story of the Glittering Plain* (Kelmscott, 1894)

Figure 6.2 William Morris, from *The Story of the Glittering Plain* (Kelmscott, 1894)

apparently as fundamental as those between letters. Imagination's power as a socialist desideratum derives from its capacity to register the diversity of human experiences only insofar as the prospect of a shared vision highlights the potential agreement in aesthetic judgment between all people. In Morris's actual world of disaggregated liberal subjects, imagination is necessarily more constrained than in a world where the complicated meaning of both "Song of the Shirt" and of "earls" and "carles" has been lost. Readers are therefore asked to embrace an aesthetic attunement to small differences, along with an ideology that looks to the end of those differences. On the one hand, the fine distinctions that Morris himself notates; on the other, the delighted laughter of the residents of Nowhere when they hear Guest trying to make subtle, but meaningless, pronouncements about distinctions between "city" and "country" people.

Although Morris is known as a poet of "the People," and his "socialist chants" vaunt the struggling masses at the expense evil oppressors, impersonal forms of judgment always form the basis for his visions of triumphant cohesion. In Morris's romances, like his late socialist "chants," enemies are defined only positionally: triumph comes not in conquest, but in the transformation that makes opposition between persons only the result of a semantic mistake.[83] The result is that language itself can come to be represented as a common property, common enough that distinctions between persons dissolve without characters needing to notice such dissolution. This ideal mutuality—in, for example, *The Dream of John Ball* (1886)—entails imagining human beings sharing a world so intimately that they might know one another's speech better even than they know their own.

At one point in *The Dream of John Ball*, the dreaming narrator is asked what his own place is in John Ball's army. The question is asked by way of what might be called a shibboleth, a triggering cue verse to which he is expected to know the password response. Someone recites to him: "John the Miller, that ground small, small, small." His response is automatic: "From between my lips *without my mind forming any meaning* came the words, 'The king's son of heaven shall pay for all.' "[84] Speech is the medium in which meaning is suspended, but that meaning need not pass through the individual consciousness to be transmitted. Rather, it is best understood as a memorized verse or an object so well known it passes below the threshold of attention.

Morris pursues an art that is visionary precisely because it is resistant to the artistic verities of his own day. Walter Pater in 1868 could already discern this trend in Morris's early poetry: "Into this kingdom of reverie, and with it into a paradise of ambitious refinements, the earthly love enters, and becomes a prolonged somnambulism. Of religion it learns the art of directing toward an imaginary object sentiments whose natural direction is toward objects of sense."[85] That is, Morris has found a way to capture in writing not so much the *features* of the world as its *feel*: not the social spaces we move through, but the sensory traces those movements produce. This perhaps is Morris's closest connection to Hardy, the sign that both are writers attuned to a new aesthetics of sensation, unwilling to look through sensory to eternal truths, reluctant to parse reactions to the "skin and surface" of the physical world (and to other human beings) as betokening some form of deeper moral engagement beneath.

Conclusion

Morris's awareness of the historical durability of somatic and social differences, then, is not an impediment to, but rather an inspiration for, his strenuous efforts to avoid seeing (contingent, limited, and remediable) differences as tokens of perdurable distinctions within a fundamentally shared humanity. The movement toward an "equality of condition" suggests Morris's wish to avoid turning etymological or historical difference into something essentially divisive. Yet the rich variety woven into his design work suggests his discomfort with homogeneity, if by "homogeneity" is meant the erasure of all surface distinction. It is contrast, after all, that makes his ornaments what they are. The diversity that is woven into his fabrics reflects something about his conception of endlessly diverse human life, and its infinite potential. His designs, with their multifoliate variations on ornament, on color, on torqued geometrical shapes, establish a matrix that is beautiful precisely by virtue of such variations. Rather than consisting of a backdrop that frames or half-conceals particular beautiful objects, Morris's designs are beautiful in how they arrange objects not in themselves necessarily beautiful.[86]

Why, then, has Morris's utopian jeremiad against inegalitarian, oppressive difference not attracted or persuaded latter-day readers? In evacuating depth from his characters Morris has created a "no-place" that relies on a rigorous conceptual distinction between sympathetic novelistic representation and an art responsive to "the skin and surface of the earth." Perhaps it was impossible in Morris's day (perhaps it is still impossible) for readers to appreciate a prose genre that so relentlessly conceptualized its refusal of personhood, that refused to pursue avenues by which a socialist-all-over aesthetics might be intertwined with or even nourish a revivified form of sympathetic novelistic representation. Like Chartist fiction, then, Morris's might have been an experiment not only doomed, but even designed to fail, because Morris was angry enough with what came before him to be unwilling to see a compromise as the way forward, an

aesthetic design that incorporated both novelistic modes for depicting idiosyncratic personhood and his new vision for an artist's socialism.[87]

That Morris's work did not lead directly to any novelistic fusion forms,
however, should not lead us to conclude that the romances were themselves failures. The late romances are infused throughout with Morris's
mastery of the art of intertwining bodies and intermingling landscapes,
and in that sense they are the vital artistic legacy of his final decade. Morris's textual genealogy of the differences embedded in etymology is of
a piece with his visual commitment to variation and diversity upon the
continuous, flat, two-dimensional space of the page itself. A manuscript
might feature an illuminated initial letter, entwined with tendrils that (in
the illustration above) pierce its top bar to make it legible as a "t" rather
than an "a" or an "o." The letter does remain legible, though, and the
tendrils, rather than being pure visual information, do contribute toward
allowing us to read figure as text.[88]

The final word has yet to be wrriten, however, on why these experiments came about at the time they did, and in the form they did. How
should we understand Morris's experiment in "equality of condition,"
his insistence on finding new ways to envision diversity and uniformity
as equally indispensable components of an artwork? One spur to the experiment might have been the linguistic division occurring all across Europe in the later nineteenth century as the word "people" came to mean
two entirely divergent things—the citizenry in general, on one hand, and
the mere common "mob," on the other.[89] Perhaps the romances take on
such an explicitly antiparticularizing form because Morris believes that
the only way to prevent the deadly particularization that results in a politics of division and exclusion is to annihilate all foundational distinctions
between persons, along with all distinctions between places. Morris's turn
toward the seemingly archaic "no-place" of the utopian romances stems
from his conviction that the fate of the working classes, the insignificant
"people," would become the fate of their citizen counterparts as well,
once the lexical and the conceptual meanings of "people" had been successfully bifurcated. Accept that "churl" and "earl" are truly distinct, and
the battle is lost.

Portability must vanish in Morris's work, then, not only because there
is nothing for individuals to carry that will make them meaningfully different from other individuals, but also because there is nowhere different
to go with that portable property. This is most graphically demonstrated
in Morris's final novel, *The Sundering Flood*, in which a river divides two
lovers and two communities from one another. The lover who sets out to
cross the river arrives, finally, to find that there is, and can be, no difference between those living on one side of the river and the other. The river's
purpose was simply to generate the proper form of love—his love for his

beloved, his community's love for the community on the other side of the river. All sunderings are effectively joinings.

Morris's romances assume that a true social life, rich in aesthetically mediated differences, can reemerge only when the "people" is not etymologically and conceptually broken in two. This movement from particularities to beautiful, formally general solutions colored even Morris's private life. Overcome with jealousy by his wife's affair with Rossetti, Morris—in a letter to an old friend—reminded himself of a larger universe within which his sorrows could radically diminish: "O how I long to keep the world from narrowing on me, and to look at things bigly and kindly!"[90] "Bigly" here means with a kind of universal comprehension of love in all its forms, and "kindly" means not only with compassion, but also "in kind." That is, with an eye for the homologous love he is looking for, a universal attachment to the skin and surface of the earth, a love broadened and strengthened, rather than attenuated, by its global application.

Where do Morris's experiments against portability ultimately lead? His romances seem to mark one potential terminus to the novel's logic of portability, which had insisted that the most enduring kinds of sympathy, and of understanding, could be attained only by keeping particular affinities intact in transit, keeping their application narrow even when the object to be loved or understood (a sweetheart, a country, a particular street in London) was far distant. The enviable forgetting practiced in *News from Nowhere* is one way to put an end to the circulation of stubbornly local patriotism. Another way, more suited for Morris's unradiant present, might be crafting Kelmscott books—at once objects and tales—with the power to persuade readers that cultural durability, like individual idiosyncrasy, has been systematically misunderstood and overvalued in a sad period that can only be brought to an end by a shared vision.[91]

Taken in tandem with Hardy's stubborn parsing of the myriad ways by which a local identity might be constructed, Morris's new socialist aesthetic demonstrates the powerful pressures bearing down on the logic of portable properties. Hardy's and Morris's accounts of the problems attached to auratic commodities and the detachable locales they purport to embody suggest some of the ways in which the sentimental freight associated with a sealed letter, a monogrammed handkerchief, or an inscribed Bible starts to seem (to more writers than just Oscar Wilde) both laughable and offensive. And yet, whether the portability Hardy and Morris saw as both pernicious and outworn was replaced or replaceable in the culture at large remained an open question. That Morris's was a potential terminus to portability does not indicate that portability had come to the end of any line.

As I suggested in the introduction, portability's logic still rules in Margaret Oliphant's *Kirsteen* (1890). Like his Chartist forebears, then, Morris made a foray that could have worked, that would have worked, had the readers of his age only begun to view the novel in a different way. That they did not do so says less about Morris's talents as a writer, I am arguing, than it does about the continuing affinity between the novel and the powerful appeal of portable property.

Is Portability Portable?

> Germany is overseas.
> The United States is overseas.
> But England is another thing.
> What this other thing is, has never been clear to anyone.
> —Ama Ata Aidoo, *Our Sister Killjoy; Or, Reflections from a Black-Eyed Squint*, 1977

> All the books they had read, their whole introduction to something called culture, all of it, in the form of words, came from outside: Dickens, Jane Austen, Kipling and that sacred gang. The West Indian's education was imported in much the same way that flour and butter are imported from Canada.
> —George Lamming, *The Pleasures of Exile*, 1960

Victorian Portability as "Traveling Theory"

How durable was Victorian portability? I have been describing a coherent set of representational practices and aesthetic assumptions that flourished in England and Greater Britain between 1830 and 1870, then continued in various vigorous forms at least until the end of the century. A variety of economic and political forces sustained it, and its continued allure is evidenced in lacunae as much as it is by extant texts: the failure of American-style regionalism to take root in England between 1870 and 1900, I argued in chapter 4, results from the imperial requirement for representations of a coherent, uniform, and thus readily exportable England. Portability's reign is by no means uniform and absolute, but exceptions and objections during this seventy-year span lead to no radical changes. The vehement protests against the logic of portability that fundamentally shape the writing of Hardy and Morris attest ultimately to portability's continued vitality, not its demise.

It might appear tempting to read the failure of those revolts against portability as proof of its entirely diachronic vitality. Perhaps cultural portability of the "traveling-Englishness" variety is a new universal, a product of modernity that (like racial thinking) could be here to stay. Might it make sense, then, to conclude this study by moving away from historical specificity toward a theoretical account of cultural portability as a timeless phenomenon? Eschewing for the moment the specificities of Victorian cultural mobility, such an account might be able to offer a general account of how ideas become portable property.

Edward Said's "Traveling Theory" is one attempt at a universal theory of intellectual filiation:

> First, there is a point of origin, or what seems like one, a set of initial circumstances in which the idea came to birth or entered discourse. Second, there is a distance traversed, a passage through the pressure of various contexts as the idea moves from an earlier point to another time and place where it will come into a new prominence. Third, there is a set of conditions—call them conditions of acceptance or, as an inevitable part of acceptance, resistances—which then confronts the transplanted theory or idea, making possible its introduction or toleration, however alien it might appear to be. Fourth, the now full [*sic*] (or partly) accommodated (or incorporated) idea is to some extent transformed by its new uses, its new position in a new time and place.[1]

Said's understandable worry about the scale of his claims—"It is obvious that any satisfactorily full account of these stages would be an enormous task"—leads him to alter the essay's course midway, into a modest reading of how certain theoretical notions descend circuitously from Lukács to Foucault.[2] In light of what historical contingencies can do to intellectual pathways, Said's diminishing of his claims strikes me as necessary, not contingent. Given how entirely notions of traveling culture changed over the mere seventy years covered by this study, any attempt to indicate the structural parameters for all such movements is certain to run up against some of the same limits on generalization that Said encountered.

It hardly seems satisfactory, though, to refuse all abstraction about cultural portability. To stick resolutely to the claim that Victorian portability is only English, and confined to the nineteenth-century, would be to overstate the force of the categories by which retrospective ordering occurs. Classifiers like "Victorian," "English," and "novel" might say as much about present-day mindsets as nineteenth-century realities. Indeed, my account of cultural portability itself suggests why this must be so: a notion of cultural portability, of Englishness capable of following trade patterns around the globe, arises precisely because the question of what defines a text's "true" identity (site of origin? race of readership? author's intent? value as trade good?) is itself perennially disputable. Studying how art objects are nationally marked in their global peregrinations perpetually reminds us that divisions between places, times, or cultures constantly change, and the identity of any one person, any one text (to whom it belongs, where it belongs), is mutable.

Victorian cultural portability evolves, in fact, precisely to redefine boundaries between places and nations that no longer seem self-evident: how else could exemplary English novels be written by the Indian-born, Vermont-dwelling Rudyard Kipling? One way that Victorian novels take this flux and flexibility of national status into account, as I argued in chapters 2 and 3, above, is in their explorations of the blurred boundary between Englishness and Jewishness. Both Emily Eden and George Eliot create fictional characters who can be satisfactorily classified neither as fully Jewish nor fully English—in fact, it is their possible involvement in the rules that govern cultural transmissibility in *either* nation (is Daniel English because he knows his Milton, or Jewish because he recognizes the Shema?) that makes such characters worth representing.

This capacity to fracture easy boundaries—to reconceive a work as belonging to a culture, a tradition, a family, or a nation that might be thousands of miles, or years, away from the site of its creation—is exactly what Victorian cultural portability ended up either offering (to certain texts and certain readerships) or foreclosing upon (for other, less privileged readerships). All worries about overgeneralization notwithstanding, the flexibility that cultural portability itself engendered makes it seem impossible to conclude this study without at least glancing beyond the seventy-year domain I have tried to map. The logic of portability that allows Carlyle to claim Shakespeare for an English Indian Empire demands that we at least consider the possibility that Carlyle, and his contemporaries, too, might belong not to their own age, but to that age's inheritors, however conceived.

How, then, to avoid offering a problematically timeless account of "traveling theory" once the known territory of the Victorian age receded? I initially thought of ending with a cautious glance into the early twentieth century, tracing the palpable residues of Victorian one-way traffic both in the modernism of Little England and in the emergent nationalism of British colonies overseas. Evelyn Waugh's "The Man Who Loved Dickens," for instance—in which the illiterate, dark-skinned Mr Tod captures the Englishman Tony Last, turning him into a reader of Dickens and native informant on English mores—could be juxtaposed with Nirad Chaudhuri's account of an Indian education that left him with such "English" heroes as "Napoleon, Shakespeare, and Raphael."[3] If the danger of setting up an abstraction like "traveling theory" is that historical specifics get replaced by ungrounded generalizations, however, taking small steps away from the Victorian poses the opposite risk. It can make the cultural portability I am describing look like a process of continual development, as slow and steady as Darwinian gradualism.

Yet what is perpetually astonishing about Victorian notions of cultural portability is how extremely durable, pervasive, and stable they were—

until violent ruptures bore them away. I have described the fiction of Morris and Hardy as a site of insurrection against portability's reign, but I have also argued that the basic apparatus for understanding Englishness as a moveable whole survived those rejections. In this conclusion, I argue that the most durable part of the Victorian notion of national cultural portability does not come under a radical assault until George Lamming's fiction of the 1950s.

Lamming's striking innovation is to anatomize, dissect, and do away with notional cultural *asymmetry*—that is, that English culture can flow to the periphery, but the reverse neither should nor can occur—which is the most enduring, and damaging, legacy of Victorian portability. Until Lamming makes the case that such asymmetry is an absurdity that has blossomed into a pseudo-fact in colonized (and postcolonial) minds, imperial asymmetry remains the tail that wags portability's dog. Portability endures, that is, as the important afterlife of a Victorian idea that had (as I argue in the introduction) come into being during debates about economic fungibility, but lingered on into the late nineteenth century and beyond to shape ideas about expatriate national and racial identities.

Making proper sense of Lamming's riposte to Victorian portability requires a look back at what I have argued are the four salient features that distinguish Victorian novels from their predecessors: *auratic commodities*, *moveable localities*, *quasi-materiality*, and the *asymmetrical flow of portable properties*. It also requires recollecting the objections Hardy and Morris raise to each.

Auratic Commodities

Certain choice moveable objects are, without relinquishing their exchange value, imbued with sentiment only a few can discern: the bank notes extracted from a long-hoarded letter in *Kirsteen*, the Moonstone's irresistible "moony glow," the semiprivate letters that mean so much in both *Cranford* and *Lorna Doone*. The crucial assumption of any account of cultural portability is that moving objects can serve as a constitutive basis for a shared (but potentially bounded) community, so that Shakespeare's works bound in green cloth can have a trade value and a resonant national identity at once. What if those same works, though, possess a value to readers outside the narrowly construed community, like the diffusive works of melodrama that both Newell and Joshi have described attracting subaltern readerships, or the movement of Bunyan through Africa that Isabel Hofmeyr charts, or *Vanity Fair*'s allure to the young C. L. R. James? That possibility, within the logic of a strictly enforced domain of cultural portability, can only be a dangerous challenge (or at best a sinister counterpart) to the "bounded" circulation of nationally significant works of art: think of (in chapter 2, above) A.U.'s fear of a Christianized India.

Hardy and Morris raise distinct objections to such auratic commodities. The inherent disarray of individual acts of perception by Thomas Hardy's account undercuts the notion of a shareable common culture transmittable by way of mementoes, novels, or luggage; Hardy, that is, disbelieves in the notion of a "culture" cohesive enough that objects could become a basis for shared meaning. By contrast, William Morris finds the specification of objects either as possessions or as bearers of national culture repulsive and politically oppressive, since it allows for "neighborhoods" of shared sensibility that rule out not only common human sensibility, but even agreement in judgment and cognition. His fantastic spaces presume a purely universal human community, in which pipes are equally valued by smokers and nonsmokers, and a beloved's green shoe is equally beautiful to her lover and to an indifferent bystander. There is a potentially infinite amount of uncommodified beauty in Morris, but without the particularizing "local" affection that figures so prominently in the novels (*Vanity Fair* is one) he fulminates against.[4] Morris believes that aesthetic apprehensions, including reactions to personal beauty, have the force they do precisely on account of the separation between aesthetic response and any particular fact—nation, class, beliefs, even gender— about the reader.

Moveable Localities

Cultural portability generates definitions of "neighborhood" that have become detached from geography, so that "local space" can itself become a portable notion. Emily Eden's cognitive map of India, for example, is so dominated by Anglo-Indians that she at one point complains charity is impossible in India because there are no poor people to be found there. Hardy, I argue in chapter 5, above, rejects the idea of such notionally portable regions because he thinks that individuals striving to make sense of the world possess a "locale" defined by their perceptions, not their baggage. For the astronomer Swithin in *Two on a Tower*, any spot on the same meridian where he can locate a telescope is essentially the same place, while for his peasant counterpart Amos nothing makes sense beyond his two well-known fields.

Morris's diametrically opposed premise leads to the same conclusions: there is no way to carry one's neighborhood from one place to another because there is no real difference between places. His last romance, *The Sundering Flood*, is premised on a false division between East and West Dale opened up by an impassable river. When the novel ends with solidarity between the two reestablished, the seeming split the river had made turns out to mark, not impede, the actual homology of all the Dale folk. According to the logic of Morris's romances, all such differences between persons and places will eventually become nondifferences.

Quasi-materiality

This term refers to the blurring of the line between simple physical transportability, and a more abstruse, or metaphorical, form of portability: for example, Gurney's phrase "portable evidence of Christianity," which comes to refer both to the physical Bible and its spiritual message. Like novels themselves, such "properties" are half-material, half-abstraction; that is, they are understood partially as pieces of physical property, and partially as weightless bearers of the message that they contain. It is not resolution but rather irresolution that such objects provide. Certain pieces of portable property had the impact they did among Victorian readers not because they were universally available and readily legible, but because they resisted or deferred the process of making complete sense of them (for example, those half-photographic illustrations I discuss in chapter 4, above, in which a sweetly featureless Lorna Doone floats above the photorealistic Exmoor waterfall).

Hardy's objections to this notion of partial portability stem from his sense that individuals carry such distinct sensations and perceptions with them (Amos knows his fields, Swithin the skies above) that no given object can mandate meaning in that doubled way: in "Green Slates," the association between slates and a lost beloved belongs to the speaker alone. Morris's objections are simpler still: since no depth exists in an artwork, there can be nothing quasi-material about it. The real nature of any given object, any given image, any given word (as the interplay between ornamental lineation and lettering in the Kelmscott pages discussed in the previous chapter suggest) exists on the page's surface at all times; significance and substance are inextricably conjoined.

Asymmetrical Flow of Portable Properties

While English Bibles (or even containers of salad oil packed in London) can arrive glowing overseas, there are other objects—among them Indian cotton and Irish potatoes—that best conform to the logic of imperial portability by showing up in England as nothing more than unresonant, unromantic commodities. This aspect of Victorian portability—its most imperial, and also, in many ways, its oddest—also seems to suggest that without an empire, portability must come to an end. After all, if everything that makes portability a distinctive and potent explanatory apparatus depends on an imperial asymmetry—so that only colonizers can deploy portability, and it always involves the neglect, refusal, or annihilation of portability in reverse—what sort of portability persists when its governmental guarantee is lifted by the withdrawal of British sovereignty? But on this final question, Hardy and Morris can shed very little light. In certain ways they still write from within the belly of the whale, with no way of gauging the remarkable durability of the notion of asymmetrical flow in cultural value. Why, after all, should the belief that ideas, identities, and values are flung outward from the metropole to its various peripheries have endured into the postcolonial late twentieth century?

I have argued that novels found themselves at an authoritative epicenter in a world where that conception of an outward-moving culture seemed desirable, or if not desirable, at least accurately descriptive of how culture flows actually worked—it is the elective affinity between novels and the notion of cultural portability, in fact, that lies behind much of the genre's dominance in the nineteenth and early twentieth centuries. But once the British Empire disintegrated (between 1947 and 1965), many factors militated against that form of literary hegemony enduring. What exactly was the status of the objects, artworks, and signifying practices that had long been used to signify Englishness once the British governmental infrastructure departed?

This conclusion aims to make the case that George Lamming is in certain structural ways a successor to Morris and to Hardy in their efforts to undo the basic lineaments of cultural portability. Like his predecessors, Lamming discerns binding restrictions (largely racial in nature) in the imaginative notion of an endlessly reiterated and seamlessly exportable national culture. His innovation—highly distinct from the sort of spatio-temporal logic present either in Morris or in Hardy—is to make the case for the impossibility of the sort of asymmetrical culture flow on which Victorian portability's success had always implicitly depended. The final claim I will advance, then, is that George Lamming does to the notion of asymmetrical flow what Hardy and Morris had done to the notions of moveable localities and auratic commodities, respectively: he sets out to prove that it never had worked as its practitioners believed. Understanding how he does this and why can shed additional light on the Victorian predilection for cultural portability—and its surprising ongoing afterlife.

Postcolonial Portability

> "Migration" was not a word I would have used to describe
> what I was doing when I sailed with other West Indians to
> England in 1950. We simply thought that we were going to

an England which had been planted in our childhood
consciousness as a heritage and a place of welcome.
—George Lamming, "Introduction," *In the Castle of
My Skin*, 1983

Cultural portability did not die with the empire, after all. Portable British
culture continues to fascinate and horrify an astounding range of African,
West Indian, and South Asian writers. Every Commonwealth writer of
the late twentieth century might not have grown up "reading *Vanity Fair*
on the average once every three months,"[5] but it is hard to find one whose
vision of Englishness is not mediated through the simultaneously uplifting
and downtreading influence of "Dickens, Jane Austen, Kipling and that
sacred gang."[6] When Salman Rushdie describes a radio as "made as England," the joke is about the capacity of residual imperial objects, after
imperial retreat, to go on performing their signifying function.[7] When he
describes the Indian inheritors of English houses in Bombay rapidly falling
into the habit of five o'clock gin-and-tonics on the verandah, the somewhat darker joke is about the capacity of imperial subjects to do the same
thing.[8] Similarly, when V. S. Naipaul has a West Indian character describe
a vivid childhood memory of giving his teacher an apple (even though
"we had no apples on Isabella") he is reflecting on how vividly "mimic
men" can incorporate a distant "motherland" into their imaginations,
how entirely their minds will recapitulate that motherland's practices, its
treasures, even its fruit.[9] Both Rushdie and Naipaul (the one satirically, the
other reverentially) perceive a kind of diminished residue of the colonial
encounter, a force that came, conquered, and departed—leaving behind
writers who both accept the logic of portability, and recognize their own
distance from the centers where such portability begins.

To Barbadian George Lamming, the joke has been on colonial subjects
all along.[10] Colonials had persisted in believing in portable British culture,
despite the fact that it had never arrived and never performed any of the
functions both colonizers and colonized believed it performed. Lamming
does not suggest fighting against portability. Lamming suggests there is
only one way out of the trap that avoids reverting to its structuring assumptions in another form: to maintain that there is nothing to fight, because there never was any such thing as transplantable English culture.[11]

The radical nature of Lamming's critique is not obvious from his best-
known nonfiction work, *The Pleasures of Exile* (1960), in which English
imports both physical and metaphysical, from butter to Jane Austen, seem
capable of transforming colonies into miniaturized versions of the colonizing country. Lamming's first novel, though, *In the Castle of My Skin*
(1953), depicts British objects operating in a quite different way.[12] If the
novel represents Barbados (or "Little England") as "a tense site of unrec-

ognized class and racial division . . . [in which] the people [attempt] to hold on to their small shreds of misguided dignity, some spurious sense of self buried deep within the castle of the skin,"[13] it also asks an unsettling question: What if the "England" that made and shaped these colonials bears no relation to England itself? If so, then English objects in the imperial hinterland can produce not an internalized hegemony, but an odd kind of imaginative freedom.

A debate about British pennies distributed to schoolboys at a prize-day frames the problem of imported culture.[14] As soon as the boys get their pennies, they start debating:

> Some said it was really a photograph of the king stuck on some kind of background and then coloured with copper. . . . Could you have a penny without a face? . . . Some said it was a drawing of the king made with a pin while the copper was soft. . . . It was a long and patient undertaking. But it had to be done if there was going to be any money at all, and everyone knew how important money was. . . . [Others said] it was very silly to argue that such a job would be done by sensible people. And the English who were the only people in the world to deal with pennies were very sensible.[15]

The challenge is to read the mind of the imperium, and the question is who can successfully ventriloquize the penny. Theories proliferate among the boys:

> One penny, that is the first penny ever made, was the real penny, and all the others were made by a kind of stamp. You simply had to get the first penny and the necessary materials and thousands followed. That meant, someone asked, that you couldn't spend the first penny. Someone wanted to know how that first penny was made. . . . [The penny was made and heated] and finally sent to the king who pressed it on one side of his face.[16]

The absurdity of each theory about the penny's origin is not merely incidental, but central to the meaning of these debates. The incredible quality of the boys' explanations is exactly the point.[17] Ngugi wa Thiong'o reads the explanations in this passage as moving toward a real understanding of the colonial condition. He argues that in this novel, "[T]he yardstick is England. Everything that affects the tender minds of children is geared toward veneration of England and the British throne."[18] In truth, though, the yardstick here is an imaginary England, which the children have made into a monstrous but wonderful reality.

The final thesis advanced by one of the children is that the king is not responsible for that image, because "the king was never seen,"[19] and that all images flow only from a kind of "shadow king." That notion of an invisible but omnipotent shadow king points to Lamming's real intent here. The wholesale importation of England to the island that knows itself as "Little England" has produced a kind of "shadow" Englishness, and that shadow's relationship to its original is fundamentally unmappable. Just as the offspring of a "shadow king" will have no genetic relationship to the "real king," the daydreams sparked by these shadow imports will have, Lamming supposes, no true relationship to their putative origin. Lamming conjures up a world in which the creation of a plausible past for the imported artifact is fatally compromised by the very act of imagination that is required to constitute the object as a lesson of the empire. All the meaning that seems to inhere in the object is actually conjured up by its interpreter.

Lamming's parable of the pennies thereby turns a seeming deficit into a hidden strength. Barbados's distance from the metropole is precisely what endows its residents with a powerful imaginative life. The West Indian imagination, by this account, is only putatively engaged in interpreting England's objects. The very moment at which colonial subjects might seem most invested in their imperial antecedents is the moment at which they have already broken with that empire.[20] It is not that the colonial objects really bring England with them, nor is it the case that they lie in seeming to do so. Rather, they offer a set of dreams anyone can imitate— but dreams that have everything to do with Barbados itself. Provincial life is shaped not by imported objects, but by the illusion that life is shaped by these imported objects. Lamming's portability from below, then, begins to look like a pure form of antiportability, as pure as Morris's.

Nor does Lamming stop there. His most compelling account of the force of such necessary illusions comes in his last novel, *Natives of My Person* (1972). As titles for novels, the phrases "in the castle of my skin" and "natives of my person" might initially appear almost identical. Both assert a kind of corporate unity that underlies the apparent disaggregation of persons: each suggests that all these voices that you hear in the novel, scattered all over the social map, are in reality joined together within "my" experience. Yet the context within which the phrase "native of my person" appears in the later novel suggests ways in which the corporatism of *In the Castle of My Skin* has been replaced by a kind of twisted or impeded solidarity that is quite a bit more difficult to parse.

At the conclusion of *Natives of My Person*, the wives and lovers of the novel's three central characters, stranded somewhere in the New World, speak of the way that their lives as women are defined by submission to another's will. Submitting is what forms their subjectivity, because their decision to make another's life a resident part of their own means they can understand their own actions as belonging to another:

SURGEON'S WIFE: It was what I had to do. He was a piece of my person.
STEWARD'S WIFE: It is the same. My husband had become that too:
   a native of my person. Whenever there is a crisis, we must choose
   against our interests.[21]

These characters, though, have been dissevered from those imagined natives of their person: unbeknownst to them, their husbands are already dead. They see themselves as the extension of others who no longer exist. Lamming maintains that in order to live, people require the impression that they are working for those persons and objects endowed with a life beyond their own. Thus even at the moment in which their connection to those others has been severed, they continue to imagine those others inhabiting them. Be the other the king's penny or the dead husband, the form of imaginary connection is equally strong.

Finally, though, all these seeming inhabitations of one's thoughts by the mind of another, or by the imported objects that make up a world, are a productive illusion. The telling pluralization—so that one "native of my person" in the line of dialogue turns into "natives of my person" in the title—suggests that Lamming contains all of his characters as beloved natives. It also suggests, however, that his own relationship to those others whom his prose ought to contain (and even speak for) is profoundly unsettled, as illusory, and as productive, as the imagined affinity to a distant England that in *In the Castle of My Skin* had been mediated through pennies.

Natives of My Person fantasizes the discovery that all our imagined connections to those who hold sway over us—our husbands, our kings, our coinage, our nations—are a delusion from the beginning. Having recognized that delusion, one realizes that one was never subservient to that authority, that the force contained in those guiding British precepts and objects was all along a product of one's own mind, not inherent in the things themselves. In *Natives of My Person*, the seeming triumph of asserting that one contains another as a "native of one's person" is the psychological corollary to the state of colonization. Both hinge on the delusion that objects and messages can traverse the ocean unimpeded, bearing with them a perfect replica of original intent. Lamming tells the story of portable treasures that do not portage any meaning with them; he tells the story of "incorporation" founded on lies or on mistakes. In so doing, he returns to the foundational conceit of overseas colonies, and crafts a response that is devastating not because it topples an old order, but because it suggests that that old order itself had never existed.

Peter Hulme has argued that Lamming's interest in "the shaping of national consciousness" depends upon "an imaginative reassessment of the relationship between metropolis and ex-colony."[22] *Natives of My Per-*

son goes further still, proposing that the shaping of a modern conscious-ness will come about not by rejecting the colonial culture, but only with the recognition that one's seeming ingestion of that culture had all along been an illusion. Victorian portability must not just cease working, it must cease ever having worked.

One way to read Lamming's gesture of negation is via Deleuze and Guattari's account of "deterritorialization," which they associate with "minor literature" in their memorable remarks on Kafka. By their ac-count, deterritorialization is related to the way that a minor literature (a literature of the oppressed in the oppressor's tongue) is "something impossible—the impossibility of not writing, the impossibility of writing in [the conquering tongue], the impossibility of writing otherwise." Deter-ritorialization eventually works to "disperse" even the ruling culture, be-cause once a minor literature has established that "impossibility" is in fact the necessary condition for any writing, there ceases to be any culture that is not traveling culture, just as there ceases to be any territory that is not deterritorialized.[23]

Deterritorialization offers one account of the interdependence of "major" and "minor" literatures within a coherent system. I have argued that the successful circulation of portable culture relied all along not upon a strong motherland transmitting wisdom to its expectant children, but upon the pervasive interaction of center and periphery, dominant and sub-ordinate culture. The spatially dispersed constitution of a seemingly co-herent culture did occur: the value of Shakespearean quotation was estab-lished in the Raj, after all, and Jane Austen became the incarnation of Englishness only by traveling overseas. That dispersion was necessarily disguised, however, because Victorian culture came to be depicted as mov-ing always from the center of its society to its edges: hence the impossibil-ity of reverse portability. This asserted asymmetry is what sustains Eden on a diet of Shakespeare and London gossip in Barrackpore. It is also what Rushdie, and many other writers of the era after decolonization, have satirized, denounced, and recapitulated. It is an act of remarkable imagination on Lamming's part to suggest that all along that portability, with its ban on "counterflow," simply did not exist.[24]

Lamming, like Hardy and Morris before him, offers a new way out. Still, the sheer oddity of Lamming's writing—its refusal of so many of the mechanisms whereby novels attempt to naturalize themselves in their surroundings and establish a comfortable relationship to social milieu—reveals how difficult it is to envision a postcolonial culture that would do without some version of cultural portability as the Victorians dreamed it up. Deterritorialized or not, dispersed or not, the Anglophone writers of the twentieth century display an astonishing reluctance to cast its guiding paradigms aside. To do so might involve asserting, for example, that geography determines who one's neighbors are, or that the sensation of living in an exiled-but-thriving diaspora tells one more about one's actual homeland than one's imaginary one—that neither pennies nor radios can be "made as England," and that the boy who dreams he gave his teacher an apple, when all he had was an orange, had only found a way to fool himself.

This conclusion—neither entirely diachronic nor comfortably Victorian—has aimed at understanding how Victorian notions of cultural portability could go on shaping people's thoughts and actions long after the material conditions (both economic and imperial) that gave that model its initial vigorous life died away. Lamming's austere refusal to see his work in terms of portable English culture can shed a great deal of light on the ways in which such portability might disappear, and even suggest, like Morris's socialist fantasies, what might be gained when portability's afterlife faded. It is impossible to avoid, though, comparing Lamming's perennially limited readership to the popularity of Naipaul, or Walcott, or the many other West Indian writers who have treated traveling English culture as an inheritance, as a garment to be worn, cast off, or publicly torn. The ongoing dream-life of portability is neither lunacy nor aberration. The terminal quality of Lamming's experiment in antiportability suggests how very portable Victorian portability continues to be.

Notes

PREFACE: GETTING HOLD OF PORTABLE PROPERTY

1. Letter to Charlotte Greville, October 1834, in Emily Eden, *Miss Eden's Letters*, ed. Violet Dickinson (London: Macmillan, 1919), 255, 257.

2. Letter to Lady Campbell, August 1835; letter to Mrs Lister, Oct. 2, 1837, both in ibid., 253, 291.

3. Letter to Mrs Lister, March 24, 1836, in ibid., 267.

4. For hair and photographs, see Geoffrey Batchen, *Forget Me Not: Photography & Remembrance* (New York: Princeton Architectural Press, 2004).

5. Letter to Charlotte Greville, November 13, 1838, in Eden, *Letters*, 305.

6. Lady Campbell to Eden, September 1, 1835, in ibid., 255.

7. Immanuel Maurice Wallerstein, *World-Systems Analysis: An Introduction* (Durham, N.C.: Duke University Press, 2004). The simultaneous centrality of London as financial capital and of the overseas Empire is affirmed by both Arrighi and Bayly, from divergent ideological and methodological standpoints. See Giovanni Arrighi, *The Long Twentieth Century: Money, Power, and the Origins of Our Times* (London: Verso, 1994), and C. A. Bayly, *The Birth of the Modern World, 1780–1914: Global Connections and Comparisons* (Malden: Blackwell, 2004).

8. J. G. A. Pocock has influentially argued against the dominance of a purely economic conception of the social realm in the nineteenth century, discerning "an astonishing unity and solidarity in the uneasiness and mistrust it evinces toward money as the medium of exchange. . . . Those thinkers of the seventeenth through nineteenth centuries who argued on individualist, capitalist or liberal premises that the market economy might benefit and transform human existence appear to be the great creative heretics and dissenters" ("The Mobility of Property and the Rise of Eighteenth-Century Sociology," in *Virtue, Commerce, and History: Essays on Political Thought and History, Chiefly in the Eighteenth Century* [New York: Cambridge University Press, 1985], 103–4). Cf. the discussion of Pocock in Ian Baucom, *Specters of the Atlantic: Finance Capital, Slavery, and the Philosophy of History* (Durham, N.C.: Duke University Press, 2005), 56–79. Catherine Gallagher, *The Body Economic: Life, Death, and Sensation in Political Economy and the Victorian Novel* (Princeton: Princeton University Press, 2005), and Boyd Hilton, *The Age of Atonement: The Influence of Evangelicalism on Social and Economic Thought, 1795–1865* (Oxford: Clarendon, 1988) are two recent accounts of Victorian economic thinking that complicate the relationship between utilitarianism and such other currents of Victorian thought as evangelicalism and Malthusianism.

9. Mary Poovey, *The Financial System in Nineteenth-Century Britain* (New York: Oxford University Press, 2003), 2.

10. Ibid.

11. Richard Mabey, *Gilbert White: A Biography of the Author of the Natural History of Selborne* (London: Century, 1986), 6, quoted in Tobias Menely, "Traveling in Place: Gilbert White's Cosmopolitan Parochialism," *Eighteenth-Century Life* 28, no. 3 (2004): 50; cf. Martha Adams Bohrer, "Tales of Locale: The Natural History of Selborne and Castle Rackrent," *Modern Philology* 100, no. 3 (2003). Despite White's early popularity, however, his emblematic status as a "man of place" begins in the Victorian, not the Romantic era. Menely has recently noted, for example, that an early White biographer "locates the origin of the 'cult of White' in an anonymous review of the republished *Selborne* in the *New Monthly Magazine* of 1830." Menely also argues that Victorian émigrés who wrote local natural histories of their new homes very frequently modeled them upon White's Selborne. Menely, "Traveling," 48, 61.

12. Charles Dickens, *Great Expectations*, ed. Margaret Cardwell (Oxford: Clarendon, 1993), 201.

13. Charles Dickens, *Our Mutual Friend* (New York: Penguin, 1997), 138.

14. Marcia Pointon discusses the value inherent in memorial rings, which are at once intensely personalized (given, usually in a will, so that a friend will mourn for one) and fully commodified (produced by job lot at values ranging from five shillings to ten pounds). Marcia Pointon, "Intriguing Jewellery: Royal Bodies and Luxurious Consumption," *Textual Practice* 11, no. 3 (1997), and "Jewelry in Eighteenth Century England," in *Consumers and Luxury: Consumer Culture in Europe 1650–1850*, ed. Maxine Berg and Helen Clifford (Manchester: Manchester University Press, 1999).

15. Similarly, black mourning suits, Davidoff and Hall report, allowed bereaved men, but not women, to return relatively quickly to their mundane business. Leonore Davidoff and Catherine Hall, *Family Fortunes: Men and Women of the English Middle Class, 1780–1850* (Chicago: University of Chicago Press, 1987).

INTRODUCTION: THE GLOBAL, THE LOCAL, AND THE PORTABLE

1. The genealogy of object obsession dates as far back as Dorothy Bendon Van Ghent, *The English Novel, Form and Function* (New York: Rinehart, 1953); more recent work includes Asa Briggs, *Victorian Things* (London: B. T. Batsford, 1988); Lara Kriegel, "Britain by Design: Industrial Culture, Imperial Display, and the Making of South Kensington, 1835–1872" (Phd. Diss., Johns Hopkins University, 2000); Elaine Freedgood, *The Ideas in Things: Fugitive Meaning in the Victorian Novel* (Chicago: University of Chicago Press, 2006).

2. Deborah Cohen, *Household Gods: The British and Their Possessions* (New Haven: Yale University Press, 2006), esp. x–xvii.

3. Thad Logan, *The Victorian Parlour* (New York: Cambridge University Press, 2001).

4. The word "terrarium" only dates from 1890, but the "Wardian Case" (also called a vivarium or a glass garden) was a popular fixture of Victorian parlors, in which plant or even animal specimens from around the world could be cultivated; "aquarium" was coined in 1854. Cf. Bernd Brunner, *The Ocean at Home: An Illustrated History of the Aquarium* (New York: Princeton Architectural Press,

2005). For beetles, see Julia Charlotte Maitland, *Letters from Madras During the Years 1836–1839*, ed. Alyson Price (Otley: Woodstock, 2003), discussed at greater length in chapter 2, below. Also worth noting are the numerous Victorian pamphlets extolling steam baths, fire extinguishers, bathtubs, gas lights, traction engines, and even, intriguingly, in 1884, *On Portable Railways*. Friedrich Gustav Ernst, *The Portable Gymnasium: A Manual of Exercises, Arranged for Self-Instruction in the Use of the Portable Gymnasium* (London, 1861); John Bartholomew, "The Portable Atlas, Consisting of (Sixteen) Maps" (Edinburgh and Glasgow, 1869); Elizabeth Kent, *Flora Domestica, or the Portable Flower-Garden*, ed. James Henry Leigh Hunt (London: Taylor and Hessey, 1825); and Henri Jomini, *A Portable Atlas for the Use of Those Who Desire to Explore the Fields of Battle of Waterloo and Ligny* (Brussels: H. Gérard, 1851).

5. Respectively: Shakespeare, in Thomas Carlyle, *On Heroes, Hero-Worship, & the Heroic in History*, ed. Michael K. Goldberg, Joel J. Brattin, and Mark Engel (Berkeley: University of California Press, 1993); necklace, in Elizabeth Cleghorn Gaskell, *Cranford*, ed. Patricia Ingham (London: Penguin, 2005); beetles, in Maitland, *Letters*; teapot, in George Eliot, *The Mill on the Floss*, ed. Gordon Sherman Haight (Oxford: Oxford University Press, 1980); moonstone, in Wilkie Collins, *The Moonstone* (Baltimore: Penguin, 1966); shawl, in Emily Eden, *The Semi-Detached House*, in Eden, *The Semi-Attached Couple and the Semi-Detached House* (London: Virago, 1979); chest, in George Eliot, *Daniel Deronda* (Oxford: Oxford University Press, 1988); ruby ring, in Jane Ellen Panton, *Dear Life* (New York: D. Appleton, 1886); and handkerchief, in Margaret Oliphant, *Kirsteen: The Story of a Scotch Family Seventy Years Ago* (London: Dent, 1984).

6. England and Englishness are the operative terms in this book because, although Scottish, Irish, and Welsh versions of Britishness are important, the writers I study (even when resident overseas) identify themselves and are generally identified not as Britons but as Englishmen and women. The topic of English provincialism and its relationship both to Great Britain and Greater Britain is explored throughout the book, but especially at the conclusion of chapter 2 and in chapter 4, below.

7. Cohen, *Household*, xi.

8. Cf. Lynn M. Festa, *Sentimental Figures of Empire in Eighteenth-Century Britain and France* (Baltimore: The Johns Hopkins University Press, 2006).

9. Christopher Flint, "Speaking Objects: The Circulation of Stories in Eighteenth-Century Prose Fiction," *PMLA: Publications of the Modern Language Association of America* 113 (1998). Also see Deidre Lynch *The Economy of Character: Novels, Market Culture, and the Business of Inner Meaning* (Chicago: University of Chicago Press, 1998).

10. Jane Austen, *Emma* (Oxford: Oxford University Press, 2003), 265, emphasis in original.

11. Ibid., 265, 239, 265.

12. Peter Short, *The Psalter or Psalms of Dauid, after the Translation of the Great Bible, Pointed as It Shal Be Said or Sung in Churches: With the Morning & Euening Praier, and Certaine Additions of Collects, and Other the Ordinarie Seruice, Gathered out of the Booke of Common Praier. Also a Briefe Table Declaring*

the True Vse of Euerie Psalme, Made by Master Theod. Beza. Newlie Printed in a Smal and Portable Volume or Manual (London, 1600).

13. The *Oxford English Dictionary* cites a first metaphorical usage from 1655 ("FULLER *Ch. Hist.* VII. i. §31 'These Psalms were therefore translated, to make them more portable in peoples memories'") but it seems to remain uncommon until the early nineteenth century. Other usages now quite common are surprisingly slow to catch on. In 1885 "portable" begins to appear as an abbreviation for "a piece of machinery that is portable; usu. ellipt. for *portable camera, computer, gramophone, radio, typewriter,* etc." And it was only in 1965 that "portable" was used to refer to "rights, privileges, information, etc., capable of being transferred or adapted in changed circumstances."

14. Joseph John Gurney, *Hints on the Portable Evidence of Christianity* (London, 1832), v–vi. In this passage, Gurney (a Quaker reformer and associate of Wilberforce) is quoting Thomas Chalmers.

15. Ibid., 1–2.

16. Cf. Robert Douglas-Fairhurst, *Victorian Afterlives: The Shaping of Influence in Nineteenth-Century Literature* (New York: Oxford University Press, 2002); William Flesch, "Quoting Poetry," *Critical Inquiry* 18, no. 1 (1991). In a discussion of literary quotations linked to particular tourist sites, James Buzard notes the rearrangement or bowdlerizing of Romantic poetry to suit tourism to a particular site. For example, he describes Murray turning Byron's *The Prisoner Of Chillon* into useful locodescription: "[T]his reconstructed Byron pervades Murray's handbooks, well suited to the brief and disconnected emotive-aesthetic responses which tourists sought to display. As the Murray guides grew in authority, their atmospheric Byron became the version of the poet most widely circulated" (*The Beaten Track: European Tourism, Literature, and the Ways to Culture, 1800–1918* [New York: Oxford University Press, 1993], 127). I discuss Emily Eden's extensive use of out-of-context quotation in chapter 2, below.

17. Novels are, however, arguably the receivers of quoted material par excellence, which makes them the logical locus for analysis of how the process of extractive quotation actually works, such as the reading of Emily Eden's *The Semi-Detached House* that I offer in chapter 2, below.

18. Henry James, *Notes and Reviews* (Freeport: Books for Libraries Press, 1968), 167–68, cited in Sally Mitchell, *Dinah Mulock Craik* (Boston: Twayne, 1983).

19. Fielding credits Geoffrey Hartman with inspiring this argument. Penny Fielding, "Burns's Topographies," in *Scotland and the Borders of Romanticism,* ed. Leith Davis, Ian Duncan, and Janet Sorensen (Cambridge: Cambridge University Press, 2004), 174.

20. Brad Evans, *Before Cultures: The Ethnographic Imagination in American Literature, 1865–1920* (Chicago: University of Chicago Press, 2005), 109–51.

21. Richard Daniel Altick, *The English Common Reader: A Social History of the Mass Reading Public, 1800–1900* (Chicago: University of Chicago Press, 1957), 301–2.

22. John Sutherland, *The Stanford Companion to Victorian Fiction* (Stanford: Stanford University Press, 1989), 589–90.

23. Jack Simmons, *The Victorian Railway* (New York: Thames and Hudson, 1991), 247.

24. Bill Bell, "Bound for Australia: Shipboard Reading in the Nineteenth Century," in *Journeys through the Market: Travel, Travellers and the Book Trade*, ed. Robin Myers and Michael Harris (New Castle, Del.: Oak Knoll, 1999), 119–20.

25. Ibid., 138.

26. Cf. also Garrett Stewart, *The Look of Reading: Book, Painting, Text* (Chicago: University of Chicago Press, 2006).

27. Carlyle, *Heroes*, 230.

28. Recent criticism that makes the case for the importance of poetry within the political and ideological debates of the Victorian era often explores the blurring of boundaries between text and reader; however, the poem's own status as a material object seems considerably less at issue than is the case for Victorian novels. That is, there appears to be a critical consensus that poetry is germane to the series of debates about the interplay between public and private, domestic and political, and that it is useful to see poetry as mediating relations between individual experience and national identity: cf. Isobel Armstrong, *Victorian Poetry: Poetry, Poetics, and Politics* (London: Routledge, 1993); Matthew Reynolds, *The Realms of Verse, 1830–1870: English Poetry in a Time of Nation-Building* (New York: Oxford University Press, 2001). By the same token, when Stephanie Kuduk Weiner traces a genealogy of Republican poetry through the period, she justifies an intriguing combination of historical and formal analysis by arguing that "poetry's contribution to Republican politics inhered not so much in advancing its arguments as in the intellectual and imaginative negotiation that took place in poetry, at particular moments in time, between political ideas and poetic forms" (*Republican Politics and English Poetry, 1789–1874* [New York: Palgrave, 2005], 178). Diverse as they are in approach, all three books share the assumption that poets and readers understand the importance of poetry to be located between poetic form and political ideology: between, that is, the poem's status as a sign-system in its own right and its place in a larger political sign-system. Around the Victorian novel, I am arguing by contrast, there rages a fierce, ongoing debate about whether novels exist as tangible, material objects, or whether their life is entirely suspended in a widely disseminated readership (as James puts it, "in a million innocent breasts").

29. See, however, Leah Price, "Reader's Block: Response," *Victorian Studies: An Interdisciplinary Journal of Social, Political, and Cultural Studies* 46, no. 2 (2004), for a subtle and far-reaching account of how books, journals, and newspapers took on a separate Victorian life as material props for forestalling various kinds of social interaction.

30. Eliot, *Mill*, 178.

31. "[Maggie] kept a Fetish which she punished for all her misfortunes. This was the trunk of a large wooden doll, which once stared with the roundest of eyes above the reddest of cheeks; but was now entirely defaced by a long career of vicarious suffering. Three nails driven into the head commemorated as many crises in Maggie's nine years of earthly struggle; that luxury of vengeance having been suggested to her by the picture of Jael destroying Sisera in the old Bible" (ibid., 25, 24–25).

32. Ibid., 186–87.

33. My thanks to Nicola Nixon for comments on this issue apropos of an earlier version of this chapter.

34. Catherine Gallagher, in *The Body Economic*, has recently described Eliot's relationship to economic thinking as partially shaped by her desire to establish that her own (female, writerly) genius lay in a kind of willed suspension of the self. By this reading, Eliot's interest in the unappealing, primitively selfish attachment to writing that Mrs Tulliver retains might help us see her as a kind of antitype to the sort of portable cultural value Eliot thinks may be achieved with her own self-effacement, including the replacement of Mary Ann Evans with "George Eliot."

35. Cf. Catherine Gallagher, "George Eliot and Daniel Deronda: The Prostitute and the Jewish Question," in *Sex, Politics, and Science in the Nineteenth-Century Novel*, ed. Ruth Bernard Yeazell (Baltimore: The Johns Hopkins University Press, 1986).

36. Miller argues that "Gaskell resists understanding material culture as the instigator of unsettling appetites and, simultaneously, works to represent female subjectivity as open and flexible rather than insular, fungible, and threatened. . . . Material culture does not, finally, 'hold' either Gaskell or the inhabitants of Cranford . . . [and its] episodic experience encourages episodic narratives." He insightfully relates Gaskell's interest in flexibility and recuperative (if often fragmentary) storytelling to De Certeau's notion of an "art of the weak." Andrew H. Miller, *Novels Behind Glass: Commodity, Culture, and Victorian Narrative* (New York: Cambridge University Press, 1995), 92, 93, 98, 105.

37. Gaskell, *Cranford*, 206.

38. Hilary M. Schor has rightly drawn attention to the masculinizing of Johnson and the implicit feminizing of the novel, and of Dickens as novelist, in this structure. Here, the crux of the gendering of this comparison is temporal—eighteenth-century essays and open-ended address (male) give way to the delightful (female) inwardness of "Household Words." Cf. Hilary Margo Schor, *Scheherezade in the Marketplace: Elizabeth Gaskell and the Victorian Novel* (New York: Oxford University Press, 1992). On the Victorian refusal of eighteenth-century notions of general or impersonal verisimilitude, see Lorraine Daston and Peter Galison, "The Image of Objectivity," *Representations* 40 (1992).

39. Cf. Jon P. Klancher, *The Making of English Reading Audiences, 1790–1832* (Madison: University of Wisconsin Press, 1987).

40. Benedict Anderson, *Imagined Communities: Reflections on the Origin and Spread of Nationalism*, rev. and exp. ed. (London: Verso, 1991), 62, 87, and 163–86.

41. Eliot, *Daniel Deronda*, 618, 620.

42. These portable properties serve as the receptacle neither for misplaced psychic energy (Freud) nor for misrecognized labor power (Marx). Elaine Freedgood has recently argued that "commodity culture" both was preceded and "survived by what I call a Victorian 'thing culture': a more extravagant form of object relations than ours." Freedgood's work is offered as a corrective to a merely commodified (and hence flattening) reading of "things" in Victorian novels: a reading initiated, she argues, by the eagerness of novelists themselves to erase certain

embarrassing traces that adhere to the objects in their novels. Although we approach the task very differently, I share her wish to bring back into view a distinctively Victorian way of understanding what it might mean to be attached, or overly attached, to objects for reasons unrelated to their status as commodities. See Freedgood, *Ideas*, 8. For a different approach, see Bill Brown, *A Sense of Things: The Object Matter of American Literature* (Chicago: University of Chicago Press, 2003).

43. Elisabeth Jay has recently called *Kirsteen* "a novel which enjoys high repute." Recent critical work includes Young's argument that in *Kirsteen* "needlework as paid employment—conventionally constructed as the means of women's economic enslavement in the nineteenth century—emerges as a means to articulate the possibilities of a woman's vocational commitment;" Heilmann, however, accuses Oliphant of depicting a needlework sweatshop as if it were a domestic idyll, while Peterson argues that *Kirsteen* "appropriates male forms of action for her heroines." See Elisabeth Jay, *Mrs. Oliphant, "A Fiction to Herself": A Literary Life* (New York: Oxford University Press, 1995), 196; Arlene Young, "Workers' Compensations: (Needle)Work and Ideals of Femininity in Margaret Oliphant's *Kirsteen*," in *Famine and Fashion: Needlewomen in the Nineteenth Century*, ed. Beth Harris (Aldershot: Ashgate, 2005); Ann Heilmann, "Mrs Grundy's Rebellion: Margaret Oliphant between Orthodoxy and the New Woman," *Women's Writing* 6, no. 2 (1999); Linda Peterson, "The Female Bildungsroman: Tradition and Revision in Oliphant's Fiction," in *Margaret Oliphant: Critical Essays on a Gentle Subversive*, ed. D. J. Trela (Selinsgrove, Pa.: Susquehanna University Press, 1995). I am grateful to Leah Price for directing me to the novel initially.

44. Margaret Oliphant, *Kirsteen: The Story of a Scotch Family Seventy Years Ago* (London: Dent, 1984), 19.

45. Ibid., 109.

46. In J. M Barrie's 1889 *A Window in Thrums*—a novel in which garments are often named after their price in shillings—a more mawkish version of the same overlay recurs. A son returned from London to the Scottish hinterland presents his mother with a crumpled five-pound note as the ultimate index of his love: "I do not know the history of that five-pound note, but well aware I am that it grew slowly out of pence and silver, and that Jamie denied his passions many things for this great hour. His sacrifices watered his young heart and kept it fresh and tender. Let us no longer cheat our consciences by talking of filthy lucre. Money may always be a beautiful thing. It is we who make it grimy" (*A Window in Thrums* [Edinburgh: Saltire Society, 2005 (1889)], 44, 90).

47. Cf. Robert J. Foster, "Making National Cultures in the Global Ecumene," *Annual Review of Anthropology* 20 (1991): 236–37.

48. Annette B. Weiner, *Inalienable Possessions: The Paradox of Keeping-While-Giving* (Berkeley: University of California Press, 1992), 6.

49. Maurice Godelier, *The Enigma of the Gift* (Chicago: University of Chicago Press, 1999), 36, emphasis in original.

50. Elizabeth Emma Ferry, "Inalienable Commodities: The Production and Circulation of Silver and Patrimony in a Mexican Mining Cooperative," *Cultural Anthropology* 17, no. 3 (2002).

51. Nancy Munn, a quarter-century ago, made a similar case for viewing objects caught up in gift exchange as nonetheless simultaneously endowed with an unchangeable essence attached to original maker. For example, "The canoe that has disappeared southward has been converted into an object that ideally can both travel away from Gawa forever, and—as a permanent possession—always return home. This capacity is in fact predicated on the power of possession, since a man's special control over his *kitomu* is what makes it infinitely reproducible in exchange" ("Spatiotemporal Transformations of Gawa Canoes," *Journal de la Societe des Oceanistes* [1977]: 46).

52. For example, C. A. Bayly sharply distinguishes between worldwide capital flow/political domination, on one hand, and geographically demarcated spaces, on the other. That sharp distinction, though, impoverishes his explanation of the ways in which "rapidly developing connections between different human societies during the nineteenth century created many hybrid polities [while also engendering] antagonism, between people in different societies, and especially between their elites." My claim is that by the logic of portable cultures, such ironies are not only feasible but almost inevitable. See Bayly, *Birth*, 2, 1.

53. Arjun Appadurai, "The Thing Itself," *Public Culture* 18, no. 1 (2006): 17, 19.

54. Ibid., 21.

55. Ibid.

56. Cf. Susan Stewart, *On Longing: Narratives of the Miniature, the Gigantic, the Souvenir, the Collection* (Baltimore: The Johns Hopkins University Press, 1984); Lewis Hyde, *The Gift: Imagination and the Erotic Life of Property* (New York: Vintage, 1983); as well as in the seminal collection, *The Social Life of Things: Commodities in Cultural Perspective*, ed. Arjun Appadurai (Cambridge: Cambridge University Press, 1986).

57. And yet, the imaginary showdown between moveable consumers and rooted locals flourishes. Zygmunt Baumann's generally nuanced work on the sociology of development deploys the unwieldy portmanteau word "glocalization" in order to conjure up a world dominated, as he sees it, by globe-trotting cosmopolites and impoverished Third-World stay-at-homes. "Glocalization," Bauman writes, "polarizes mobility—that ability to use time to annul the limitation of space. That ability—or disability—divides the world into the globalized and the localized." By Bauman's odd account, the poor are always in one place, whereas the wealthy inhabit interchangeable spaces all over the globe. See Zygmunt Baumann, "Globalization and the New Poor," in *The Baumann Reader*, ed. Peter Beilharz (Malden: Blackwell, 2001), 307. Nor are Benjamin Barber (*Jihad vs. McWorld*) and Thomas Friedman (*The Lexus and the Olive Tree*) the only popularizers to pose Manichaean choices between a global (often shallowly materialistic) culture and purely autochthonous ones, which draw their strength from their rootedness and blind attachment to the past. See Benjamin R. Barber, *Jihad vs. McWorld* (New York: Times Books, 1995), and Thomas L. Friedman, *The Lexus and the Olive Tree* (New York: Farrar, Straus, Giroux, 1999). Recent work exploring the conceptual problems with this kind of division includes Bill Maurer and Gabriele Schwab, eds., *Accelerating Possession: Global Futures of Property and Personhood* (New York: Columbia University Press, 2006).

58. Gauri Viswanathan, *Masks of Conquest: Literary Study and British Rule in India* (New York: Columbia University Press, 1989), 3. The key texts on this phenomenon, Viswanathan's book and Crawford's edited collection, are not always in perfect accord: for example, Robert Crawford accuses Viswanathan of being "quite unaware of the developments in literary teaching in the Scottish universities" in the late eighteenth century. Issues of Indian or Scottish primacy aside, however, Crawford largely agrees with Viswanathan's approach: "As the chapters of this present book indicate, the university teaching of literary texts written in English has been bound up with issues of colonialism (both internal and external) from its origins in eighteenth-century Scotland, and in its subsequent exporting abroad, and it continues to be so" (Robert Crawford, *The Scottish Invention of English Literature* [Cambridge: Cambridge University Press, 1998], 16, 17).

59. Another alternative to the sequestration I am examining was presented by English Christian missionary activity among the colonies, often understood as directly in conflict with both the colonial state and with English business interests; this topic is powerfully explored, for example, in Catherine Hall, *Civilising Subjects: Metropole and Colony in the English Imagination, 1830–1867* (Cambridge, Mass.: Polity, 2002).

60. Cf. Judith Plotz's discussion of "The Jane Function" in Emily Eden, and in Rudyard Kipling's "The Janeites." See Judith Plotz, "Jane Austen Goes to India: Emily Eden's Semi-Detached Home Thoughts from Abroad," in *The Postcolonial Jane Austen* (London: Routledge, 2000), and Rudyard Kipling, "The Janeites," in *Debits and Credits* (Garden City, N.Y.: Doubleday, Page, 1926).

61. Flora Annie Webster Steel, *On the Face of the Waters* (Rahway, N.J.: Mershon, 1896); Harriet Tytler, *An Englishwoman in India: The Memoirs of Harriet Tytler 1828–1858*, ed. Anthony Sattin (Oxford: Oxford University Press, 1986), 14.

62. Anderson, *Imagined*; Benedict Anderson, "Exodus," *Critical Inquiry* 20, no. 2 (1994). The attempt to understand the true lineaments of domestic Englishness by studying what happens when it is projected upon an overseas "New England" stretches as far back as the 1790s at least. As Will Verhoeven has recently argued—in a reading of Imlay's *The Emigrants* and an anonymous reactionary novel written in response, *Berkeley Hall*— "[T]he struggle over England's future ideological space was conducted in the shape of a debate over a geographically and temporally displaced English countryside," whereby "both radicals and conservatives project[ed] England's 'green and pleasant land' on to the map of contemporary America" ("'Some Corner of a Foreign Field That Is Forever England': The Transatlantic Construction of the Anglo-American Landscape," in *Green and Pleasant Land*, ed. Amanda Gilroy [Leuven: Peeters, 2004], 157).

63. Linda Colley, *Britons: Forging the Nation, 1707–1837* (New Haven: Yale University Press, 1992); David Armitage, *The Ideological Origins of the British Empire* (New York: Cambridge University Press, 2000); Katie Trumpener, *Bardic Nationalism: The Romantic Novel and the British Empire* (Princeton: Princeton University Press, 1997), esp. "The Abbotsford Guide to India," 242–92.

64. Pierre Lanfranchi and Matthew Taylor, *Moving with the Ball: The Migration of Professional Footballers* (Oxford: Berg, 2001).

65. A recent comparison of baseball and football (here as elsewhere in the book I use the globally accepted term "football" to denote the sport known in the

United States as "soccer") suggests that the latter's spread was precisely predi-cated on the English losing key matches early and often; by contrast, American dominance at baseball (for example, pummeling the Swedish team, 13–3, in an Olympic exhibition match in 1912) helped keep baseball from spreading. See Ste-fan Szymanski and Andrew S. Zimbalist, *National Pastime: How Americans Play Baseball and the Rest of the World Plays Soccer* (Washington, D.C.: Brookings Institution Press, 2005).

66. Alan Black bemoans the fact that Scotland is remembered each year with National Tartan Day, but that the Scottish contribution to "roads, bridges, penicil-lin, the TV and the telephone" is forgotten. By Black's account, tartan has re-mained unpopular enough—except among Scots—for its national character to be recalled. But Fleming's antibiotic and Bell's talking machine are popular enough to have entirely slipped the bounds of affiliation. See Alan Black, "Scotland the Grave," Salon.com, April 6, (2006), available online at http://salon.com/opinion/feature/2006/04/06/scotland/.

67. It is possible to find instances of the English doing just that, glorying in what no one else could possibly love about their country. See, for instance, a very popular and yet accurately titled gift book, filled with images of motorways, rest stops, and chemical plants in dreary scrubland: Martin Parr, *Boring Postcards* (London: Phaidon, 1999).

68. Although Appadurai's account of imperial cultural legacies offers two rather than three ways of understanding colonial export (that is, it omits the porta-bility I am locating in cricket, and calls it, like football, a "soft" cultural form), the analysis I am offering here both responds to and is informed by Arjun Appadurai, *Modernity at Large: Cultural Dimensions of Globalization* (Minneapolis: Univer-sity of Minnesota Press, 1996), 90 et seq.

69. Carlyle, *Heroes*, 113.

70. Cf. Cyril Lionel Robert James, *Beyond a Boundary* (London: Hutchinson, 1963), 255, and Nirad C. Chaudhuri, *The Autobiography of an Unknown Indian* (New York: Macmillan, 1951). Cricket became somewhat less markedly English in the twentieth century. A few have even made the case than in the late twentieth century the sport becomes much less English: for example, a former Jamaican prime minister's effort to reinvent cricket as a counterpart to baseball that princi-pally showcases West Indian "individuality . . . [and] free moving, free-striking, lithe athleticism," and owes only a very small debt to British colonizers who were, in any event, less oppressors than they were "exemplars of modern values appro-priate to the Industrial Revolution" (Michael Manley, *A History of West Indies Cricket* [London: Deutsch, 1988], 13, 381–83, 319). Most commentators seem to agree, though, that cricket's colonial residue lingered far longer than football's; an engaging account of what factors determined the diffusion (that is "transmis-sion, adoption, and eventual acculturation of an innovation by a recipient popula-tion" [83]) of cricket into various English-ruled countries is offered in Jason Kauf-man and Orlando Patterson, "Cross-National Cultural Diffusion: The Global Spread of Cricket," *American Sociological Review* 70, no. 1 (2005). Acute as Patterson and Kaufman's analysis of comparative diffusion rates is, their study's interest in diffusion, with success defined by a nation's taking up the sport (the choice they pose in the opening sentence is a simple binary, "Why do some foreign

practices take root while others arrive dead in the water or take hold only to wither and die?" [82]) means that to some extent they neglect what seems to me a crucial distinction between those traveling sports which shed their initial national residue (such as football) and those that, like cricket, travel with strong associations to their country of origin intact.

The counterexample to cricket's durable Englishness is the massively altered version played in the Trobriand Islands, documented in Jerry Leach's film *Trobriand Cricket: An Ingenious Response to Colonialism* (1979). But Trobriand cricket makes such a good film topic precisely because of how the syncretic Trobriand game differs from the remarkably durable homogeneity of cricket everywhere else in the world.

71. James Buzard, *Disorienting Fiction: The Autoethnographic Work of Nineteenth-Century British Novels* (Princeton: Princeton University Press, 2005), esp. 1–70.

72. That is indeed what Dilke optimistically hoped would occur—but only in the United States. I analyze both Dilke and Acton's account of this expansion of Englishness overseas in the conclusion to chapter 2.

73. Evans, *Before*, 65–68. Like Buzard, Evans is building on important earlier work by Stocking and Herbert: George W. Stocking, *Victorian Anthropology* (New York: Free Press, 1987), and Christopher Herbert, *Culture and Anomie: Ethnographic Imagination in the Nineteenth Century* (Chicago: University of Chicago Press, 1991).

74. Evans, *Before*, 194–95.

75. Cf. Ian Baucom, *Out of Place: Englishness, Empire, and the Locations of Identity* (Princeton: Princeton University Press, 1999).

76. I am interested in the ways in which portability endows novels with a curious durability that makes them surprisingly resistant to translation outside the Greater British context. My project is accordingly distinct from—but by no means opposed to—the wide range of impressive recent work that aims to treat crucial historical events or documents as "global phenomen[a]" and to map the "global afterlives" of such events or documents. See David Armitage, *The Declaration of Independence: A Global History* (Cambridge, Mass.: Harvard University Press, 2007), 4, 139.

77. J. R. Seeley, *Expansion of England* (London: Macmillan, 1883), 9.

78. Ibid., 9, 8. See also Armitage, *Ideological*, and idem., "Greater Britain: A Useful Category of Historical Analysis?," *American Historical Review* 104, no. 2 (1999). Porter has recently studied "how uneven, complex, and changeable the relationship between Britons and their empire was" and argues that "imperial Britain was generally a *less* imperial society than is often assumed" (Bernard Porter, *The Absent-Minded Imperialists: Empire, Society, and Culture in Britain* [New York: Oxford University Press, 2004], xv).

79. E. M. Collingham, *Imperial Bodies: The Physical Experience of the Raj, 1800–1947* (Cambridge, Mass.: Polity, 2001), 69; cf. my extended discussion in chapter 2, below.

80. A great deal of important work on the question of whether such trade flows are also available for cultural traffic is contained within the multigenerational debate (including seminal accounts by Max Weber and Georg Lukács) that parses

Marx's claim that "all that is solid melts into air." Recent memorable explorations the relationship between commodity and fetish (work asking, among other things, whether the commodity itself is indeed a fetish formation), include William Pietz, "The Problem of the Fetish [Parts 1, 2, and 3]," *Res: Journal of Anthropology and Aesthetics* 9, 13, 16 (1985, 1987, 1988), and Yoon Sun Lee, *Nationalism and Irony: Burke, Scott, Carlyle* (New York: Oxford University Press, 2004).

81. Nicholas Daly, for example, notes that "the mummy story emplots the new relations of subjects and commodities, articulating the connections between the national economy and its less visible imperial extensions, and so providing a sort of narrativized commodity theory" "That Obscure Object of Desire: Victorian Commodity Culture and Fictions of the Mummy," *Novel: A Forum on Fiction* 28, no. 1 (1994): 26. Cf. Tom Flynn and T. J. Barringer, eds., *Colonialism and the Object: Empire, Material Culture, and the Museum* (New York: Routledge, 1998); and Annie E. Coombes, *Reinventing Africa: Museums, Material Culture, and Popular Imagination in Late Victorian and Edwardian England* (New Haven: Yale University Press, 1994).

82. While little discussed with regards to mid-Victorian writing, this phenomenon has been analyzed in fin-de-siècle texts: Stephen D. Arata, for instance, sees *Dracula* exemplifying "the period's [1880–1900] most important and pervasive narrative of decline, a narrative of reverse colonization"; he finds similar reversals in Haggard, Doyle, Wells, and "the numerous adventure novels of G. A. Hope, Henry S. Merriman, and John Buchan" ("The Occidental Tourist: Dracula and the Anxiety of Reverse Colonization," *Victorian Studies: A Journal of the Humanities, Arts and Sciences* 33, no. 4 [1990]: 623).

83. Nupur Chaudhuri has argued that Anglo-Indian "memsahibs" were an important vector for bringing redolent items back to India: Nupur Chaudhuri, "Shawls, Jewelry, Curry, and Rice in Victorian Britain," in *Western Women and Imperialism: Complicity and Resistance*, ed. Nupur Chaudhuri and Margaret Strobel (Bloomington: Indiana University Press, 1992). I am grateful to Shayna Skarf for bringing this article to my attention. See my further discussion in chapter 2, below. Cf. also Jordanna Bailkin, "Indian Yellow: Making and Breaking the Imperial Palette," *Journal of Material Culture* 10, no. 2 (2005).

84. Charles Wentworth Dilke, *Greater Britain: A Record of Travel in English-Speaking Countries During 1866 and 1867* (London: Macmillan, 1869), 512.

85. "The English fly is the best possible fly of the whole world, and will naturally beat down and exterminate, or else starve out, the merely provincial Maori fly" (ibid., 275). See my further discussion of Dilke in chapter 2, below.

86. Examples of the imperial residue that is associated with canonical British literature in the postcolonial world could be multiplied almost endlessly—for example, in Derek Walcott, V. S. Naipaul, C. L. R. James, or Nirad Chaudhuri. In the conclusion, I examine what that exportability of English literary culture looks like from a colonial perspective, and explore the ways in which postcolonial writers like Barbadian George Lamming reject the most basic premises of imperial portability, exploring in its place a kind of deterritorialized imaginative capacity that neither mimics nor mirrors the colonial legacy.

87. Philip Fisher, "Local Meanings and Portable Objects: National Collections, Literatures, Music, and Architecture," in *The Formation of National Collections*

of Art and Archaeology, ed. Gwendolyn Wright (Washington, D.C.: National Gallery of Art, 1996).

88. See Catherine Hall, *White, Male, and Middle-Class: Explorations in Feminism and History* (New York: Routledge, 1992), and Anthony Appiah, *In My Father's House: Africa in the Philosophy of Culture* (New York: Oxford University Press, 1992). See also the discussion of how cultural portability might evolve into a form of racial identity in *Daniel Deronda* in chapter 4, below.

89. Isabel Hofmeyr has recently described the "Englishing" of John Bunyan, showing that in the early twentieth century he no longer appeared, as he had for centuries, a universal evangelizer whose text was at home anywhere, but rather as representative of his own small corner of England. Isabel Hofmeyr, *The Portable Bunyan: A Transnational History of the* Pilgrim's Progress (Princeton: Princeton University Press, 2004).

90. In "The Political Economy of Reading" (and in his recent book *The Reading Nation in the Romantic Period*) William St Clair has made the case against "exclusively text-based approaches" to understanding how ideas permeate and define a culture. He argues for the study of publication and distribution information so as to discover when books were narrowly read, widely read, and not read at all. He hopes that this will help us to "conceive of past culture not as a parade or as a parliament but as a dynamic system with many interacting agents, into which the writing, publication, and subsequent reading of a text were interventions that had consequences. . . . [T]he engagement between competing texts occurred mainly in the minds of readers" ("The Political Economy of Reading," *John Coffin Memorial Lecture in the History of the Book* [2005], available online at http://ies.sas.ac.uk/publications/johncoffin/stclair.pdf).

CHAPTER ONE: DISCREET JEWELS: VICTORIAN DIAMOND NARRATIVES AND THE PROBLEM OF SENTIMENTAL VALUE

1. Recent contributions to this nascent field by Daniel Tiffany, Simon Schaeffer, Joseph Koerner, Charity Scribner, Peter Galison, and others are collected in Bill Brown, ed., *Things* (Chicago: University Of Chicago Press, 2004), and in Lorraine Daston, ed., *Things That Talk: Object Lessons from Art and Science* (New York: Zone, 2004). The following five sentences are a reworking of material originally published in John Plotz, "Can the Sofa Speak? A Look at Thing Theory," *Criticism* 47, no. 1 (2005).

2. Phil Harris's chart-topping 1950 song about an unnamable horror (indicated only by an ominous drumming: "Get out of here with that—RAT-TAT-TAT—and don't come back no more") was called "The Thing" for good reason; "thingamagummy" and "thingamabob" also testify to the word's inherent amorphousness.

3. Thing theory, then, is not a theory about the cultural significance of *objects*. There is no shortage of social scientific methods for appraising objects (or even "property") as they circulate inside a society. Anthropological discourse has systematically analyzed the eloquent signifiers by which a culture makes itself known to itself, ever since Bronislaw Malinowski's accounts of "ka" exchange in the

Pacific Islands—Nicholas Thomas, Marilyn Strathern, and Maurice Godelier being among the prime exporters of "gift theory" to scholars in other disciplines. Such work, however, generally hears objects saying nothing that the ambient culture has not carefully instilled. Clifford Geertz sees no slippage, and no divergence of opinions, when he pins down, for example, a cock's poetic associations in his memorable article on "Deep Play." See Bronislaw Malinowski, *Argonauts of the Western Pacific* (London: G. Routledge and Sons, 1922); Marcel Mauss, *The Gift: Forms and Functions of Exchange in Archaic Societies*, trans. Ian Cunnison (Glencoe, Ill.: Free Press, 1954); Godelier, *Enigma* ; Nicholas Thomas, *Entangled Objects: Exchange, Material Culture, and Colonialism in the Pacific* (Cambridge, Mass.: Harvard University Press, 1991); Marilyn Strathern, *The Gender of the Gift: Problems with Women and Problems with Society in Melanesia* (Berkeley: University of California Press, 1988); and "Deep Play: Notes on the Balinese Cockfight" in Clifford Geertz, *The Interpretation of Cultures: Selected Essays* (New York: Basic, 1973).

4. Peter Galison, "Images of Self," in *Things That Talk: Object Lessons from Art and Acience*, ed. Lorraine Daston (New York: Zone, 2004), 271, emphasis in original.

5. Ibid.

6. Georg Simmel, "Adornment," in *The Sociology of Georg Simmel*, ed. and trans. Kurt H. Wolff (Glencoe, Ill.: Free Press, 1950 [1908]).

7. The passage continues: "Metal Jewelry . . . is always new; in untouchable coolness, it stands above the singularity and destiny of its wearer. . . . Style is always something general. It brings the contents of personal life and activity into a form shared by many and accessible to many" (ibid., 340–41).

8. Van Ghent, *English*; on speaking puddings, see Kriegel, "Britain."

9. Cohen, *Household*, xi, xvii.

10. The next four sentences are also adapted from Plotz, "Can the Sofa Speak."

11. Geoffrey Batchen, "Ere the Substance Fade: Photography and Hair Jewelry," in *Photographs Objects Histories: On the Materiality of Images*, ed. Elizabeth Edwards and Janice Hart (New York: Routledge, 2005), 34.

12. Batchen argues that these hairy photos are crux points where the weakness of the guarantees of Truth show through and hence sites where people are forced to redescribe what it is they are looking for in an art "object." Batchen might be right to emphasize the "deconstructive" force of these hybrid image/substances, but it also seems crucial to stress the sheer ordinariness of this practice, its unproblematic relationship at the time to other mundanely realistic forms of representation. See Batchen, *Forget*, 73–76.

13. Charles Johnston, *Chrysal: Or, the Adventures of a Guinea* (London: T. Cadell, 1794).

14. Cf. the essays collected in Mark Blackwell, ed., *The Secret Life of Things: Animals, Objects, and It-Narratives in Eighteenth-Century England* (Lewisburg, Maine: Bucknell University Press, 2007).

15. Adam Smith, *The Theory of Moral Sentiments*, ed. Knud Haakonssen, Cambridge Texts in the History of Philosophy (New York: Cambridge University Press, 2002).

16. Cynthia Wall, "The Rhetoric of Description and the Spaces of Things," in *Eighteenth-Century Genre and Culture*, ed. Dennis Todd and Cynthia Wall (Newark: University of Delaware Press, 2001), 261.

17. For example, Christopher Flint observes that "[m]oney tales, then, are particularly emblematic of eighteenth-century literary attitudes about publishing: they fuse linguistic and material exchange" ("Speaking," 220). Cf. the important accounts of eighteenth-century object-narratives in Lynch, *Economy*, and in Festa, *Sentimental*.

18. Peregrine Oakley, *Aureus: Or, the Life and Opinions of a Sovereign* (London: G. Wightman, 1824), v.

19. Object narratives about purely economic, purely fungible objects do persist into the nineteenth century, but only as pointedly didactic occasional pieces, like an 1851 squib from *Household Words*; see Sydney Laman Blanchard, "A Biography of a Bad Shilling," in *The Financial System in Nineteenth-Century Britain*, ed. Mary Poovey (New York: Oxford University Press, 2003).

20. The book was also published under the title *The Wonder of Common Things*. Annie Carey, *Autobiographies of a Lump of Coal; a Grain of Salt; a Drop of Water; a Bit of Old Iron; a Piece of Flint* (London: Cassell, Petter and Galpin, 1870), 104.

21. Arthur Conan Doyle, "The Adventure of the Blue Carbuncle," in *Victorian Tales of Mystery and Detection*, ed. Michael Cox (New York: Oxford University Press, 1992), 202.

22. Ruskin's account of how the eyesight of the lace-makers of Bruges is converted into adornment for the noble is exceptionally gruesome, as is his account of the nervous system of the glass-makers of Murano, destroyed in exchange for baubles: "Glass beads are utterly unnecessary, and there is no design or thought employed in their manufacture. . . . The men who chop up the rods sit at their work all day, their hands vibrating with a perpetual and exquisitely timed palsy, and the beads dropping beneath their vibration like hail. . . . Every young lady, therefore, who buys glass beads is engaged in the slave-trade" (John Ruskin, "The Nature of Gothic," in *The Works of John Ruskin*, ed. Edward Cook and Alexander Wedderburn [London: G. Allen, 1904], 197). Joseph Conrad's *Victory* (1915), too, opens by remarking upon that "deplorable lack of concentration in coal. Now, if a coal-mine could be put into one's waistcoat pocket—but it can't!" (*Victory* [New York: Doubleday, Page, 1924], 3).

23. Many thanks to Jordanna Bailkin for the reference.

24. Christina Rossetti, "Hero," in *Victorian Love Stories: An Oxford Anthology*, ed. Kate Flint (New York: Oxford University Press, 1996), 141.

25. Ibid., 143.

26. Consider, for example, a wedding present imperiously requested in *The Eustace Diamonds*, with an eye to its ready resale: a "thirty-guinea ring" (Trollope, *Eustace Diamonds*, 306).

27. A more complete version of this chapter would ideally spend some time with the curious diamond pin that, thrown by Rawdon, "cut him [Becky's lover Steyne] on his bald forehead," leaving a scar that he wore "to his dying day." That diamond-scar daily reminds Steyne of the humiliation of the Becky affair, ensuring that Lord Steyne will attempt to destroy Becky if he sees her again. The

moment in which the diamond pin cuts Steyne thus marks a radical break from the usual economy of *Vanity Fair*, for it allows objects and bodies to interact in a way that money never had (even wrapped in Becky's clothes) and that Amelia's two fetish images of her husband (his portrait, that is, and also his son) never could. Indeed, Rawdon likes what this pin can do when turned from symbol into weapon so well that he conceives the idea of returning to Steyne a £1000 note (he believes Steyne used it to pay Becky for their affair) wrapped around the bullet he means to kill him with. See William Makepeace Thackeray, *Vanity Fair*, ed. Nicholas Dames (New York: Barnes and Noble, 2003), 525, 531.

28. "We had supposed that in Lady Eustace we were to have Mr Trollope's equivalent for Thackeray's 'Becky Sharp'"; review of Anthony Trollope, *The Eustace Diamonds*, *Spectator*, October 26, 1872, 1365.

29. Trollope, *Eustace Diamonds*, 689.

30. Ibid., 590.

31. Ibid., 686.

32. Ibid., 520.

33. See Lee Holcombe, *Wives and Property: Reform of the Married Women's Property Law in Nineteenth-Century England* (Toronto: University of Toronto Press, 1983), for an account of the four sorts of property treated in the various Married Women's Property Acts.

34. Trollope, *Eustace Diamonds*, 695.

35. Ibid.

36. D. A. Miller, *The Novel and the Police* (Berkeley: University of California Press, 1988), 114.

37. Trollope, *Eustace Diamonds*, 63.

38. Ibid., 64.

39. Ibid., 753.

40. My reading of Trollope's relationship to such adhesive objects is consonant with Lauren Goodlad's recent argument (in her forthcoming *Victorian Internationalisms: Literary Encounters with "The South"*) that "Trollope's notion of the heirloom thus describes a form of property that accumulates particular ethical and cultural worth in excess of abstract economic value and, in so doing, binds rather than atomizes."

41. Gallagher, *Body*, 89–90.

42. Ibid., 123–24.

43. On the question of Mill's own thinking about classical economics and what later modifications to it were entailed by his political philosophy, see (infra alia) Donald Winch, *Riches and Poverty: An Intellectual History of Political Economy in Britain, 1750–1834* (Cambridge: Cambridge University Press, 1996), 409–22, which also contains a suggestive analysis of "the underlying *cultural* reasons for the long history of misunderstanding [of classical economics generally] which began with the romantic attack on Malthus" (419).

44. Gallagher, *Body*, 118–29.

45. Cf. Kathy Alexis Psomiades's wide-ranging and fascinating ,"Heterosexual Exchange and Other Victorian Fictions: *The Eustace Diamonds* and Victorian Anthropology," *Novel: A Forum on Fiction* 33 (1999).

46. Sharon Marcus, *Between Women: Friendship, Desire, and Marriage in Victorian England* (Princeton: Princeton University Press, 2007), illuminates the Victorian novel's interest in representing (proper) female friendship as an aid and catalyst to marriage, rather than an impediment. My argument is that Lucinda's passionate attachment to her aunt is not represented as a dangerous *substitute* to her marrying a man, but rather as a pathological state that will eventually destroy even her homosocial attachment to her aunt.

47. Trollope, *Eustace Diamonds*, 62.

48. Ibid., 133.

49. Ibid., 224.

50. Ibid., 222.

51. Ibid., 223. Marcia Pointon's account of the royal diamonds of Queen Charlotte stresses the double role that diamonds can play: in highlighting the beauty of a young female body (and marking a young woman's agency in refusing traffic in that body), or in contrasting, unfavorably, with her fading beauty as she ages. Marcia Pointon, "Intriguing Jewellery; Royal Bodies and Luxurious Consumption," *Textual Practice* 11, no. 3 (1997): 510–12.

52. Anthony Trollope, *An Autobiography*, ed. Bradford Allen Booth (Berkeley: University of California Press, 1947), 287.

53. Ibid., 276.

54. Nicholas Dames kindly reminded me of this passage.

55. Anthony Trollope, *Can You Forgive Her?* (New York: Oxford University Press, 1973), 2:59.

56. Ibid., 2:63.

57. Ibid.

58. Karl Marx, "Capital: Volume 1," in *Capital: An Abridged Edition*, ed. David McLellan (Oxford: Oxford University Press, 1995), 1:32.

59. Trollope, *Eustace Diamonds*, 320.

60. Ibid., 634.

61. Trollope does not explicitly mention *The Moonstone* in discussing the writing of *The Eustace Diamonds* in *An Autobiography*, but his reference to how Collins would have handled the same situation makes it clear that the novel was on his mind: "Wilkie Collins would have arranged [necklace thefts] with infinite labour, preparing things present so that they should fit in with things to come" (Trollope, *An Autobiography*, 286).

62. Ian Duncan, "*The Moonstone*, the Victorian Novel, and Imperialistic Panic," *Modern Language Quarterly* 55, no. 3 (1994): 300.

63. Review of Wilkie Collins, *The Moonstone*, *Nation*, September 17, 1868, 235.

64. The Raj was associated not simply with malevolent opposition to British rule, but also with supernatural forces that might operate throughout the empire. Roger Luckhurst has recently argued that "at the edges of empire . . . narratives concerning occult relation, uncanny methods of communication and instances of telepathic rapport abounded." Thus Stead believed that the "telephone [had been] anticipated by Wild Indians," while Charles Bray in 1866 asserted that "[i]mportant news travels faster in India by Mental Telegraph than by Electric Telegraph," and as late as the 1880s many commentators placed credence in some sort

of Indian "Secret Mail" ("Knowledge, Belief and the Supernatural at the Imperial Margin," in *The Victorian Supernatural*, ed. Nicola Bown, Carolyn Burdett, and Pamela Thurschwell [New York: Camridge University Press, 2004], 198, 204, 205–6).

65. Collins, *Moonstone*, 70.

66. "Considering him merely as a real, marketable, tangibly-useful possession [Shakespeare is the only thing] ... that can keep all these [English emigrants] together into virtually one Nation. ... [The] Indian Empire will go, at any rate [but] ... Indian Empire or no Indian Empire, we cannot do without Shakespeare!" (Carlyle, *Heroes*, 58).

67. "The accounts that [Pandita Ramabai, Cornelia Sorabji, and Behramji Malabari] left of their experiences in the British Isles in the 1880s and 1890s suggest that the United Kingdom could be as much of a 'contact zone' as the colonies themselves. Their experiences also provide historical evidence of how imperial power was staged at home and how it was contested by colonial 'natives' at the heart of the empire itself" (Antoinette Burton, *At the Heart of the Empire: Indians and the Colonial Encounter in Late-Victorian Britain* [Berkeley: University of California Press, 1998], 1). Cf. also Neil Parsons, *King Khama, Emperor Joe, and the Great White Queen: Victorian Britain through African Eyes* (Chicago: University of Chicago Press, 1998).

68. Antoinette Burton, "Tongues Untied: Lord Salisbury's 'Black Man' and the Boundaries of Imperial Democracy," *Comparative Studies in Society and History* 42, no. 3 (2000).

69. Cf. Antoinette Burton's account of one twentieth-century offshoot of such optimism about the reversibility of cultural flows: the "Cold War cosmopolitanism" that made expatriate Santha Rama Rau into a spokeswoman in America for an enlightened (because already Anglicized) India. Cf. the work of Srinivas Aravamudan, who has recently described other Indian expatriates who were able to travel freely and successfully in the West because they brought a palatable brand of "Guru English" with them. See Antoinette Burton, *The Postcolonial Careers of Santha Rama Rau* (Durham, N.C.: Duke University Press, 2007), and Srinivas Aravamudan, *Guru English: South Asian Religion in a Cosmopolitan Language* (Princeton: Princeton University Press, 2005).

70. Thanks to an anonymous reader for Princeton University Press for advice on this point.

71. On the gradual de-Nabobization of British attitudes toward India—that is, from the 1820s onward, decreasing English willingness to claim that one has "become" Indian while living there—see Collingham, *Imperial*.

CHAPTER TWO: THE FIRST STRAWBERRIES IN INDIA: CULTURAL PORTABILITY ABROAD

1. Harriet Tytler, *An Englishwoman in India: The Memoirs of Harriet Tytler 1828–1858*, ed. Anthony Sattin (Oxford: Oxford University Press, 1986), 33.

2. Tytler is best remembered for having given birth in a besieged redoubt during the 1857 siege of Delhi. Her inveterate identification of herself as English rather

than Indian, though, is characteristic of Anglo-Indian "memsahibs" generally. See Tytler, *Englishwoman*, 14–15.

3. " 'Contact zone' . . . I use to refer to the space of colonial encounters, the space in which peoples geographically and historically separated come into contact with each other and establish ongoing relations, usually involving conditions of coercion, radical inequality, and intractable conflict. . . . By using the term 'contact,' I aim to foreground the interactive, improvisational dimensions of colonial encounters so easily ignored or suppressed by diffusionist accounts of conquest and domination" (Mary Louise Pratt, *Imperial Eyes: Travel Writing and Transculturation* [New York: Routledge, 1992], 6–7).

4. Margot C. Finn, "Colonial Gifts: Family Politics and the Exchange of Goods in British India, C. 1780–1820," *Modern Asian Studies* 40, no. 1 (2006): 210; see also Collingham's recent argument "trac[ing] the transformation of the early nineteenth-century nabob from the flamboyant, effeminate and wealthy East India Company servant, open to Indian influence and into whose self-identity India was incorporated, to the sahib, a sober, bureaucratic representative of the crown" (*Imperial*, 3).

5. Finn goes on to make a persuasive case that "collective kin obligations" among elite English families ruling India, exemplified by "exchanges of gifts, commodities and other signifying artifacts," remain, throughout the nineteenth century, crucial in understanding how power was mediated in ways inadequately described by the habitual historical focus upon contractual relationships and "possessive individualism." Finn, "Colonial," 230–31.

6. Sara Jeannette Duncan, *The Crow's-Nest* (New York: Dodd, Mead, 1901), in Duncan, *The Imperialist*, ed. Misao Dean (Orchard Park, N.Y.: Broadview, 2005), 305, 307.

7. Gauri Viswanathan, "Raymond Williams and British Colonialism," *Journal of English and Foreign Languages* 7–8 (1991): 81.

8. Amartya Sen, *The Argumentative Indian: Writings on Indian Culture, History, and Politics* (New York: Farrar, Straus, Giroux, 2005), 141.

9. Benita Parry finds little evidence in the Indian colonial encounter for "assenting and equally situated parties conducting colloquies," seeing instead "cultural solipsism and not cultural conversation." She has recently argued, against Mary Louise Pratt and others, that, in British India at least, there is scant evidence anywhere for "transculturation . . . through continuous negotiations." Benita Parry, *Delusions and Discoveries: India in the British Imagination, 1880–1930*, 2nd ed. (London: Verso, 1998), 8.

10. Naipaul has memorably argued that "The truth is that *Indians do not see*, [but Gandhi] looked at India as no Indian was able to; his vision was direct. . . . He sees exactly what the visitor sees; he does not ignore the obvious. . . . He sees the Indian callousness, the Indian refusal to see." My argument is that throughout the Victorian era a similar sort of blindness played a protective role in *Anglo*-Indian society. V. S. Naipaul, *An Area of Darkness* (New York: Macmillan, 1965), 75, 77, 78.

11. Caroline Elkins and Susan Pedersen, "Introduction," in *Settler Colonialism in the Twentieth Century: Projects, Practices, Legacies*, ed. Caroline Elkins and Susan Pedersen (New York: Routledge, 2005), 2.

12. Patrick Wolfe, "Land, Labor and Difference: Elementary Structures of Race," *American Historical Review* 106, no. 3 (2001); Angela Woollacott, *To Try Her Fortune in London: Australian Women, Colonialism, and Modernity* (New York: Oxford University Press, 2001), 5, see also 19–46.

13. Janet C. Myers, "Antipodal England: Emigration, Gender, and Portable Domesticity in Victorian Literature and Culture" (Ph.D. Diss., Rice University, 2000), 2.

14. "The paradox is that we today can without much trouble read Mary Rowlandson *as* American precisely because, in captivity, she saw English fields before her" (Anderson, "Exodus," 315).

15. My argument is that India is distinct from other settler colonies less in the quality of its settler-indigenous interactions than in the influence that books about those interactions had upon other settler colonies. Woollacott's is one recent nuanced account (among a growing number) of the growth of national consciousness in settler colonies such as Australia, Canada, and South Africa; it is notable for its memorable account of how the (faux) aboriginal cry "Coo-ee" became a shibboleth of white Australian identity, a nativist appropriation of the culture of people whose dispossession and virtual eradication was necessary for the Australian nation to be born. Woollacott, *To Try*, 175–80. I am grateful to an anonymous reader from *Victorian Studies* and to Isabel Hofmeyr for guidance on this point.

16. In a recent article, Dipesh Chakrabarty reiterates the importance of remembering two aspects of British colonial rule. On the one hand, that there were, particularly in the second half of the nineteenth century, "Europeans, official and nonofficial, who took their liberalism seriously and agonized over the contradictions between colonial rule and liberalism." But, on the other hand, "colonial sovereignty" required colonial authorities to respond to any crisis in authority by "reminding Indians of who was in charge." Dipesh Chakrabarty, " 'In the Name of Politics': Democracy and the Power of the Multitude in India," *Public Culture* 19, no. 1 (2007): 43.

17. It is significant, for example, that the South African National Library—descendant of the "South African Library" founded in Capetown in 1818—has held, apparently since their first publication, all three of Emily Eden's books about India (including her *Portraits of the Princes and Peoples of India*, of which fewer than thirty copies exist), but owns neither of her far more widely circulated novels. Isabel Hofmeyr has suggested (in a personal communication) that the early presence of Emily Eden's three published works on India signals the importance of *transimperial* communication in the Victorian era, whereby prolific writers of English India were studied eagerly in other imperial peripheries.

18. Focusing on India also highlights the Victorian insistence on regarding colonial subjects as rooted in specific territories, despite the evident importance of migrant labor throughout British domains. That insistence is worth comparing to certain kinds of presumptive deterritorialization that shape representations of colonial subjects. I am thinking of the notional denationalization of black subjects of British novels, not only in the twentieth century, when migration comes to seem a matter of course, but even in earlier epochs. Catherine Gallagher has argued, for example, that in Romantic-era novels attacking the slave trade, the national or geographic rootedness of black subjects is readily undone, so that even their

birthplaces are deliberately obscured, and they are frequently imagined as permanently displaced and deracinated. It might be argued, though, that with the cessation of slave trading and slavery in the British Empire by the mid-1830s (to place a historical terminus to such Romantic-era denationalizations of black slaves), the assignment of any black subject to a specific nation may have become easier, and the rooted territoriality of both Britons and their colonial inferiors correspondingly more straightforward. Catherine Gallagher, "Floating Signifiers of Britishness in the Novels of the Anti-Slave-Trade Squadron," in *Dickens and the Children of Empire*, ed. Wendy S. Jacobson (New York: Palgrave, 2000).

19. Cf., for example, Burton, *Heart*.

20. Salman Rushdie, *Midnight's Children* (New York: Penguin, 1991), 305.

21. Robert Young's new book, *The Idea of English Ethnicity* (Oxford: Blackwell, 2007), which was not yet available when this book went to press, seems to address similar issues, exploring the notion that nineteenth-century Englishness is a long-distance result of overseas Britishness.

22. H. R. Panckridge, *A Short History of the Bengal Club, 1827–1927* (Calcutta: H. R. Panckridge, 1927), 1, quoted in Mrinahlini Sinha, "Britishness, Clubbability, and the Colonial Public Sphere," in *Bodies in Contact: Rethinking Colonial Encounters in World History*, ed. Tony Ballantyne and Antoinette Burton (Durham, N.C.: Duke University Press, 2005), 184.

23. Sinha, "Britishness," 184.

24. Ibid., 184, 187.

25. Sinha argues that such measures as the shipping of poor whites back to Britain exemplify how strongly everyday Anglo-Indian life had to be manipulated to maintain an effective simulacrum of British life among elite whites. Ibid., 186, 188.

26. On the bungalow itself as a bit of portable culture, see Anthony D. King, *The Bungalow: The Production of a Global Culture* (Boston: Routledge and Kegan Paul, 1984).

27. Chaudhuri, "Shawls," 232.

28. Ibid., 239.

29. Quoted in Collingham, *Imperial*, 69.

30. Maitland, *Letters*, 96–97.

31. For Murray's global reach, see the checklist and discussion of Australian distribution in Graeme Johanson, *Colonial Editions in Australia, 1843–1972* (Wellington: Elibank, 2000), 211–53, 307–12. For a discussion of Murray's comparative failure and Macmillan's success, see Priya Joshi, *In Another Country: Colonialism, Culture, and the English Novel in India* (New York: Columbia University Press, 2002), 93–139.

32. John Kaye, quoted in Joshi, *Another*, 94. One of the many achievements of Joshi's work is that it sketches out opportunities to study various pathways of diffusion and transmission of English culture in the British empire, pathways that might or might not follow the portability paradigm I am proposing here to explain Anglo-Indian works. James Buzard has recently argued compellingly for an attention to the autoethnographic work that English novels perform for English readers, but there is no reason to take that call as an excuse to leave off the vital work

of understanding how various forms of mutual self-constitution defined acts of colonial exchange.

33. Emma Roberts, *Scenes and Characteristics of Hindoostan, with Sketches of Anglo-Indian Society* (London: W. H. Allen, 1835), quoted in Joshi, *Another*, 105. Writing of a slightly earlier era (1780–1820), Finn associates lent books with sentimental gifts such as jewelry: "Like the miniatures, portraits, sleeve-buttons and strands of hair that circulated as mementoes of distant or departed kin, volumes of Romantic poetry were compact, scarce and saturated with emotive sentiments" (Finn, "Colonial," 227).

34. Maitland, *Letters*, 94.

35. Ibid., 41.

36. Ibid., 105, emphasis in original.

37. Ibid., 54.

38. Maitland's effort to establish her collecting credibility via approval from the British Museum illustrates one of the key problems associated with any kind of amateur scientific work done in the colonies. As Luckhurst has recently argued, "[F]or much of the nineteenth century, the person in the field was judged as a lowly and unreliable figure, whose information had to be returned to the imperial centre and judged by experts before reaching the threshold of legitimate knowledge. Reports from missionaries were likely to be biased by prepossession, it was felt, but even professional collectors trained in scientific observation were regarded with suspicion" (Luckhurst, "Knowledge," 212).

39. A later letter to the friend who received her specimens reveals another side to that unease: "I am very glad those insects I sent were so curious, and that you gave the new specimens to the British Museum. No doubt I shall be able to send you plenty more: I do not at all recollect which they were, but in future I will keep numbered duplicates, that I may learn their names. Pray, ask Mr Samouelle what names were given to the five new species, and let me know" (Maitland, *Letters*, 186).

40. Ibid., 47.

41. Cf. John Plotz, "Virtually Being There: Edmund Wilson's Suburbs," *Southwest Review* 87, no. 1 (2002).

42. Maitland, *Letters*, 49.

43. "I fell asleep recalling what I 'used to do' when I was at Miss Havisham's; as though I had been there weeks or months, instead of hours; and as though it were quite an old subject of remembrance, instead of one that had arisen only that day" (Dickens, *Great Expectations*, 73).

44. Interestingly, an 1845 notice in the *Quarterly Review* praised Maitland's capacity to describe not India itself, but rather Anglo-Indian life: "[T]he very lightest work that has ever appeared from India, yet it tells us more of what everybody cares to know than any other" (quoted in Penelope Carson, "Letters from Madras During the Years 1836–1839 (Book)," *Journal of Imperial and Commonwealth History* 32, no. 2 [2004]: 150).

45. Parry does not actually discuss the work; the two scholarly references I know cite it as a source for Anglo-Indian received ideas about servants, which seems perfectly apt. Nupur Chaudhuri, "Memsahibs and Motherhood in Nineteenth-Century Colonial India," *Victorian Studies* 31, no. 4 (1988): 519, 520,

522, 525; Mary A. Procida, *Married to the Empire: Gender, Politics and Imperialism in India, 1883–1947* (Manchester: Manchester University Press, 2002), 197.

46. A.U., *Overland*, 92–93.

47. Catherine Hall discusses the internal tensions within the British émigré community in the West Indies, while Viswanathan tracks a broader range of concerns about conversion, apostasy, and the durability of various syncretic belief systems in India: Hall, *Civilising*; Gauri Viswanathan, *Outside the Fold: Conversion, Modernity, and Belief* (Princeton: Princeton University Press, 1998). And Gyan Prakash describes Indian religious reform movements, exploring the difficult ironies and paradoxes built into religious alteration in a "contact zone": Gyan Prakash, *Another Reason: Science and the Imagination of Modern India* (Princeton: Princeton University Press, 1999).

48. A.U., *Overland*, 157.

49. Ibid., 185.

50. Ibid., 73.

51. "*semi-detached*. A. *adj.* . . . . b. *spec.* Designating either of a pair of houses joined together and forming a block by themselves. [1859] E. EDEN, *The Semi-Detached House*" (*Oxford English Dictionary*, 2nd ed. [Oxford: Oxford University Press, 1989]).

52. Emily Eden wrote two Austen-inflected novels, *The Semi-Detached House* (1859) and *The Semi-Attached Couple* (drafted 1830, rewritten and published 1860). The novels were, however, substantially outsold by her 1866 *Up the Country*, which printed (extensively edited) letters, mostly to her sister Eleanor, describing her life as part of her brother's 6,000-person traveling "darbar" between 1835 and 1842. Janet Dunbar, *Golden Interlude: The Edens in India, 1836–1842* (Boston: Houghton Mifflin, 1956), 228–31.

Eden's latter-day reception ranges from censure for her grand-dame racism—Edward Thompson's 1930 annotations to her letters, as well as Thalassa Ali's censorious 2001 historical novel—to Deirdre David's praise of Eden for undermining the Whiggish certainty of a bureaucratically governed India. David praises Eden's "remarkable perception of the fragility and sheer implausibility of the British Enterprise." By her account, Eden's perception of fragility should be contrasted to the unflinching certainty of a male administrator such as Macaulay; where Macaulay sees Indians skilled enough to follow orders, Eden sees them ready to cut off British heads. Tom Stoppard, too, seemingly aligns Eden with a later generation of British advocates of decolonization when he ends his 1995 play *Indian Ink* with an 1839 Eden letter about the seeming passivity of Indian subalterns witnessing an English ball in Simla: "I sometimes wonder they do not cut all our heads off and say nothing more about it." (I am grateful to Antoinette Burton for the reference). Edward Thompson, "Introduction and Notes," in *Emily Eden's Up the Country: Letters Written to Her Sister from the Upper Provinces of India*, ed. Edward Thompson (London: Oxford University Press, 1930); Thalassa Ali, *A Singular Hostage* (New York: Bantam Books, 2002); Deirdre David, *Rule Britannia: Women, Empire, and Victorian Writing* (Ithaca: Cornell University Press, 1995), 40; Tom Stoppard, *Plays*, 5vols. (London: Faber and Faber, 1999), 5:482.

53. Plotz, "Jane," 168. I am grateful to Judith Plotz for advice on Eden stretching over many years.

54. Angelia Poon, for instance, stresses Eden's curious doubleness as Indian traveler, at once reveling in imperial power and indulging in a masochistic sense of the fragility, the tininess, of her own presence in India. Poon argues that, for Eden, "the rapid ascent of European power despite their smallness in numbers . . . serves to add a sort of *piquancy* [italics Poon's] to colonial dominance." Poon also stresses Eden's interest in contrasting the "public grandeur" of British imperial rule to the "private discomfort" that she had to undergo as an exemplary Anglo-Indian. Angelia Poon, "Seeing Double: Performing English Identity and Imperial Duty in Emily Eden's *Up the Country* and Harriet Martineau's *British Rule in India*," *Women's Writing* 12, no. 3 (2005): 460, 456, emphasis in original.

55. Dunbar, *Garden*, 222.

56. For instance, beside a thoroughly unremarkable picture of an elephant-back procession: "The Raja of Putteealla is chief of the largest of the Sikh principalities on the South Bank of the Sutlej, which owe allegiance to the British government, and are under its protection. These principalities were saved from subjection to the Ranjeet Singh, in the year 1809, through the interference of the British Government. Lord Minto was then Governor-General, and Sir Charles Metcalfe was the Envoy deputed by him to restrain Ranjeet Singh in his conquests south of the Sutlej. The revenues of the Rajah of Putteealla are supposed to be from £300,000 to £400,000 a year" (Emily Eden, *Portraits of the Princes and People of India* [London: J. Dickinson, 1844], pl. 6).

57. Ibid.

58. Ibid., pl. 10.

59. Ibid., pl. 24.

60. Eden, *Up the Country: Letters Written to Her Sister from the Upper Provinces of India*, ed. Edward Thompson (London: Oxford University Press, 1930), 393.

61. Ibid.

62. Ibid., 147.

63. Jo Robertson makes the point that Eden's encounter with mortality in India poses a direct, carnal challenge to her comfortable identity as the witty, literate sister of the Governor-General: "[T]he personal experience of illness, demoralization, and death undermines Eden's public voice, as the distance between a metropolitan poetic discourse about imperial service and the embodied colonial discourse of that sacrifice becomes literally unspeakable 'out loud'" ("Anxieties of Imperial Decay: Three Journeys in India," in *In Transit: Travel, Text, Empire*, ed. Helen Gilbert and Anna Johnston [New York: P. Lang, 2002], 115).

64. Eden, *Up the Country*, 147–48.

65. It is a commonplace among English writers to represent Indian jewels as precious goods that have been not so much crafted as spoiled by Indian workmanship. Harriet Tytler's observation at a banquet in the mid-1850s is typical: "Some of the emeralds were the size of large marbles, but so badly cut that they only looked like bits of glass. The diamonds, too, though immense, were cut into thin, flat ones and made no more show than pieces of crystal would have done" (Tytler, *Englishwoman*, 65).

66. Eden, *Up the Country*, 374–75.

67. Ibid., 319–20, emphasis in original.

68. Eden might have known (although the book by Emma Roberts she cites on Skinner has only an unrevealing single paragraph classing him as one of the "European residents in India") that James Skinner (1778–1841) had fought both for and against the British in his long, distinguished career, and that his parents were a Scotch lieutenant colonel and his Rajput mistress (I am indebted to an anonymous reader for *Victorian Studies* for directing me to the details of Skinner's life). Roberts, *Scenes*, 289; Stephen Wheeler, "Skinner, James (1778–1841)," in *Oxford Dictionary of National Biography: In Association with the British Academy: From the Earliest Times to the Year 2000*, ed. H. C. G. Matthew and Brian Howard Harrison (Oxford: Oxford University Press, 2004).

69. Judith Plotz describes Eden's "desperate homesickness," sickness, detestation of the climate, aesthetic dissatisfaction, and most of all, her "boredom." She also notes an 1866 review of *Up the Country* in the *Saturday Review* praising Eden for her unique understanding of "how monotonous Indian life is." Plotz, "Jane," 170–74, 186.

70. Eden, *Up the Country*, 144, emphasis in original.

71. Ibid., 63.

72. Ibid., 63–64.

73. Ibid., 65. William Shakespeare, *Romeo and Juliet*, ed. Jill Levenson. (Oxford: Oxford University Press, 2000), 5.1.72; reference is to act, scene, and line, respectively.

74. Eden, *Semi-Detached*, 121.

75. Ibid., 230.

76. Ibid.

77. Ibid., 203. William Shakespeare, *Macbeth*, ed. A. R. Braunmuller (New York: Cambridge University Press, 1997), III.4.50–51.

78. Eden, *Semi-Detached*, 210.

79. Paul Carter has recently drawn a similar set of suggestive analogies between "gloomy over-furnished interiors of suburban London . . . [and] the mundane drama of colonization" en route to an argument for the importance, in analogous ways, of occultism to suburbs and colonial peripheries. Carter argues that "domestic interiors reproduced the interiors of exotic countries; they were populated with sub-rational beings—spirit doubles, unruly children, illnesses and unhappinesses" ("Turning the Tables—or Grounding Post-Colonialism," in *Text, Theory, Space: Land, Literature and History in South Africa and Australia*, ed. Kate Darian-Smith, Elizabeth Gunner, and Sarah Nuttall [London: Routledge, 1996], 24).

80. Lawrence Zygmunt, " 'This Particular Web': George Eliot, Emily Eden, and Locale in Multiplot Fiction," in *Teaching British Women Writers, 1750–1900*, ed. Jeanne Moskal and Shannon R. Wooden (New York: P. Lang, 2005), 117.

81. Seeley was the great popularizer of the phrase "Greater Britain," viewing "British expansion rather than liberal democracy . . . as . . . the hidden coordinator of British history" (James Epstein, "Under America's Sign: Two Nineteenth-Century British Readings," *European Journal of American Culture* 24, no. 3

[2005]: 215). Cf. also Armitage, "Greater Britain: A Useful Category of Historical Analysis?".

82. David Nicholls, *The Lost Prime Minister: A Life of Sir Charles Dilke* (London: Hambledon, 1995).

83. Dilke, *Greater*, 274.

84. Ibid., 513.

85. Epstein, "Under America's Sign," 211.

86. Dilke, *Greater*, ix.

87. Ibid.

88. "In speaking of the physical and moral characteristics of the populations descended from the English you sometimes express yourself almost as if there were no sources of national character but race and climate—as if whatever does not come from climate must come from race. But you shew, in many parts of your book, a strong sense of the good and bad influences of education, legislation, and social circumstances" (John Stuart Mill, letter of February 9, 1869, in *The Later Letters of John Stuart Mill, 1849–1873*, ed. Francis Edward Mineka and Dwight N. Lindley [Toronto: University of Toronto Press, 1972], 563).

89. Epstein remarks that "[t]o say that Dilke's vision was often confused or unresolved is merely to state the obvious. . . . What is interesting is the uncertain quality of his race theory." Epstein links Dilke's racial theorizing to later Anglo-Saxonists such as James Bryce, J. A. Froude, and E. A. Freeman. "By the late nineteenth century, Dilke's Anglo-Saxonism, which had left unresolved the relative weight of the biological as distinct from the cultural, hardened into a more essentialist racial mode within imperial thought which also subordinated radical populist elements to a conservative nationalism" ("Under America's Sign," 214, 216, 218).

90. John Emerich Acton, "Nationality," in *The History of Freedom, and Other Essays* (London: Macmillan, 1907), 286.

91. Ibid., 283–85, 299–300.

92. Ibid., 288–90.

93. Ibid., 294.

94. Ibid., 290, 298.

95. Ibid., 292.

96. Appadurai, *Modernity*, 178.

97. Ian Duncan, "The Provincial or Regional Novel," in *A Companion to the Victorian Novel*, ed. Patrick Brantlinger and William B. Thesing (Oxford: Blackwell, 2002).

CHAPTER THREE: SOMEONE ELSE'S KNOWLEDGE: RACE AND PORTABLE CULTURE IN *DANIEL DERONDA*

1. David Harvey uses the phrase "flexible accumulation" to describe economic and cultural structures that promote accumulation but also discourage overadherence to any particular commodity. That is, treasure a family heirloom if you must, but avoid getting attached to that rotary phone.

2. The word "imperialism" enters English in 1858, designating "an imperial system of government; the rule of an emperor, esp. when despotic or arbitrary." It is not until 1878, however, that the word is used in the more specific form that remained dominant for the next half-century: "The principle or spirit of empire; advocacy of what are held to be imperial interests. In nineteenth-century British politics, the principle or policy (1) of seeking, or at least not refusing, an extension of the British Empire in directions where trading interests and investments require the protection of the flag; and (2) of so uniting the different parts of the empire having separate governments, as to secure that for certain purposes, such as war-like defence, internal commerce, copyright, and postal communication, they should be practically a single state" (s.v., *Oxford English Dictionary*, 2nd ed.).

3. Cf. Stocking, *Victorian*; Herbert, *Culture*; Nancy Henry, *George Eliot and the British Empire* (New York: Cambridge University Press, 2002).

4. Gaskell, *Cranford*, 206.

5. The English, she writes, "do not call ourselves a dispersed and a punished people: we are a colonising people, and it is we who have punished others." The capacity to be a "colonising people" seems to mean that the English are, like the Jews, able to carry their own lore and law wherever they go. George Eliot, "The Modern Hep! Hep! Hep!," in *Impressions of Theophrastus Such*, ed. Nancy Henry (Iowa City: University of Iowa Press, 1994), 146. The Jewish-English analogy, however, is not meant to open the floodgates for comparisons to all peripatetic nations. Deborah Epstein Nord has located Eliot among those writers who portrayed Jews as "conscious of their history and aware of their origin"; by contrast, Nord argues that Eliot portrays Gypsies as lacking a "rich and solid basis" for an "idea of a place of origin or fantasy of return" (*Gypsies and the British Imagination, 1807–1930* [New York: Columbia University Press, 2006], 6–7, 100–101). Cf. Ian Duncan, "Wild England: George Borrow's Nomadology," *Victorian Studies* 41 (1998).

6. This is a long way from the well-known letter to John Sibree in February 1848 that inveighs against pride in Jewishness per se and concludes that "everything specifically Jewish is of a low grade" (George Eliot, *George Eliot's Life as Related in Her Letters and Journals*, ed. J. W. Cross [New York: Harper and Brothers, 1885], 1:125).

7. Eliot, *Daniel*, 408.

8. George Eliot, *Middlemarch*, ed. Bert G. Hornback (New York: Norton, 2000), 67.

9. "Cf. Charming as were all Mrs Radcliffe's works, and charming even as were the works of all her imitators, it was not in them perhaps that human nature, at least in the midland counties of England, was to be looked for" (Jane Austen, *Northanger Abbey*, ed. Marilyn Butler [New York: Penguin, 2003], 188).

10. Duncan, "Provincial," 332.

11. William Baker and J. C. Ross, *George Eliot: A Bibliographical History* (New Castle, Del.: Oak Knoll, 2002), 316.

12. Eliot, *Daniel*, 16.

13. The opening paragraph of Conrad's *Victory* refers to "the age in which we are camped like bewildered travellers in a garish, unrestful hotel" (3). Compare also Conrad's *Lord Jim* (1900), Ford Madox Ford's *The Good Soldier* (1915),

Thomas Mann's *Felix Krull* (1911), and the film *Grand Hotel* (1932), modernist works in which hotels represent the "transcendental shelterlessness" (Lukács's term) of the human condition.

14. Eliot, *Daniel Deronda*, 3.

15. Ibid., 16.

16. Ibid., 156.

17. Ibid., 308.

18. "What Daniel teaches Gwendolen and the other English is that one need not have had any direct experience of the culture proper to one's ethnicity (as Gwendolen has not) so long as that culture is somehow held in trust, preserved in the collective memory of the race, until the moment one decides to begin learning how to act like what one is." In a footnote, Buzard also argues (contra Baucom) that in Eliot "English locale" does not protect against "imperial contamination": "race, not place, is finally the one 'secure' determinant of national identity" (Buzard, *Disorienting*, 296, 297).

19. Hall, *White*, 255–95.

20. Mary Poovey argues that racial categories "stabilized" in the 1840s, and Charlotte Sussman argues that "after 1838, appeals to a universal sensibility—mutual emotions discovered in sympathy and tears across vast distances—began to disappear from British conceptions of cultural difference, to be replaced by a more essentialist and 'scientific' understanding of 'race'" (Sussman, *Consuming Anxieties: Consumer Protest, Gender, and British Slavery, 1713–1833* [Stanford: Stanford University Press, 2000], 193); Mary Poovey, *Making a Social Body: British Cultural Formation, 1830–1864* (Chicago: University of Chicago Press, 1995), 2. On the late nineteenth-century rise of both "extrinsic" and "intrinsic" racism, and its formative influence on both Zionism and Pan-Africanism, see Appiah, *Father's*, esp. 3–26.

21. I thank Sarah Gracombe (personal communication) for a set of intriguing hypotheses about how far the implicit parallel between Englishness and Jewishness extends. Yet Englishness finally does not seem to me to be presented as a masked cultural legacy in the same way as Jewishness. Although there is a theoretical symmetry between a character's discovering a Jewish or an English identity, in Eliot there is no formal mechanism available for the narrator to disavow knowledge of the interior contents of Englishness, as can be done for Judaism. I look forward, however, to Gracombe's forthcoming work on Eliot, which should illuminate this range of questions from a different vantage point.

22. Eliot, *Daniel Deronda*, 315.

23. Ibid.

24. Ibid., 316.

25. Cf. Irene Tucker's illuminating discussion of the way that Daniel's quest to establish his paternity (and hence his patrimony) is transformed into the uncovering of *maternal* secrets (since Judaism traces descent through the mother). Irene Tucker, *A Probable State: The Novel, the Contract, and the Jews* (Chicago: University of Chicago Press, 2000). On the ways that Judaism and Jewishness came to be defined via a female domestic space in Victorian England, see Michael Galchinsky, *The Origin of the Modern Jewish Woman Writer: Romance and Reform in Victorian England* (Detroit: Wayne State University Press, 1996).

26. Eliot, *Daniel Deronda*, 316.
27. Ibid.
28. Ibid.
29. Ibid., 694.
30. Ibid., 693.
31. My hypothesis that Eliot wants to mark certain areas as "intrinsically Jewish," and hence off limits, even for her own speculations, also offers a new way to approach the question of whether Daniel is circumcised. Consider the Alcharisi's contemptuous dismissal of the idea that culture might be written onto the body: "I rid myself of the Jewish tatters and gibberish that make people nudge each other at sight of us, as if we were tattooed under our clothes" (ibid., 544). This suggests Eliot is uncomfortable with instances where culture (the external world) impinges physically on the body (the natural and internal world). Circumcision, arguably, is what inscribes custom on the body. The point, then, is not so much that Daniel was (or was not) circumcised, but that the reader's (and Eliot's) state of ignorance about his foreskin is exactly the novel's point. Daniel's foreskin is a sort of Schrodinger's cat, both present and absent. Cf. Mary Wilson Carpenter, "'A Bit of Her Flesh': Circumcision and 'the Signification of the Phallus' in *Daniel Deronda*," *Genders* 1 (1988); Cynthia Chase, "The Decomposition of the Elephants: Double-Reading *Daniel Deronda*," *PMLA: Publications of the Modern Language Association of America* 93, no. 2 (1978); and John Sutherland, *Can Jane Eyre Be Happy?: More Puzzles in Classic Fiction* (New York: Oxford University Press, 1997), 169–79.
32. Eliot, *Daniel Deronda*, 695.
33. I am grateful to Irene Tucker (personal communication) for pointing out that the very fact of allusions to canonical English literary texts about Jewish suffering (like the novel's repeated references to Ruth and Naomi) gestures to an ongoing conversation—mediated through literary texts—in which Eliot's imagined English readers would participate. That conversation, though, is *about*, rather than *with*, Jews, whose own cultural referents are treated as existing in a different realm altogether.
34. Eliot, *Daniel Deronda*, 679.
35. Michael Fried, *Absorption and Theatricality: Painting and Beholder in the Age of Diderot* (Chicago: University of Chicago Press, 1988).
36. There is no evidence either that Eliot ever read Flaubert, or vice versa (I am grateful to Susan Hoyle and Rosemarie Bodenheimer for assistance on this question). Cf. John Rignall, *Oxford Reader's Companion to George Eliot* (Oxford: Oxford University Press, 2000), 124–25.
37. Cf. the illuminating use of this term in Miller, *Novel*, 207.
38. This is not to say that the novel would only be read by Christians. Lewes is notably quick to embrace the idea of a substantial Jewish readership, writing to Blackwood that "[t]he Jews seem to be very grateful for *Deronda*—and will perhaps make up for the deadness of so many Christians to that part of the book which does not directly concern Gwendolen. When the cheap edition is issued we shall perhaps see the effect of this Jewish sympathy. The Jews ought to make a good public—as the doctors did for *Middlemarch*" (Lewes, letter to George Eliot, October 29, 1876, in Eliot, *The George Eliot Letters*, 303). Eliot, though, seems

more reluctant to imagine herself writing for Jews in general (although, as I discuss below, the possibility of a few choice Jewish interlocutors evidently appealed to her). In a letter written five days after the one from Lewes, quoted above, she is still speculating about a Christian readership whom she will educate: "A statesman who shall be nameless has said that I first opened to him a vision of Italian life, then of Spanish, and now I have kindled in him a quite new understanding of the Jewish people. This is what I wanted to do—to widen the English vision a little in that direction and let in a little conscience and refinement" (Eliot, letter of November 3, 1876, in *The George Eliot Letters*, 304).

39. F. R. Leavis, *The Great Tradition: George Eliot, Henry James, Joseph Conrad* (New York: G. W. Stewart, 1948), 122, emphasis in original.

40. One notable exception to this puzzlement is Raymond Williams, whose dissatisfaction with the novel stems not from its being a break with the novel as usual, but from its striking him as acquiescing to the usual English novel's "narrowing of people and situations to those capable, in traditional terms, of limitation to an individual moral action, the fading-out of all others. . . . [T]he re-creation . . . of a country-house England" (*The Country and the City* [New York: Oxford University Press, 1973], 180). Williams's strangely cloistered account (as if he had only read Leavis's *Gwendolen*) suggests that even as recently as 1973 the Jewish plot—and with it the late Victorian turn toward questions of national identity understood in either racial or ethnic terms—might remain invisible even to an exceptionally sensitive critic, if that critic parsed questions of class and caste struggles to the exclusion of the questions of national belonging that, from the late 1860s onward, gradually begin to define the novel.

41. *Spectator*, July 29, 1876, in David Carroll, *George Eliot: The Critical Heritage* (London: Routledge and Kegan Paul, 1971), 370, emphasis in original.

42. "*Daniel Deronda*: A Conversation." *Atlantic Monthly*, December 1876, reprinted in Leavis, *Great*, 249–66, 264. See the discussion in Daniel Novak, "A Model Jew: 'Literary Photographs' and the Jewish Body in *Daniel Deronda*," *Representations* 85 (2004). One extreme manifestation of this early anti-Semitic response to the novel is an American sequel that has Daniel turning from Judaism in disgust: *Gwendolen, Or Regained* (Boston: 1876), discussed in John M. Picker, "George Eliot and the Sequel Question," *New Literary History* 37, no. 2 (2006).

43. Cf. Audrey Jaffe, *Scenes of Sympathy: Identity and Representation in Victorian Fiction* (Ithaca: Cornell University Press, 2000).

44. Gallagher, *Body*, 132.

45. Eliot, *Daniel Deronda*, 189.

46. Cf. the central tale in an eighteenth-century portmanteau novel, in which an Indian/European woman discovers that her mother was Christian (and learns how to become a Christian herself) by discovering her mother's memoir and prayerbooks in her jewelry box after her death. *The Lady's Drawing-Room* (London: 1744).

47. Eliot, *Daniel Deronda*, 617.

48. Ibid., 688, emphasis in original.

49. George Eliot, review of *The Progress of the Intellect*, *Westminster Review* 54, no. 107 (1851): 178. Cf. also: "A certain consciousness of our entire past and our imagined future blends itself with all our moments of keen sensibility"

(George Eliot, *Adam Bede*, ed. Stephen Charles Gill [New York: Penguin, 1980], 199). I am grateful to Deb Gettelman for the reference from *Adam Bede*.

50. Eliot, *Daniel Deronda*, 566.

51. Ibid., 537.

52. Ibid., 687.

53. Ibid., 537.

54. Ibid., 659. Cf. the notion of "hysterical repetitive time" in Mary Jacobus, *Reading Woman: Essays in Feminist Criticism* (New York: Columbia University Press, 1986); I am grateful to Pam Thurschwell for the reference.

55. Eliot, *Daniel Deronda*, 691.

56. Ibid.; all ellipses in original.

57. The review goes on to say that "the consummate literary artist has degenerated into the student of social psychology" (review of George Eliot, *Impressions of Theophrastus Such*, *Athenaeum*, June 7, 1879, 719). W. H. Mallock was still less charitable, calling them "wraiths . . . hardly human beings at all . . . shapes seen in a dream" (review of *Impressions of Theophrastus Such*, *Edinburgh Review* (1879): 574).

58. With at least eighteen major reviews, and sales not less than 5,800 copies within four months of publication in the United Kingdom alone (and similar print-runs reported in the United States, as well as evidence of strong sales on the Continent), *Theophrastus Such* might, simply by virtue of Eliot's magisterial reputation at the time, have had a far wider readership than later critical reception might suggest. Although a projected German translation was eventually issued in 1880 containing only "The Modern Hep!, Hep!, Hep!," a complete Dutch translation did appear in 1879. Such figures, however, do little to offset the impression given by Mallock's crushing article in the *Edinburgh Review* that both critical and popular reception was dismal in comparison to that accorded to even the slightest of her fictions. See Baker and Ross, *George*, 355–72.

59. "Three Small Books by Great Writers," *Fraser's* 115 (1879): 106; review of Eliot, *Impressions of Theophrastus Such*, *Athenaeum*, 719.

60. Some reviewers felt that such special pleading could be better done when speaking through a Jewish character than in propria persona: "How far inferior is this defence [of Jews and Judaism] appealing to the intellect" declared the *Athenaeum*, "when compared with exactly the same arguments as urged by the passionate rhetoric of Mordecai in the book itself." By contrast, a short notice in the *Times* observed sympathetically that the book's "last and most eloquent" essay "traces out certain affinities and directs attention to some of the contrasts between the English and Jewish races" (review of Eliot, *Impressions of Theophrastus Such*, *Athenaeum*, 720; review of Eliot, *Impressions of Theophrastus Such*, *Times*, June 5, 1879).

61. Eliot, "Modern," 164.

62. This rebuke of Mill by Eliot resonates with a recent reading of *Daniel Deronda* as endorsing "partiality" in preference to Mill's calls for "impartiality." Suzy Anger, *Victorian Interpretation* (Ithaca: Cornell University Press, 2005), 129. By Anger's account, the novel endorses "sympathetic understanding" rather than simply racial connection; my argument is that the channels through which such sympathetic understanding can flow are shaped by the advantages that a shared

cultural heritage can provide in abetting the sharing of understanding—as well as by the barriers that the absence of racial connection throws up between would-be sympathizers and the object of their sympathy.

63. Alexander Welsh has a cogent account of the absence of grounds for disagreement in *Daniel Deronda*: "Ideas are designed for particular adherents and not for dissemination far and wide, at least not at present (one reason they are not very generously supplied to the reader). There have to be adherents and nonadherents for an ideology to take hold, to gather energy from the choosing of sides. The scenario is entirely different from the constant exchange and adjustment of opinion at large assumed by Mill in *On Liberty*" (*George Eliot and Blackmail* [Cambridge, Mass.: Harvard University Press, 1985], 311).

64. Compare Benedict Anderson's distinction between "bounded" (for example, national or racial) and "unbounded" (for example, aesthetic, vocational, or elective) seriality as an adhesive factor between individuals. Benedict Anderson, "Nationalism, Identity, and the Logic of Seriality," in *The Spectre of Comparisons: Nationalism, Southeast Asia, and the World* (New York: Verso, 1998).

65. For example, Eliot's letter to Asher Isaac Myers points out that Mordecai ought not be confused with "the Jew named Cohn. . . . Cohn being a keen dialectician and a highly impressive man, but without any specifically Jewish enthusiasm. His type was rather that of Spinoza whose metaphysical system attracted his subtle intellect, and in relation to Judaism Spinoza was in contrast with my *conception* of Mordecai" (George Eliot, letter of January 18, 1879, in *Selections from George Eliot's Letters*, ed. Gordon Sherman Haight [New Haven: Yale University Press, 1985], 503).

66. Eliot, letter of May 31, 1877, in *The George Eliot Letters*, 379.

67. Gallagher, *Body*, 144.

Chapter Four: Locating *Lorna Doone*: R. D. Blackmore, F. H. Burnett, and the Limits of English Regionalism

1. I am grateful to Elaine Freedgood (personal communication) for elucidating the intriguing connection to Victorian antiquarianism.

2. By comparison, Mrs Humphrey Ward's *Robert Elsmere* (1888) sold 70,000 copies in its first decade; data from Altick, *English*, 385–86. The assertion that the 1895 print-run sold out within a week is in Waldo Hilary Dunn, *R. D. Blackmore: The Author of* Lorna Doone: *A Biography* (New York: Longmans, Green, 1956), 134. At least eleven film adaptations exist; Theodore Marston's 1911 short is the first of five made prior to 1923. Margaret Oliphant, review of *Lorna Doone*, *Blackwood's Edinburgh Magazine*, January 1871, 43. Blackmore's popularity is compared to such bestselling contemporaries as Braddon and Haggard in Simon Eliot, *A Measure of Popularity: Public Library Holdings of Twenty-Four Popular Authors 1883–1912* (Oxford: Open University, 1992).

3. Max Keith Sutton, *R. D. Blackmore* (Boston: Twayne, 1979) is the best-known Blackmore monograph; other scholarly work includes Dunn, *R. D. Blackmore*, and Kenneth George Budd, *The Last Victorian: R. D. Blackmore and His Novels* (London: Centaur, 1960). See also William E. Buckler, "Blackmore's Nov-

els before *Lorna Doone*," *Nineteenth-Century Fiction* 10, no. 3 (1955), and Peter Merchant, "Rehabilitating *Lorna Doone*," *Children's Literature in Education* 18, no. 4 (1987).

4. In America, reviews were somewhat more sympathetic to the land-and-lore side of Blackmore's writing.

5. George Marnett Smith, "Mr Blackmore's Novels," *International Review*, September 1879.

6. Review of *Lorna Doone*, *Athenaeum*, April 17, 1869, 534.

7. Oliphant's observation that "[w]e are as much interested in the way he [John Ridd] digs out his sheep from the snow as in his rescue of Lorna from the hands of her clan" does suggest her perception of the importance of agricultural and natural detail to Blackmore ("Review," 43, 44, 47).

8. The most recent book-length discussion of the nineteenth-century evolution of "local" novels from the days of Mary Russell Mitford's *Our Village* is Franco Moretti, *Graphs, Maps, Trees: Abstract Models for a Literary History* (New York: Verso, 2005).

9. Recent criticism on Oliphant's Carlingford novels has generally read them as provincial fictions readily comparable to Trollope or to early Eliot: for example, Elsie B. Michie, "Buying Brains: Trollope, Oliphant, and Vulgar Victorian Commerce," *Victorian Studies: An Interdisciplinary Journal of Social, Political, and Cultural Studies* 44, no. 1 (2001); Janice Carlisle, "The Smell of Class: British Novels of the 1860s," *Victorian Literature and Culture* 29, no. 1 (2001); and Margarete Rubik, "The Subversion of Literary Clichés in Oliphant's Fiction," in *Margaret Oliphant: Critical Essays on a Gentle Subversive*, ed. D. J. Trela (Selinsgrove, Pa.: Susquehanna University Press, 1995). Jay's argument about Oliphant's partially successful effort to master the intricacies of English small-town life also tends in the same direction; Jay, *Mrs Oliphant*, 198–200. There is, however, some recent work placing Oliphant in a Scottish tradition: cf. Young, "Workers"; Adrianne Noel Bender, "Mapping Scotland's Identities: Representations of National Landscapes in the Novels of Scott, Stevenson, Oliphant, and Munro" (Ph.D. Diss., New York University, 2001); and Pam Perkins, "'We Who Have Been Bred Upon Sir Walter': Margaret Oliphant, Sir Walter Scott, and Women's Literary History," *English Studies in Canada* 30, no. 2 (2004).

10. Dunn, *R. D. Blackmore*, 142, quoted in Sally Shuttleworth, "Introduction," in *Lorna Doone: A Romance of Exmoor* (New York: Oxford University Press, 1989), ix.

11. For a discussion of provincialism and provinciality that frames the issue through England's "provinciality" in Europe in the eighteenth century, see Alok Yadav, *Before the Empire of English: Literature, Provinciality, and Nationalism in Eighteenth-Century Britain* (New York: Palgrave Macmillan, 2004); for a theoretical overview of provincialism as a problem of colonial-imperial relations, see Dipesh Chakrabarty, *Provincializing Europe: Postcolonial Thought and Historical Difference* (Princeton: Princeton University Press, 2000).

12. Duncan, "Provincial," 322. See also Ian Duncan, *Scott's Shadow* (Princeton: Princeton University Press, forthcoming), esp. chapter 3, "Economies of National Character." An earlier scholarly analysis less attuned than are Duncan or Gilmour to the ironies and contradictions built into the provincial novel is John

Lucas, *The Literature of Change: Studies in the Nineteenth-Century Provincial Novel* (New York: Barnes and Noble, 1977).

13. Franco Moretti, *Atlas of the European Novel, 1800–1900* (New York: Verso, 1999), 40. The division of the nineteenth century into these three periods can, according to Gilmour, be traced back as far as Lucien Leclaire's work of the mid-twenieth-century. Robin Gilmour, "Regional and Provincial in Victorian Literature," in *The Literature of Region and Nation*, ed. R. P. Draper (Basingstoke: Macmillan, 1989), 53; Lucien Leclaire, *Le Roman Régionaliste Dans Les Iles Britanniques, 1880–1950* (Clermont-Ferrand: G. de Bussac, 1954).

14. Duncan, "Provincial," 323.

15. Two remarks in Eliot's letters can be taken as emblematic of her comparative indifference to fine distinctions between one English provincial locale and another. The first comes in a letter to William Allingham of March 8, 1877: "I was born and bred in Warwickshire, and heard the Leicestershire, North Staffordshire and Derbyshire dialects during visits made in my childhood and youth. These last are represented (mildly) in *Adam Bede*. . . . [D]ialect, like other living things, tends to become mongrel, especially in a central fertile and manufacturing region attractive of migration." The second is in a letter to John Blackwood of September 19, 1873, apropos of her having used the name Lowick in *Middlemarch*: "I did not know that there was really a Lowick, in a midland county too" (both letters are included in Eliot, *Selections*, 481, 424).

16. Elizabeth Cleghorn Gaskell, *Wives and Daughters* (New York: Penguin, 1997), 5.

17. The detachment Arnold advocates in place of provincialism is revealingly charted in Amanda Anderson, *The Powers of Distance: Cosmopolitanism and the Cultivation of Detachment* (Princeton: Princeton University Press, 2001), 91–118.

18. Matthew Arnold, "The Literary Influence of Academies," in *Essays in Criticism, First Series*, ed. Thomas Marion Hoctor (Chicago: University of Chicago Press, 1968), 42.

19. See the helpful discussion of Arnold's essay in Gilmour, which also cites an 1865 article by James Hannay, "Provincialism." "If the railways bring the country into London, they also carry London into the country. The Londoner sees more of his own country and other countries than he used to do, and cockneyism diminishes from the same cause which diminishes the rusticity of the provincial" ("Regional," 53).

20. Arnold, "Literary," 42, 44, 45.

21. Emily's commitment to the grainy particularities of local landscape and custom (cf. Nancy Armstrong, "Emily's Ghost: The Cultural Politics of Victorian Fiction, Folklore, and Photography," *Novel: A Forum on Fiction* 25 [1992]) might match Blackmore's. Charlotte's redaction of and apology for Emily's "rude . . . strange . . . unintelligible, and . . . repulsive" world of the moors, though, helps explain Charlotte's comparative success in her own day: Jonathan Grossman refers to *Wuthering Heights*, by contrast (personal communication), as "the twentieth century's favorite nineteenth-century novel." Jane Eyre's willingness to let herself be bundled from place to place like a stagecoach parcel (cf. Sharon Marcus, "The Profession of the Author: Abstraction, Advertising, and Jane Eyre," *PMLA: Publications of the Modern Language Association of America* 110, no. 2 [1995])

is, for instance, consistent with Charlotte's appreciation for strong characters capable of traveling long distances unchanged, a trope much more typical of provincial than regional writing. I am grateful to Eileen Gillooly, Eric Gray, and Sharon Marcus for conversations on this point.

22. Cf. Amanda Claybaugh's call for "a transatlanticism that is as attentive to the connections across national boundaries as to the differences between nations" ("Toward a New Transatlanticism: Dickens in the United States," *Victorian Studies* 48, no. 3 [2006]: 439). Influential attempts at "deprovincializing American literary studies" (the phrase is from Lawrence Buell, "Rethinking Anglo-American Literary History," *Clio* 33, no. 1 [2003]) include Robert Weisbuch, *Atlantic Double-Cross: American Literature and British Influence in the Age of Emerson* (Chicago: University of Chicago Press, 1986), and Paul Giles, *Virtual Americas: Transnational Fictions and the Transatlantic Imaginary* (Durham, N.C.: Duke University Press, 2002).

23. I am grateful to Susan Pedersen and Amanda Claybaugh for conversations on this point.

24. Sutton, *R. D. Blackmore*, 131.

25. Amy Kaplan, "Nation, Region, and Empire," in *The Columbia History of the American Novel*, ed. Emory Elliott (New York: Columbia University Press, 1991); Richard H. Brodhead, *Cultures of Letters: Scenes of Reading and Writing in Nineteenth-Century America* (Chicago: University of Chicago Press, 1993). For a persuasive account of this, and of related work by Nancy Glazener, Carrie Bramen, Laurie Shannon, and Bill Brown, see Evans, *Before*, 109–19.

26. Josiah Royce, "Provincialism," in *Race Questions, Provincialism, and Other American Problems* (New York: Macmillan, 1908), 61.

27. Ibid., 71–72.

28. Ibid., 65–67.

29. Nancy Glazener, *Reading for Realism: The History of a U.S. Literary Institution, 1850–1910* (Durham, N.C.: Duke University Press, 1997); Brodhead, *Cultures*; Philip Fisher, *Still the New World: American Literature in a Culture of Creative Destruction* (Cambridge, Mass.: Harvard University Press, 1999); Philip Joseph, *American Literary Regionalism in a Global Age* (Baton Rouge: Louisiana State University Press, 2006).

30. Philip Fisher, "Democratic Social Space: Whitman, Melville, and the Promise of American Transparency," *Representations* 24 (1988), emphasizes Jeffersonian republicanism's commitment to replicability that can, as in the work of Whitman, proceed by way of the disavowal of cultural depth. The persistence of strong racial demarcation in America, however, coupled with the rise in nostalgic forms of reinvigorated attention to "cultural preservation" throughout the late nineteenth century and beyond demonstrate the continuing American belief in identity defined by cultural and historical depth; on this point, see Stephen Michael Best, *The Fugitive's Properties: Law and the Poetics of Possession* (Chicago: University of Chicago Press, 2004), and Walter Benn Michaels, *Our America: Nativism, Modernism, and Pluralism* Durham, N.C.: Duke University Press, 1995). One implication of such adherence to depth is a fascination with the profound wells of residual culture that backwaters (for example, Appalachia, Down-East Maine) can supply.

31. That *The Virginians* is explicitly marked as a sequel to Thackeray's *Henry Esmond* (about Henry's grandsons) is of a piece with the logic of American "local color": America assembles itself from salvageable bits of traveling culture, which may come from the English canon or (as I argue below) the Sears catalogue.

32. Evans, *Before*, 111, 113.

33. The Scottish kailyard novelists, J. M Barrie especially, might seem evidence for a newly emergent British regional tradition, but their ties to evangelical meliorism suggest how far they are from a return to the separatist strand in Romantic-era national tales. Gillian Shepherd even goes so far as to attack "kailyard novelists" because "for one brief but crucial span of Scottish history they [Ian McLaren, S. R. Crockett, and J. M. Barrie] sought to thwart a national consciousness that might have been, and to divert attention from the appalling problems of an emerging and maturing industrial nation. It was not national infantilism; it was attempted national infanticide" ("The Kailyard," in *The History of Scottish Literature, Vol. 3: Nineteenth Century*, ed. Douglas Gifford [Aberdeen: Aberdeen University Press, 1988], 317).

34. Buzard's innovation is not the word, which Pratt had coined to describe the way that colonized nations might write their own stories, but the suggestion that even a colonizing and imperial nation would contain writers who turned the ethnographic lens (*avant la lettre*) upon the metropole itself. Buzard, *Disorienting*, 8–19.

35. Michael A. Elliott, *The Culture Concept: Writing and Difference in the Age of Realism* (Minneapolis: University of Minnesota Press, 2002), 45.

36. Frances Hodgson Burnett, *Louisiana* (New York: C. Scribner's Sons, 1880), 2, 6.

37. Ibid., 163.

38. This warehousing of Louisiana's authentic past is perfectly coincident with her own name: like Owen Wister's "Virginian," she is named for a natal state that never appears in the novel and has no discernible impact on her current actions.

39. Cf. Gretchen Gerzina, *Frances Hodgson Burnett: The Unexpected Life of the Author of the Secret Garden* (New Brunswick: Rutgers University Press, 2004); James Malcolm Nelson, "The Stage Adaptation of *That Lass O'Lowrie's* and Mid-Victorian Plays of Factory and Mine," *Dalhousie Review* 61, no. 4 (1981).

40. Frances Hodgson Burnett, *That Lass O' Lowrie's* (New York: Scribner, Armstrong, 1877), 1–2.

41. The two were even published together in a single volume by Macmillan in 1880, in what appears to be the first English publication of *Louisiana*.

42. Burnett, *Lass*, 261.

43. Ibid., 269.

44. Cf. Trumpener, *Bardic*, and Duncan, *Scott's Shadow*. My argument for separating out the Irish and Scottish cases is developed in the introduction, and (in note 33, above) I argue that the fiction of the kailyard school proves ultimately amenable to the logic of English/British provincialism.

45. On the conceptual division of England into North and South, see Roberto M. Dainotto, "Lost in an Ancient South: Elizabeth Gaskell and the Rhetoric of

Latitudes," in *Place in Literature: Regions, Cultures, Communities* (Ithaca: Cornell University Press, 2000), 75–102.

46. Similarly, critiques of decadent aristocracy mingle with stirring fights with brigands: head villain Carver Doone's best friend is an effete aristocrat, the Marwood of Whichehalse. Shuttleworth has an excellent account both of Lorna's ornamentalism and of the various ersatz capitalist plot devices that shape the latter half of the novel. Shuttleworth, "Introduction," vix–xvi.

47. Blackmore, *Lorna Doone*, 147.

48. June 8, 1875. Blackmore's reply of June 11, saying that it is generous of Hardy "to be pleased with one who works in your own field," is probably a pun on the professional and pastoral meanings of "field." Thomas Hardy, letter to Blackmore, August 6, 1875, in *Collected Letters of Thomas Hardy: Volume One (1840–1892)*, ed. Richard Little Purdy and Michale Millgate (Oxford: Clarendon, 1978), 38.

49. Blackmore, *Lorna Doone*, 299.

50. Ibid., 15, 134.

51. Ibid., 56.

52. Sutton, however, makes the case that *The Prelude* was (along with *Waverley* and *Henry Esmond*) a great influence upon *Lorna Doone*. Indeed, both Blackmore's sensibility and syntax often seem shaped by *The Prelude*'s treatment of "spots of time." Max Keith Sutton, " 'The Prelude' and *Lorna Doone*," *Wordsworth Circle* 13, no. 4 (1982).

53. R. D. Blackmore, *Alice Lorraine, a Tale of the South Downs* (London: S. Low, Marston, Searle, and Rivington, 1883), 1.

54. Ibid. Compare the argument that "the possibility of a new social valuation of landscape [that is, aesthetic appreciation after the Romantic model] is contingent upon the large-scale transformation of the countryside in the wake of agricultural capitalism, and, in particular, as a consequence of successive waves of enclosure and consequent depopulation" (John Guillory, "The English Common Place: Lineages of the Topographical Genre," *Critical Quarterly* 33, no. 4 [1991]: 5, drawing on John Barrell, *The Idea of Landscape and the Sense of Place, 1730–1840: An Approach to the Poetry of John Clare* [Cambridge: University Press, 1972]).

55. Blackmore, *Alice Lorraine*, 2.

56. Blackmore, *Lorna Doone*, 210.

57. Ibid., 562.

58. Ibid., 563.

59. "All this was done in pencil, but as plain as plain could be. In my coffin it shall lie, with my ring, and something else. Therefore I will not expose it to every man who buys this book, and haply thinks that he has bought me to the bottom of my heart" (ibid., 584).

60. Review of Blackmore, *Lorna Doone*, *Saturday Review*, November 5, 1870, 503.

61. Blackmore, *Lorna Doone*, 589.

62. Ibid., 642. My notion of Lorna's unpersonality is informed by the cogent account of Scott's interest in protagonists without "character" in Alexander Welsh, *The Hero of the Waverley Novels* (New Haven: Yale University Press, 1963).

63. It is noteworthy that the chapter describing the shooting of Lorna was originally titled "Driven Beyond Endurance"— that is, the salience of the shooting is what it does to John, not to Lorna.

64. R. D. Blackmore, *Lorna Doone, a Romance of Exmoor. With a Special Introduction by the Author, Illustrated from Drawings by W. Small, and from Photographs by Clifton Johnson* (New York and London: Harper and Bros., 1900), 446, 450.

65. There are many photographs in the book that show signs of subtle touch-ups—skylines illuminated, the outline of birds strengthened, and so forth. But the few instances of juxtaposition I have in mind are glaringly evident, different in kind from such silent emendations.

66. Examining photographs by Clifton Johnston in his various travel books (for example, *New England and its Neighbors* [1902] and *The New England Country* [1915]), I have noted his repeated use of what I believe to be blurry photographs with sharply rendered figures in the foreground. In all of his works, such blurry photographs with superimposed figures are clearly distinguished both from pure landscape photography and from evident pen-and-ink drawings. Whatever their technical specifications (colleagues have suggested both that they might be simply specially prepared photographs and that they are simply drawings), they are evidently meant to be distinguishable both from his drawings and his unmodified photographs.

67. For example, one acolyte writes of "his *enthralling power of fancy* . . . the purity and limpid transparency of his imagery and playful fancy." The proof for this "fancy" lies in an unremarkable, factually descriptive passage; the author then praises Blackmore because "this is the Charles Parsonage, the home of his boyhood . . . this the rookery, the cawing of which lingered in his memory for sixty years" (Anonymous, "Richard Dodd Blackmore: Secretive Genius of the Moors," in *Echoes of Exmoor: A Record of the Discussions and Doings of the Men-of-Exmoor Club. Fourth Series* [London: Simpkin and Marshall, 1926], 21, emphasis in original).

68. Blackmore, *Lorna Doone*, 663.

69. Burnett, *Louisiana*, 163.

70. Royce, "Provincialism," 66.

71. Dated 1890, the poem appears in an American edition of 1900. R. D. Blackmore, "Preface to Harper's Edition," in *Lorna Doone, a Romance of Exmoor*, xii.

72. John Meade Falkner, *Moonfleet*, ed. Brian Alderson (New York: Oxford University Press, 1993).

73. Duncan argues that "a regionalist discourse is established, in the early decades of the nineteenth century, in national and historical novels by Irish and Scottish writers. . . . [In the 1840s] regionalism decisively loses its ideological ability to stabilize the figure of the nation [and English provincialism triumphs]. But the novel [in the economic depressions of 1870–1885] abandons the stabilizing equation of provincial with national life and resumes a variety of regionalisms, all of which articulate a centrifugal relation to the historical form of the nation" ("Provincial," 325–26).

74. A telling example here is the overdetermined failure of the work, both fictional and essayistic, of the microlocalist (with one fantastical exception) Richard Jefferies.

75. Kipling, who called England "my favorite foreign country," spent a total of nearly two decades in India, various intervals in South Africa and elsewhere, and lived in Vermont between 1893 and 1899. Burnett spent roughly thirty of her seventy-five years in England, and the remainder in America.

76. Frances Hodgson Burnett, *The Secret Garden*, ed. Dennis Butts (New York: Oxford University Press, 2000).

77. "I had every opportunity for knowing her well, at least. We were born on the same day, we learned to toddle about together, we began our earliest observations of the world we lived in at the same period, we made the same mental remarks on people and things, and reserved to ourselves exactly the same rights of private personal opinion" (Burnett, *The One I Knew the Best of All* [New York: Arno, 1980], 1).

78. Anna Krugovoy Silver, "Domesticating Brontë's Moors: Motherhood in *The Secret Garden*," *Lion and the Unicorn: A Critical Journal of Children's Literature* 21, no. 2 (1997); Susan E. James, "*Wuthering Heights* for Children: Frances Hodgson Burnett's *The Secret Garden*," *Connotations: A Journal for Critical Debate* 10, no. 1 (2000).

79. Burnett, *Secret Garden*, 269, 232.

CHAPTER 5: GOING LOCAL: CHARACTERS AND ENVIRONMENTS IN
THOMAS HARDY'S WESSEX

1. Thomas Hardy, *Tess of the D'Urbervilles*, ed. John Paul Riquelme (Boston: Bedford, 1998), 384; Michael Millgate, *Thomas Hardy: A Biography Revisited* (New York: Oxford University Press, 2004), 122.

2. Henry James, review of *Far from the Madding Crowd*, *Nation*, December 24, 1874, in R. G. Cox, ed., *Thomas Hardy, the Critical Heritage* (London: Routledge and Kegan Paul, 1970), 27–31, 30.

3. Thomas Hardy, *The Return of the Native*, ed. Simon Gatrell, Nancy Barrineau, and Margaret R. Higonnet (New York: Oxford University Press, 2005), 3.

4. "Hardy the Degenerate," *World*, November 13, 1895, quoted in Millgate, *Thomas Hardy*, 341. Millgate has a helpful account of Hardy's early exposure to Darwin and to positivism in *Thomas Hardy*, 89, 122.

5. "The Wessex Labourer," *Examiner* July 15, 1876. On the parallels between imperial and internal peripheries, cf. R. Radhakrishnan, "Cultural Theory and the Politics of Location," in *Views Beyond the Border Country: Raymond Williams and Cultural Politics*, ed. Dennis L. Dworkin and Leslie G. Roman (New York: Routledge, 1993).

6. Tom Paulin, for example, cites a note Hardy made in August 1865: "[T]he poetry of a scene varies with the minds of the perceivers. Indeed, it does not lie in the scene at all." Paulin traces, through Shelley, the influence upon Hardy of Hume's "reducing the self to a heap of different perceptions which lack a simple identity . . . so the human mind becomes a random assemblage of what it per-

ceives, the sum of its memories and perceptions" (*Thomas Hardy, the Poetry of Perception* [Totowa, N.J.: Rowman and Littlefield, 1975], 15–16). See also Samuel Hynes, *The Pattern of Hardy's Poetry* (Chapel Hill: University Of North Carolina, 1961), esp. 109–29.

7. Florence Emily Hardy, *The Early Life of Thomas Hardy, 1840–1891* (New York: Macmillan, 1928), 177. Although both volumes of the *Life* are published under Florence's name, and written in her voice (which explains why Hardy's reported speech and journal entries are often set off as quotations, as in the passages above), Millgate and others have demonstrated that both volumes were "very largely written by Thomas Hardy himself"—in fact, nearly entirely so. Richard Purdy, quoted in Michael Millgate, "Introduction," in *The Life and Work of Thomas Hardy*, ed. Michael Millgate (Athens: University of Georgia Press, 1985), x. This particular passage also appears unaltered in Millgate's edition, which gives authorial credit directly to Hardy himself. Hardy, *Life and Work*, 139. One fictional counterpoint to the scene can be found in a description of Granny Martin in *Two on a Tower* "quietly re-enacting in her brain certain of the long chain of episodes, pathetic, tragical, and humorous, which had constituted the parish history for the last sixty years" (Thomas Hardy, *Two on a Tower: A Romance*, ed. Sally Shuttleworth [New York: Penguin, 1999], 16).

8. Hardy, *Tess*, 32.

9. Ibid., 99–100.

10. I believe that my account applies to Hardy's later poetry, as well, but I make my case only by way of that first book in 1898. For some of the recent work on Hardy's relationship to regionalism, see, infra alia, Ralph Pite, *Hardy's Geography: Wessex and the Regional Novel* (New York: Palgrave, 2002), and Simon Gatrell, *Thomas Hardy's Vision of Wessex* (New York: Palgrave, 2003). Duncan reads Hardy as disavowing provincialism in favor of regionalism or something akin to regionalism. Duncan, "Provincial," 335.

11. "Dorset in London" (1908), reprinted in Thomas Hardy, *Personal Writings: Prefaces, Literary Opinions, Reminiscences*, ed. Harold Orel (Lawrence: University Press of Kansas, 1966), 224–25, 220.

12. Hardy consistently rejected the idea that there was anything more to knowing a place than spending time there. In the *Life*, Hardy is described (which is to say, describes himself) as "knowing every street and alley west of St. Paul's like a born Londoner, which he was often supposed to be; an experience quite ignored by the reviewers of his later books, who, if he only touched on London in his pages, promptly reminded him not to write of a place he was unacquainted with, but to get back to his sheepfolds" (Hardy, *Early Life*, 82).

13. Ibid., 50.

14. Ibid., 53.

15. One work that treats *The Mayor of Casterbridge* in the context of a global marketplace is Michael Valdez Moses, *The Novel and the Globalization of Culture* (New York: Oxford University Press, 1995).

16. Even to Lea, however, Hardy complained that "he had been unknowingly 'Kodaked' while visiting the Higher Bockhampton cottage" (Millgate, *Thomas Hardy*, 389).

17. Horace Moule, review of Thomas Hardy, *Under the Greenwood Tree*, *Saturday Review*, September 28, 1872; Andrew Lang, review of Thomas Hardy, *Far from the Madding Crowd*, *Academy*, January 2, 1875; review of Hardy, *Far from the Madding Crowd*, *Athenaeum*, December 5, 1874; all three reviews reprinted in Cox, ed., *Thomas*, 11–14, 35–39, 19–20, 11, 35, 20. Cf. Raymond Williams's gloss on this tendency: "It is common to reduce Hardy's fiction to the impact of an urban alien on the 'timeless pattern' of English rural life" (Williams, *Country*, 200).

18. For example, "The Dorsetshire Labourer," *Longman's Magazine* (July 1883), 252–69, reprinted in Hardy, *Personal*.

19. For example, in his "General Preface to the Novels and Poems" (1911; reprinted in Hardy, *Tess*).

20. Even as a Naturalist, though, Hardy is an anomaly, given his clear interest in the divergence of individual experiences from any overarching social norm. Gillian Beer has drawn attention to Hardy's interest in the relationship between the individual contingency of plot outcomes and the general fact of the universe's determined course (the "gratuitous and the inexorable"). In Hardy, she insightfully argues, "Deterministic systems are placed under great stress: a succession of ghost plots is present. The persistent almost-attained happy alternatives are never quite obliterated by the actual terrible events" (*Darwin's Plots: Evolutionary Narrative in Darwin, George Eliot, and Nineteenth-Century Fiction* [London and Boston: Routledge and Kegan Paul, 1983], 239, cf. 239–58).

21. Thomas Hardy, *Poems of the Past and the Present* (London: Harper and Bros., 1902), vi.

22. Jonathan Crary, *Suspensions of Perception: Attention, Spectacle, and Modern Culture* (Cambridge, Mass.: The MIT Press, 1999), 1.

23. Ibid., 4.

24. "In late-nineteenth-century psychology and philosophy . . . attention seemed to be a subjective activity affecting our perception of things and thus worth investigating" (Gerald E. Myers, *William James, His Life and Thought* [New Haven: Yale University Press, 1986], 185).

25. Stein Notebooks, YCAL 76, Box 39, folders 814–15 (c. 1909) . I thank Sean McCann for the reference, and for help in contextualizing it.

26. Crary's account of the complementary relationship between aesthetic absorption and the worker's concentration on industrial processes is helpful on this point.

27. Tim Armstrong, *Haunted Hardy* (Basingstoke: Palgrave, 2000), 30.

28. Thomas Hardy, "The Profitable Reading of Fiction [from *Forum*, 1888]," in *Thomas Hardy's Personal Writings*, ed. Harold Orel (Lawrence: University Press of Kansas, 1966), 117.

29. "Afterwards" (1917) in Hardy, *The Complete Poems of Thomas Hardy*, ed. James Gibson (New York: Macmillan, 1978), 553.

30. Paulin traces this pattern through several related poems in which "the perception of a thing, rather than the thing itself, has disappeared" (*Thomas*, 97).

31. This despite Hardy's own insistence that the boundaries of Wessex are heuristic of, rather than intrinsic to, the place itself: "The geographical limits of the stage here trodden were not absolutely forced upon the writer by circumstances;

he forced them upon himself from judgment" (Hardy, "General Preface to the Novels and Poems," 21).

32. John Barrell, "Geographies of Hardy's Wessex," in *The Regional Novel in Britain and Ireland, 1800–1990*, ed. K. D. M. Snell (Cambridge: Cambridge University Press, 1998 [1982]), 113, 118.

33. Cf. "Hardy's aesthetics of disjunction was a fundamental principle of his art, a mode he used throughout his poetry and fiction" (Vern B. Lentz, "Disembodied Voices in Hardy's Shorter Poems," *Colby Literary Quarterly* 23, no. 2 [1987]: 65).

34. Hardy, *Mayor*, 157.

35. Williams, *Country*, 200.

36. Ibid., 213. Elaine Scarry's important account of work's centrality in Hardy also persuasively stresses continuity, not just between various sorts of labor, but also between laborers and the surfaces of the material world. Such continuity seems to me compatible with Hardy's commitment to representing diverse ways of noticing that material world. "Work and the Body in Hardy and Other Nineteenth-Century Novelists," *Representations* 3 (1983).

37. Williams, *Country*, 214.

38. Crary, *Suspensions*, 4.

39. "The Dorsetshire Labourer."

40. Thomas Hardy, *The Trumpet-Major and Robert His Brother* (New York: Penguin, 1984), 149–50.

41. Hardy, *Tess*, 150.

42. Thomas Hardy, *Desperate Remedies: A Novel* (London: Macmillan, 1975), 44. One of the determinedly hostile reviews that greeted that novel singled out this scene to praise Hardy's talent for "sensitiveness to scenic and atmospheric effects, and to their influence on the mind, and the power of rousing similar sensitiveness in his readers." That formulation is interesting because it collapses the difference that Hardy works so hard to establish between things as they occur in the world and the effect they have upon those who perceive them. Review of *Desperate Remedies*, *Spectator*, April 22, 1871, reprinted in Cox, *Thomas*, 3–5, 4.

43. Hardy, *Tess*, 285.

44. Ibid., 318. I discuss Hardy's thinking about the forms of perception attached to portable professions in John Plotz, "Motion Slickness: Spectacle and Circulation in Thomas Hardy's 'On the Western Circuit,' " *Studies in Short Fiction* 33, no. 3 (1996).

45. Simmel's "The Stranger" is a useful guide to the domestic alienness that defines the indispensable role that the outsider has to play in such provincial novels.

46. I am grateful to James Buzard and Mary Jean Corbett for conversations (March 2004) clarifying the significance of different sorts of "local" attention in Hardy.

47. Hardy, *Two Towers*, 231–32.

48. Hardy, "Profitable Reading," 124.

49. "He could see fractional parts of the dancers . . . together with about three-fifths of the band in profile, including the restless shadow of a fiddler's elbow and the tip of a bass viol bow" (Hardy, *Mayor*, 375).

50. Beer, *Darwin's*, 246.

51. Thomas Hardy, *The Woodlanders*, ed. Patricia Ingham (New York: Penguin, 1998), 9.

52. Ibid.

53. Cf. "[t]he separation of the two forms of Hardy's art is primarily a convenient fiction" (Catherine Robson, " 'Where Heaves the Turf': Thomas Hardy and the Boundaries of the Earth," *Victorian Literature and Culture* 32, no. 2 [2004]: 501). I have in mind here astronomical parallax, the "[d]ifference or change in the apparent position or direction of an object as seen from two different points" (s.v. "parallax," *Oxford English Dictionary*, 2nd edition), rather than the neo-Hegelian dialectical notion of "an insurmountable *parallax gap*, the confrontation of two closely linked perspectives between which no neutral common ground is possible" (Slavoj Zizek, *The Parallax View* [Cambridge, Mass.: The MIT Press, 2006], 4).

54. Quoted in Donald Davie, "Thomas Hardy and British Poetry," in *With the Grain: Essays on Thomas Hardy and Modern British Poetry*, ed. Clive Wilmer (Manchester: Carcanet, 1998), 23.

55. In distinguishing between the poems that anatomize the diversity of perception and those that do not, it might even seem tempting to follow Hynes and say that "Hardy was two poets." Hynes distinguishes between the Hardy who "attached himself to the literary high culture of his time" and wrote bad public poetry, and the good Hardy, who "took poetry to be an ordinary but private activity, like meditation, or day-dreaming, or despair." I am interested in the difficulties involved in sharing private sensations and memories within what Hynes calls "good Hardy" poetry. Samuel Hynes, "On Hardy's Badness," in *Critical Essays on Thomas Hardy's Poetry*, ed. Harold Orel (New York: G. K. Hall, 1995 [1983]), 80.

56. "Alike and Unlike" (1925), in Hardy, *Complete Poems*, 739.

57. Ralph Pite, *Thomas Hardy: The Guarded Life* (London: Picador, 2006), 349.

58. Hardy, *Complete Poems*, 712.

59. J. Hillis Miller analyzes Hardy's "recognition of the mute detachment of external objects" (*Thomas Hardy: Distance and Desire* [Cambridge, Mass.: Harvard University Press, 1970], 4).

60. Edmund Chambers, quoted in Trevor Johnson, "Introduction," in Thomas Hardy, *Wessex Poems and Other Verses* (Keele: Keele University Press, 1995), 45; Millgate, *Thomas Hardy*, 363.

61. By 1903, the poem had been retitled "She: At His Funeral." Thomas Hardy, *Wessex Poems and Other Verses, with Thirty Illustrations by the Author* (London: Harper and Bros., 1903), 19.

62. Ibid., 21.

63. Marjorie Levinson, "Object-Loss and Object Bondage: Economies of Representation in Hardy's Poetry," *ELH* 73, no. 2 (2006): 550.

64. Hardy, *Wessex*, 195.

65. Analyzing another poem "organized by its many images of perception," Geoffrey Harvey describes Hardy as finding a way to reconcile "place and the eye

of vision, which both perceives and half creates" ("Thomas Hardy: Moments of Vision," in Orel, *Critical Essays*, 41).

66. Hardy, "General Preface to the Novels and Poems," 23.

67. Hardy, *Personal*, 9–10.

CHAPTER SIX: NOWHERE AND EVERYWHERE: THE END OF PORTABILITY IN WILLIAM MORRIS'S ROMANCES

1. As Dorothy Van Ghent memorably writes: "The fictional hypothesis is peculiar in that it has to carry at every moment the full weight of all its concrete experimental data. . . . The particular body that a thing has is of the very greatest importance to the whole fictional structure. Does it squeak, is it scared, is it brown, is it round, is it chilly, does it think, does it smash? . . . The procedure of the novel is to individualize." (Van Ghent, *English*, 4).

2. Catherine Gallagher, "George Eliot: Immanent Victorian," *Representations*, no. 90 (2005).

3. Christoph Menke-Eggers explores the tension within Kantian aesthetics between imagining art as staking out an entire separate way of looking at the world, and imagining art as an alternative pathway to the same apprehension of the world that analytic judgment provides. Alain Badiou has recently criticized philosophical misapprehensions about analytically parsing the truth found in aesthetic objects, and proposed instead that aesthetic truths are to be found in art's resistance to philosophical paraphrase, since art is "the thinking of the thought that it itself is." Menke-Eggers, *The Sovereignty of Art: Aesthetic Negativity in Adorno and Derrida* (Cambridge, Mass.: The MIT Press, 1998), and Alain Badiou, *Handbook of Inaesthetics*, trans. Alberto Toscano (Stanford: Stanford University Press, 2005), 14.

4. Hannah Arendt, *Lectures on Kant's Political Philosophy*, ed. Ronald Beiner (Brighton: Harvester, 1982).

5. Hannah Arendt, *The Human Condition* (Chicago: University of Chicago Press, 1998 [1958]), 23–73.

6. William Morris, *News from Nowhere*, in *The Collected Works of William Morris*, ed. M. Morris (London: Longmans, Green, 1910–1915; reprinted London: Routledge/Thoemmes, 1992), 16:22.

7. Ibid., 16:158, 151.

8. Morris, "The Lesser Arts," in M. Morris, *Collected Works of William Morris*, 22:4.

9. E. P. Thompson, *William Morris: Romantic to Revolutionary* (London: Lawrence and Wishart, 1955), and Fiona McCarthy, *William Morris: A Life for Our Times* (London: Faber and Faber, 1994) are the biographies of record. On questions of design, see Peter Stansky, *Redesigning the World: William Morris, the 1880s, and the Arts and Crafts* (Palo Alto, Calif.: Society for the Promotion of Science and Scholarship, 1996), and Peter Faulkner, *Against the Age: An Introduction to William Morris* (Boston: Allen and Unwin, 1980). Recent work on Morris's poetry also includes Herbert Tucker, "All for the Tale: The Epic Macropoetics of Morris' *Sigurd the Volsung*," *Victorian Poetry* 34, no. 3 (1996), and

Jeffrey Skoblow, *Paradise Dislocated: Morris, Politics, Art* (Charlottesville: University Press of Virginia, 1993).

10. Morris, "The Lesser Arts," 22:4.

11. Morris, *News*, 16:132.

12. George Lamming, *Natives of My Person* (Ann Arbor: University of Michigan Press, 1992 [1970]). This may help to explain why, as C. S. Lewis puts it, Morris was damned or faintly praised in his day as "faint," "shadowy, "decorative": in Lewis's terms, "nineteenth-century criticism was unconsciously dominated by the novel, and could praise only with reservations work which does not present analysed characters . . . in a naturalistic setting" ("William Morris," in *Rehabilitations and Other Essays* [London: Oxford University Press, 1939], 43).

13. Cf. Anderson, *Powers*, and George Lewis Levine, *Dying to Know: Scientific Epistemology and Narrative in Victorian England* (Chicago: University of Chicago Press, 2002), on the late Victorian interest in impersonality. Anderson genealogizes the "detached" intellectual; Levine investigates instances of scientific knowledge seemingly only attainable by renouncing personhood.

14. Alex Woloch, *The One Vs. The Many: Minor Characters and the Space of the Protagonist in the Novel* (Princeton: Princeton University Press, 2004), 13.

15. Ibid., 15.

16. Ibid., 14.

17. Ibid., 13.

18. I have found almost no modern editions of the romances apart from a small flurry a generation ago, among which are William Morris, *The Story of the Glittering Plain* (San Bernadino, Calif.: Borgo, 1980); Morris, *The Sundering Flood* (Seattle: Unicorn, 1973); and Morris, *The Well at the World's End: A Tale*, ed. Lin Carter (New York: Ballantine, 1970).

19. The following two paragraphs draw on my article, "Chartist Literature," in David Scott Kastan, ed., *The Oxford Encyclopedia of British Literature* (Oxford: Oxford University Press, 2006), 1:440–44.

20. The authoritative recent account is contained in Ian Haywood, *The Revolution in Popular Literature: Print, Politics, and the People, 1790–1860* (New York: Cambridge University Press, 2004).

21. Haywood, *Working-Class Fiction: From Chartism to Trainspotting* (Plymouth: Northcote House, 1997), 16.

22. In the same way that the lost girl of De Quincey's *Confessions of an English Opium Eater*, Ann(e), might have been named after the parish, St. Anne's, in which De Quincey describes her living. Grevel Lindop, *The Opium-Eater: A Life of Thomas De Quincey* (New York: Taplinger, 1981).

23. Thomas Martin Wheeler, "Sunshine and Shadow," in *Chartist Fiction*, ed. Ian Haywood (Aldershot: Ashgate, 1999), 192.

24. Ibid.

25. Anne F. Janowitz, *Lyric and Labour in the Romantic Tradition* (Cambridge: Cambridge University Press, 1998). This topic is also explored in Michael Sanders, "Poetic Agency: Metonymy and Metaphor in Chartist Poetry, 1838–1852," *Victorian Poetry* 39, no. 2 (2001). Kuduk Weiner, *Republican*, is another admirable recent account of Chartist poetry.

26. That they are ignored is proven not just by the extreme paucity of critical material on them (Kelvin, Silver, and a few others excepted), but by the feeble sales they have enjoyed over the years. *The Sundering Flood*, for example, though it might be imagined to have benefited from a surge in interest occasioned by Morris's death, apparently had a total print-run (across three editions, excluding the *Collected Works*) of about 2,000 copies in its first decade. Similarly, *The Water of the Wondrous Isles*, excluding those copies in the *Collected Works*, had a total print-run of 2,250 prior to a Longmans Pocket Library edition of 1914; and prior to a 1913 Longmans Pocket Library edition of 2,050 copies, only 1,850 copies of *The Well at the World's End* (excluding the *Collected Works*) were printed. Eugene D. LeMire, *A Bibliography of William Morris* (New Castle, Del.: Oak Knoll, 2006), 201–23. I am grateful to Mark Samuels Lasner (and members of the SHARP-L listserve) for guidance on this and other bibliographic matters.

27. Jürgen Habermas, *The Structural Transformation of the Public Sphere: An Inquiry into a Category of Bourgeois Society*, trans. Thomas Burger (Cambridge, Mass.: Polity, 1989), 137.

28. Arendt, *Human*, 39, but compare additional discussion of the novel's relationship to "storytelling," 50–51.

29. William Morris, *The Water of the Wondrous Isle*, in M. Morris, *The Collected Works of William Morris*, 20:158. No scholarly edition of the prose romances exists.

30. For an argument describing the evolution of "taste" as a quintessential component of Whig and liberal aesthetics, see Linda C. Dowling, *The Vulgarization of Art: The Victorians and Aesthetic Democracy* (Charlottesville: University Press of Virginia, 1996).

31. Morris, *News*, 16:37.

32. This helps explain, for example, the curious coolness that Morris's characters often exhibit in the face of palpable suffering near them. The dwellers near the steep, dangerous mountains that shield the World's End from the ordinary world in *The Well at the World's End* are inexplicably tormented. But Ralph and Ursula can remain apart from these sufferings, which arise from residents' doomed infatuation with the sublime dreadfulness of their native mountains.

33. Of Heaven or Hell I have no power to sing,
   I cannot ease the burden of your fears,
   Or make quick-coming death a little thing,
   Or bring again the pleasure of past years,
   Nor for my words shall ye forget your tears,
   Or hope again for aught that I can say,
   The idle singer of an empty day.

("The Earthly Paradise," I. Apology, ll. 1–7, in William Morris, *The Earthly Paradise*, ed. Florence Saunders Boos, 2 vols. [New York: Routledge, 2002], 1:52).

34. Ellen, for example, says reprovingly to a fan of Thackeray, "But I say flatly that in spite of all their cleverness and vigour, and capacity for story-telling, there is something loathsome about [Victorian novels]" (Morris, *News*, 16:151).

35. Ibid., 16:102.

36. Morris, "The Lesser Arts," 22:4.

37. Carolyn Lesjak, although she is dissatisfied with "surface mirrorings of existing conditions (present gender inequalities)" in *News from Nowhere*, also persuasively describes that novel as reaching toward a state in which, although "it constitutes the basis of sociality," "labor has ceased to be a commodity." By my account, labor arrives at that decommodified state in Morris only once the earth's "skin and surface" become both narrative's telos and its location. Carolyn Lesjak, *Working Fictions: A Genealogy of the Victorian Novel* (Durham, N.C.: Duke University Press, 2006), 174, 146, 168.

38. Morris, *News*, 16:66.

39. "Song of the Shirt," ll. 327–32, in Thomas Hood, *Selected Poems of Thomas Hood*, ed. John Clubbe (Cambridge, Mass.: Harvard University Press, 1970), 305.

40. Hannah Arendt, *On Revolution* (London: Faber and Faber, 1963); see also Deborah Nelson, "The Virtues of Heartlessness: Mary McCarthy, Hannah Arendt, and the Anesthetics of Empathy," *American Literary History* 18, no. 1 (2006). Cf. "[p]lurality is the condition of human action because we are all the same, that is, human, in such a way that nobody is ever the same as anyone else who ever lived, lives, or will live" (Arendt, *Human*, 8).

41. Morris, *News*, 16:192–93.

42. Ibid., 16:173, 198.

43. James Buzard charts in *News from Nowhere* a kind of ethnographic imagination and obsessive focus on "the role of interruption in fiction" that makes it a critique of the novel that "brought to heightened self-consciousness important formal problems arising from nineteenth-century conjunctions of narrative, history and collective identity" ("Ethnography as Interruption: *News from Nowhere*, Narrative and the Modern Romance of Authority," *Victorian Studies: A Journal of the Humanities, Arts and Sciences* 40, no. 3 [1997]: 447, 446).

44. To the socialist Richard Norman Shaw, Morris was "a great man who somehow delighted in glaring wallpapers," while to many of his artistic admirers his socialism is a continuing embarrassment or a nonsequitur. Quoted in *William Morris by Himself: Designs and Writings*, ed. Gillian Naylor (London: Macdonald Orbis, 1988), 315.

45. Phillippa Bennett, "Rediscovering the Topography of Wonder: Morris, Iceland and the Last Romances," *Journal of the William Morris Society* 16, no. 2–3 (2005).

46. Critical appraisals of Morris's romances are scarce; important recent work includes Norman Kelvin, "*News from Nowhere* and *The Spoils of Poynton*: Interiors and Exteriors," in , *William Morris: Centenary Essays: Papers from the Morris Centenary Conference Organized by the William Morris Society at Exeter College, Oxford, 30 June-3 July 1996* ed. Peter Faulkner, Peter Preston (Exeter: University of Exeter Press, 1999), 107–21; Norman Talbot, "William Morris and the Bear" in Faulkner, Preston, and Society, *Centenary*, 94–106; Carole G. Silver, *The Romance of William Morris* (Athens: Ohio University Press, 1982); and the essays collected in Florence Saunders Boos and Carole G. Silver, eds., *Socialism and the Literary Artistry of William Morris* (Columbia: University of Missouri Press, 1990).

47. William Morris, *The Well at the World's End*, vols. 16–19, in M. Morris, *Collected Works of William Morris*, 17:270.

48. Ibid.

49. This occurs, on his account, because the masses had ceded "criticism and control . . . [to] the private sphere of civil society [who rule by means of] their power of control over the means of production" (Habermas, *Structural*, 128).

50. This is a rupture that could only be overcome when "private persons came to be the private persons of a public rather than a public of private persons" (ibid., 128–29). Cf. Georg Lukács, "Reification and the Consciousness of the Proletariat," in *History and Class Consciousness: Studies in Marxist Dialectics* (Cambridge, Mass.: The MIT Press, 1971).

51. Georg Lukács, "Narrate or Describe?" in *"Writer and Critic" and Other Essays*, ed. Arthur D. Kahn (New York: Grosset and Dunlap, 1971), 127.

52. David Baguley stresses Naturalism's antiexceptionalism—that there are no grounds for distinguishing human experience from any other natural phenomena: "materialistic in its ontology, mechanistic in its cosmology, empirical in its epistemology and relativistic in its ethics, and its main direction is toward reconciling, even to the point of assimilating, the natural world and human experience" (*Naturalist Fiction: The Entropic Vision* [Cambridge: Cambridge University Press, 1990], 44). Jennifer Fleissner shows how Naturalism may be present as motif, theme, and ideology in works not generically classifiable as Naturalist, in Jennifer Fleissner, *Women, Compulsion, Modernity: The Moment of American Naturalism* (Chicago: University of Chicago, 2004).

53. Letter to Andreas Scheu, September 5, 1883, quoted in Morris, *Himself*, 17.

54. For the tradition of British socialist fiction, see H. Gustav Klaus, *The Socialist Novel in Britain: Toward the Recovery of a Tradition* (New York: St. Martin's, 1982).

55. William Morris, "How I Became a Socialist," in M. Morris, *Collected Works of William Morris*, 22:277.

56. Morris, *Water*, 20:258.

57. Ibid.

58. Kelvin also instructively contrasts Morris's attention to surfaces with the attention to psychological depths in Henry James's *The Spoils of Poynton* in "Interiors and Exteriors," 107–21, in Faulkner, Preston, and Society, eds., *Centenary*.

59. Morris, *News*, 16:182.

60. Ibid.

61. This seems a very good reason to follow Patrick Brantlinger in calling *News from Nowhere* an "antinovel" and "deliberate work of non-art" ("*News from Nowhere*: Morris' Socialist Anti-Novel," *Victorian Studies: A Journal of the Humanities, Arts and Sciences* 19 [1975]: 39–40).

62. Silver, *Romance*.

63. W. H. Hudson, *A Crystal Age* (London: T. F. Unwin, 1887), 12–13.

64. The phrase is from William Morris, review of *Looking Backward*, *Commonweal*, June 22, 1889, 194–95.

65. Morris, *Water*, 20:210.

66. Morris, *Well*, 19:253.

67. William Morris, *The Novel on Blue Paper*, ed. Penelope Fitzgerald (London: Journeyman, 1982), 73.

68. Morris, *News*, 16:211.

69. Morris's romances are a near-perfect antithesis to the most durable bit of pastiche medievalism of his day, a novel that is essentially defined by the ironic juxtaposition of past and present: Mark Twain's *Connecticut Yankee in King Arthur's Court* (1889). Twain's transparently allegorical send-up of the problems that the postwar American South (Camelot) poses to a greedy and inventive carpetbagger from the money-mad industrial North (the Yankee) works by juxtaposing two different temporalities, which meet with the grinding of gears: the book's defining image is Lancelot mounted on a bicycle. It is this sort of satire-via-overlay Morris makes impossible when he places his romance world in a realm cognitively distinct from our present day, visitable only through an act of imaginative transplantation. The Yankee brings his pistol with him, but Morris's reader (with the quasi-exception of Guest in *News from Nowhere*) does not even bring along a subject position.

70. Jones's work is eloquently described in Sally Ledger, "Chartist Aesthetics in the Mid Nineteenth Century: Ernest Jones, a Novelist of the People," *Nineteenth Century Literature* 57, no. 1 (2002).

71. Chris Waters, "Marxism, Medievalism and Popular Culture," in *History and Community: Essays in Victorian Medievalism*, ed. Florence Saunders Boos (New York: Garland, 1992), makes an interesting analogy to Nietzsche's axiomatic insistence on creative forgetting.

72. "Society of the Future," in Morris, *News and Selected Writings*, 191.

73. For example, Morris, *Well*, 19:174, and passim.

74. Ibid., 19:245.

75. "The Folk-Mote by the River," ll. 212–17, in William Morris, *Selected Poems*, ed. Peter Faulkner (Manchester: Fyfield, 1992), 147–55. Cf. Chris Waters, "Morris's 'Chants' and the Problems of Socialist Culture," 127–46, in Boos and Silver, *Socialist*.

76. Lewis, "William Morris," 39.

77. Morris, *News*, 16:88.

78. Richard Chenevix Trench, *On the Study of Words* (New York: Redfield, 1852), 33. For Gerard Manley Hopkins, things and sounds partook of the same objective realm—from which only human consciousness and our own subjective graspings after meaning are excluded. This leads to an insistence on the import of etymology that, while dissimilar ideologically from Trench's, resembles it at least in the passion for recovering lost linguistic information as if it were foundational to essential being, rather than, as Morris proposes, a lamentable historical residuum. Cf. Isobel Armstrong, *Language as Living Form in Nineteenth-Century Poetry* (Brighton: Harvester, 1982).

79. Trench, *Study*, 33–34.

80. Like Carlyle (in *On Heroes* and *Chartism*, especially), Trench presumes that migration is the quintessential English national experience. Although the novel itself comes to seem, to many Victorian writers, the one cultural phenomenon that can overcome the dangers of dissolution associated with national migration, for Trench language is the true balm and bond: "It was something for the children of Israel, when they came into Canaan, to enter upon wells which they digged not and vineyards which they had not planted, and houses which they had not built; but how much greater a boon, how much more glorious a prerogative, for any one generation to enter upon the inheritance of a language, which other

generations by their truth and toil have made already a receptacle of choicest treasures, a storehouse of so much unconscious wisdom, a fit organ for expressing the subtlest distinctions, the tenderest sentiments, the largest thoughts, and the loftiest imaginations, which at any time the heart of man can conceive" (*Study*, 36). To Morris, the conception of linguistic inheritance as treasure is precisely what leaves the English in thrall to history's corrosive force. In effect, Trench is configuring portability as the thing that makes a language a living storehouse. Morris grants the principle of weighty accumulation, but denies that it serves any function other than the purely negative one of obscuring the unadorned everyday reality of what he sees in its place: egalitarian and ecumenical solidarity.

81. Most of Morris's romances were published initially in much cheaper editions, often serialized in the pages of *Commonweal* magazine. Morris seems not to have felt a contradiction, focused as he was in making his books available to all readers in some feasible form.

82. Jerome McGann argues that Morris is interested in reminding readers that the space of imagination depends upon the flinty edges of distinct signs—the deadly space between them. Jerome J. McGann, " 'Thing to Mind': The Materialist Aesthetic of William Morris," in *Black Riders: The Visible Language of Modernism* (Princeton: Princeton University Press, 1993).

83. Morris does retain an attenuated notion of national identity, but it is striking how little real importance attaches to the "English and Jutish blood" of *News from Nowhere*, or to the difference between blonde farming folk and brunette "Cheaping-town" residents in *The Well at the World's End*. The purpose of physical distinction is not so much to racialize communities as it is to diversify the "skin and surface" of the earth. Morris, *News*, 16:62; Morris, *Well*, 16:8–16.

84. William Morris, *A Dream of John Ball*, in M. Morris, *Collected Works of William Morris*, vol. 16:220, emphasis added.

85. Walter Pater, "Poems by William Morris," *Westminster Review* n.s. 34 (1868): 301.

86. Cf. Caroline Arscott, "William Morris: Decoration and Materialism," in *Marxism and the History of Art: From William Morris to the New Left*, ed. Andrew Hemingway (London: Pluto, 2006). The artist David Mabb, by selectively painting Mayakovsky-like white squares over Morris wallpapers and fabrics (but not painting over one design element—for example, the primrose flower) has shown the very different aesthetic effect of isolating individual elements within Morris works. David Mabb, Caroline Arscott, and Steve Edwards, *William Morris* (Manchester: Whitworth Art Gallery, 2004).

87. I am grateful to Alex Woloch for conversation on this point.

88. By contrast, the "decorations" that Aubrey Beardsley is attaching to his work at this time—for example, the Morte D'Arthur he produced during 1893 and 1894—often work by exaggerated or elaborated borders that quite overwhelm the text they purportedly illuminate or complement. Seemingly, the idea of "decoration" in Beardsley is at least partially to remind the reader that what strikes one initially as sense (words) can also be seen as simply markings on the page. Cf. Nicholas Frankel, "Aubrey Beardsley 'Embroiders' the Literary Text," in *The Victorian Illustrated Book*, ed. Richard Maxwell (Charlottesville: University Press of Virginia, 2002).

89. Giorgio Agamben, *Homo Sacer: Sovereign Power and Bare Life*, trans. Daniel Heller-Roazen (Stanford: Stanford University Press, 1998 [1995]), 144, 144–53.

90. William Morris to Aglaia Coronio, letter of November 25, 1872, in William Morris, *The Collected Letters of William Morris*, ed. Norman Kelvin (Princeton: Princeton University Press, 1984), 173.

91. The Kelmscott books are, you might say, not so much portable properties as relics, containing the whole world's beauty *in parvo*. They are in that sense kissing cousins to the medieval painted books Morris treasured so much that (Burne Jones reports) he would have saved one rather than saved the world— since "no one can run a railway through a book." Dowling, *Vulgarization*, 68.

CONCLUSION: IS PORTABILITY PORTABLE?

1. Traveling Theory, 226–47, in Edward W. Said, *The World, the Text, and the Critic* (Cambridge, Mass.: Harvard University Press, 1983), 226–27. A similarly ambitious attempt to offer a general formula is Stefan Collini's analysis of John Stuart Mill's latter-day (English) reception, which, by Collini's account, exemplifies the four stages whereby ideas become portable for latter-day thinkers. Stefan Collini, "From Dangerous Partisan to National Possession: John Stuart Mill in English Culture, 1873–1933," 311–41, in Collini, *Public Moralists: Political Thought and Intellectual Life in Britain, 1850–1930* (New York: Oxford University Press, 1991).

2. Said, *The World, the Text, and the Critic*, 227.

3. Chaudhuri, *Autobiography*, 101.

4. Morris, "News," 158, 151.

5. James, *Beyond*, 17.

6. Lamming, *The Pleasures of Exile*, 27.

7. Rushdie, *Midnight's Children*, 305. In *A Bend in the River*, V.S. Naipaul is grimmer, seeing the disappearance of colonial rule as a descent into chaos, against which the durability of Western trade goods looks like a macabre joke. The perfect emblem for the diminished flow of culture is imported zinc basins, "in demand because they were good for keeping grubs alive in, packed in damp fibre and marsh earth" (Naipaul, *A Bend in the River* [New York: Knopf, 1979], 40).

8. Rushdie, *Midnight's Children*, 109–11.

9. V. S. Naipaul, *The Mimic Men* (London: Deutsch, 1967), 90.

10. George Lamming, born in Barbados in 1927, is the author of many influential essays, especially those collected in *The Pleasures of Exile* (1960), as well as six novels: *In the Castle of My Skin* (1953); *The Emigrants* (1954); *Of Age and Innocence* (1958); *Season of Adventure* (1960); *Water with Berries* (1972); and *Natives of My Person* (1972). He has published no fiction (and very little nonfiction) in the last thirty-five years.

11. The reading of Lamming that follows is partially adapted from John Plotz, "One-Way Traffic: George Lamming and the Portable Empire," 308–23, in *After the Imperial Turn: Thinking with and through the Nation*, ed. Antoinette Burton (Durham, N.C.: Duke University Press, 2003).

12. Important recent critical work on Lamming includes Supriya Nair, *Caliban's Curse: George Lamming and the Revisioning of History* (Ann Arbor: University of Michigan Press, 1996); Sandra Pouchet Paquet, *The Novels of George Lamming* (London: Heinemann, 1982), Avis G. McDonald, "'Within the Orbit of Power': Reading Allegory in George Lamming's *Natives of My Person*," *Journal of Commonwealth Literature* 22, no. 1 (1987); and Peter Hulme, "Reading from Elsewhere: George Lamming and the Paradox of Exile," in *The Tempest and Its Travels*, ed. Peter Hulme, William H. Sherman, and Robin Kirkpatrick (Philadelphia: University of Pennsylvania Press, 2000).

13. Jonathan Goldberg, *Tempest in the Caribbean* (Minneapolis: University of Minnesota Press, 2004), 28.

14. Jessica Damián has recently argued that the absence of authoritative literary texts as British antecedents within the world of *In the Castle of My Skin* redoubles the importance of those purely bureaucratic-administrative tokens of British control: the church, the schoolroom, money. "Minting the Face of Empire: Coinage and the Shadow King in George Lamming's *In the Castle of My Skin*," *Anthurium: A Caribbean Studies Journal* 2, no. 1 (2004).

15. George Lamming, *In the Castle of My Skin* (Ann Arbor: University of Michigan Press, 1991 [1953]), 53.

16. Ibid., 53–54.

17. Neil ten Kortenaar suggests that the underlying question is, "Where is the authority that mints the pennies, that guarantees the currency on which everything in a capitalist economy depends?" To Kortenaar, the boys have no chance of approaching that answer, while to Damián, at this moment "Little England dreams of stepping outside of Columbus's machine." Neil ten Kortenaar, "George Lamming's *In the Castle of My Skin*: Finding Promise in the Land," *ARIEL: A Review of International English Literature* 22, no. 2 (1991): 48; Damián, "Minting," 16.

18. Ngugi wa Thiong'o, "George Lamming's *In the Castle of My Skin*," in *Homecoming: Essays on African and Caribbean Literature, Culture and Politics* (London: Heinemann, 1972), 115.

19. Lamming, *In the Castle of My Skin*, 54.

20. Cf. Homi Bhabha, "Of Mimicry and Man: The Ambivalence of Colonial Discourse," *October* 28 (1984).

21. Lamming, *Natives of My Person*, 328.

22. Peter Hulme, "George Lamming and the Postcolonial Novel," 120–36, in *Recasting the World: Writing after Colonialism*, ed. Jonathan White (Baltimore: The Johns Hopkins University Press, 1993), 131.

23. Gilles Deleuze and Félix Guattari, *Kafka: Toward a Minor Literature* (Minneapolis: University of Minnesota Press, 1986), 22–25.

24. Cf. a much later Lamming essay, "Western Education and the Caribbean Intellectual" (1985), which argues that "the Caribbean may be defined as the continuum of a journey in space and consciousness: through various stages of crossing from original homeland to island enclave; from enclave to enclave, or the fugitive erratic pursuit of fortune and meaning within each enclave" (in George Lamming, *Coming, Coming Home: Conversations II* (Philipsburg, St. Martin: House of Nehesi, 2000), 24.

Bibliography

Reviews of Primary Sources

Review of R. D. Blackmore, *Lorna Doone. Athenaeum,* April 17, 1869, 534–35.
Review of R. D. Blackmore, *Lorna Doone. Saturday Review,* November 5, 1870, 503–4.
Review of Wilkie Collins, *The Moonstone. Nation,* September 17, 1868, 235.
Review of George Eliot, *Impressions of Theophrastus Such. Times,* June 5, 1879.
Review of George Eliot, *Impressions of Theophrastus Such. Athenaeum,* June 7, 1879, 719–20.
Review of Thomas Hardy, *Desperate Remedies. Spectator,* April 22, 1871, 481–83.
Review of Thomas Hardy, *Far from the Madding Crowd. Athenaeum,* December 5, 1874, 747–48.
Review of Anthony Trollope, *The Eustace Diamonds. Spectator,* October 26, 1872, 1365–66.

Primary and Secondary Sources

Acton, John Emerich "Nationality." In *The History of Freedom, and Other Essays,* 270–300. London: Macmillan, 1907.
Agamben, Giorgio. *Homo Sacer: Sovereign Power and Bare Life.* Translated by Daniel Heller-Roazen. Stanford: Stanford University Press, 1998 [1995].
Aidoo, Ama Ata. *Our Sister Killjoy: Or, Reflections from a Black-Eyed Squint.* London: Longmans, 1977.
Ali, Thalassa. *A Singular Hostage.* New York: Bantam, 2002.
Altick, Richard Daniel. *The English Common Reader: A Social History of the Mass Reading Public, 1800–1900.* Chicago: University of Chicago Press, 1957.
Anderson, Amanda. *The Powers of Distance: Cosmopolitanism and the Cultivation of Detachment.* Princeton: Princeton University Press, 2001.
Anderson, Benedict. "Exodus." *Critical Inquiry* 20, no. 2 (1994): 314–27.
———. *Imagined Communities: Reflections on the Origin and Spread of Nationalism.* Rev. and expanded ed. London: Verso, 1991.
———. "Nationalism, Identity, and the Logic of Seriality." In *The Spectre of Comparisons: Nationalism, Southeast Asia, and the World,* 29–45. New York: Verso, 1998.
Anger, Suzy. *Victorian Interpretation.* Ithaca: Cornell University Press, 2005.
Anonymous. "Richard Dodd Blackmore: Secretive Genius of the Moors." In *Echoes of Exmoor: A Record of the Discussions and Doings of the Men-of-Exmoor Club. Fourth Series,* 1–21. London: Simpkin and Marshall, 1926.

Appadurai, Arjun. *Modernity at Large: Cultural Dimensions of Globalization*. Minneapolis: University of Minnesota Press, 1996.

——., ed. *The Social Life of Things: Commodities in Cultural Perspective*. Cambridge: Cambridge University Press, 1986.

——. "The Thing Itself." *Public Culture* 18, no. 1 (2006): 15–22.

Appiah, Anthony. *In My Father's House: Africa in the Philosophy of Culture*. New York: Oxford University Press, 1992.

Arata, Stephen D. "The Occidental Tourist: Dracula and the Anxiety of Reverse Colonization." *Victorian Studies: A Journal of the Humanities, Arts and Sciences* 33, no. 4 (1990): 621–45.

Aravamudan, Srinivas. *Guru English: South Asian Religion in a Cosmopolitan Language*. Princeton: Princeton University Press, 2005.

Arendt, Hannah. *The Human Condition*. Chicago: University of Chicago Press, 1998 [1958].

——. *Lectures on Kant's Political Philosophy*. Edited by Ronald Beiner. Brighton: Harvester, 1982.

——. *On Revolution*. London: Faber and Faber, 1963.

Armitage, David. *The Declaration of Independence : A Global History*. Cambridge, Mass.: Harvard University Press, 2007.

——. "Greater Britain: A Useful Category of Historical Analysis?" *American Historical Review* 104, no. 2 (1999): 427–45.

——. *The Ideological Origins of the British Empire*. New York: Cambridge University Press, 2000.

Armstrong, Isobel. *Language as Living Form in Nineteenth-Century Poetry*. Brighton: Harvester, 1982.

Armstrong, Nancy. "Emily's Ghost: The Cultural Politics of Victorian Fiction, Folklore, and Photography." *Novel: A Forum on Fiction* 25 (1992): 245–67.

Armstrong, Tim. *Haunted Hardy*. Basingstoke: Palgrave, 2000.

Arnold, Matthew. "The Literary Influence of Academies." In *Essays in Criticism, First Series*, edited by Thomas Marion Hoctor, 31–52. Chicago: University of Chicago Press, 1968.

Arrighi, Giovanni. *The Long Twentieth Century: Money, Power, and the Origins of Our Times*. London: Verso, 1994.

Arscott, Caroline. "William Morris: Decoration and Materialism" In *Marxism and the History of Art: From William Morris to the New Left*, edited by Andrew Hemingway, 9–27. London: Pluto, 2006.

Austen, Jane. *Emma*. Oxford: Oxford University Press, 2003.

——. *Northanger Abbey*. Edited by Marilyn Butler. New York: Penguin, 2003.

Badiou, Alain. *Handbook of Inaesthetics*. Translated by Alberto Toscano. Stanford: Stanford University Press, 2005.

Baguley, David. *Naturalist Fiction: The Entropic Vision*. Cambridge: Cambridge University Press, 1990.

Bailkin, Jordanna. "Indian Yellow: Making and Breaking the Imperial Palette." *Journal of Material Culture* 10, no. 2 (2005): 197–214.

Baker, William, and J. C. Ross. *George Eliot: A Bibliographical History*. New Castle, Del.: Oak Knoll, 2002.

Barber, Benjamin R. *Jihad vs. McWorld*. New York: Times, 1995.

Barrell, John. "Geographies of Hardy's Wessex." In *The Regional Novel in Britain and Ireland, 1800–1990*, edited by K. D. M. Snell, 99–118. Cambridge: Cambridge University Press, 1998 [1982].

———. *The Idea of Landscape and the Sense of Place, 1730–1840: An Approach to the Poetry of John Clare*. Cambridge: Cambridge University Press, 1972.

Barrera, A. de. *Gems and Jewels: Their History, Geography, Chemistry and Ana.: From the Earliest Ages Down to the Present Time*. London: Richard Bentley, 1860.

Barrie, J. M. *A Window in Thrums*. Edinburgh: Saltire Society, 2005 [1889].

Bartholomew, John. "The Portable Atlas, Consisting of (Sixteen) Maps." Edinburgh and Glasgow, 1869.

Batchen, Geoffrey. "Ere the Substance Fade: Photography and Hair Jewelry." In *Photographs Objects Histories: On the Materiality of Images*, edited by Elizabeth Edwards and Janice Hart. New York: Routledge, 2005.

———. *Forget Me Not: Photography and Remembrance*. New York: Princeton Architectural Press, 2004.

Baucom, Ian. *Out of Place: Englishness, Empire, and the Locations of Identity*. Princeton: Princeton University Press, 1999.

———. *Specters of the Atlantic: Finance Capital, Slavery, and the Philosophy of History*. Durham, N.C.: Duke University Press, 2005.

Baumann, Zygmunt. "Globalization and the New Poor." In *The Baumann Reader*, edited by Peter Beilharz, 298–333. Malden: Blackwell, 2001.

Bayly, C. A. *The Birth of the Modern World, 1780–1914: Global Connections and Comparisons*. Malden: Blackwell, 2004.

Beer, Gillian. *Darwin's Plots: Evolutionary Narrative in Darwin, George Eliot, and Nineteenth-Century Fiction*. Boston: Routledge and Kegan Paul, 1983.

Bell, Bill. "Bound for Australia: Shipboard Reading in the Nineteenth Century." In *Journeys through the Market: Travel, Travellers and the Book Trade*, edited by Robin Myers and Michael Harris, 119–40. New Castle, Del.: Oak Knoll, 1999.

Bender, Adrianne Noel. "Mapping Scotland's Identities: Representations of National Landscapes in the Novels of Scott, Stevenson, Oliphant, and Munro." Ph.D. Diss., New York University, 2001.

Bennett, Phillippa. "Rediscovering the Topography of Wonder: Morris, Iceland and the Last Romances." *Journal of the William Morris Society* 16, no. 2–3 (2005): 31–48.

Best, Stephen Michael. *The Fugitive's Properties: Law and the Poetics of Possession*. Chicago: University of Chicago Press, 2004.

Bhabha, Homi. "Of Mimicry and Man: The Ambivalence of Colonial Discourse." *October* 28 (1984): 125–33.

Black, Alan. "Scotland the Grave." Salon.com, April 6, 2006), available online at http://salon.com/opinion/feature/2006/04/06/scotland/.

Blackmore, R. D. *Alice Lorraine, a Tale of the South Downs*. London: S. Low, Marston, Searle, and Rivington, 1883.

———. *Lorna Doone, a Romance of Exmoor. With a Special Introduction by the Author, Illustrated from Drawings by W. Small, and from Photographs by Clifton Johnson*. New York and London: Harper and Bros., 1900.

Blackmore, R. D. *Lorna Doone: A Romance of Exmoor.* Edited by Sally Shuttleworth. New York: Oxford University Press, 1989.

———. "Preface to Harper's Edition." In *Lorna Doone, a Romance of Exmoor. With a Special Introduction by the Author, Illustrated from Drawings by W. Small, and from Photographs by Clifton Johnson.* New York and London: Harper and Bros., 1900.

Blackwell, Mark, ed. *The Secret Life of Things: Animals, Objects, and It-Narratives in Eighteenth-Century England.* Lewisburg, Maine: Bucknell University Press, 2007.

Blanchard, Sydney Laman. "A Biography of a Bad Shilling." In *The Financial System in Nineteenth-Century Britain,* edited by Mary Poovey, 60–70. New York: Oxford University Press, 2003.

Bohrer, Martha Adams. "Tales of Locale: The Natural History of Selborne and Castle Rackrent." *Modern Philology* 100, no. 3 (2003): 393.

Boos, Florence Saunders, and Carole G. Silver, eds. *Socialism and the Literary Artistry of William Morris.* Columbia: University of Missouri Press, 1990.

Brantlinger, Patrick. "*News from Nowhere:* Morris's Socialist Anti-Novel." *Victorian Studies: A Journal of the Humanities, Arts and Sciences* 19 (1975): 35–49.

Briggs, Asa. *Victorian Things.* London: B. T. Batsford, 1988.

Brodhead, Richard H. *Cultures of Letters: Scenes of Reading and Writing in Nineteenth-Century America.* Chicago: University of Chicago Press, 1993.

Brown, Bill. *A Sense of Things: The Object Matter of American Literature.* Chicago: University of Chicago Press, 2003.

———, ed. *Things.* Chicago: University Of Chicago Press, 2004.

Buckler, William E. "Blackmore's Novels before *Lorna Doone.*" *Nineteenth-Century Fiction* 10, no. 3 (1955): 169–87.

Budd, Kenneth George. *The Last Victorian: R. D. Blackmore and His Novels.* London: Centaur, 1960.

Buell, Lawrence. "Rethinking Anglo-American Literary History." *Clio* 33, no. 1 (2003): 65–72.

Burnett, Frances Hodgson. *Louisiana.* New York: C. Scribner's Sons, 1880.

———. *The One I Knew the Best of All.* New York: Arno, 1980.

———. *The Secret Garden.* Edited by Dennis Butts. New York: Oxford University Press, 2000.

———. *That Lass O' Lowrie's.* New York: Scribner, Armstrong, 1877.

Burton, Antoinette. *At the Heart of the Empire: Indians and the Colonial Encounter in Late-Victorian Britain.* Berkeley: University of California Press, 1998.

———. *The Postcolonial Careers of Santha Rama Rau.* Durham, N.C.: Duke University Press, 2007.

———. "Tongues Untied: Lord Salisbury's 'Black Man' and the Boundaries of Imperial Democracy." *Comparative Studies in Society and History* 42, no. 3 (2000): 632–61.

Buzard, James. *The Beaten Track: European Tourism, Literature, and the Ways to Culture, 1800–1918.* New York: Oxford University Press, 1993.

———. *Disorienting Fiction: The Autoethnographic Work of Nineteenth-Century British Novels.* Princeton: Princeton University Press, 2005.

———. "Ethnography as Interruption: *News from Nowhere*, Narrative and the Modern Romance of Authority." *Victorian Studies: A Journal of the Humanities, Arts and Sciences* 40, no. 3 (1997): 445–74.

Carey, Annie. *Autobiographies of a Lump of Coal; a Grain of Salt; a Drop of Water; a Bit of Old Iron; a Piece of Flint.* London: Cassell, Petter, and Galpin, 1870.

Carlisle, Janice. "The Smell of Class: British Novels of the 1860s." *Victorian Literature and Culture* 29, no. 1 (2001): 1–19.

Carlyle, Thomas. *On Heroes, Hero-Worship, and the Heroic in History.* Edited by Michael K. Goldberg, Joel J. Brattin, and Mark Engel. Berkeley: University of California Press, 1993.

Carpenter, Mary Wilson. "'A Bit of Her Flesh': Circumcision and 'the Signification of the Phallus' in *Daniel Deronda*." *Genders* 1 (1988): 1–23.

Carroll, David. *George Eliot: The Critical Heritage.* London: Routledge and Kegan Paul, 1971.

Carson, Penelope. "Letters from Madras During the Years 1836–1839 (Book)." *Journal of Imperial and Commonwealth History* 32, no. 2 (2004): 150–51.

Carter, Paul. "Turning the Tables—or Grounding Post-Colonialism." In *Text, Theory, Space: Land, Literature and History in South Africa and Australia*, edited by Kate Darian-Smith, Elizabeth Gunner, and Sarah Nuttall, 23–36. London: Routledge, 1996.

Chakrabarty, Dipesh. "'In the Name of Politics': Democracy and the Power of the Multitude in India." *Public Culture* 19, no. 1 (2007): 35–57.

———. *Provincializing Europe: Postcolonial Thought and Historical Difference.* Princeton: Princeton University Press, 2000.

Chase, Cynthia. "The Decomposition of the Elephants: Double-Reading *Daniel Deronda*." *PMLA: Publications of the Modern Language Association of America* 93, no. 2 (1978): 215–27.

Chaudhuri, Nirad C. *The Autobiography of an Unknown Indian.* New York: Macmillan, 1951.

Chaudhuri, Nupur. "Memsahibs and Motherhood in Nineteenth-Century Colonial India." *Victorian Studies* 31, no. 4 (1988): 517–35.

———. "Shawls, Jewelry, Curry, and Rice in Victorian Britain." In *Western Women and Imperialism: Complicity and Resistance*, edited by Nupur Chaudhuri and Margaret Strobel, 231–46. Bloomington: Indiana University Press, 1992.

Claybaugh, Amanda. "Toward a New Transatlanticism: Dickens in the United States." *Victorian Studies* 48, no. 3 (2006): 439–60.

Cohen, Deborah. *Household Gods: The British and Their Possessions.* New Haven: Yale University Press, 2006.

Colley, Linda. *Britons: Forging the Nation, 1707–1837.* New Haven: Yale University Press, 1992.

Collingham, E. M. *Imperial Bodies: The Physical Experience of the Raj, C. 1800–1947.* Cambridge, Mass.: Polity, 2001.

Collini, Stefan. *Public Moralists: Political Thought and Intellectual Life in Britain, 1850–1930.* New York: Oxford University Press, 1991.

Collins, Wilkie. *The Moonstone.* Baltimore: Penguin, 1966.

Conrad, Joseph. *Victory*. New York: Doubleday, Page, 1924.

Coombes, Annie E. *Reinventing Africa: Museums, Material Culture, and Popular Imagination in Late Victorian and Edwardian England*. New Haven: Yale University Press, 1994.

Cox, R. G., ed. *Thomas Hardy, the Critical Heritage*. London: Routledge and Kegan Paul, 1970.

Crary, Jonathan. *Suspensions of Perception: Attention, Spectacle, and Modern Culture*. Cambridge, Mass.: The MIT Press, 1999.

Crawford, Robert. *The Scottish Invention of English Literature*. Cambridge: Cambridge University Press, 1998.

Dainotto, Roberto M. "Lost in an Ancient South: Elizabeth Gaskell and the Rhetoric of Latitudes." In *Place in Literature: Regions, Cultures, Communities*, 75–102. Ithaca: Cornell University Press, 2000.

Daly, Nicholas. "That Obscure Object of Desire: Victorian Commodity Culture and Fictions of the Mummy." *Novel: A Forum on Fiction* 28, no. 1 (1994): 24–51.

Damián, Jessica. "Minting the Face of Empire: Coinage and the Shadow King in George Lamming's *In the Castle of My Skin*." *Anthurium: A Caribbean Studies Journal* 2, no. 1 (2004).

Daston, Lorraine, ed. *Things That Talk: Object Lessons from Art and Science*. New York: Zone, 2004.

Daston, Lorraine, and Peter Galison. "The Image of Objectivity." *Representations* 40 (1992): 81–128.

David, Deirdre. *Rule Britannia: Women, Empire, and Victorian Writing*. Ithaca: Cornell University Press, 1995.

Davidoff, Leonore, and Catherine Hall. *Family Fortunes: Men and Women of the English Middle Class, 1780–1850*. Chicago: University of Chicago Press, 1987.

Davie, Donald. "Thomas Hardy and British Poetry." In *With the Grain: Essays on Thomas Hardy and Modern British Poetry*, edited by Clive Wilmer, 21–170. Manchester: Carcanet, 1998.

Deleuze, Gilles, and Félix Guattari. *Kafka: Toward a Minor Literature*. Minneapolis: University of Minnesota Press, 1986.

Dickens, Charles. *Great Expectations*. Edited by Margaret Cardwell. Oxford: Clarendon Press, 1993.

———. *Our Mutual Friend*. New York: Penguin, 1997.

Dilke, Charles Wentworth. *Greater Britain: A Record of Travel in English-Speaking Countries During 1866 and 1867*. London: Macmillan, 1869.

Douglas-Fairhurst, Robert. *Victorian Afterlives: The Shaping of Influence in Nineteenth-Century Literature*. New York: Oxford University Press, 2002.

Dowling, Linda C. *The Vulgarization of Art: The Victorians and Aesthetic Democracy*. Charlottesville: University Press of Virginia, 1996.

Doyle, Arthur Conan. "The Adventure of the Blue Carbuncle." In *Victorian Tales of Mystery and Detection*, edited by Michael Cox, 195–213. New York: Oxford University Press, 1992.

Dunbar, Janet. *Golden Interlude: The Edens in India, 1836–1842*. Boston: Houghton Mifflin, 1956.

Duncan, Ian. "*The Moonstone*, the Victorian Novel, and Imperialistic Panic." *Modern Language Quarterly* 55, no. 3 (1994): 297–319.

———. "The Provincial or Regional Novel." In *A Companion to the Victorian Novel*, edited by Patrick Brantlinger and William B. Thesing, 318–35. Oxford: Blackwell, 2002.

———. *Scott's Shadow*. Princeton: Princeton University Press, forthcoming.

———. "Wild England: George Borrow's Nomadology." *Victorian Studies* 41 (1998): 381–404.

Duncan, Sara Jeannette. *The Crow's-Nest*. New York: Dodd, Mead, 1901.

———. *The Imperialist*. Edited by Misao Dean. Orchard Park, N.Y.: Broadview, 2005.

Dunn, Waldo Hilary. *R. D. Blackmore: The Author of* Lorna Doone: *A Biography*. New York: Longmans, Green, 1956.

Eden, Emily. *Miss Eden's Letters*. Edited by Violet Dickinson. London: Macmillan, 1919.

———. *Portraits of the Princes and People of India*. London: J. Dickinson, 1844.

———. *The Semi-Attached Couple and the Semi-Detached House*. London: Virago, 1979.

———. *Up the Country: Letters Written to Her Sister from the Upper Provinces of India*. Edited by Edward Thompson. London: Oxford University Press, 1930.

Eliot, George. *Adam Bede*. Edited by Stephen Charles Gill. New York: Penguin, 1980.

———. *Daniel Deronda*. Oxford: Oxford University Press, 1988.

———. *George Eliot's Life as Related in Her Letters and Journals*. Edited by J. W. Cross. New York: Harper and Bros., 1885.

———. *The George Eliot Letters*. Edited by Gordon Sherman Haight. 9 vols. New Haven: Yale University Press, 1954.

———. *Middlemarch*. Edited by Bert G. Hornback. New York: Norton, 2000.

———. *The Mill on the Floss*. Edited by Gordon Sherman Haight. Oxford: Oxford University Press, 1980.

———. "The Modern Hep! Hep! Hep!" In *Impressions of Theophrastus Such*, edited by Nancy Henry, 143–65. Iowa City: University of Iowa Press, 1994.

———. Review of *The Progress of the Intellect*. *Westminster Review* 54, no. 107 (1851): 177–85.

———. *Selections from George Eliot's Letters*. Edited by Gordon Sherman Haight. New Haven: Yale University Press, 1985.

Eliot, Simon. *A Measure of Popularity: Public Library Holdings of Twenty-Four Popular Authors, 1883–1912*. Oxford: Open University, 1992.

Elkins, Caroline, and Susan Pedersen. "Introduction." In *Settler Colonialism in the Twentieth Century: Projects, Practices, Legacies*, edited by Caroline Elkins and Susan Pedersen, 1–23. New York: Routledge, 2005.

Elliott, Michael A. *The Culture Concept: Writing and Difference in the Age of Realism*. Minneapolis: University of Minnesota Press, 2002.

Epstein, James. "Under America's Sign: Two Nineteenth-Century British Readings." *European Journal of American Culture* 24, no. 3 (2005): 205–19.

Ernst, Friedrich Gustav. *The Portable Gymnasium: A Manual of Exercises, Arranged for Self-Instruction in the Use of the Portable Gymnasium*. London, 1861.

Evans, Brad. *Before Cultures: The Ethnographic Imagination in American Literature, 1865–1920*. Chicago: University of Chicago Press, 2005.

Falkner, John Meade. *Moonfleet*. Edited by Brian Alderson. New York: Oxford University Press, 1993.

Faulkner, Peter. *Against the Age: An Introduction to William Morris*. Boston: Allen and Unwin, 1980.

Faulkner, Peter, Peter Preston, and William Morris Society, eds. *William Morris: Centenary Essays: Papers from the Morris Centenary Conference Organized by the William Morris Society at Exeter College Oxford, 30 June-3 July 1996*. Exeter: University of Exeter Press, 1999.

Ferry, Elizabeth Emma. "Inalienable Commodities: The Production and Circulation of Silver and Patrimony in a Mexican Mining Cooperative." *Cultural Anthropology* 17, no. 3 (2002): 331–58.

Festa, Lynn M. *Sentimental Figures of Empire in Eighteenth-Century Britain and France*. Baltimore: The Johns Hopkins University Press, 2006.

Fielding, Penny. "Burns's Topographies." In *Scotland and the Borders of Romanticism*, edited by Leith Davis, Ian Duncan, and Janet Sorensen, 170–87. Cambridge: Cambridge University Press, 2004.

Finn, Margot C. "Colonial Gifts: Family Politics and the Exchange of Goods in British India, C. 1780–1820." *Modern Asian Studies* 40, no. 1 (2006): 203–31.

Fisher, Philip. "Democratic Social Space: Whitman, Melville, and the Promise of American Transparency." *Representations* 24 (1988): 60–101.

———. "Local Meanings and Portable Objects: National Collections, Literatures, Music, and Architecture." In *The Formation of National Collections of Art and Archaeology*, edited by Gwendolyn Wright, 15–28. Washington, D.C.: National Gallery of Art 1996.

———. *Still the New World: American Literature in a Culture of Creative Destruction*. Cambridge, Mass.: Harvard University Press, 1999.

Fleissner, Jennifer. *Women, Compulsion, Modernity: The Moment of American Naturalism*. Chicago: University of Chicago, 2004.

Flesch, William. "Quoting Poetry." *Critical Inquiry* 18, no. 1 (1991): 42–63.

Flint, Christopher. "Speaking Objects: The Circulation of Stories in Eighteenth-Century Prose Fiction." *PMLA: Publications of the Modern Language Association of America* 113 (1998): 212–26.

Flynn, Tom, and T. J. Barringer, eds. *Colonialism and the Object: Empire, Material Culture, and the Museum*. New York: Routledge, 1998.

Foster, Robert J. "Making National Cultures in the Global Ecumene." *Annual Review of Anthropology* 20 (1991): 235–60.

Frankel, Nicholas. "Aubrey Beardsley 'Embroiders' the Literary Text." In *The Victorian Illustrated Book*, edited by Richard Maxwell, 259–81. Charlottesville: University Press of Virginia, 2002.

Freedgood, Elaine. *The Ideas in Things: Fugitive Meaning in the Victorian Novel*. Chicago: University of Chicago Press, 2006.

Fried, Michael. *Absorption and Theatricality: Painting and Beholder in the Age of Diderot*. Chicago: University of Chicago Press, 1988.

Friedman, Thomas L. *The Lexus and the Olive Tree*. New York: Farrar, Straus, Giroux, 1999.

Galchinsky, Michael. *The Origin of the Modern Jewish Woman Writer: Romance and Reform in Victorian England*. Detroit: Wayne State University Press, 1996.

Galison, Peter. "Images of Self." In *Things That Talk: Object Lessons from Art and Science*, edited by Lorraine Daston, 256–95. New York: Zone, 2004.

Gallagher, Catherine. *The Body Economic: Life, Death, and Sensation in Political Economy and the Victorian Novel*. Princeton: Princeton University Press, 2005.

———. "Floating Signifiers of Britishness in the Novels of the Anti-Slave-Trade Squadron." In *Dickens and the Children of Empire*, edited by Wendy S. Jacobson, 78–93. New York: Palgrave, 2000.

———. "George Eliot and *Daniel Deronda*: The Prostitute and the Jewish Question." In *Sex, Politics, and Science in the Nineteenth-Century Novel*, edited by Ruth Bernard Yeazell, 39–62. Baltimore: The Johns Hopkins University Press, 1986.

———. "George Eliot: Immanent Victorian." *Representations*, no. 90 (2005): 61–74.

Gaskell, Elizabeth Cleghorn. *Cranford*. Edited by Patricia Ingham. London: Penguin, 2005.

———. *Wives and Daughters*. New York: Penguin, 1997.

Gatrell, Simon. *Thomas Hardy's Vision of Wessex*. New York: Palgrave, 2003.

Geertz, Clifford. *The Interpretation of Cultures: Selected Essays*. New York: Basic, 1973.

Gerzina, Gretchen. *Frances Hodgson Burnett: The Unexpected Life of the Author of* The Secret Garden. New Brunswick: Rutgers University Press, 2004.

Gilbert, William, and Arthur Sullivan. "For He Is an Englishman." In *Complete Plays of Gilbert and Sullivan*, 112. New York: Norton, 1941.

Giles, Paul. *Virtual Americas: Transnational Fictions and the Transatlantic Imaginary*. Durham, N.C.: Duke University Press, 2002.

Gilmour, Robin. "Regional and Provincial in Victorian Literature." In *The Literature of Region and Nation*, edited by R. P. Draper, 51–60. Basingstoke: Macmillan, 1989.

Glazener, Nancy. *Reading for Realism: The History of a U.S. Literary Institution, 1850–1910*. Durham, N.C.: Duke University Press, 1997.

Godelier, Maurice. *The Enigma of the Gift*. Chicago: University of Chicago Press, 1999.

Goldberg, Jonathan. *Tempest in the Caribbean*. Minneapolis: University of Minnesota Press, 2004.

Guillory, John. "The English Common Place: Lineages of the Topographical Genre." *Critical Quarterly* 33, no. 4 (1991): 3–27.

Gurney, Joseph John. *Hints on the Portable Evidence of Christianity*. London, 1832.

Habermas, Jürgen. *The Structural Transformation of the Public Sphere: An Inquiry into a Category of Bourgeois Society*. Translated by Thomas Burger. Cambridge, Mass.: Polity, 1989.

Hall, Catherine. *Civilising Subjects: Metropole and Colony in the English Imagination, 1830.–1867*. Cambridge, Mass.: Polity, 2002.

———. *White, Male, and Middle-Class: Explorations in Feminism and History*. New York: Routledge, 1992.

Hardy, Florence Emily. *The Early Life of Thomas Hardy, 1840–1891*. New York: Macmillan, 1928.

Hardy, Thomas. *The Complete Poems of Thomas Hardy*. Edited by James Gibson. New York: Macmillan, 1978.

———. *Desperate Remedies: A Novel*. London: Macmillan, 1975.

———. "Letter to Blackmore, August 6, 1875." In *Collected Letters of Thomas Hardy: Volume One (1840–1892)*, edited by Richard Little Purdy and Michael Millgate. Oxford: Clarendon, 1978.

———. *The Life and Work of Thomas Hardy*. Edited by Michael Millgate. Athens: University of Georgia Press, 1985.

———. *The Mayor of Casterbridge: The Life and Death of a Man of Character*. Edited by Keith Wilson. New York: Penguin, 2003.

———. *Personal Writings: Prefaces, Literary Opinions, Reminiscences*. Edited by Harold Orel. Lawrence: University Press of Kansas, 1966.

———. *Poems of the Past and the Present*. London: Harper and Bros., 1902.

———. "The Profitable Reading of Fiction" In *Thomas Hardy's Personal Writings*, edited by Harold Orel, 110–25. Lawrence: University Press of Kansas, 1966.

———. *The Return of the Native*. Edited by Simon Gatrell, Nancy Barrineau, and Margaret R. Higonnet. New York: Oxford University Press, 2005.

———. *Tess of the D'Urbervilles* Edited by John Paul Riquelme. Boston: Bedford, 1998.

———. *The Trumpet-Major and Robert His Brother*. New York: Penguin, 1984.

———. *Two on a Tower: A Romance*. Edited by Sally Shuttleworth. New York: Penguin, 1999.

———. *Wessex Poems and Other Verses, with Thirty Illustrations by the Author*. London: Harper and Bros., 1903.

———. *The Woodlanders*. Edited by Patricia Ingham. New York: Penguin, 1998.

Harvey, Geoffrey. "Thomas Hardy: Moments of Vision." In *Critical Essays on Thomas Hardy's Poetry*, edited by Harold Orel, 35–46. New York: G. K. Hall, 1995 [1986].

Haywood, Ian. *The Revolution in Popular Literature: Print, Politics, and the People, 1790–1860*. New York: Cambridge University Press, 2004.

———. *Working-Class Fiction: From Chartism to Trainspotting*. Plymouth: Northcote House, 1997.

Heilmann, Ann. "Mrs Grundy's Rebellion: Margaret Oliphant between Orthodoxy and the New Woman." *Women's Writing* 6, no. 2 (1999): 215–37.

Henry, Nancy. *George Eliot and the British Empire*. New York: Cambridge University Press, 2002.

Herbert, Christopher. *Culture and Anomie: Ethnographic Imagination in the Nineteenth Century*. Chicago: University of Chicago Press, 1991.

Hilton, Boyd. *The Age of Atonement: The Influence of Evangelicalism on Social and Economic Thought, 1795–1865*. Oxford: Clarendon, 1988.

Hofmeyr, Isabel. *The Portable Bunyan: A Transnational History of the* Pilgrim's Progress. Princeton: Princeton University Press, 2004.

Holcombe, Lee. *Wives and Property: Reform of the Married Women's Property Law in Nineteenth-Century England*. Toronto: University of Toronto Press, 1983.

Hood, Thomas. *Selected Poems of Thomas Hood*. Edited by John Clubbe. Cambridge, Mass.: Harvard University Press, 1970.

Hudson, W. H. *A Crystal Age*. London: T. F. Unwin, 1887.

Hulme, Peter. "George Lamming and the Postcolonial Novel." In *Recasting the World: Writing after Colonialism*, edited by Jonathan White, 120–36. Baltimore: The Johns Hopkins University Press, 1993.

———. "Reading from Elsewhere: George Lamming and the Paradox of Exile." In *The Tempest and Its Travels*, edited by Peter Hulme, William H. Sherman, and Robin Kirkpatrick, 220–35. Philadelphia: University of Pennsylvania Press, 2000.

Hyde, Lewis. *The Gift: Imagination and the Erotic Life of Property*. New York: Vintage, 1983.

Hynes, Samuel. "On Hardy's Badness." In *Critical Essays on Thomas Hardy's Poetry*, edited by Harold Orel, 72–81. New York: G. K. Hall, 1995 [1983].

———. *The Pattern of Hardy's Poetry*. Chapel Hill: University Of North Carolina, 1961.

Jacobus, Mary. *Reading Woman: Essays in Feminist Criticism*. New York: Columbia University Press, 1986.

Jaffe, Audrey. *Scenes of Sympathy: Identity and Representation in Victorian Fiction*. Ithaca: Cornell University Press, 2000.

James, Cyril Lionel Robert. *Beyond a Boundary*. London: Hutchinson, 1963.

James, Henry. *Notes and Reviews*. Freeport: Books for Libraries Press, 1968.

———. Review of *Far from the Madding Crowd*. *Nation*, December 24, 1874.

James, Susan E. "*Wuthering Heights* for Children: Frances Hodgson Burnett's *The Secret Garden*." *Connotations: A Journal for Critical Debate* 10, no. 1 (2000): 59–76.

Janowitz, Anne F. *Lyric and Labour in the Romantic Tradition*. Cambridge: Cambridge University Press, 1998.

Jay, Elisabeth. *Mrs. Oliphant, "A Fiction to Herself": A Literary Life*. New York: Oxford University Press, 1995.

Johanson, Graeme. *Colonial Editions in Australia, 1843–1972*. Wellington: Elibank, 2000.

Johnson, Trevor. "Introduction." In Thomas Hardy, *Wessex Poems and Other Verses*, 1–58. Keele: Keele University Press, 1995.

Johnston, Charles. *Chrysal: Or, the Adventures of a Guinea*. London: T. Cadell, 1794.

Jomini, Henri. *A Portable Atlas for the Use of Those Who Desire to Explore the Fields of Battle of Waterloo and Ligny*. Brussels: H. Gérard, 1851.

Joseph, Philip. *American Literary Regionalism in a Global Age*. Baton Rouge: Louisiana State University Press, 2006.

Joshi, Priya. *In Another Country: Colonialism, Culture, and the English Novel in India*. New York: Columbia University Press, 2002.

"Kailyard." In *The History of Scottish Literature, Vol. 3: Nineteenth Century*, edited by Douglas Gifford, 309–18. Aberdeen: Aberdeen University Press, 1988.

Kaplan, Amy. "Nation, Region, and Empire." In *The Columbia History of the American Novel*, edited by Emory Elliott, 240–66. New York: Columbia University Press, 1991.

Kaufman, Jason and Orlando Patterson, "Cross-National Cultural Diffusion: The Global Spread of Cricket," *American Sociological Review* 70, no. 1 (2005): 82–110.

Kastan, David Scott, ed. *The Oxford Encyclopedia of British Literature*. Vol. 1. Oxford: Oxford University Press, 2006.

Kent, Elizabeth. *Flora Domestica, or the Portable Flower-Garden*. Edited by James Henry Leigh Hunt. London: Taylor and Hessey, 1825.

King, Anthony D. *The Bungalow: The Production of a Global Culture*. Boston: Routledge and Kegan Paul, 1984.

Kipling, Rudyard. "The Janeites." In *Debits and Credits*, 124–49. Garden City, N.Y.: Doubleday, Page, 1926.

Klancher, Jon P. *The Making of English Reading Audiences, 1790–1832*. Madison: University of Wisconsin Press, 1987.

Klaus, H. Gustav. *The Socialist Novel in Britain: Toward the Recovery of a Tradition*. New York: St. Martin's, 1982.

Kortenaar, Neil ten. "George Lamming's *In the Castle of My Skin*: Finding Promise in the Land." *ARIEL: A Review of International English Literature* 22, no. 2 (1991): 43–53.

Kriegel, Lara. "Britain by Design: Industrial Culture, Imperial Display, and the Making of South Kensington, 1835–1872." Ph.D. Diss., Johns Hopkins University, 2000.

Kuduk Weiner, Stephanie. *Republican Politics and English Poetry, 1789–1874*. New York: Palgrave, 2005.

Lady's Drawing-Room, The. N.P., London, 1744.

Lamming, George. *Coming, Coming Home: Conversations II*. Philipsburg, St. Martin: House of Nehesi, 2000.

———. *In the Castle of My Skin*. Ann Arbor: University of Michigan Press, 1991.

———. "Introduction" [1983]. In Lamming, *In the Castle of My Skin*. Ann Arbor: University of Michigan Press, 1991.

———. *Natives of My Person*. Ann Arbor: University of Michigan Press, 1992.

———. *The Pleasures of Exile*. Ann Arbor: University of Michigan Press, 1992.

Lanfranchi, Pierre, and Matthew Taylor. *Moving with the Ball: The Migration of Professional Footballers*. Oxford: Berg, 2001.

Lang, Andrew. Review of Thomas Hardy, *Far from the Madding Crowd. Academy*, January 2, 1875, vii, 9.

Larkin, Philip. *Collected Poems*. Edited by Anthony Thwaite. New York: Farrar, Straus, Giroux, 2004.

Leavis, F. R. *The Great Tradition: George Eliot, Henry James, Joseph Conrad*. New York: G. W. Stewart, 1948.

Leclaire, Lucien. *Le Roman Régionaliste Dans Les Iles Britanniques, 1880–1950*. Clermont-Ferrand: G. de Bussac, 1954.

Ledger, Sally. "Chartist Aesthetics in the Mid-Nineteenth Century: Ernest Jones, a Novelist of the People." *Nineteenth Century Literature* 57, no. 1 (2002): 31–63.

Lee, Yoon Sun. *Nationalism and Irony: Burke, Scott, Carlyle*. New York: Oxford University Press, 2004.

LeMire, Eugene D. *A Bibliography of William Morris*. New Castle, Del.: Oak Knoll, 2006.

Lentz, Vern B. "Disembodied Voices in Hardy's Shorter Poems." *Colby Literary Quarterly* 23, no. 2 (1987): 57–65.

Lesjak, Carolyn. *Working Fictions: A Genealogy of the Victorian Novel*. Durham, N.C.: Duke University Press, 2006.

Levine, George Lewis. *Dying to Know: Scientific Epistemology and Narrative in Victorian England*. Chicago: University of Chicago Press, 2002.

Levinson, Marjorie. "Object-Loss and Object-Bondage: Economies of Representation in Hardy's Poetry." *ELH* 73, no. 2 (2006): 549–80.

Lewis, C. S. "William Morris." In *Rehabilitations and Other Essays*, 37–55. London: Oxford University Press, 1939.

Lindop, Grevel. *The Opium-Eater: A Life of Thomas De Quincey*. New York: Taplinger, 1981.

Logan, Thad. *The Victorian Parlour*. New York: Cambridge University Press, 2001.

Lucas, John. *The Literature of Change: Studies in the Nineteenth-Century Provincial Novel*. New York: Barnes and Noble, 1977.

Luckhurst, Roger. "Knowledge, Belief and the Supernatural at the Imperial Margin." In *The Victorian Supernatural*, edited by Nicola Bown, Carolyn Burdett, and Pamela Thurschwell, 197–216. New York: Cambridge University Press, 2004.

Lukács, Georg. "Narrate or Describe?" In *"Writer and Critic," and Other Essays*, edited by Arthur D. Kahn, 110–48. New York: Grosset and Dunlap, 1971.

———. "Reification and the Consciousness of the Proletariat." In *History and Class Consciousness: Studies in Marxist Dialectics*, 83–221. Cambridge, Mass.: The MIT Press, 1971.

Lynch, Deidre. *The Economy of Character: Novels, Market Culture, and the Business of Inner Meaning*. Chicago: University of Chicago Press, 1998.

Mabb, David, Caroline Arscott, and Steve Edwards. *William Morris*. Manchester: Whitworth Art Gallery, 2004.

Mabey, Richard. *Gilbert White: A Biography of the Author of the Natural History of Selborne*. London: Century, 1986.

Maitland, Julia Charlotte. *Letters from Madras During the Years 1836–1839*. Edited by Alyson Price. Otley: Woodstock, 2003.

Malinowski, Bronislaw. *Argonauts of the Western Pacific*. London: G. Routledge and Sons, 1922.

Mallock, W. H. Review of George Eliot, *Impressions of Theophrastus Such*. *Edinburgh Review* (1879): 557–86.

Manley, Michael. *A History of West Indies Cricket*. London: Deutsch, 1988.

Marcus, Sharon. *Between Women: Friendship, Desire, and Marriage in Victorian England*. Princeton: Princeton University Press, 2007.

Marcus, Sharon. "The Profession of the Author: Abstraction, Advertising, and *Jane Eyre*." *PMLA: Publications of the Modern Language Association of America* 110, no. 2 (1995): 206–19.

Marx, Karl. "Capital: Volume 1." In *Capital: An Abridged Edition*, edited by David McLellan. Oxford: Oxford University Press, 1995.

Masson, David. "Politics of the Present, Foreign and Domestic." *Macmillan's* 1 (1859): 1–10.

Maurer, Bill, and Gabriele Schwab, eds. *Accelerating Possession: Global Futures of Property and Personhood*. New York: Columbia University Press, 2006.

Mauss, Marcel. *The Gift: Forms and Functions of Exchange in Archaic Societies*. Translated by Ian Cunnison. Glencoe, Ill.: Free Press, 1954.

McCarthy, Fiona. *William Morris: A Life for Our Times*. London: Faber and Faber, 1994.

McDonald, Avis G. "'Within the Orbit of Power': Reading Allegory in George Lamming's *Natives of My Person*." *Journal of Commonwealth Literature* 22, no. 1 (1987): 73–86.

McGann, Jerome J. "'Thing to Mind': The Materialist Aesthetic of William Morris." In *Black Riders: The Visible Language of Modernism*, 47–75. Princeton: Princeton University Press, 1993.

Menely, Tobias. "Traveling in Place: Gilbert White's Cosmopolitan Parochialism." *Eighteenth-Century Life* 28, no. 3 (2004): 46–65.

Menke-Eggers, Christoph. *The Sovereignty of Art: Aesthetic Negativity in Adorno and Derrida*. Cambridge, Mass.: The MIT Press, 1998.

Merchant, Peter. "Rehabilitating *Lorna Doone*." *Children's Literature in Education* 18, no. 4 (1987): 240–52.

Michaels, Walter Benn. *Our America: Nativism, Modernism, and Pluralism*. Durham, N.C.: Duke University Press, 1995.

Michie, Elsie B. "Buying Brains: Trollope, Oliphant, and Vulgar Victorian Commerce." *Victorian Studies: An Interdisciplinary Journal of Social, Political, and Cultural Studies* 44, no. 1 (2001): 77–97.

Mill, John Stuart. *The Later Letters of John Stuart Mill, 1849–1873*. Edited by Francis Edward Mineka and Dwight N. Lindley. Toronto: University of Toronto Press, 1972.

Miller, Andrew H. *Novels Behind Glass: Commodity, Culture, and Victorian Narrative*. New York: Cambridge University Press, 1995.

Miller, D. A. *The Novel and the Police*. Berkeley: University of California Press, 1988.

Miller, J. Hillis. *Thomas Hardy: Distance and Desire*. Cambridge, Mass.: Harvard University Press, 1970.

Millgate, Michael. "Introduction." In *The Life and Work of Thomas Hardy*, edited by Michael Millgate, x–xxix. Athens: University of Georgia Press, 1985.

———. *Thomas Hardy: A Biography Revisited*. New York: Oxford University Press, 2004.

Mitchell, Sally. *Dinah Mulock Craik*. Boston: Twayne, 1983.

Moretti, Franco. *Atlas of the European Novel, 1800–1900*. New York: Verso, 1999.

———. *Graphs, Maps, Trees: Abstract Models for a Literary History*. New York: Verso, 2005.

Morris, William. *The Collected Letters of William Morris*. Edited by Norman Kelvin. Princeton: Princeton University Press, 1984.

———. *A Dream of John Ball*. In *The Collected Works of William Morris*, edited by May Morris, 16:213–70. London: Longmans, Green, 1910–1915. Reprinted London: Routledge/Thoemmes, 1992.

———. *The Earthly Paradise*. Edited by Florence Saunders Boos. 2 vols. New York: Routledge, 2002.

———. "How I Became a Socialist." In *The Collected Works of William Morris*, edited by May Morris, 23:277–81. London: Longmans, Green, 1910–1915. Reprinted London: Routledge/Thoemmes, 1992.

———. "The Lesser Arts." In *The Collected Works of William Morris*, edited by May Morris, 22:3–28. London: Longmans, Green, 1910–1915. Reprinted London: Routledge/Thoemmes, 1992.

———. *News from Nowhere*. In *The Collected Works of William Morris*, edited by May Morris, 16:3–211. London: Longmans, Green, 1910–1915. Reprinted London: Routledge/Thoemmes, 1992.

———. *News from Nowhere and Selected Writings and Designs*. Edited by Asa Briggs. London: Penguin, 1962.

———. *The Novel on Blue Paper*. Edited by Penelope Fitzgerald. London: Journeyman, 1982.

———. Review of Edward Bellamy, *Looking Backward*. *Commonweal*, June 22, 1889, 194–95.

———. *Selected Poems*. Edited by Peter Faulkner. Manchester: Fyfield, 1992.

———. *The Story of the Glittering Plain*. San Bernadino, Calif.: Borgo, 1980.

———. *The Sundering Flood*. Seattle: Unicorn, 1973.

———. *The Water of the Wondrous Isle*. In *The Collected Works of William Morris*, edited by May Morris. Vol. 20. London: Longmans, Green, 1910–1915. Reprinted London: Routledge/Thoemmes, 1992.

———. *The Well at the World's End*. In *The Collected Works of William Morris*, edited by May Morris. Vols. 18–19. London: Longmans, Green, 1910–1915. Reprinted London: Routledge/Thoemmes, 1992.

———. *The Well at the World's End: A Tale*. Edited by Lin Carter. New York: Ballantine, 1970.

———. *William Morris by Himself: Designs and Writings*. Edited by Gillian Naylor. London: Macdonald Orbis, 1988.

Moses, Michael Valdez. *The Novel and the Globalization of Culture*. New York: Oxford University Press, 1995.

Moule, Horace. Review of Thomas Hardy, *Under the Greenwood Tree*. *Saturday Review*, September 28, 1872, 34, 417.

Munn, Nancy. "Spatiotemporal Transformations of Gawa Canoes." *Journal de la Societe des Oceanistes* (1977): 39–52.

Myers, Gerald E. *William James, His Life and Thought*. New Haven: Yale University Press, 1986.

Myers, Janet C. "Antipodal England: Emigration, Gender, and Portable Domesticity in Victorian Literature and Culture." Ph.D. Diss. Rice University, 2000.

Naipaul, V. S. *A Bend in the River*. New York: Knopf, 1979.

———. *An Area of Darkness*. New York: Macmillan, 1965.

———. *The Mimic Men*. London: Deutsch, 1967.

Nair, Supriya. *Caliban's Curse: George Lamming and the Revisioning of History*. Ann Arbor: University of Michigan Press, 1996.

Nelson, Deborah. "The Virtues of Heartlessness: Mary McCarthy, Hannah Arendt, and the Anesthetics of Empathy." *American Literary History* 18, no. 1 (2006): 86–101.

Nelson, James Malcolm. "The Stage Adaptation of *That Lass O'Lowrie's* and Mid-Victorian Plays of Factory and Mine." *Dalhousie Review* 61, no. 4 (1981): 698–717.

Nicholls, David. *The Lost Prime Minister: A Life of Sir Charles Dilke*. London: Hambledon, 1995.

Nord, Deborah Epstein. *Gypsies and the British Imagination, 1807–1930*. New York: Columbia University Press, 2006.

Novak, Daniel. "A Model Jew: 'Literary Photographs' and the Jewish Body in *Daniel Deronda*." *Representations* 85 (2004): 58–97.

Oakley, Peregrine. *Aureus: Or, the Life and Opinions of a Sovereign*. London: G. Wightman, 1824.

Oliphant, Margaret. Review of R. D. Blackmore, *Lorna Doone*. *Blackwood's Edinburgh Magazine*, January 1871, 43–47.

———. *Kirsteen: The Story of a Scotch Family Seventy Years Ago*. London: Dent, 1984.

Oxford English Dictionary, 2nd Edition. Oxford: Oxford University Press, 1989.

Panckridge, H. R. *A Short History of the Bengal Club, 1827–1927*. Calcutta: H. R. Panckridge, 1927.

Panton, Jane Ellen. *Dear Life*. New York: D. Appleton, 1886.

Paquet, Sandra Pouchet. *The Novels of George Lamming*. London: Heinemann, 1982.

Parr, Martin. *Boring Postcards*. London: Phaidon, 1999.

Parry, Benita. *Delusions and Discoveries: India in the British Imagination, 1880–1930*. 2nd ed. London: Verso, 1998.

Parsons, Neil. *King Khama, Emperor Joe, and the Great White Queen: Victorian Britain through African Eyes*. Chicago: University of Chicago Press, 1998.

Pater, Walter. "Poems by William Morris." *Westminster Review* n.s. 34 (1868): 300–312.

Paulin, Tom. *Thomas Hardy, the Poetry of Perception*. Totowa, N.J.: Rowman and Littlefield, 1975.

Perkins, Pam. "'We Who Have Been Bred Upon Sir Walter': Margaret Oliphant, Sir Walter Scott, and Women's Literary History." *English Studies in Canada* 30, no. 2 (2004): 90–104.

Peterson, Linda. "The Female Bildungsroman: Tradition and Revision in Oliphant's Fiction." In *Margaret Oliphant: Critical Essays on a Gentle Subversive*, edited by D. J. Trela, 66–89. Selinsgrove, Pa.: Susquehanna University Press, 1995.

Picker, John M. "George Eliot and the Sequel Question." *New Literary History* 37, no. 2 (2006): 361–88.

Pietz, William. "The Problem of the Fetish [Parts 1, 2, and 3]." *Res: Journal of Anthropology and Aesthetics* 9, 13, 16 (1985, 1987, 1988): 5–17, 23–45, 105–23.

Pite, Ralph. *Hardy's Geography: Wessex and the Regional Novel.* New York: Palgrave, 2002.

———. *Thomas Hardy: The Guarded Life.* London: Picador, 2006.

Plotz, John. "Can the Sofa Speak? A Look at Thing Theory." *Criticism* 47, no. 1 (2005): 109–18.

———. "Motion Slickness: Spectacle and Circulation in Thomas Hardy's 'On the Western Circuit.'" *Studies in Short Fiction* 33, no. 3 (1996): 369–86.

———. "One-Way Traffic: George Lamming and the Portable Empire." In *After the Imperial Turn: Thinking with and through the Nation,* edited by Antoinette Burton, 308–23. Durham, N.C.: Duke University Press, 2003.

———. "Virtually Being There: Edmund Wilson's Suburbs." *Southwest Review* 87, no. 1 (2002): 10–28.

Plotz, Judith. "Jane Austen Goes to India: Emily Eden's Semi-Detached Home Thoughts from Abroad." In *The Postcolonial Jane Austen,* 163–87. London: Routledge, 2000.

Pocock, J. G. A. "The Mobility of Property and the Rise of Eighteenth-Century Sociology." In *Virtue, Commerce, and History: Essays on Political Thought and History, Chiefly in the Eighteenth Century,* 103–23. New York: Cambridge University Press, 1985.

Pointon, Marcia. "Intriguing Jewellery: Royal Bodies and Luxurious Consumption." *Textual Practice* 11, no. 3 (1997): 493–516.

———. "Jewelry in Eighteenth Century England." In *Consumers and Luxury: Consumer Culture in Europe, 1650–1850,* edited by Maxine Berg and Helen Clifford, 120–46. Manchester: Manchester University Press, 1999.

Poon, Angelia. "Seeing Double: Performing English Identity and Imperial Duty in Emily Eden's *Up the Country* and Harriet Martineau's *British Rule in India.*" *Women's Writing* 12, no. 3 (2005): 453–72.

Poovey, Mary. *The Financial System in Nineteenth-Century Britain.* New York: Oxford University Press, 2003.

———. *Making a Social Body: British Cultural Formation, 1830–1864.* Chicago: University of Chicago Press, 1995.

Porter, Bernard. *The Absent-Minded Imperialists: Empire, Society, and Culture in Britain.* New York: Oxford University Press, 2004.

Prakash, Gyan. *Another Reason: Science and the Imagination of Modern India.* Princeton: Princeton University Press, 1999.

Pratt, Mary Louise. *Imperial Eyes: Travel Writing and Transculturation.* New York: Routledge, 1992.

Price, Leah. "Reader's Block: Response." *Victorian Studies: An Interdisciplinary Journal of Social, Political, and Cultural Studies* 46, no. 2 (2004): 231–42.

Procida, Mary A. *Married to the Empire: Gender, Politics and Imperialism in India, 1883–1947.* Manchester: Manchester University Press, 2002.

Psomiades, Kathy Alexis. "Heterosexual Exchange and Other Victorian Fictions: *The Eustace Diamonds* and Victorian Anthropology." *Novel: A Forum on Fiction* 33 (1999): 93–118.

Radhakrishnan, R. "Cultural Theory and the Politics of Location." In *Views Beyond the Border Country: Raymond Williams and Cultural Politics*, edited by Dennis L. Dworkin and Leslie G. Roman, 275–94. New York: Routledge, 1993.

Rignall, John. *Oxford Reader's Companion to George Eliot*. Oxford: Oxford University Press, 2000.

Roberts, Emma. *Scenes and Characteristics of Hindoostan, with Sketches of Anglo-Indian Society*. London: W. H. Allen, 1835.

Robertson, Jo. "Anxieties of Imperial Decay: Three Journeys in India." In *In Transit: Travel, Text, Empire*, edited by Helen Gilbert and Anna Johnston, 103–23. New York: P. Lang, 2002.

Robson, Catherine. "'Where Heaves the Turf': Thomas Hardy and the Boundaries of the Earth." *Victorian Literature and Culture* 32, no. 2 (2004): 495–503.

Rossetti, Christina. "Hero." In *Victorian Love Stories: An Oxford Anthology*, edited by Kate Flint, 138–50. New York: Oxford University Press, 1996.

Royce, Josiah. "Provincialism." In *Race Questions, Provincialism, and Other American Problems*, 57–108. New York: Macmillan, 1908.

Rubik, Margarete. "The Subversion of Literary Clichés in Oliphant's Fiction." In *Margaret Oliphant: Critical Essays on a Gentle Subversive*, edited by D. J. Trela, 49–65. Selinsgrove, Pa.: Susquehanna University Press, 1995.

Rushdie, Salman. *Midnight's Children*. New York: Penguin, 1991.

Ruskin, John. "The Nature of Gothic." In *The Works of John Ruskin*, edited by Edward Cook and Alexander Wedderburn, vol. 10, 180–269. London: G. Allen, 1904.

Said, Edward W. *The World, the Text, and the Critic*. Cambridge, Mass.: Harvard University Press, 1983.

Sanders, Michael. "Poetic Agency: Metonymy and Metaphor in Chartist Poetry 1838–1852." *Victorian Poetry* 39, no. 2 (2001): 111–35.

Scarry, Elaine. "Work and the Body in Hardy and Other Nineteenth-Century Novelists." *Representations* 3 (1983): 90–123.

Schor, Hilary Margo. *Scheherezade in the Marketplace: Elizabeth Gaskell and the Victorian Novel*. New York: Oxford University Press, 1992.

Seeley, J. R. *Expansion of England*. London: Macmillan, 1883.

Sen, Amartya. *The Argumentative Indian: Writings on Indian Culture, History, and Politics*. New York: Farrar, Straus, Giroux, 2005.

Shakespeare, William. *Macbeth*. Edited by A. R. Braunmuller. New York: Cambridge University Press, 1997.

Short, Peter. *The Psalter or Psalms of Dauid, after the Translation of the Great Bible, Pointed as It Shal Be Said or Sung in Churches: With the Morning & Euening Praier, and Certaine Additions of Collects, and Other the Ordinarie Seruice, Gathered out of the Booke of Common Praier. Also a Briefe Table Declaring the True Vse of Euerie Psalme, Made by Master Theod. Beza. Newlie Printed in a Smal and Portable Volume or Manual*. London, 1600.

Shuttleworth, Sally. "Introduction." In R. D. Blackmore, *Lorna Doone: A Romance of Exmoor*, ix–xxv. New York: Oxford University Press, 1989.

Silver, Anna Krugovoy. "Domesticating Brontë's Moors: Motherhood in *The Secret Garden*." *Lion and the Unicorn: A Critical Journal of Children's Literature* 21, no. 2 (1997): 193–203.

Silver, Carole G. *The Romance of William Morris*. Athens: Ohio University Press, 1982.

Simmel, Georg. "Adornment." In *The Sociology of Georg Simmel*, edited by Kurt H. Wolff, 338–44. Glencoe, Ill.: Free Press, 1950.

Simmons, Jack. *The Victorian Railway*. New York: Thames and Hudson, 1991.

Sinha, Mrinahlini. "Britishness, Clubbability, and the Colonial Public Sphere." In *Bodies in Contact: Rethinking Colonial Encounters in World History*, edited by Tony Ballantyne and Antoinette Burton, 183–200. Durham, N.C.: Duke University Press, 2005.

Skoblow, Jeffrey. *Paradise Dislocated: Morris, Politics, Art*. Charlottesville: University Press of Virginia, 1993.

Smith, Adam. *The Theory of Moral Sentiments*. Edited by Knud Haakonssen. Cambridge Texts in the History of Philosophy. New York: Cambridge University Press, 2002.

Smith, George Marnett. "Mr Blackmore's Novels." *International Review*, September 1879, 406–26.

St Clair, William. "The Political Economy of Reading." *John Coffin Memorial Lecture in the History of the Book* (2005), available online at http://ies.sas.ac.uk/Publications/johncoffin/stclair.pdf.

Stansky, Peter. *Redesigning the World: William Morris, the 1880s, and the Arts and Crafts*. Palo Alto, Calif.: Society for the Promotion of Science and Scholarship, 1996.

Steel, Flora Annie Webster. *On the Face of the Waters*. Rahway, N.J.: Mershon, 1896.

Stewart, Garrett. *The Look of Reading: Book, Painting, Text*. Chicago: University of Chicago Press, 2006.

Stewart, Susan. *On Longing: Narratives of the Miniature, the Gigantic, the Souvenir, the Collection*. Baltimore: The Johns Hopkins University Press, 1984.

Stocking, George W. *Victorian Anthropology*. New York: Free Press, 1987.

Stoppard, Tom. *Plays*. 5 vols. London: Faber and Faber, 1999.

Strathern, Marilyn. *The Gender of the Gift: Problems with Women and Problems with Society in Melanesia*. Berkeley: University of California Press, 1988.

Sussman, Charlotte. *Consuming Anxieties: Consumer Protest, Gender, and British Slavery, 1713–1833*. Stanford: Stanford University Press, 2000.

Sutherland, John. *Can Jane Eyre Be Happy?: More Puzzles in Classic Fiction*. New York: Oxford University Press, 1997.

———. *The Stanford Companion to Victorian Fiction*. Stanford: Stanford University Press, 1989.

Sutton, Max Keith. "'The Prelude' and *Lorna Doone*." *Wordsworth Circle* 13, no. 4 (1982): 193–97.

———. *R. D. Blackmore*. Boston: Twayne, 1979.

Szymanski, Stefan, and Andrew S. Zimbalist. *National Pastime: How Americans Play Baseball and the Rest of the World Plays Soccer*. Washington, D.C.: Brookings Institution Press, 2005.

Talbot, Norman. "'Whilom, as Tells the Tale': The Language of the Prose Romances." *Journal of the William Morris Society* 8, no. 2 (1989): 16–26.

Thackeray, William Makepeace. *Vanity Fair.* Edited by Nicholas Dames. New York: Barnes and Noble, 2003.

Thiong'o, Ngugi wa. "George Lamming's *In the Castle of My Skin.*" In *Homecoming: Essays on African and Caribbean Literature, Culture and Politics,* 110–26. London: Heinemann, 1972.

Thomas, Nicholas. *Entangled Objects: Exchange, Material Culture, and Colonialism in the Pacific.* Cambridge, Mass.: Harvard University Press, 1991.

Thompson, E. P. *William Morris: Romantic to Revolutionary.* London: Lawrence and Wishart, 1955.

Thompson, Edward. "Introduction and Notes." In *Emily Eden's Up the Country: Letters Written to Her Sister from the Upper Provinces of India,* edited by Edward Thompson. London: Oxford University Press, 1930.

"Three Small Books by Great Writers." *Fraser's* 115 (1879): 103–24.

Trench, Richard Chenevix. *On the Study of Words.* New York: Redfield, 1852.

Trollope, Anthony. *An Autobiography.* Edited by Bradford Allen Booth. Berkeley: University of California Press, 1947.

———. *Can You Forgive Her?* New York: Oxford University Press, 1973.

———. *The Eustace Diamonds.* Edited by Stephen Gill and John Sutherland. Baltimore: Penguin, 1969.

Trumpener, Katie. *Bardic Nationalism: The Romantic Novel and the British Empire.* Princeton: Princeton University Press, 1997.

Tucker, Herbert. "All for the Tale: The Epic Macropoetics of Morris' *Sigurd the Volsung.*" *Victorian Poetry* 34, no. 3 (1996): 373–432.

Tucker, Irene. *A Probable State: The Novel, the Contract, and the Jews.* Chicago: University of Chicago Press, 2000.

Tytler, Harriet. *An Englishwoman in India: The Memoirs of Harriet Tytler 1828–1858.* Edited by Anthony Sattin. Oxford: Oxford University Press, 1986.

U.A. *Overland, Inland, and Upland: A Lady's Notes of Personal Observation and Adventure.* London, 1873.

Van Ghent, Dorothy Bendon. *The English Novel, Form and Function.* New York: Rinehart, 1953.

Verhoeven, Will. "'Some Corner of a Foreign Field That Is Forever England': The Transatlantic Construction of the Anglo-American Landscape." In *Green and Pleasant Land,* edited by Amanda Gilroy, 155–72. Leuven: Peeters, 2004.

Viswanathan, Gauri. *Masks of Conquest: Literary Study and British Rule in India.* New York: Columbia University Press, 1989.

———. *Outside the Fold: Conversion, Modernity, and Belief.* Princeton: Princeton University Press, 1998.

———. "Raymond Williams and British Colonialism." *Journal of English and Foreign Languages* 7–8 (1991): 79–102.

Wall, Cynthia. "The Rhetoric of Description and the Spaces of Things." In *Eighteenth-Century Genre and Culture,* edited by Dennis Todd and Cynthia Wall, 261–79. Newark: University of Delaware Press, 2001.

Wallerstein, Immanuel Maurice. *World-Systems Analysis: An Introduction.* Durham, N.C.: Duke University Press, 2004.

Waters, Chris. "Marxism, Medievalism and Popular Culture." In *History and Community: Essays in Victorian Medievalism*, edited by Florence Saunders Boos, 137–68. New York: Garland, 1992.

———. "Morris's 'Chants' and the Problems of Socialist Culture." In *Socialism and the Literary Artistry of William Morris*, edited by Florence Saunders Boos and Carole G. Silver, 127–46. Columbia: University of Missouri Press, 1990.

Weiner, Annette B. *Inalienable Possessions: The Paradox of Keeping-While-Giving*. Berkeley: University of California Press, 1992.

Weisbuch, Robert. *Atlantic Double-Cross: American Literature and British Influence in the Age of Emerson*. Chicago: University of Chicago Press, 1986.

Welsh, Alexander. *George Eliot and Blackmail*. Cambridge, Mass.: Harvard University Press, 1985.

———. *The Hero of the Waverley Novels*. New Haven: Yale University Press, 1963.

"The Wessex Labourer." *Examiner*, July 15, 1876.

Wheeler, Thomas Martin. "Sunshine and Shadow." In *Chartist Fiction*, edited by Ian Haywood, 65–193. Aldershot: Ashgate, 1999.

Williams, Raymond. *The Country and the City*. New York: Oxford University Press, 1973.

Winch, Donald. *Riches and Poverty: An Intellectual History of Political Economy in Britain, 1750–1834*. Cambridge: Cambridge University Press, 1996.

Wolfe, Patrick. "Land, Labor, and Difference: Elementary Structures of Race." *American Historical Review* 106, no. 3 (2001): 866–905.

Woloch, Alex. *The One Vs. The Many: Minor Characters and the Space of the Protagonist in the Novel*. Princeton: Princeton University Press, 2004.

Woollacott, Angela. *To Try Her Fortune in London: Australian Women, Colonialism, and Modernity*. New York: Oxford University Press, 2001.

Yadav, Alok. *Before the Empire of English: Literature, Provinciality, and Nationalism in Eighteenth-Century Britain*. New York: Palgrave Macmillan, 2004.

Young, Arlene. "Workers' Compensations: (Needle)Work and Ideals of Femininity in Margaret Oliphant's *Kirsteen*." In *Famine and Fashion: Needlewomen in the Nineteenth Century*, edited by Beth Harris, 41–51. Aldershot: Ashgate, 2005.

Žižek, Slavoj. *The Parallax View*. Cambridge, Mass.: The MIT Press, 2006.

Zygmunt, Lawrence. "'This Particular Web': George Eliot, Emily Eden, and Locale in Multiplot Fiction." In *Teaching British Women Writers, 1750–1900*, edited by Jeanne Moskal and Shannon R. Wooden, 110–18. New York: Peter Lang, 2005.

Index